Illinois History

A Reader

EDITED BY MARK HUBBARD

A collection of articles from
Journal of the Illinois State Historical Society

COMMON THREADS

An anthology from the
University of Illinois Press

Note: Articles, including author biographies, are presented as originally published.

Library of Congress Control Number: 2018935344
ISBN 978-0-252-08364-8 (paperback)
ISBN 978-0-252-05068-8 (e-book)

Contents

Introduction

MARK HUBBARD

THE YEAR 2018 MARKS THE BICENTENNIAL of the state of Illinois, and like all historical anniversaries, this one prompts the professional historian and layperson alike to reflect upon current scholarship in the field. My primary goal in putting together *Illinois History—A Reader* is to present the student with a snapshot of the state of the field, as it were, through selected articles previously published in the *Journal of the Illinois State Historical Society*, of which I currently serve as editor-in-chief. The fourteen essays offered here—spanning the colonial era to the very recent past—represent some of the best work published in the *Journal* over the last three or so decades.

I would be remiss if I did not acknowledge a rather large caveat: no single collection of previously published essays can hope to encompass in its entirety the rich diversity of Illinois's past. For one thing, the state of the field, like all fields of history, remains fluid and subject to ongoing revision as new questions are asked, new sources emerge, and new ways of conceptualizing existing sources develop. For another, the themes and subjects that historians have already documented are too numerous, the methodological and interpretive approaches that have shaped historical research and writing on the Prairie State in the last few decades too wide-ranging, to be captured fully in one volume of essays.[1] The idea here is thus more modest: to introduce students and researchers to the burgeoning field of fascinating subjects opened up by studying Illinois history. In this sense, I hope, this volume can serve as an accessible and useful complement to several of the Illinois history textbooks taught at colleges and

---

1. For a comprehensive survey of scholarship on Illinois history, see the essays in the commemorative double issue "Illinois History—A Bicentennial Appraisal," *Journal of the Illinois State Historical Society* 111: 1–2 (Spring/Summer, 2018).

universities today.[2] The articles at hand offer students and researchers greater granularity and complexity in understanding and interpreting some of the key issues that have shaped the Prairie State. I seek to enhance students' knowledge of selected topics and offer a breadth of chronological coverage consistent with the survey approach to Illinois history often found in university-level courses.

The fourteen essays in this volume were selected for their thematic relevance to the study of Illinois's past. The overarching theme is relationships of power and their historical dimensions; and the forms of political conflict such relationships generated through time.[3] When viewed across centuries, Illinois evolved through several stages, each marked by distinctive patterns of demography, social and economic development, and political conflict. Before the arrival of Europeans to North America, Illinois Country was a distinctive cultural and ecological zone occupied by diverse (and sometimes loosely confederated) Indian tribes that had prospered on and shaped the land in ways barely perceptible to the Europeans who arrived in the late seventeenth century and after. The Europeans brought new ideas such as Christianity, as well as new goods and trading opportunities to the Indians. They also mapped onto Illinois Country a new geopolitical context defined by Old World rivalries. By the eighteenth century, competing Spanish, French, and British colonial claims in North America turned Illinois Country into a battleground of clashing cultures and imperial ambitions. The opening essays by Raymond Hauser and Reginald Horsman offer case studies in the complex economic and political relationships among Indian and European powers that evolved in Illinois Country during this period. Indian and European peoples alike calculated their interests and pursued strategies that promised, from their perspective, to advance themselves in relation to rival groups. Rather than seeing early Illinois history as a triumphal story of inevitable civilization brought by Anglo-Europeans, the essays by Hauser and Horsman underscore the interactive, syncretic, and highly contested character of life in Illinois Country before American independence.

---

2. Among the single-volume surveys of state history currently available, the best is Roger Biles, *Illinois: A History of the Land and Its People* (DeKalb: Northern Illinois University Press, 2005). A very useful summary of the state's history, complete with rich and visually striking illustrations, is Gerald A. Danzer, *Illinois: A History in Pictures* (Urbana: University of Illinois Press, 2011). Other single-volume textbooks that remain useful, though dated in their content and analytical approach, include Robert P. Howard, *Illinois: A History of the Prairie State* (Grand Rapids, MI: Eardmans, 1972); and Richard J. Jensen, *Illinois: A History* (New York: Norton, 1978).

3. Put differently, the emphasis here is on politics, broadly defined to include both formal and informal (and sometimes extralegal) acts of political protest and expression. Perhaps a second volume in the Common Threads series can draw on the back issues of the *Journal* to elucidate in greater detail the state's economic, social, and cultural history. There is certainly no shortage of excellent work in these subfields.

The American Revolution assured that the history of Illinois would thenceforth take place in a new context defined by economic abundance, staggering geographic and social mobility, ethnic and cultural pluralism, and a constitutional order in theory devoted to individual liberty and democratic equality. In a sense, the history of Illinois—from its territorial stage up to the present—can be viewed as a long struggle to define what liberty and equality meant in practice, not just in theory, for the increasingly diverse people who came to call Illinois home. In the first half of the nineteenth century, the state remained a rural frontier, attractive to settlers seeking cheap land and a new life on the prairie. The essay by Robert Sutton illustrates some of the political and cultural conflicts that ensued as waves of new Anglo-American settlers arrived in the early decades of the nineteenth century. By midcentury new settler groups from both New England and Western and Northern Europe made Illinois more diverse, and the rise of Chicago and other smaller cities in the 1850s heralded the coming of large-scale industry and agribusiness to the Prairie State. It was during this stage that Illinois also stood at the center of the nation's defining conflict over slavery and the place of black folk in American life. The essays by Paul Finkelman and Robert Sampson trace the competing ideologies over slavery, race, and the Civil War that emerged in Illinois, and show too how demographic and economic growth in the middle decades of the nineteenth century shaped those conflicting attitudes.

In the decades after the Civil War, Illinois cemented its status as the Midwest's preeminent industrial and commercial state; Chicago in particular, with a population over one million in 1890, became the nation's central link in a chain of people, trade, and communication networks that bound together an entire continent. By the late nineteenth and early twentieth centuries, industrialization developed in tandem with the spread of urban life; both processes relied on cheap labor supplied by successive waves of new immigrants—this time mostly from Central and Southern Europe. Illinoisans—like Americans generally—confronted a new world of stark inequalities of wealth and political power. The second essay by Robert Sampson and the essay by Shirley Portwood offer case studies in how Illinoisans confronted the problems of both class and racial inequality in this period. The essays by Suellen Hoy and Thomas Pegram illustrate some of the ways in which Illinois men and women created new modes of political influence in the late nineteenth and early twentieth centuries.

As the twentieth century unfolded, Illinois became more modern and even more heterogeneous, as African Americans, followed by Latinos and, later, Asians, migrated in large numbers to Illinois. The struggle for racial equality—dating back to the nation's colonial roots—reached a new phase in northern cities like Chicago, where blacks could vote. While FDR promoted his Four Freedoms as justification for America's entry into World War II, activists like

A. Philip Randolph and James Farmer launched a new age of black militancy. The essays by Lionel Kimble, Jr., and Ronald Shaw detail some of the strategies Illinois blacks employed to obtain equal rights, and also illustrate the practical difficulties of confronting *de facto* discrimination and systemic racism in the North. The essays by Lilia Fernandez and Judson Jeffries show some of the ways that the civil rights movement inspired other communities of color to new heights of activism and consciousness, forever reshaping the political and cultural landscape of Chicago and beyond. In seminal ways, the 2008 election of President Barack Obama, a community activist in Chicago's South Side before his entry into electoral politics, was a product of the political awakenings of post-WWII era. Yet as Illinois emerged from the tumultuous years of the 1960s, its diverse peoples faced the challenge of adapting to an increasingly global economy. The decline of Decatur, as recounted by Roger Biles in this volume's final essay, illustrates many of the themes of recent state history and many of the problems Illinoisans face today. Decatur is a place with an uncertain future, an observation few would have made only two generations ago. This tragic story is a case study in the economic, social, and political consequences of globalization in the Prairie State.

1. The Fox Raid of 1752

Defensive Warfare and the Decline of the Illinois Indian Tribe

RAYMOND E. HAUSER

ON JUNE 1, 1752, THE FOX INDIANS led an intertribal force of between four hundred and five hundred raiders on a surprise attack against the Cahokia and Michigamea Illinois Indian village located on the east bank of the Mississippi River, a short distance north of Fort de Chartres.[1] Specialists have long recognized that American Indian raiding warfare expeditions grew larger after contact

RAYMOND E. HAUSER completed his undergraduate studies at Western Illinois University. He received a graduate fellowship from the Illinois State Historical Society, which enabled him to complete a doctoral dissertation at Northern Illinois University. The author has published several articles on the Illinois Indian tribe, including "The Illinois Indian Tribe: From Autonomy and Self-Sufficiency to Dependency and Depopulation," which appeared in this *Journal* in 1976. Hauser is a member of the history faculty and director of the honors program at Waubonsee Community College. This article was originally presented at the Twelfth Annual Illinois History Symposium in 1991.

1. Major Macarty Mactigue, the French commandant in the Illinois country, clearly identified June 1 as the date of the attack; Macarty to Pierre Rigaud de Vaudreuil de Cavagnal, Sept. 2, 1752, in Theodore Calvin Pease and Ernestine Jenison, eds., *Illinois on the Eve of the Seven Years' War, 1747–1755*, Collections of the Illinois State Historical Library, Vol. 29 (Springfield: Illinois State Historical Library, 1940), pp. 654, 687. Father Alexis F. X. de Guyenne confirmed the date in Guyenne to Vaudreuil, Sept. 10, 1752 (ibid., p. 720). Jean-Bernard Bossu erred when he claimed that the attack occurred on June 6, but internal evidence (a reference to "the holiday of Corpus Christi") also identifies June 1 (see Bossu, *Travels in the Interior of North America, 1751–1762*, trans. and ed. Seymour Feiler [Norman: University of Oklahoma Press, 1962], p. 79). Carl Ekberg confirmed that this holiday was celebrated on June 1 in 1752 (Ekberg to author, March 16, 1990).

Illinois Historical Journal Vol. 86, No. 4 (Winter 1993): 210–224

Fort de Chartres, from a mural in the Illinois State Capitol.

with Europeans, but the size and composition of that particular raiding party even caught the attention of French cartographer Jacques Nicolas Bellin in 1755.[2]

While scholars have often referred to the raid, their purposes have not required a thorough examination of it or its implications.[3] In one of the more extensive and error-laden reviews of the attack, Lawrence Henry Gipson, an influential twentieth-century historian, employed it as an example of the difficulty encountered by the French while attempting to control their Indian allies, and he was probably incorrect here, also.[4] The Fox raid of 1752 was a significant event for the Illinois Indian tribe because it emphasizes the inadequate implementation of defensive raiding warfare precautions, it sheds light

2. Harold E. Driver, *Indians of North America* (Chicago: University of Chicago Press, 1961), p. 370; Bellin, "Partie du Cours du Fleuve St. Louis ou Mississippi," in *Indian Villages of the Illinois Country, Part 1, Atlas*, comp. Sara Jones Tucker, Scientific Papers, Vol. 2 (Springfield: Illinois State Museum, 1942), pl. XXIV.

3. The raid is often mentioned, but scholars have met their objectives by employing just one of the two major sources, Macarty and Bossu. For example, only two of the eighteen publications consulted that refer to the attack cite both sources; they utilize only Bossu, however; see Wayne C. Temple, *Indian Villages of the Illinois Country, Part 2, Historic Tribes*, Scientific Papers, Vol. 2, rev. ed. (Springfield: Illinois State Museum, 1966), p. 46; John A. Walthall and Elizabeth D. Benchley, *The River l'Abbe Mission: A French Colonial Church for the Cahokia Illini on Monks Mound*, Studies in Illinois Archaeology, No. 2 (Springfield: Illinois Historic Preservation Agency, 1987), pp. 11–12.

4. Gipson, *Zones of International Friction: North America, South of the Great Lakes Region, 1748–1754* (New York: Knopf, 1939), p. 146.

on Indian-white relations, and it focuses attention on the role warfare played in explaining the population decline of the Illinois.

The subtribes of the Illinois and their neighbors must have maintained a fully developed raiding warfare tradition for at least a generation prior to the arrival of the Europeans. The influence of Europeans caused Native Americans to adapt their concept of war to include communal war during the protohistoric period[5] and to adapt raiding warfare by including firearms and much larger raiding expeditions early in the historic period. While the Illinois launched and received larger expeditions prior to 1752, the raid executed by the Fox and their allies from various northern tribes offers a clear example of how inadequate defensive raiding warfare had become, compared to the devastating dimensions of postcontact offensive operations.

The Cahokia and Michigamea constituted subtribes of the Illinois, which also included the Kaskaskia, Moingwena, Peoria, and Tamaroa.[6] The Illinois had been subdividing into separate tribes when the arrival of Louis de Jolliet and Jacques Marquette in 1673 opened the historic period in the Illinois country, but that process was halted and then reversed by conditions that attended contact. The tribe occupied most of the present state of Illinois from at least the late 1630s until "the middle of the eighteenth century."[7] The Illinois suffered a disastrous population decline during the historic period,[8] and pressures from other tribes encouraged the Peoria eventually to settle on the Illinois River at Lake Peoria. The Kaskaskia, Cahokia, and Michigamea moved southwest to the American Bottom along the east bank of the Mississippi River below the mouth of the Missouri. The French built forts close to all four of those Illinois villages.

---

5. Hauser, "Warfare and the Illinois Indian Tribe During the Seventeenth Century: An Exercise in Ethnohistory," *Old Northwest*, 10 (1984–1985), 367–87.

6. For a comprehensive list of Illinois subtribes, see Hauser, "The Illinois Indian Tribe: From Autonomy and Self-Sufficiency to Dependency and Depopulation," *Journal of the Illinois State Historical Society*, 69 (1976), 130; Charles Callender, "Illinois," in Bruce G. Trigger, ed., *Handbook of North American Indians: Northeast*, Vol. 15 (Washington, D.C.: Smithsonian Institution, 1978), pp. 673, 680.

7. Joseph Jablow, "A Study of Indian Tribes in . . . Illinois and Indiana, 1640–1832," in *Illinois, Kickapoo and Potawatomi Indians* (New York: Garland, 1974), p. 43; see also Margaret Kimball Brown, *Cultural Transformations Among the Illinois: An Application of a Systems Model*, Publications of the Museum, Anthropological Series, Vol. 1, No. 3 (East Lansing: Michigan State University, 1979), p. 252.

8. Father Louis Vivier estimated the Illinois population in 1750 at two thousand; Vivier to [a friend], June 8, 1750, in *The Jesuit Relations and Allied Documents*, ed. Reuben Gold Thwaites (1896–1901; rpt. New York: Pageant Book Co., 1959), LXIX, 149 (hereafter cited as *Jesuit Relations*). This number suggests an 83 percent decline from the 1680 population of twelve thousand, which is based on Emily J. Blasingham's total of 10,500 plus an estimated population of fifteen hundred for the Michigamea; see Blasingham, "The Depopulation of the Illinois Indians," *Ethnohistory*, 3 (1956), 365; Hauser, "Illinois," p. 134.

This painting by Robert Thorn, which hangs in the Illinois State Historical Library, depicts the arrival of Father Louis de Jolliet and Jacques Marquette, the first Europeans to make contact with the Indians of the Illinois country.

As Prairie Siouan culture peoples, the Fox and the Illinois shared the same traditional raiding warfare practices. Among the Illinois, for example, military success provided warriors with status recognized in victory ceremonies, martial tattoos, and burial rights. The Illinois regularly fought the Fox, Sioux, and five or six other tribes in a continuous state of war in which peace was only a temporary truce. The primary motive was revenge, but prestige, adventure, and economic advantage were additional factors. War chiefs were self-selected, and warriors volunteered to participate in their war parties in numbers that varied between six or seven and twenty. Raiders employed tactics that emphasized stealth, surprise, and ambush, and their weapons included bows, arrows, knives, clubs, and shields. War parties traveled as far as 1,250 or fifteen hundred miles, moved cautiously at night in enemy territory, and attacked at dawn. They killed enemy women and children on the spot, but retreated quickly with warriors, who were usually tortured to death at the Illinois village.[9]

---

9. Hauser, "Warfare," pp. 368–71; Callender, "Illinois," p. 676; Brown, *Cultural Transformations*, pp. 236–37, 241, 244–45. For reviews of Fox warfare, see Wendell H. Oswalt, *This Land Was Theirs: A Study of the North American Indian* (New York: John Wiley and Sons, 1966), pp. 212–13; Charles Callender, "Fox," in Trigger, ed., pp. 640–42.

Contact with Europeans brought fundamental changes in warfare, which included communal or raid-in-force expeditions, targeting women and children as prisoners; younger warriors; metal arrow heads, knives, and clubs; and, of course, firearms. Warfare thus became much more deadly.[10]

The stealth, ambush, and surprise elements of raiding warfare conditioned Illinois defensive efforts. They built their semipermanent summer villages in river valley locations, with the cabins arranged along the banks of the river or on the edge of a prairie in order to avoid surprise attacks and facilitate launching retaliatory pursuit.[11] The Illinois despised men who were reluctant to pursue raiders, considering them cowards.[12] Defenders utilized the same weapons employed by raiders, and civil chiefs—relying on their own military experience—probably organized defensive arrangements. The presence of enemies was often discovered by women working in fields, by hunters, and by scouts returning from enemy territory. Even with numerous dogs, village defenses were usually quite lax. Enemies alerted to their peril were considered so dangerous, however, that the raiders "would need [a] ten to one [advantage]; and moreover, on those occasions each one [of the raiders] avoids being the first to advance."[13]

Traditional Illinois defensive maneuvers also included moving villages to island locations, combining villages, removing them from the proximity of dangerous foes, and organizing defensive alliances against particularly troublesome enemies. Despite the increasing danger from raiders following contact, the Illinois did not often construct protective stockades around their villages prior to 1752.[14] The French instructed the Illinois "in the art of fortification" as early as 1680,[15] but the Illinois economic cycle, which required frequent moves, probably

---

10. Hauser, "Warfare," pp. 368–71.

11. Brown, Cultural Transformations, pp. 238, 252; [Pierre Deliette], "Memoir of De Cannes Concerning the Illinois Country [ca. 1702]," in *The French Foundations, 1680–1693*, ed. Theodore Calvin Pease and Raymond C. Werner, Collections of the Illinois State Historical Library, Vol. 23 (Springfield: Illinois State Historical Library, 1934), p. 308; J. F. Buisson de St. Cosme [to Bishop Laval], Jan. 2, 1699, in *Early Narratives of the Northwest*, 1634–1699, ed. Louise Phelps Kellogg (1917; rpt. New York: Barnes, 1967), p. 356. See also Deliette, pp. 325, 378, 395; Napoleon A. Chagnon, *Yanomamo: The Fierce People*, 3rd ed. (New York: Holt, 1983), p. 176.

12. Bossu, p. 82; Chagnon, p. 183.

13. Gabriel Marest to Barthe1emi Germon, Nov. 9, 1712, in *Jesuit Relations*, LXVI, 273.

14. Two sources challenge Blasingham's conclusion that the Illinois did not erect stockades (p. 395): M. Bergier, April 13, 1701, in Edward Joseph Fortier, "The Establishment of the Tamarois Mission," *Transactions of the Illinois State Historical Society, 1908* (Springfield: Illinois State Historical Library, 1909), p. 238; C. C. du Tisne, Jan. 14, 1725, in *The French Regime in Wisconsin—I, 1634–1727*, ed. Reuben Gold Thwaites, Collections of the State Historical Society of Wisconsin, Vol. 16 (Madison: Wisconsin State Historical Society, 1902), p. 461.

15. Mary Borgias Palm, *The Jesuit Missions of the Illinois Country, 1673–1763* (Cleveland: n.p., 1933), p. 18.

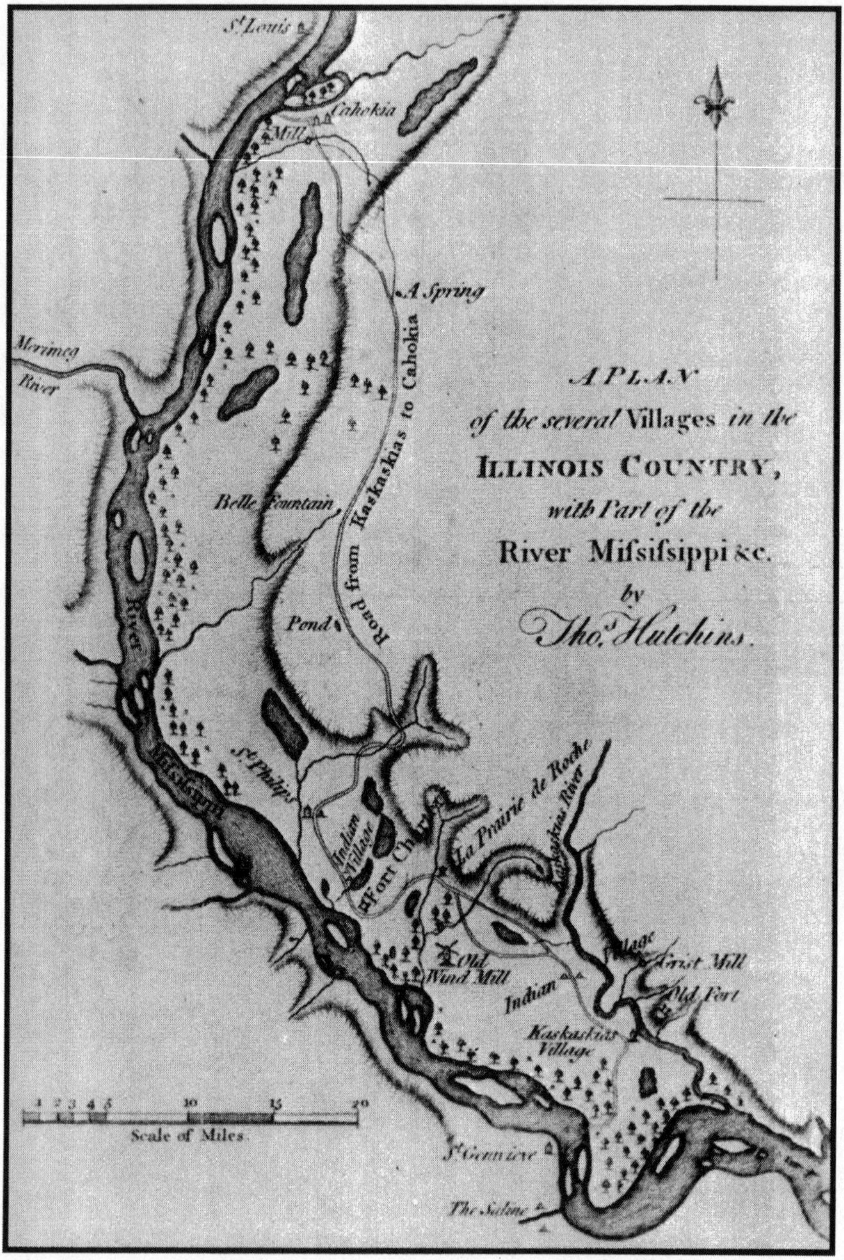

This 1771 map of the Illinois country by Captain Thomas Hutchins shows the proximity of the Indian villages to the French forts and settlements.

discouraged them from expending the effort required to erect palisades. They continued to rely on the presence of French military power—including French forts—for protection. Dependence on French forts required timely warning in the event that several small war parties or a large raid-in-force was directed against them.[16] That warning was unavailable on June 1, 1752.

The declared origins of the 1752 raid-in-force may be found in the culture-driven competition of raiding warfare. The Fox rationalized that the immediate reason for the attack was the Cahokia aggression of 1751, which violated a peace with the northern tribes arranged by the French. While the Cahokia were "out on a hunting trip," they captured seven Fox and tortured them. Jean-Bernard Bossu, a French officer and the only eyewitness to write an account of the raid, does not explain where the Cahokia executed the captives, but he does relate the experiences of the Fox prisoner who escaped and endured tremendous hardships during the journey to rejoin his tribe.[17]

The Fox were, of course, distressed at the news that the survivor brought, and they determined to carry out a remarkable revenge. Even if the provocation had not been so compelling, the Fox would have retaliated because of raiding warfare traditions, the economic and military alliance between the Illinois and the French, and the desirable geographic position occupied by the Illinois. According to Bossu, the Fox chief "assembled his men [after the return of the survivor], for nothing is done without a council, and they decided to send bundles of twigs to the chiefs of allied tribes . . . who [eventually] marched as auxiliary troops under the standard of the Foxes."[18] Although it is not possible to estimate the number of warriors contributed to the venture by the various tribes, the number of Illinois prisoners awarded the Sauk after the attack suggests that they made up a considerable part of the expedition.

The Cahokia expected a Fox retaliatory raid. Deciding that their village position and numbers placed them in some jeopardy, they abandoned the village located

16. Temple, pp. 39, 20, 32, 40, 86; Blasingham, p. 395; Callender, "Illinois," p. 678; Palm, p. 18. See also Macarty to Vaudreuil, p. 677.

17. Jablow, p. 217; Bossu, pp. 77–78; Macarty to Vaudreuil, pp. 654–55. Bossu's account, written from memory, contains numerous errors: the date of the attack, the year the Cahokia tortured several Fox, the number of Fox tortured, the distance between the Michigamea village and Fort de Chartres, and estimates of the size of the Fox force and the number of Illinois casualties. He may also have exaggerated his role during the attack. As a source, therefore, Bossu's details become suspect, but internal evidence concerning the date, the number of raider casualties, the death of a Sioux chief, and the references to Chicagou suggest that his broad account remains dependable.

18. Bossu, p. 78.

since 1735 about nine miles north of the French village also named Cahokia.[19] The Seminary of Foreign Missions had maintained a missionary program in the Cahokia-Illinois village.[20] The Cahokia took a traditional defensive step when they moved about forty-five miles south and relocated with their Michigamea relatives in the village positioned just one and a quarter miles north of Fort de Chartres, a distance probably required in order to promote harmony between the two communities.[21] Nevertheless, in 1721, Father Pierre de Charlevoix noted that "the French are now beginning to settle the country between this fort [de Chartres] and the first mission."[22] The Michigamea, who had occupied that summer village for more than thirty years, extended refuge to the Cahokia because they shared a "fear of being attacked by the Foxes in reprisal," and they also hoped to share the security offered by the larger population of a combined village.[23]

The Cahokia and Michigamea village had a population that might be estimated at fewer than four hundred "of all ages."[24] A village of four hundred would have had an adult male population of about ninety-six who were "capable of bearing arms," and would have contained approximately twenty-four or twenty-five large cabins.[25] The Michigamea had entertained Jesuit missionaries in their village, but because the Illinois had not accepted Catholicism in sufficient numbers and because of the unavailability of a missionary, the village was without one by 1750.[26]

---

19. Walthall and Benchley, pp. 9–10. See also J. Joseph Bauxar, "History of the Illinois Area," in Trigger, ed., p. 596. The village "was built . . . near the confluence of Cahokia and Canteen creeks on the first terrace of Monks Mound" in what today is the Cahokia Mounds State Historic Site (see Walthall and Benchley, p. 10).

20. Vivier to [a friend], p. 149; Pease and Jenison, eds., p. xiii; Walthall and Benchley, p. 10.

21. Bossu, p. 81; n.a., ca. 1720, in Fortier, p. 238. See also J. P. Mercier to Vaudreuil, April 20, 1743, in *Old Cahokia: A Narrative and Documents Illustrating the First Century of Its History*, ed. John F. McDermott (St. Louis: St. Louis Historical Documents Foundation, 1949), p. 79; Walthall and Benchley, p. 8; Clarence Walworth Alvord, *The Illinois Country, 1673–1818* (1922; rpt. Chicago: Loyola University Press, 1965), pp. 222–23.

22. Charlevoix, *Journal of a Voyage to North America* (1761; rpt. Ann Arbor, Mich.: University Microfilms, 1966), II, 221. See also Palm, p. 50.

23. Macarty to Vaudreuil, p. 654; Charles Edward Orser, Jr., "The Kolmer Site: An Eighteenth Century Michigamea Village," p. 70, Midwestern Archaeological Research Center, Illinois State University, Normal; Brown, *Cultural Transformations*, p. 225. Some of the Cahokia may have joined Wabash Valley tribes who were associated with the English (see Pierre de la Rue, Abbe de L'Isle Dieu to Antoine-Louis Rouille, Comte de Jouy, March 28, 1752, in Pease and Jenison, eds., p. 567); see also Walthall and Benchley, p. 10.

24. Vivier provided enough information in 1750 to allow for an estimation of the combined village's 1752 population (see Vivier to [a friend], pp. 145, 149).

25. Blasingham, p. 364; see also Brown, *Cultural Transformations*, p. 228n; Letter by Vivier, Nov. 17, 1750, in *Jesuit Relations*, LXIX, 221; Blasingham, p. 364; Vivier to [a friend], p. 147.

26. Vivier to [a friend], p. 149; see also Palm, p. 94.

The village probably had its dwellings arranged in "the lineal pattern of the Illinois" that was "spread out, scattered along the bank" of the Mississippi.[27] The Michigamea did not protect the village with a palisade. It was placed so that it "was surrounded by woods and a ravine."[28] Agapit Chicagou served the Michigamea as village or peace chief. He was an experienced political leader who had been chief for more than twenty-five years, and he was also well acquainted with the French, having visited King Louis XV at the royal apartments at Fontainbleau in 1725.[29]

The Fox assembled a huge raiding party of "four hundred or five hundred" warriors that included representatives from such northern tribes as the Sioux, Sauk, Potawatomi, Winnebago, Menominee,[30] and Kickapoo.[31] The main body of raiders traveled south down the Mississippi River in a convoy of sixty canoes; a vanguard of the finest Fox runners functioned as scouts. The stealthy raiders passed Fort Cahokia without alerting the French, and they concealed themselves from Adamville, the French commander in the Peoria area,[32] when they discovered him along their route. They said later that they neglected to present themselves to Macarty Mactigue, the French commander in the Illinois country, because they feared that the Illinois would then discover their purpose or that Macarty would prevent them from attacking.[33] The raiders "landed" about

---

27. Brown, *Cultural Transformations*, pp. 257–58, 242. Traditionally they may have arranged their cabins "in rows on 'streets'" (ibid., p. 241).

28. Brown to author, Aug. 9, 1991; Bossu, pp. 78–79.

29. Macarty to Vaudreuil, pp. 665, 672; Bossu, p. 81; Richard N. Ellis and Charlie R. Steen, eds., "An Indian Delegation in France, 1725," *Journal of the Illinois State Historical Society*, 67 (1974), 385–405; see also Virgil Vogel, "Chicagou," in *Indians of the Chicago Area*, ed. Terry Straus (Chicago: NAES College, 1989), pp. 33–36.

30. Macarty to Vaudreuil, pp. 654, 655. Macarty repeated the list, except for the Potawatomi (ibid., p. 665). Vaudreuil accepted Macarty's list of tribes (see Vaudreuil to Rouille, Sept. 28, 1752, in Pease and Jenison, eds., p. 726). L'Isle Dieu, apparently relying on Macarty, did not mention either the Potawatomi or the Winnebago (see L'Isle Dieu to Rouille, Sept. 5, 1753, in ibid., p. 832).

31. Bossu added the Kickapoo to the Fox, Sauk, and Sioux (p. 78). Father Michel Baudouin included the Kickapoo, too, along with the Fox and Sauk, but he also added the Mascouten (see Baudouin to L'Isle Dieu, June 28, 1754, in Pease and Jenison, eds., p. 874). Because those on the scene did not include either the Mascouten or the Chippewa, who were included on a 1755 map, those tribes have not been included in the list of Fox allies (see Bellin, pl.. XXIV).

32. Bossu, p. 82. For identification of Adamville, see Alvord, pp. 235–36; Pease and Jenison, eds., p. 655n.

33. Macarty to Vaudreuil, p. 655. Macarty's reports frustrate scholars because his comments are so opaque. Unfortunately, his detailed account of the Fox raid, written to Vaudreuil on June 2, 1752, is not extant, and specialists must, therefore, rely on his summary account of Sept. 2, 1752.

six-tenths of a mile from the target village, a location permitting "the invaders to come within musket shot of the unsuspecting Michigameas."[34]

Although the combined warrior population of the Cahokia-Michigamea village could not have been more than 20 to 25 percent of the strength of the attacking party, the Fox developed a plan that would reduce the target population to an even more desirable advantage. They scheduled their attack for a day when many Illinois were absent from the village because of a Roman Catholic religious observance, "the holiday of Corpus Christi," at Fort de Chartres.[35]

The Fox began the attack on Sunday night[36] with a ruse that sent a dozen warriors, who were among their "fastest runners," rushing into the village. "[S]houting a death cry" and killing everyone they encountered, the decoy party quickly withdrew as soon as each of the attackers had discharged his firearm. The enraged Illinois immediately raced after the retreating Fox and into an ambush laid by the main raiding force. Concealed by tall grass, the Fox and their allies fired their guns at the advancing Illinois, killing twenty-eight of them. The raiders then charged the village in order to burn it and kill or capture as many men, women, and children as possible.[37]

The raiders "burned ten or twelve cabins [about half of the village], and scattered about the limbs of the dead," a possible reference to the ultimate act of disdain or contempt: desecrating the graves of those Illinois buried in an adjacent graveyard.[38] While the hasty withdrawal of the raiders was part of the raiding tradition, it might also have been encouraged by the proximity of the French at Fort de Chartres, the Europeans located between the village and the fort,[39] and the anticipated return of the visiting villagers.

Removing thirty scalps, the raiders quickly withdrew, taking about forty prisoners with them as insurance against Illinois retaliation. Within a day the raiders tortured three or four captives to death (presumably included in the total of thirty dead).[40] The Fox and their allies suffered only four losses, including "a bemedaled chief of the Sioux."[41]

---

34. Bossu, p. 79.

35. Ibid.

36. Macarty to Vaudreuil, pp. 654, 655.

37. Bossu, p. 79. The number killed in the ambush may have been an exaggeration; Bossu also counted "about eighty Michigamea . . . killed or taken prisoner" (p. 80).

38. Macarty to Vaudreuil, p. 654; Brown, *Cultural Transformations*, p. 243; Blasingham, p. 379.

39. The raiders took precautions to avoid injuring the only Frenchman they encountered during the raid because it would have compromised their relations with the Europeans. Bossu made this point, but it might also serve as an example of the complaint that he exaggerated his role in the events he described (see Bossu, p. 79; Palm, p. 116n).

40. Macarty to Vaudreuil, pp. 655, 672.

41. Bossu, p. 79; see also Macarty to Vaudreuil, p. 655.

The exultant raiders proceeded back up the Mississippi River without any of the caution that had marked their descent or lament over their losses. They placed their captives in the leading canoes. "As they came up to the French fort of the Cahokias, they fired a salvo with their muskets," Bossu reported. "The Fox chief flew the French colors from his canoe and could not have been prouder of his victory if he had conquered an entire empire."[42] The raiders again encountered Adamville on the river, about seven and a half miles from French Cahokia, but that time they had no qualms about discussing their attack.[43]

The surviving Illinois sought refuge at Fort de Chartres.[44] When the raiders destroyed about half of the village, they dislocated between 163 and 196 Illinois. The panic caused by the attack, "the lack of a fort to which they could retire in case of alarm," and the loss of household goods quickly induced a number of families to move in with Peoria relatives some two hundred miles away on Lake Peoria.[45]

Six days after the attack, the Illinois who had retreated to Fort de Chartres were again thrown into a panic when a Frenchman named Roulier arrived from French Cahokia with news that the reinforced Fox raiding party was returning and would attack the "next morning." At the direction of French authorities, the Illinois men, women, and children marched all that cold and rainy night the fifteen miles required to join their Kaskaskia relatives and to reach French Kaskaskia. The French authorities there, however, refused to offer the Illinois sustenance, yet prevented them from leaving, fearing an alliance with the Miami. A French priest eventually supplied the destitute with shelter and food, and Macarty discovered that Roulier had lied about the impending attack. The frightened Illinois finally left Kaskaskia on June 11, only to receive another "sharp alarm" the next day, "while going [back] to the village of the Michigamea."[46]

The French authorities did make an effort to obtain the release of the forty Illinois captives. One band of Sauk held thirteen prisoners, and another—led by Le Chat Blanc—retained six women even after releasing "a [Michigamea] man, three women, and a child" to the Peoria. The remaining survivors were distributed among the other members of the alliance, except for the Sioux, who were only interested in scalps and held no prisoners. The French effort on behalf of the Illinois apparently included dissuading the Peoria from launching a retaliatory attack against the Sauk.[47] By 1754, the commandant at Green Bay,

---

42. Bossu, p. 79.
43. Macarty to Vaudreuil, p. 655.
44. Guyenne to Vaudreuil, p. 720. See also L'Isle Dieu to Rouille, Sept. 5, 1753, p. 832.
45. Guyenne to Vaudreuil, p. 718.
46. Macarty to Vaudreuil, pp. 657–58; Guyenne to Vaudreuil, pp. 720–22.
47. Macarty to Vaudreuil, p. 664.

Joseph de la Marque, Sieur de Marin, secured the release of four Illinois women from the Fox, bringing the known total of repatriated captives to nine.[48]

The impact of the raid on the Illinois was, of course, quite devastating. Seventy inhabitants of the combined village had been killed or captured, the raiders continued to hold thirty-one prisoners two years after the attack, and the loss of those captives plus the thirty killed during and after the raid meant that of a total population of nearly four hundred, about 340 villagers survived the attack.

A number of those survivors joined relatives in other villages. Other survivors eventually reestablished a smaller Michigamea village about a quarter of a mile from Fort de Chartres, "on a ridge in the midst of an open meadow," and they protected it with a palisade.[49] "The structures within the village may have been in rows with 'streets' between them," but they were "not oriented in any particular direction." Archaeologist Margaret Kimball Brown estimated a "village of only 20–25 structures" with only a "possible four to eight persons per cabin, . . . [which] would indicate a maximum of 80 to 200 persons." The size of the village suggests that it did not contain all of the surviving Michigamea and that others may have found refuge with relatives in other villages.[50]

The Illinois must have concluded that their situation had become even more desperate when they learned that their allies and defenders, the French, had betrayed them by exposing them to the Fox and their other enemies among the northern tribes. The first reports of the involvement of French Commander Macarty were treated as unfounded rumor by the French. Macarty might be best described as an alcoholic with a bad temper; he was also irascible, arrogant, tactless, and inconsiderate. He was quite incapable of addressing the problems faced by France, and the governors of New France and Louisiana complained about his failures with the Indians. Bossu, it should be noted, denied the accusation against Macarty.[51]

Evidence implicating Macarty more directly, however, is rather convincing, if not conclusive. On July 26, Le Chat Blanc, the Sauk chief, "secretly told the [Illinois] prisoners [he released to the Peoria] that it was the French who were

48. Michel-Ange, Marquis Duquesne de Menneville to Rouille, Oct. 31, 1753, in Pease and Jenison, eds., p. 850; Blasingham, p. 380.

49. Bossu, p. 81; Brown, "The Search for the Michigamea Indian Village," *Outdoor Illinois*, March, 1972, pp. 19, 26; Orser, p. 66.

50. Brown, "Waterman Site Report," MS, rev. ed., pp. 94–96, Cahokia Mounds State Historic Site, Collinsville, Ill.

51. Macarty to Vaudreuil, pp. 663–64; William P. McCarthy, "The Chevalier Macarty Mactigue," *Journal of the Illinois State Historical Society*, 61 (1968), 53; Bossu, p. 80. See also Pease and Jenison, eds., p. xiiin.

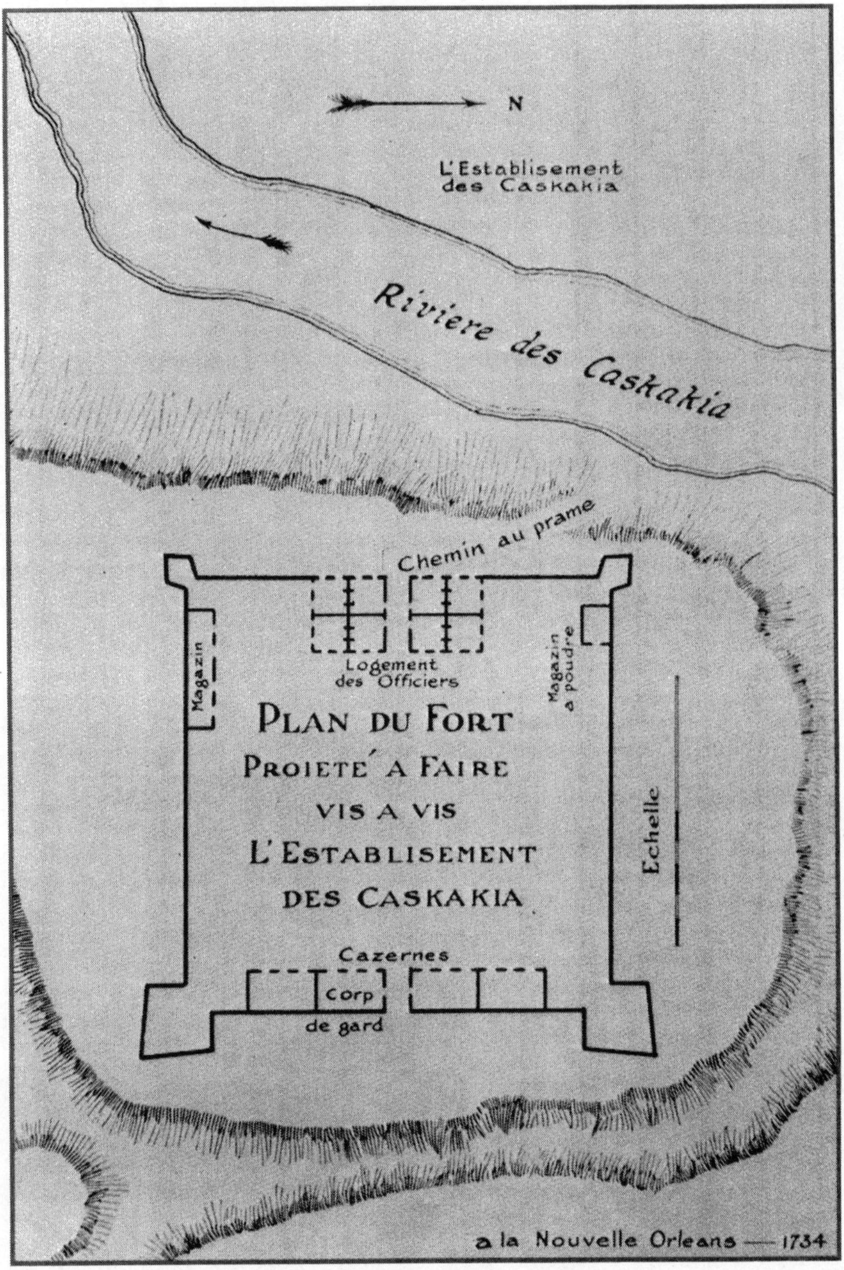

Fort Kaskaskia was built not only to protect French economic interests in the area but also to provide some security to the Indian villages nearby.

the cause of the attack." The Wabash tribes also reported, "It was the French who caused them [the Illinois] to be eaten by the tribes."[52]

Macarty certainly had enough motives to implicate him in a scheme to betray the Illinois. He understood that "the country of the Illinois, in a sense was the keystone of the arch of French imperialism" and that the Illinois Indians remained "a key factor in any anti-French enterprise in the Illinois country." The French position was precarious, and Macarty hoped to prevent further deterioration when he sought to keep the Illinois from joining an English conspiracy involving the tribes of the Wabash Valley. English rum and trade goods were more available, often of better quality, and even cheaper than French brandy and trade goods. Therefore, the Illinois were considering abandoning their longtime French allies.[53]

As might have been expected, no documentary evidence has been found that explains how Macarty encouraged the Fox to attack. He understood the enmity that the Fox, the other northern tribes, and the Illinois shared for one another as a consequence of raiding warfare practices, and it seems reasonable to assume that he played on that animosity. He might easily have had an agent explain that French forces would not protect the Illinois if the Fox launched a covert strike of massive proportions. Of course, the assault had to be conducted with the secrecy that accompanied traditional raiding expeditions. The French plan to retain Illinois support would have been frustrated if the Fox attack had become exposed prematurely because the French would have been required to oppose it.[54]

In a September 2, 1752, letter to Pierre Riguad de Vaudreuil de Cavagnal, the governor of Louisiana, Macarty reported news from Father Alexis F. X. de Guyenne, a Jesuit missionary who worked among the Kaskaskia. The priest indicated "that the chiefs of all the tribes were invited to meet together in the spring [of 1753] to deliberate on the means of defending themselves, and avenging themselves for the tyranny of the French who stirred them up against each other to their destruction."[55] For two reasons, Macarty probably felt constrained to include information in his dispatches that indicted him. First, the charges were known by and reported on by other Frenchmen, like Guyenne; second, the information could have served as a means of informing his superiors of activities he considered shrewd without directly acknowledging culpability.

On June 28, 1754, two years after the attack, Father Michel Baudouin praised a young officer named Pierre Joseph de Neyon de Villiers as a possible successor to

52. Macarty to Vaudreuil, pp. 672, 669.

53. Pease and Jenison, eds., p. xv; Jablow, pp. 208–16; Alvord, pp. 188, 234–35. See also R. David Edmunds, "Old Briton," in *American Indian Leaders: Studies in Diversity*, ed. Edmunds (Lincoln: University of Nebraska Press, 1980), pp. 1–20.

54. Bossu, p. 80.

55. Macarty to Vaudreuil, p. 685.

Saukie and Fox Indians on the Beach near St. Louis by Karl Bodmer. The Sauk joined the Fox on the 1752 raid against the Illinois Indians.

Macarty. The Jesuit saw Neyon as "the only one proper in present circumstances when it is a question of regaining the confidence of our domiciled [Illinois] Indians which has been much abated, not to say entirely lost, by the attack. . . . We tried to persuade them that this blow was made without our knowledge," claimed Baudouin, "but they learned from the very people who attacked them that it had been brought about by [Macarty,] the commandant of the Illinois [country]." The priest hoped that "replacing the man who caused this disgrace, will be very proper to make them forget it."[56]

The argument that focuses on Macarty's role in the attack is based on circumstantial evidence involving motive, means, opportunity, and Jesuit testimony, but it is quite plausible, and it is reinforced by the commander's own statements. The charges leveled against Macarty by the northern and Wabash tribes might be discounted because of the conflicting interests that would have seen them quite satisfied with any Illinois alienation from the French. The accusations of the Jesuits, especially Baudouin, require the most serious consideration, however. Illinois suspicions concerning the French role in the attack of 1752 and other raids appear to have been based on "some truth."[57]

---

56. Baudouin to L'Isle Dieu, p. 874.
57. Pease and Jennison, eds., p. xiv.

By encouraging the Fox attack, Macarty made the Illinois even more dependent and retained their services for France. Demoralized, the Illinois saw no alternative to the French. Continued enmity separated them from the northern tribes, and French policy would not permit them to join the Wabash tribes. Furthermore, the Illinois had been allied with, related to, and living among the French for too long to sever ties because of the betrayal by one official. The Illinois, however, did become much more suspicious. While explaining the reasoning behind an Illinois effort to enlist the Osage as an ally after the 1752 raid, Macarty noted that "the Illinois are . . . always in fear of some surprise from us."[58]

Illinois suspicions were based on the losses sustained in the attack. The sixty-one Illinois killed or captured in the 1752 raid represented a 15 percent loss for the combined village population of four hundred and a 3 percent loss for the total Illinois population of two thousand. To place the loss in perspective, anthropologist John C. Ewers concluded that "during many years" small raiding parties, rather than larger forces, caused "some [Plains] tribes . . . [to lose] more than one percent of their total population from war casualties."[59] The 1752 raid-in-force was so devastating because it had such a heavy impact on the Illinois population at the same time that frequent raids against them took their customary toll. The Illinois had launched large-scale or communal war operations during the seventeenth century, when their village populations had been so much larger, but the tribe was always unable to organize tribal—as opposed to village—expeditions.[60]

Scholars have not agreed about the consequences of warfare on the depopulation of the Illinois. Influenced by eighteenth-century sources that emphasize the impact of war with the Iroquois or the northern tribes,[61] both anthropologists[62] and historians[63] have singled out warfare as among the most important factors

58. Macarty to Vaudreuil, p. 680.

59. Ewers, "When Red and White Men Met," *Western Historical Quarterly*, 2 (1971), 142.

60. Brown, *Cultural Transformations*, p. 233; Temple, pp. 39, 40, 45.

61. "Journal of Diron d'Artaguiette, Inspector General of Louisiana, 1722–1723," in *Travels in the American Colonies*, ed. Newton D. Mereness (New York: Macmillan, 1916), p. 71; Bossu, p. 77.

62. Blasingham, extending anthropologist Alfred Louis Kroeber's hypothesis, pp. 394–95; Callender, "Illinois," p. 678; Walthall and Benchley, p. 80.

63. Francis Parkman, *The Conspiracy of Pontiac* (rpt.; New York: Collier Books, 1962), pp. 56, 441; Alvord, p. 235; J. H. Schlarman, *From Quebec to New Orleans: Fort de Chartres* (Belleville, Ill.: Buechler Pub. Co., 1929), p. 296; Vogel, p. 35; Helen Hornbeck Tanner, ed., *Atlas of Great Lakes Indian History* (Norman: University of Oklahoma Press, 1987), p. 42; Indian Claims Commission, "Commission Findings Continued," in *American Indian Ethnohistory* (New York: Garland, 1974), III, 103.

that explain the Illinois decline. For example, Emily J. Blasingham pointed out that "it was the almost annual raids both by and on the Illinois which had a more lasting effect in persons killed and wounded, in destruction of food and property, and on the morale of the group as a whole."[64]

A useful approach to examining the reason behind the impact of warfare on depopulation is to focus on the French unofficial, but effective, campaign to make the Illinois dependent on them because dependency made the Illinois more vulnerable to depopulation factors—such as warfare, disease, and alcoholism—than tribes that maintained a more independent status.[65] Macarty set the Fox and their allies loose upon the Illinois in order to demonstrate to the latter that they relied on French protection in order to survive. Before the assault, the commander had emphasized their vulnerability to attack when he addressed the Kaskaskia, Cahokia, and Michigamea in March of 1752. "You are small, and your tribe few in number," he declared. "Up to now the Frenchman has sustained you. The Foxes, Sauk, Potawatomi, Sioux, and many others ask to eat you up." Macarty tied Illinois problems with him to their "trade with the English." He asked them to "remember that the Frenchman [Macarty] has preserved you as long as you can remember, that he has saved your lives, that he has redeemed you from the house of your enemies, that he has held them back from you."[66] Macarty clearly understood the Illinois dilemma. The Peoria, the most independent of the Illinois subtribes, survived more successfully than the others because they—like the Fox—maintained a geographical, religious, and political distance between themselves and the French.[67]

The 1752 raid displayed changes in Prairie Siouan warfare practices. The raid was traditional because of its declared revenge motive; the implementation of stealth, surprise, and ambush tactics; a goal that emphasized enemy prisoners and deaths; a rapid withdrawal; and the torture of captives. The changes brought by contact included firearms, larger expeditions, a night attack, women and

---

64. Blasingham, p. 394.

65. Hauser, "Illinois," p. 135; see also Callender, "Illinois," p. 678; Brown, *Cultural Transformations*, pp. 223–67 passim.

66. Macarty to Vaudreuil, pp. 541–42.

67. Physical separation was probably the most important factor. Although the Peoria were numbered by the French as among their "domiciled" allies and lived close to a few Frenchmen at Lake Peoria, the French presence was not substantial (see Macarty to Vaudreuil, p. 677). In 1752 the vicar-general of Canada and the Mississippi noted, "Religion is among the strongest motives that tie the Indian to us" (see L'Isle Dieu to Rouille, March 28, 1752, p. 568). Despite French reliance on the impact of Christianity, the religious independence of the Peoria was quite significant (see Hauser, "Illinois," p. 135; Palm, p. 94). See also John Gilmary Shea, *History of the Catholic Missions Among the Indian Tribes of the United States, 1529–1854* (1855; rpt. New York: AMS Press, 1973), pp. 424, 426, 428; Temple, p. 36.

children included among prisoners, taking captives in sufficient numbers to discourage pursuit, and a cheering rather than mourning leader, despite the loss of four members of the expedition.

The defensive ramifications of the Fox attack became painfully clear to the Illinois. Because of their dependence, the Michigamea had made themselves more vulnerable to attack by neglecting their customary defensive precautions. They failed to locate their village in the open, or close enough to the French fort, or to fortify it with palisades, and the security sought by combining village populations had not proven adequate. Mter the attack, many families left for refuge with relatives among the Peoria and other tribes, some on the Great Miami River.[68] The Peoria, who earlier had expected to take refuge in the French fort at Lake Peoria, now built a stockade around their village.[69] The Michigamea moved their village even closer to Fort de Chartres, built it out in the open, and erected a palisade around it.[70] Finally, the Illinois sought a defensive alliance with the Osage.[71]

Macarty's probable role in promoting the Fox attack illustrates how effective the French could be in manipulating their Indian allies, both the northern tribes and the Illinois. The dependent Illinois remained cautiously loyal to the French because their options were so limited, but the ultimate impact of the raid was quite devastating. Between 1750 and 1765, when the British assumed control over the Illinois country, "the Cahokia and Tamaroa villages totally lost any distinct village identity." Eventually, "the Cahokia merged into the Peoria," and the Michigamea were absorbed by the Kaskaskia.[72] Most of the Peoria began moving west of the Mississippi in 1765, and today the lineal descendants of the Illinois identify themselves as Peoria and make their homes in Oklahoma.[73]

• • •

AUTHOR'S NOTE: The author gratefully acknowledges the critiques provided by Virgil Vogel and Margaret Kimball Brown, as well as the assistance of Audrey Hauser, Carol Bannon, Susan Burch, Su Erickson, and Jill Wold.

68. Vaudreuil to Rouille, p. 727.
69. Bossu, p. 108.
70. Brown to author, Aug. 9, 1991.
71. Macarty to Vaudreuil, pp. 817, 790, 824; Bossu, p. 82; Vaudreuil to Rouille, p. 727.
72. Brown, *Cultural Transformations*, pp. 259, 258; Callender, "Illinois," p. 673.
73. Ibid. See also Blasingham, pp. 212, 391.

2. Great Britain and the Illinois Country in the Era of the American Revolution

REGINALD HORSMAN

WHEN LAWRENCE HENRY GIPSON in his monumental study of the British Empire before the American Revolution wished to depict its extreme limits in 1763, he wrote that its outposts were "scattered from Fort Marlborough on Sumatra in the Far East to the newly acquired French settlements in the Illinois Country in the New World and from the frigid wastes of Hudson Bay to the steaming tropical forests of the Bay of Honduras."[1] Gipson's linking the Illinois country with Sumatra, the wastes of Hudson's Bay, and the forests of Honduras is a useful warning to those who might think of Illinois in nineteenth- or twentieth-century terms as the heart of one of the richest and most flourishing valleys in the world. In the middle of the eighteenth century some individuals did sense the future greatness of the Mississippi Valley and conjured up images of a vast population spreading westward, but most of those individuals were residents of the New World. To the government officials in London, bedazzled by the riches of India or the wealth of the sugar islands, the Illinois country was an incredibly isolated burden.

REGINALD HORSMAN is professor of history at the University of Wisconsin–Milwaukee. He received the B.A. and M.A. degrees from the University of Birmingham, England, his native country. He came to the United States in the 1950s and obtained the Ph.D. degree from Indiana University. His books include *Expansion and American Indian Policy, 1783–1812* (1967) and *The Causes of the War of 1812* (1962).

1. Gipson, *The Triumphant Empire: New Responsibilities Within the Enlarged Empire, 1763–1766* (New York: Knopf, 1956), p. 3.

Journal of the Illinois State Historical Society Vol. 69, No. 2 (May 1976): 100–109

From 1763 until it was lost twenty years later, the Illinois country was for the most part neglected by the British government. That neglect stemmed primarily from the mercantilist nature of the British Empire and, to a lesser extent, from pressures induced by growing tensions along the eastern seaboard of America after 1765. As commercial enterprises, the colonies were expected to foster British prosperity either through the riches they produced, the goods they bought, or indirectly by the stimulus they gave to British naval power. The dynastic arrangements of 1763 left the Illinois country singularly unfitted to enhance British prosperity. If the Illinois country was to be of commercial advantage to the British, it had to be through the fur trade, and the boundary arrangements of 1763 were ill-devised to produce that effect. The overriding problem was that New Orleans was in Spanish hands. Even if the fur trade flourished, its profits seemed likely to go to the Spanish, not the British. The only hope for Great Britain was to divert the trade away from the Mississippi to the Great Lakes and the St. Lawrence. Without extensive enforcing procedures, which would cost more than they were worth, it seemed unlikely that such a diversion would take place. An additional problem was Spanish influence in the Missouri River trade. After the founding of St. Louis in 1764, traders from that post were able to compete on both banks of the Mississippi.[2] British officials quickly realized that the future of the Illinois as a prosperous commercial colony depended on the eventual British possession of New Orleans.

The idea of developing large settlements in the Illinois region, much discussed and planned in the American colonies, found little favor in England. As friction increased after the mid-1760s, the British government saw danger in the uncontrolled movement of Americans into the interior. That movement would weaken colonial ties with England, and seemed unlikely to provide economic benefits to the Mother Country.[3] What was even worse, from the British point of view, it would increase the costs of imperial administration. The financial burden of outposts in the distant Mississippi Valley influenced all British decisions about the Illinois country—both prior to and during the American Revolution. In

2. Abraham S. Nasatir, "The Anglo-Spanish Frontier in the Illinois Country during the American Revolution," *Journal of the Illinois State Historical Society*, 21 (1928), 291–92; James Alton James, *The Life of George Rogers Clark* (Chicago: University of Chicago Press, 1928), 89–91; Clarence E. Carter, *Great Britain and the Illinois Country, 1763–1774* (Washington, D.C.: American Historical Association, 1910), pp. 86–93; Clarence W. Alvord, *The Mississippi Valley in British Politics* (1917; rpt. New York: Russell & Russell, 1959), I, 77–84, 287–324.

3. Thomas P. Abernethy, *Western Lands and the American Revolution* (New York: Appleton, 1937), *passim;* Carter, pp. 96–102, 134–35; Louise Phelps Kellogg, *The British Regime in Wisconsin and the Old Northwest* (Madison: State Historical Society of Wisconsin, 1935), pp. 116–22; Jack M. Sosin, *Whitehall and the Wilderness: The Middle West in British Colonial Policy, 1760–1775* (Lincoln: University of Nebraska Press, 1961), pp. 253–54.

British thinking, the possible future profits of the fur trade in no way offset the obvious and immediate burdens of garrisons and government. The imagery of a Franklin, who could imagine a new and grander British empire arising out of a densely populated Mississippi Valley, made little impression on British officials responsible to Parliament for their expenditures. For them the balance sheet for distant American outposts showed too much red ink.

The Quebec Act of 1774, and the manner in which it was defended in England, clearly demonstrated the British desire to restrict the growth of the Illinois country, a growth that would enhance Spanish prosperity at New Orleans, increase British expenses, and weaken the bonds between England and her American colonies. When British official William Knox defended the Quebec Act against English attacks, he admitted that in placing the interior under the jurisdiction of Quebec the government had "the avowed purpose of excluding all further settlements therein."[4] Solicitor General Alexander Wedderburn answered the objection that the measure was oppressive to British subjects settled in Canada by arguing that he did not wish to see considerable numbers of British subjects going to Canada; he did not wish the colonies to be extended at the expense of Great Britain. He also hoped to dissuade Americans from crossing the Ohio and removing themselves from maritime contact with England.[5] British policy in the Illinois country during the American Revolution has to be understood against that background of restriction. The Illinois country was not profitable to the British, and efforts to win military control of that region were to be directed more by local officials influenced by Canadian fur traders than by official British orders. The only exception to that situation would arise if the opportunity came to make the Illinois country part of a viable economic unit that included the whole Mississippi Valley and New Orleans.

The American Revolution broke out before British government for the Illinois country could be implemented under the Quebec Act. Mathew Johnson, the lieutenant governor who was to be located at Kaskaskia, never arrived there; and Edward Abbott, who was appointed to that position at Vincennes, soon discovered that British indifference and unwillingness to spend money in the region placed him in an untenable position. British troops were withdrawn from Kaskaskia in 1776, and Abbott's efforts to establish a post at Vincennes lasted from only May, 1777, to February, 1778. Abbott fled from Vincennes at that time, he said, because he knew that when the Indians returned from their

4. Quoted in Sosin, p. 247.

5. J. Wright, *Debates in the House of Commons in the Year 1774 on the Bill for Making More Effectual Provision for the Government of the Province of Quebec* (1839; rpt. New York: Johnson Reprint Co., 1966), pp. 49–58. For a discussion of the Quebec Act, see Alfred L. Burt, *The Old Province of Quebec* (Minneapolis: University of Minnesota Press, 1933), pp. 177–201.

George Rogers Clark marches through flooded swamplands from Kaskaskia to Vincennes in February, 1779. Painting by George I. Parrish, Jr., from the Sesquicentennial series commissioned by Illinois Bell.

winter hunting grounds, they would be exasperated by his inability to supply them. He also pointed out, in his report to General Guy Carleton, that there was danger of the Indians entering the service of the Americans unless Great Britain paid for a garrison and provided the supplies and presents that were needed for the tribes.[6]

With Abbott's withdrawal from Vincennes, British presence or influence in the Illinois country depended on Detroit and Mackinac. Both posts were essential to the British presence in the Upper Country because they were centers of the British Great Lakes fur trade, and their peltries flowed through the Lakes and down the St. Lawrence to England. Moreover, Detroit was an important base for the harassment of the Rebels throughout the Ohio Valley region. In the early years of the Revolution the Illinois country was considered a no-man's-land, unworthy of even limited effort and expenditures by the British. They hoped it would stay that way, conveniently forgotten until the rebellion was quelled. Two major events forced a change in the British attitude: George Rogers Clark's conquest of the region and the entry of France and Spain into the war.

6. Abbott to Carleton, April 25, 1778, *Michigan Pioneer and Historical Collections* (Lansing: Michigan Historical Commission, 1874–1929), IX, 488; hereinafter cited as *Michigan Historical Collections.* See also John D. Barnhart, *Henry Hamilton and George Rogers Clark in the American Revolution, with the Unpublished Journal of Lieut. Governor Henry Hamilton* (Crawfordsville, Ind.: R. E. Banta, 1951), pp. 14–15.

Clark's conquest of the Illinois villages and Vincennes in the summer of 1778 came as a major shock to the British. The threat it posed was twofold. First, it meant that Indians throughout the Great Lakes region, impressed by the display of American power, might shift their allegiance to the Americans.[7] Second, with the Illinois country as a base, and with widespread Indian support, Clark posed a serious threat to both Detroit and Mackinac. Some British response was needed, and the manner in which it was undertaken illustrates yet another difficulty of British policy in the Illinois country and the West. As so much depended on the loyalty of the Indian tribes, the higher British command was obliged to depend on local commanders in deciding broad lines of action. Even General Frederick Haldimand, who was responsible for the Upper Country, exercised little control over the actual course of events. If Haldimand was helpless, how much more so was the British government in England.

The nature of the response to Clark's advance into the Illinois country was decided upon by Lieutenant Governor Henry Hamilton at Detroit. He did not await approval from his commanding officers in the East, nor did he wait to coordinate plans with Captain Arent de Peyster, the British military commander at Mackinac. Late in August, Haldimand instructed Hamilton that everything possible should be done to redeem the situation—if not to recover what had been lost, at least to keep the disaster from spreading further. Haldimand also asked Hamilton's advice about what might be done to recover the Illinois country.[8] Hamilton's decision was not to present alternatives but rather to proceed immediately to recover the lost areas, and in mid-September he informed Haldimand of the plan. By the time Haldimand could respond, Hamilton was on his way. When Haldimand did finally reply, his words revealed the dilemma of the British. "In the uncertainty of all things here," wrote Haldimand from Quebec, "uninformed how far this war may spread, it is impossible for me at this distance to give you orders and directions respecting the further measures to be pursued by you; of the possibility or practibility of those you embrace, you must be the best Judge and on your doing what is best for the King's service I must and do fully rely." He warned Hamilton, however, that before taking any considerable action, he should weigh very carefully the expense involved.[9]

Hamilton's decision to proceed immediately to the Illinois country had the military advantage of decisiveness and surprise; the main weaknesses in his plan were two: (1) failure to give enough warning to De Peyster at Mackinac so that assistance could be provided by the Indian tribes and (2) underestimation of

---

7. For a discussion of Clark's efforts to win Indian support, see James, pp. 127–30.
8. Haldimand to Hamilton, Aug. 26, 27, 1778, *Michigan Historical Collections,* IX, 402, 404.
9. Haldimand to Hamilton, April 8, 1779, ibid., pp. 406–7.

Clark's resourcefulness. Hamilton hoped to retake the Illinois country and, if possible, construct a fort at the junction of the Ohio and Mississippi rivers.[10] He set off from Detroit on October 7, and on December 17 took possession of Fort Sackville at Vincennes. De Peyster could be of little help; by the time he heard from Hamilton, the Indians had left Mackinac for their winter hunting grounds. De Peyster did, however, send agents to try to rally the Indians, but it proved impossible to persuade them to gather in time to be of any help to Hamilton. Hamilton's gamble failed. In February, 1779, Clark trekked across country from the Illinois villages, retook Vincennes, and captured Hamilton.[11] By acting on his own initiative and with his own resources, Hamilton had clearly hoped to gain the exclusive praise for a striking military victory. Unfortunately for him, the responsibility for defeat was also exclusively his.

Hamilton's failure posed an immediate threat to Detroit and a potential threat to Mackinac, and was compounded in a far more serious way by French entry into the war and the imminence of Spanish participation. The Spanish had been sending aid from New Orleans to the Americans, and from St. Louis they had been extending their influence among the Indians within British territory. The French posed a more formidable threat because as the British officials admitted, the Indians of the Great Lakes region looked back with nostalgia to the days of French rule. In view of British parsimony in the area after 1763 it was not surprising that the Indians hoped for the return of more bountiful presents. The British also had to reckon with the possibility of widespread disaffection among the French inhabitants of the region. Given the lack of British influence in the Illinois country, a French-Spanish-American-Indian alliance seemed both formidable and possible. In spring and summer of 1779 the British at Detroit and Mackinac believed themselves in immediate danger of attack. They had originally hoped to leave the Illinois country to itself during the American Revolution. Clark's initiative and the widening of the war in Europe made that impossible, and the British now feared that the Illinois region would serve as the base for the conquest of the whole Upper Country.

At the end of May, 1779, Captain Dietrich Brehm, who had been sent by Haldimand to investigate conditions in the Upper Country, reported that the Rebels had spread the news among the Wabash and Illinois Indians that the French, the Spanish, and even the Germans had joined with the Americans

10. Hamilton to Haldimand, Sept. 16, 22 (to Oct. 3), 1778, ibid., pp. 475–82.

11. De Peyster to Haldimand, Oct. 24, 27, 1778, ibid., pp. 374–79; De Peyster to Langlade and Gautier, Oct. 26, 1778, *Collections of the State Historical Society of Wisconsin* (Madison: State Historical Society of Wisconsin, 1885–1931), XVIII, 371–73; hereinafter cited as *Wisconsin Historical Collections.* Hamilton's own account of the expedition can be found in Barnhart, pp. 71–78; Clark's attack is described in James, pp. 136–46.

to drive the English out of North America.[12] And as De Peyster reported from Mackinac, Hamilton's defeat in February had "cooled the Indians in General."[13] By July the British confidently expected that Clark would attack Detroit by way of the Wabash and the Potawatomi settlements at St. Joseph (in what is now southwestern Michigan). De Peyster did all he could to rally the Indians on both shores of Lake Michigan, but their allegiance was doubtful.[14] The British at Detroit were to be saved less by their own exertions than by the inability of the Virginians to give Clark more support. Rumors of Clark's advance, and even reports of his route, flooded into Detroit and Mackinac in the summer of 1779, but he never actually moved. Although Haldimand reported throughout the fall and into the winter that the Upper Country was in a desperate situation, the actual state of affairs was more a stand-off than he realized.[15] Both the Americans and the British found it incredibly difficult to carry on military operations in the distant Mississippi Valley. The problems of supply and communication made any considerable offensive operations impossible.

The entry of France and Spain into the war, although posing many problems for the British, also gave the British government its first chance since 1763 for a comprehensive solution of its Mississippi Valley problems. The 1763 peace settlement, by leaving Spain in control of the Mississippi and New Orleans, ensured that the Illinois country would become an expensive white elephant for the British. The expected expense had been avoided by neglect, but the developments of 1778 and 1779 posed the danger of losing the vital British trading outlets of Detroit and Mackinac. When Spain declared war on England in June, 1779, the British could attempt to remedy the anomalous situation they had allowed to develop in 1763. Secretary of State Lord George Germain told Haldimand that the British intended to take New Orleans, gain control of the Mississippi, and simultaneously conquer the Spanish posts in the Illinois country. The British plan called for Brigadier General John Campbell to conquer New Orleans and then advance up the Mississippi and take Natchez. British posts in the northern Mississippi Valley were expected to cooperate by applying all possible pressure from the north in order to link up with General Campbell.

The manner in which those comprehensive plans were carried out illustrates again the overwhelming difficulties that confronted the British in their efforts

---

12. Brehm to Haldimand, May 28, 1779, *Michigan Historical Collections,* IX, 411; see also McKee to Lernoult, May 26, 1779, ibid., XIX, 423–24.

13. De Peyster to Haldimand, June 1, 1779, ibid., IX, 383.

14. De Peyster to Haldimand, June 27, July 9, 1779, to Major Nairne, July 9, 1779, ibid., pp. 389–90.

15. See *Wisconsin Historical Collections,* XVIII, 393–96; *Michigan Historical Collections,* X, 359–61, XIX, 463–65, 496–98.

to coordinate attacks in the vast, undeveloped North American Continent. The plan had essentially failed even before the northern posts knew it had been formulated. The basic stumbling block to the British was the energy and vigor of Governor Bernardo de Galvez. Before Campbell could launch his offensive operations, Galvez had made the whole plan impossible. In September, 1779, he had conquered Manchac and Baton Rouge, and by February, 1780, had taken Mobile. In the following year the Spanish were to take Pensacola.[16] The planned British conquest of Louisiana, which was the core of British offensive operations in the Mississippi Valley, collapsed in autumn, 1779. The Illinois country remained without a British outlet to the sea.

Germain's order that the British at Mackinac were to support the attack on Louisiana was not even sent from Detroit until January, 1780, when the general plan had already failed, but since autumn, 1779, British officials at Detroit and Mackinac had been planning offensive operations against the Illinois country. De Peyster reported in November that "the Western Nations about Michilimackinac are all well disposed, and will act with vigor against the Illinois"; the Wabash Indians, he said, would divert Clark's attention from the Mississippi. It was hoped that Lieutenant Governor Patrick Sinclair, who had assumed command at Mackinac, would be able to send the Indians of that region in an attack on St. Louis.[17] Those plans appeared to take on added significance in the new year when Sinclair received word that he should attempt to coordinate the movement of his troops with those coming from the south and thereby win the whole Mississippi Valley. Sinclair sent word in mid-February, 1780, that he would send all available Indians to attack the Spanish settlements as far down the river as possible. He had already sent messages to the Sioux, and thought that they could be used down the Mississippi as far as Natchez, even if Campbell had not yet arrived.[18] Sinclair did not know that any chance of Campbell's arriving had already disappeared.

Sinclair planned his offensive operations for the spring of 1780. He sent Emanuel Hesse, a trader and former soldier, to the Fox-Wisconsin portage in order to gather the Indians who were to attack the Illinois country. Winnebago, Menominee, Sauk and Foxes, and Chippewa were to meet there, and they would be joined at the junction of the Wisconsin and the Mississippi by nations from

16. See J. Leitch Wright, *Anglo-Spanish Rivalry in North America* (Athens: University of Georgia Press, 1971), pp. 130–31; James, pp. 198–202; Nasatir, pp. 291–92; *Wisconsin Historical Collections,* XI, 145.

17. De Peyster to McKee, Nov. 2, 1779, and letter of De Peyster, Nov. 20, 1779, *Michigan Historical Collections,* X, 370–73.

18. Sinclair to Brehm, to Haldimand, Feb. 15, 1780, *Wisconsin Historical Collections,* XI, 144–46, 147.

higher up the river. Sinclair was optimistic that the party could restore British influence in the Illinois region by capturing the Spanish fort at St. Louis. The Sioux meanwhile were to go as far down the river as possible, with the idea of helping Campbell. Sinclair expected to receive considerable assistance in the Mackinac region from traders who had been shut out of the rich fur trade of the Missouri River region.[19] The profits of the fur trade often seemed of greater importance to officers on the spot in the Upper Country than to British officials in England, who could examine the entire balance sheet of fur trade profits and military costs. The same conflict was present for the next thirty-five years. The specific interests of Upper Canada were often neglected by cost-conscious policy-makers in London, whereas British officials in Canada often felt constrained to support the desires of the people among whom they lived.

If the British had been successful on the lower Mississippi, the chance of success for the northern wing of the attack would have been considerably enhanced. Such victories would have stimulated large-scale Indian support. As it was, by the time the northern operations were launched early in May, news had already reached the Indian villages that the Spanish had been successful in attacking British posts on the lower Mississippi. At the end of April the vital villages on the St. Joseph, which had been wavering throughout the Revolution, reported that the defeats on the lower Mississippi, together with French influence, were causing major discontent among the Potawatomi. Although the Indians at St. Joseph and along the Wabash had been urged to attack the settlements at Vincennes and along the Mississippi, they were unwilling to launch such offensive operations in the spring of 1780.[20] De Peyster, then in command at Detroit, had more luck with the Indians near Detroit and south of Lake Erie. In 1780 they accompanied Captain Henry Bird on a pillaging raid against the American settlements in Kentucky. Bird's raid was intended to divert the attention of Clark and the Americans from Sinclair's operations in the Illinois country and against St. Louis.[21]

Sinclair's main expedition was launched on May 2. Some 750 men, including traders and Indians, proceeded down the Mississippi. At the same time Captain Charles de Langlade was sent to join the Indians assembled at Chicago preparatory to an attack on the Illinois River; another party was sent to patrol the region between the Wabash and the Mississippi. By those moves Sinclair was hopeful of winning complete control of the Illinois country, St. Louis, and the

---

19. Sinclair to Haldimand, Feb. 17, 1780, ibid., pp. 147–48; Kellogg, pp. 163–67.

20. See *Michigan Historical Collections,* IX, 533–38, 582; X, 391–93.

21. De Peyster to Bolton, March 10, 1780, and De Peyster to Sinclair. March 12, 1780, ibid., XIX, 501–2; IX, 580–81. See also Milo M. Quaife, "When Detroit Invaded Kentucky," *Burton Historical Collection Leaflet,* 4 (1925), 17–32.

whole Missouri River trade. He had won the support of the Mackinac traders, and, by promising them exclusive control of the Missouri trade during the coming winter, obtained their influence among the Indians; in exchange, the traders were to remain at the Spanish posts on the west side of the Mississippi. The settlements in the Illinois country were to be forced to contribute to the support of the British, either by supplying the British garrisons in the region or by sending cattle via Green Bay to Mackinac for supplying the Indians. Sinclair was to send other Indians to watch the lead mines, which Illinois residents were to be prohibited from working.[22]

Sinclair's dreams of conquering the Illinois country and St. Louis, and thereby dominating the Missouri River trade, evaporated as rapidly as had British hopes of capturing New Orleans and winning control of the entire Mississippi region. Not one of the attacks succeeded. Sinclair had hoped for surprise, but the Spanish at St. Louis knew of his plans. Fortifications were thrown up well before the British and their Indian allies arrived, and the attack was beaten off. The attack on Cahokia had the same result. The only success Sinclair could report was the kind of pillaging and scalping that had been restrained by De Peyster when he was in command at Mackinac. Those who suffered most were settlers in outlying areas, not the defenders of the forts. Sinclair reported that some seventy civilians had been killed, forty-three scalps brought in, hundreds of cattle slaughtered, and thirty or so whites and blacks taken prisoner. The Spanish complained bitterly of British atrocities. After the attacks the British and their Indian allies retreated precipitately and in some confusion.[23]

Sinclair, in his frustration, blamed some of the Indians for being lukewarm in their assaults; he was also critical of the support received from the Mackinac traders. "The Traders who would not assist in extending their Commerce," wrote Sinclair to Haldimand, "cannot complain of its being circumscribed to necessary bounds."[24] A similar complaint was leveled at traders Joseph Calve and Jean Marie Ducharme, who, according to Sinclair, had been responsible for the "treachery" of the Sauk and Foxes. He suggested that both of those men traded secretly in the Illinois region and preferred "the little underhand commerce of that country to the advantages I held out to them all, in promising them the Trade of the Missouri, provided they could gain & Garrison the Illinois."[25] In

---

22. Sinclair to Haldimand, May 29, 1780, and Sinclair to Bolton, June 4, 1780, *Wisconsin Historical Collections,* XI, 151–53; *Michigan Historical Collections,* XIX, 529–30.

23. *Wisconsin Historical Collections,* XI, 154.

24. Ibid., p. 156.

25. Sinclair to Bolton, July 4, 1870 (misdated), ibid., p. 154; Sinclair to De Peyster, July 30, 1780, *Michigan Historical Collections,* IX, 586–87.

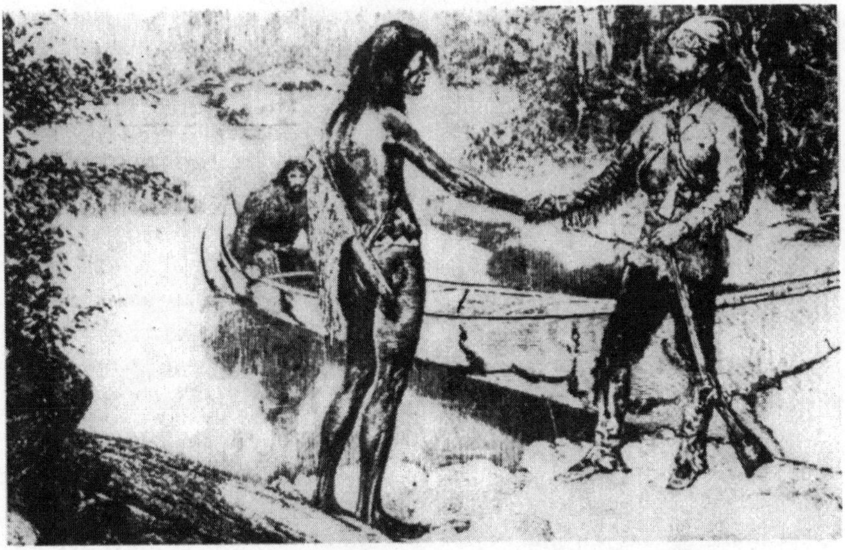

A Frederic Remington sketch of an Indian greeting a French trader

the northern wing the grand British plan to win strategic control of the whole Mississippi Valley became merely a marauding expedition designed to win control of the fur trade of the Missouri River.

By the summer of 1780 the British had no real foothold in the Illinois country. It is a commonplace of Revolutionary western history to point out that George Rogers Clark's victories in 1778 were never built on, that they were dissipated by lack of support in the later years of the Revolution, and that he had in no sense "won the West." That is all true, but it needs to be pointed out that although Clark could not build on (and even had to retreat from) his position in the Illinois country, the British were unable to replace him with military power of their own. Sinclair's expeditions of 1780 were absolute failures, and the British position on the lower Mississippi was infinitely weaker by 1780 than it had been at the beginning of the Revolution. General Haldimand, who throughout the Revolution had been pessimistic about the western situation and who had constantly stressed economy rather than military victory, continued to bombard British officials in England with reports of the problems of the West. "If the Western Indians were more attached & more interested, they might originally have prevented, & still may, the advances of the Enemy," he explained to Germain in September, 1780, "but it is in their interests to protract the War, that they may live in Indolence, receiving Presents which were at first indispensably necessary, & cannot now, with safety, be withheld from them, particularly as the Spaniards are become

Masters of the Mississippi & can by that Channel supply their wants."[26] It is not surprising that British ministers believed the region was of little importance to future British prosperity.

With the failure of the large-scale British plan to take control of the Mississippi Valley, and the inability of Sinclair's forces to take control of the Illinois country and St. Louis, initiative again shifted to England's enemies. Ironically, both the British and the Americans had lost real control of the Illinois country, and even the Spanish at St. Louis lacked the power for permanent control over the region. It thus reverted to the no-man's-land it had been when the British withdrew at the beginning of the Revolution. Into that power vacuum came Augustin Mottin de La Balme, a French officer who had offered his services to the Americans early in the Revolution. In autumn, 1780, he raised a force in the Illinois country and attacked the Indians along the Wabash. He was killed on October 5 when Indians in the British interest counterattacked. La Balme had hoped to raise enough men to attack Detroit, but the support he needed was not forthcoming and the expedition turned into a marauding raid. La Balme had also planned another small raid against St. Joseph in what is now southwestern Michigan. Part of his command, led by Jean Baptiste Hamelin, went on to that post; they timed their arrival for the absence of the Indians on their winter hunt. Hamelin's sixteen men captured traders at St. Joseph and seized a large quantity of goods, but were overtaken and defeated by a pursuing force on December 5.[27] With both the British and the Americans unable to exert control, the Illinois country reverted to a state of semi-independence.

Late in December, 1780, the Spanish at St. Louis were informed of the results of the attack on St. Joseph. The news was delivered by two chiefs from Milwaukee, El Heturno and Naquiguen, who had long been friendly to the Spanish. The chiefs urged the Spanish to attack St. Joseph and offered to assist them. The Spanish lieutenant governor, Francisco Cruzat, decided to respond to the Indian request. In that way he could demonstrate Spanish strength to the Indians, ensure their continued support, destroy the British supply base at St. Joseph, and forestall future British attacks through the Illinois country.[28]

---

26. Haldimand to Germain, Sept. 17, 1780, *Michigan Historical Collections*, X, 430–32.

27. De Peyster to Haldimand, Nov. 16, 1780, Jan. 8, 1781, ibid., pp. 448–51; ibid., XIX, 581–82, 591–92, 699; Nasatir, p. 330. Four of the sixteen were killed, two were wounded, seven taken prisoner, and three escaped.

28. Cruzat to De Galvez, Jan. 10, 1781, in Lawrence Kinnaird, ed., *Spain in the Mississippi Valley, 1765–94 . . . Part I: The Revolutionary Period, 1765–81,* Annual Report of the American Historical Association for 1945, Vol. 2 (Washington, D.C.: Government Printing Office, 1949), pp. 415–17. El Heturno was also known as Letourneau and Blackbird. His Indian name was Siggenauk.

Augustin Mottin de la Balme

Early in January, sixty-five Spanish militiamen, joined by about the same number of Indians, set out from St. Louis. For more than five weeks they traveled across the frozen northwest. There was no resistance at St. Joseph—throughout the Revolution the Indians of that region had wavered in their support of the British. All the trade goods there were either distributed among the Indians or destroyed. On February 12 the Spanish party issued a formal proclamation annexing St. Joseph and its dependencies in the name of Spain. The military party immediately withdrew to St. Louis, however.[29] (That Don Eugenio Purre's epic winter trek from St. Louis to southwest Michigan is virtually unknown, while Clark's winter journey across Illinois to Vincennes is famous, tells us much about the vagaries of nationalism and historical myth-making.)

In view of the British attitude towards the Illinois country and the interior of North America, the eventual peace settlement of the American Revolution

29. Cruzat to Miro, Aug. 6, 1781, ibid., pp. 431–34; see also pp. xxix, 418.

produced no real boundary surprises. It is not necessary to stress Franklin's diplomacy, even less the old canard of Clark's victories, to understand British willingness to yield the Old Northwest to the Americans with only token diplomatic opposition.[30] To keep the American interior without either the seaboard colonies or New Orleans would have been ludicrous from the British point of view. Although the Spanish would have favored British control of the land north of the Ohio, England herself was quite willing to yield to the Americans. The greatest danger to American possession of the Illinois country had come in 1779–1780 when the British hoped to conquer New Orleans and the Mississippi. Such a victory would clearly have given the British a firmer diplomatic stance at the peace negotiations. But Spanish victories on the lower Mississippi ended the British threat to the Americans. The conquest of New Orleans, not Kaskaskia or Cahokia, was decisive to the fate of the Illinois country.

30. Three standard accounts of the diplomacy that ended the American Revolution are Richard B. Morris, *The Peacemakers* (New York: Harper, 1965); Samuel F. Bemis, *The Diplomacy of the American Revolution* (Bloomington: Indiana University Press, 1957); and Paul C. Phillips, *The West in the Diplomacy of the American Revolution* (1913; rpt. New York: Russell & Russell, 1967).

3. Edward Coles and the Constitutional Crisis in Illinois, 1822–1824

ROBERT M. SUTTON

EDWARD COLES IS SCARCELY A HOUSEHOLD WORD among Illinoisans. There are a number of valid reasons why the name of the second governor of the state might be—perhaps even ought to be—more widely recognized. For one thing, the Edward Coles story is full of paradoxes. He was an enigma to many of his contemporaries, and he remains so to those who examine his career a century and a half later. He spent only thirteen of his eighty-two years in Illinois, but that span proved to be a curious mixture of sunlight and shadow—of success and failure, with the failures seeming to clearly outweigh the successes. Yet his years of major political activity embraced stirring times, and the high esteem accorded him today stems not so much from his own place and time in history

---

ROBERT M. SUTTON retired as a professor emeritus in 1983 after thirty-six years on the faculty of the University of Illinois at Urbana-Champaign. For the last nineteen of those years he was also director of the Illinois Historical Survey in the University Library. A former president and life member of the Illinois State Historical Society, he has been involved in a wide range of Illinois history activities, the most recent of which was service as a member of the Illinois Historic Sites Advisory Council of the Illinois Historic Preservation Agency. An earlier version of this paper was presented before a meeting of the Society for the History of the Early American Republic in Knoxville, Tennessee, on July 25, 1986.

Illinois Historical Journal Vol. 82, No. 1 (Spring 1989): 33–46

Edward Coles

but rather from the present-day acceptance of the principles and ideals that he espoused and practiced.[1]

Almost from the day of his birth, Coles was associated with the great and the near great in revolutionary American society. He was born in 1786 to a well-to-do planter family in Albemarle County, Virginia, a frontier region in the picturesque Blue Ridge that Thomas Jefferson also called home. Family wealth and position made educational opportunities available to Coles both at Hampden-Sydney and at the College of William and Mary, but there is no evidence that he was graduated from either. Already expressing strong antislavery sentiments, he was employed as private secretary to President James Madison from 1809 to 1815, and following that service he made his first trip to the Old Northwest, going as far as St. Louis and returning to his home in Virginia by way of the Mississippi River and the Atlantic.[2]

1. Elihu B. Washburne, "Sketch of Edward Coles, Second Governor of Illinois, and of the Slavery Struggle of 1823–4," in *Governor Edward Coles,* ed. Clarence Walworth Alvord, Collections of the Illinois State Historical Library, Vol. 15 (Springfield: Illinois State Historical Library, 1920), pp. 15–20; Kurt Edwin Leichtle, "Edward Coles: An Agrarian on the Frontier," Diss. University of Illinois-Chicago 1982.

2. Washburne, pp. 18–20, 36–40; Leichtle, pp. 9–13, 60–85.

As Secretary of State in the Madison administration, James Monroe sent Coles to Russia in 1816 with a letter of introduction to the United States consul in St. Petersburg. Monroe wrote of Coles: "He was lately the private secretary of the President, and is a very respectable and amiable young man."

Greatly impressed with Illinois and especially with its apparent freedom from slavery, Coles began making plans to move permanently to the West, but before that could happen, President Madison recalled him, asking that he undertake a somewhat delicate diplomatic mission to the Russian capital of St. Petersburg. This undertaking, carried out successfully in 1816 and 1817, proved to be Edward Coles's private window on the world. Feeling no urgency to hurry home, he made his leisurely way across Europe with lengthy stops in Berlin, Paris (three months!), and London. Following a tour through England, Scotland, Ireland, and Wales, he sailed for New York in the spring of 1817. He made a second trip to Illinois in the summer of 1818, when he was able to observe the deliberations of the convention at Kaskaskia that was framing a constitution as a preliminary step toward statehood. Although the issue of slavery seems to have been kept in the background during the convention, the resulting constitution with its affirmation of "neither slavery nor involuntary servitude" apparently confirmed Coles's decision to remove to the frontier.[3]

3. Washburne, pp. 36–40; Theodore Calvin Pease, *The Frontier State, 1818–1848*, Centennial History of Illinois, Vol. 2 (Springfield: Illinois Centennial Commission, 1918), pp. 47–50, 70–71.

He returned home to settle his affairs, and by April he was ready to leave for Illinois. Traveling across northwestern Virginia by wagon, he took with him the twenty slaves and their families inherited from his father. Upon reaching the Ohio River, he engaged flatboats for the remainder of the trip. During the downriver journey Coles seized a particularly striking moment on what he called "a mild, calm and lovely April day" to announce to the unsuspecting slaves that he was granting them their freedom.[4] He had apparently made the decision some years earlier and waited only for his approach to the free state of Illinois to carry out his resolve. One would surely assume that such a magnanimous act of generosity, as well as of humanity, would not only have earned for Coles the respect and approbation of his fellow citizens but also have established his credentials as a true antislavery leader in the troubled society of frontier Illinois. Indeed, those results did eventually follow, but one not familiar with the facts of the case could scarcely believe the legal harassment and personal humiliation that befell Coles at the hands of his fellow citizens as a result of the manumission. Several years later, the Madison County Circuit Court held Coles liable for violating the state law passed just prior to his arrival in Illinois—a law that had not yet been published and of which he had no knowledge. The law required anyone bringing slaves into the state for the purpose of emancipation to post a $1,000 bond for each slave thus freed. Coles had provided certificates of manumission for each one, but had failed to post the required bond. Fortunately, the Illinois Supreme Court in 1826 reversed the judgment of the circuit court and relieved him of the heavy penalties of the unfairly applied legislation.[5]

Coles settled in Illinois as the owner of six thousand acres of land in Madison and St. Clair counties (purchased on a previous trip), and he held an appointment from President James Monroe as registrar of the recently established land office at Edwardsville. From that secure economic base the transplanted Virginian was quickly drawn into the turmoil of frontier politics.

Illinois was admitted to the Union in 1818, culminating a movement begun the year before. The issue of slavery seems to have been kept in the background, both in the constitutional convention and in the first state elections. This proved to be a remarkably fortuitous decision in view of the difficulty and delay that befell Missouri when she petitioned Congress for admission only a year later. Coles's thirteen years in Illinois indisputably affected the destiny of the then infant Prairie State.[6]

---

4. Washburne, pp. 43–45.

5. Pease, *Frontier State*, pp. 47–48; *Edwardsville Spectator*, April 12, 1825, p. 2, cols. 1–5; Washburne, pp. 162–69.

6. Leichtle, p. 67; Washburne, pp. 48–49.

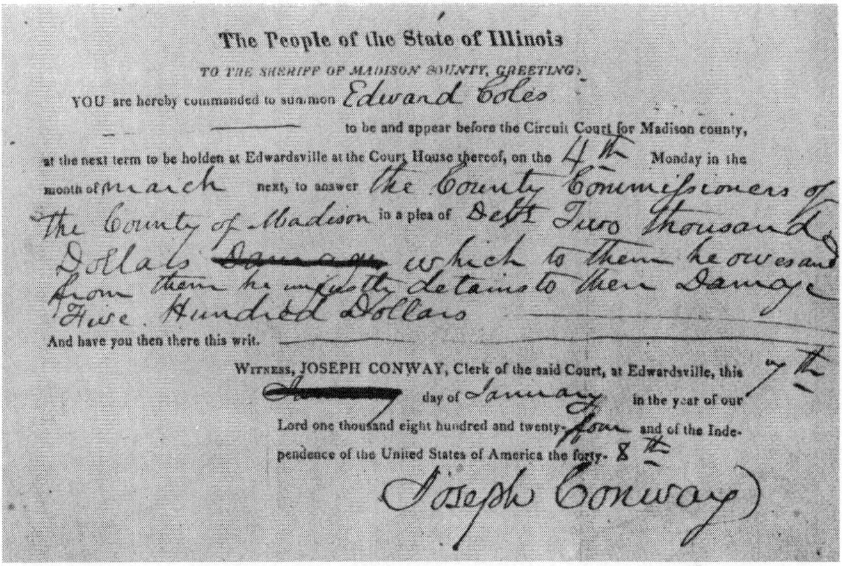

The People of the State of Illinois

TO THE SHERIFF OF MADISON COUNTY, GREETING:

YOU are hereby commanded to summon Edward Coles to be and appear before the Circuit Court for Madison county, at the next term to be holden at Edwardsville at the Court House thereof, on the 4th Monday in the month of March next, to answer the County Commissioners of the County of Madison in a plea of Debt Two thousand Dollars ~~Damage~~ which to them he owes and from them he unjustly detains to their Damage Five Hundred Dollars

And have you then there this writ.

Witness, JOSEPH CONWAY, Clerk of the said Court, at Edwardsville, this 7th day of January in the year of our Lord one thousand eight hundred and twenty-four and of the Independence of the United States of America the forty-8th

Joseph Conway

This summons was issued to Coles by the Madison County Commissioners for his failure to post bond for his emancipated slaves. The summons declared a debt of $2,000, plus $500 in damages. Under a law passed about the time Coles entered the state, a bond insuring that an emancipated Negro would not become a burden on the county was required of the former owner. Coles's penalty was eventually revoked.

Nothing illustrates so well the fluid character of frontier politics as Coles's decision to become a candidate for governor in 1822, only three years after his arrival in Illinois. Equally surprising is the fact that his candidacy was taken seriously. An explanation can be found in the confused state of slavery and antislavery issues.

Briefly stated, the facts are these. During the time that Illinois was a part of the French empire, Negro slaves were introduced into the region primarily to provide labor for the mining activities anticipated by Philippe François Renault and his Company of the Indies. The numbers of slaves were never large, but their presence was continuous; every major decision made with respect to the western territory (or back lands, as the British liked to call them) found it necessary to take into account the presence of slaves in Illinois. The British, coming into possession of the Illinois country after 1763, saw no need to interfere with the existing arrangement and indeed moved to guarantee the French the enjoyment of their laws and property rights by means of the ill-fated Quebec Act of 1774.[7]

7. Alvord, *The Illinois Country, 1673–1818,* Centennial History of Illinois, Vol. 1 (Springfield: Illinois Centennial Commission, 1920), pp. 154, 202, 303–7.

The situation did not change during the American Revolution, though in times of political or military crises affluent Frenchmen had a habit of moving across the Mississippi River with their slaves into friendly Spanish Louisiana. Almost as regularly they would move back into the Illinois country once conditions had returned to normal. Finally, after the war the American states that had claims to lands beyond the Appalachian Mountains responded favorably, one by one, to the Resolution of Congress on Public Lands, dated October 10, 1780, recommending a cession of western lands to the general government. That generous action by states with western land claims broke the deadlock that had delayed ratification of the Articles of Confederation for three and one half years. It also endowed the American government with a priceless resource—the public domain.[8]

The Virginia cession has a special significance for Illinois. Virginia's western claims were the most extensive and the strongest of any of the states, based as they were not only on the rights drawn from the royal charter but also on the military achievements of George Rogers Clark in the Illinois country in 1778, 1779, and 1780. The Virginia cession of 1783 guaranteed that French inhabitants of the Illinois villages who professed themselves citizens of Virginia "shall have their possessions and titles confirmed to them, and be protected in the enjoyment of their rights and liberties."[9] Whatever else that may say, it clearly confirmed the right to continue to own slaves.

In the meantime, Congress began to wrestle with the need for government—for some form of law and order—in the vast region between the existing states and the Mississippi River. Numerous plans were put forward, the most celebrated of which were the Land Ordinance of 1785 providing for the rectangular survey and public land sale and the Northwest Ordinance of 1787. Nothing illustrates better the ambivalent situation respecting slavery in Illinois at the time of statehood than a comparison of the Act of Cession (1783) and Article VI of the Northwest Ordinance (1787). One guarantees that the property rights of French inhabitants in Illinois (including their slaves) will be recognized and protected, and the other, the justly famous Article VI, declares: "There shall be neither slavery nor involuntary servitude in the said territory, otherwise than in the punishment of crimes, whereof the party shall have been duly convicted."[10]

How was the seeming contradiction to be reconciled? The answer is, it never really was, with the result that argument and agitation over slavery remained

8. Robert P. Howard, *Illinois: A History of the Prairie State* (Grand Rapids, Mich.: Eerdmans Pub. Co., 1972), pp. 43–46, 55–61; Henry Steele Commager, ed., *Documents of American History* (New York: S. F. Crofts, 1934), pp. 119–21.

9. Commager, ed., p. 121.

10. Emil Joseph Verlie, ed., *Illinois Constitutions,* Collections of the Illinois State Historical Library, Vol. 13 (Springfield: Illinois State Historical Library, 1919), p. 8.

as one of the continuing bones of contention throughout the territorial period. Given the skeletal governmental framework prevailing in the first stage of territorial organization, it frequently fell to the all-powerful governor to explain and implement portions of the Ordinance.

Various arguments and interpretations arose concerning the compact nature of the Ordinance. Because the controversy over slavery in different portions of the Old Northwest was particularly violent and recurrent in Illinois, the question as to whether Article VI of the Ordinance had immediate and permanent or only provisional and transitory force entered the debate from time to time.

While the earliest understanding in Illinois seems to have been that the antislavery section of the Ordinance was retrospective and that slavery existing in the Northwest Territory would be abolished, Governor Arthur St. Clair soon allayed the fears of French slaveholders and thereby contributed his share to the confusion that hovered over the scene. St. Clair, from the territorial capital in Marietta, Ohio, made his first trip out to distant Illinois in March, 1790. There, without consulting those who were more familiar with the genesis of Article VI than he was—and certainly without soliciting the opinions of first-class lawyers on the matter—St. Clair gave his opinion that Article VI was prospective in character, not retrospective, and should be interpreted as "a prohibition to any future introduction of slaves." That was a far cry from the actual language of Article VI and, perhaps, from the intentions of the framers as well. There is no evidence that St. Clair ever sought an official opinion from the Attorney General of the United States. That he should have delivered his pronouncement without even having consulted the principal legal officer of the government he represented is nothing less than amazing.[11] In our day when it seems as if any piece of legislation with even the slightest controversial twist has its constitutionality challenged in court, the fact that the Northwest Ordinance of 1787 as a whole was never subjected to judicial review seems almost incredible to us.

For the reasons detailed above, the slavery/antislavery dichotomy in Illinois was an ambiguous one, had been for a generation, and continued to be up to and including the constitutional crisis of 1822–1824. In August, 1822, Illinois would be electing its second governor, and since the constitution prevented governors from immediately succeeding themselves, incumbent Shadrach Bond was not a candidate for reelection. Exaggerated individualism with its attendant factionalism dominated Illinois politics in the 1820s. Even though the stage was set for the transition from gentlemen's politics to everyman's politics (Jacksonianism), party structure had not yet imposed its own brand of discipline upon electoral

11. Francis S. Philbrick, ed., *The Laws of Illinois Territory, 1809–1818,* Collections of the Illinois State Historical Library, Vol. 25 (Springfield: Illinois State Historical Library, 1950), pp. ccxli–ccxliii.

behavior in Illinois, and the personal factionalism of frontier politics was never better illustrated than in 1822.

Four candidates entered the race for governor in almost random fashion, and each of them seems to have had an identifiable position with respect to slavery, but that is not always easy to demonstrate. There is no question about Edward Coles; his was an avowedly antislavery position from the very start. Joseph B. Phillips, Chief Justice of the State Supreme Court and the first to announce his candidacy, was generally known to favor a constitutional convention as a means of clarifying the slavery issue. For a long time they were the only contestants in the race, but shortly before the election, Illinois Supreme Court Associate Justice Thomas C. Browne with a proslavery stance and Major General James B. Moore of the state militia, an opponent of slavery, tossed their hats into the ring.[12]

The results were as odd and as mystifying as you would expect them to be. Coles was elected governor, receiving 2,854 votes (33 percent), only 167 more than Judge Phillips. Phillips's total (representing 31 percent of the vote), in turn, was only 244 more than his judicial colleague, Thomas Browne. General Moore recorded only 622 votes (7 percent). The irony lies in the fact that Phillips and Browne, who represented similar proslavery positions, amassed between them more than five thousand votes, while Coles and Moore could command only 3,476 antislavery votes. The only satisfactory explanation that can be offered as to why those forces that wished to modify or change Illinois' position with respect to slavery would undermine their own position by allowing two candidates with such similar views to enter the race is to say that personalities still carried more weight than principles. The rivalry-fed factions, which tended to coalesce around the few federal officeholders in the state, made a strong effort to dominate local politics.[13]

Though the slavery question was the dominant issue (or, at the very least, the dominant *underlying* issue) in the campaign of 1822, there were other matters that attracted and deserved the attention of the voters. Congress was making decisions affecting the sale of public lands, Illinois citizens were deeply concerned with the need for internal improvements, and there were questions regarding the advisability of issuing more paper money in order to stabilize the always shaky State Bank of Illinois. But events would soon demonstrate that Illinois' future, either as a free state or as a newly converted slave state, was clearly hanging in the balance. For two years little else was discussed in the

---

12. Pease, *Frontier State*, pp. 74–76; *Edwardsville Spectator*, Nov. 6 (p. 1, cols. 2–5), Nov. 27 (p. 3, col. 2), 1821, and April 9, 1822, p. 3, cols. 2–4; Washburne, pp. 50–53.

13. Pease, ed., *Illinois Election Returns, 1818–1848*, Collections of the Illinois State Historical Library, Vol. 18 (Springfield: Illinois State Historical Library, 1923), pp. 14–15.

Illinois General Assembly, in the state's few newspapers, and in the churches, taverns, inns, and other public places.[14]

The Illinois General Assembly convened at Vandalia on the first Monday in December, 1822, and Governor Coles delivered what is described as a "Speech on his inauguration in the presence of both houses of the General Assembly of Illinois." Coles touched on a number of significant and timely issues, as a typical inaugural address should, but the emphatic part of his message had to do with the presence of slaves in Illinois and the treatment of blacks—both slave and free. Apparently subscribing to the theory that the best defense is a good offense, the Governor determined to confront the issue head on. Coles argued convincingly that despite the prohibition contained in the Ordinance, slavery *did* exist in Illinois and that the protection granted by the Virginia cession to French slaveholders was no longer necessary. By any stretch of the imagination few, if any, of the mature slaves owned by French masters would still be alive. From that courageous position Coles urged the legislature to abolish the institution totally, repeal the repressive Black Code, and pass additional laws that would provide much-needed protection for free blacks—especially against the heinous crime of kidnapping for the purpose of reselling them into slavery.[15]

Coles's speech to the general assembly opened up a bitter controversy, and the legislative response was imaginative and not totally unpredictable. Each house responded to the Governor's message in a different way, but the basic theme was that the abolition of slavery was beyond the power of the legislature to effect. Only a constitutional convention could do such a thing, the Senate report stated. The Senate report further argued that the convention of 1818 had been hampered, if not seriously flawed, by the provisions of the Ordinance of 1787, but now as a sovereign state in the Union, Illinois was in complete control of her destiny. With a kind of creative irony, the report thus concluded that a new constitutional convention was the only way to address the issues raised by the governor.[16]

The proposal for a constitutional convention would have to be submitted to a referendum of the people (that is, the male voters), and for that to happen the call would have to be approved by a two-thirds vote of both branches of the general assembly. Throughout this article, the terms proslavery and preconvention

---

14. Leichtle, pp. 154–56; Washburne, pp. 54–57; Eudora Ramsay Richardson, "The Virginian Who Made Illinois a Free State," *Journal of the Illinois State Historical Society,* 45 (1952), 14–15.

15. Washburne, p. 57; *Senate Journal,* 3 G.A., 1 Sess. (1822–1823), pp. 28–31; Pease, *Frontier State,* p. 77.

16. *Senate Journal,* 3 G.A., 1 Sess., pp. 43–45; Alexander Davidson and Bernard Stuvé, *A Complete History of Illinois from 1673 to 1873* (Springfield: Illinois Journal Co., 1874), pp. 318–21; Donald S. Spencer, "Edward Coles: Virginia Gentleman in Frontier Politics," *Journal of the Illinois State Historical Society,* 61 (1968), 154–55.

forces will henceforth be used interchangeably, as will the terms antislavery and anticonvention. There is no mistaking the strength of the proslavery faction. Although they had lost the governorship by what some would call a fluke, they continued to believe (with some justification) that, had their forces been united, Chief Justice Phillips would have been elected governor by a substantial majority. Furthermore, they had elected a proslavery lieutenant governor and returned decided majorities in both branches of the general assembly. It was a combination of these circumstances that led them to the conclusion that the time was right to press for a change in the constitution. Slavery advocates in the legislature set about preparing to submit the question of a convention to popular vote. There was no hesitation on the part of the Senate, where after a certain amount of logrolling and arm twisting, the resolution passed on February 10, 1823, by the required two-thirds majority on a vote of twelve to six. The progress of a similar resolution in the House was not so fortunate. A preliminary vote late in January returned twenty-two affirmative votes and fourteen negative—two short of the necessary two-thirds majority.[17]

Various pressures—some subtle, some not—were brought to bear on individual members in an effort to persuade them to change their vote. There were contracts to be let, canal commissioners to be appointed, new counties to be created, county seats to be located—all of which were used effectively by the legislative majority. Votes *were* influenced, and when the convention matter was again brought before the House on February 11, the expectation was that the required majority would be forthcoming. The anticipation and excitement of the proconvention forces was suddenly turned to surprise, shock, and indignation, however, when the vote was announced as twenty-three to thirteen—one short of the required two thirds. One member who had previously voted for the convention, Nicholas Hansen of Pike County, had switched his position and was now voting negatively. The resolution was defeated and was apparently beyond resuscitation. The fury of the convention majority seemed limitless, and cries of "the convention or death" rang throughout the State House.

Naturally, most of the indignation was directed toward Hansen. What follows is a turn of events almost too bizarre to believe. Nicholas Hansen owed his seat to a general assembly ruling after a challenged election. The very next day after his decisive negative vote, the House moved to reopen the question of his election. Not surprisingly, a majority of representatives decided that they had made a mistake; not Hansen but his opponent John Shaw should have been given the Pike County seat. Shaw's name was substituted for Hansen's, who was then turned out of his seat. Resorting to parliamentary cunning, the

17. Davidson and Stuvé, pp. 322–23; Pease, *Frontier State,* p. 77; Howard, pp. 134–36.

This mural of Edward Coles freeing his slaves is on the west wall of the first floor of the Illinois Statehouse. Installed in 1886, it was painted by an unknown artist who worked for the Phillips Decorative Company of Chicago.

House voted to reconsider the convention resolution. Sure enough, John Shaw was hurriedly summoned to Vandalia, voted with the majority, and—since no new defections occurred—the convention call passed twenty-four to twelve. The House reserved one final act of revenge for Mr. Hansen. On a motion by Alexander Field of Union County, Hansen's name was stricken from the list of canal commissioners.[18]

Initially the passage of the convention resolution in the legislature was regarded as tantamount to its being carried in the referendum; the sentiment was particularly prevalent among the proslavery advocates who were riding

18. Davidson and Stuvé, pp. 323–26; Pease, *Frontier State*, pp. 78–80; *Edwardsville Spectator*, Feb. 15 (p. 2, cols. 4–5), March 29 (p. 1, cols. 4–5, p. 2, cols. 1–3), 1823.

the crest of an emotional "high," but it also reflected a degree of consternation and discouragement on the part of the opponents of slavery. Both sides began immediately to organize for the eighteen-month-long campaign ahead of them. Not until August, 1824, would the people of the state indicate whether they favored or opposed the call for a new constitutional convention.

The opposing parties made use of every resource at their disposal. Coles immediately placed himself at the head of the anticonvention forces and moved to sway and mold public opinion in a most enlightened fashion. Local antislavery societies were organized, and an address (undoubtedly written by the Governor) was signed by fifteen legislators who had opposed the convention call. It closed by saying that should the convention forces triumph, "We should write the epitaph of free government" in Illinois.[19] Conventionists complained of the influence of the clergy; pulpits and public platforms rang with the wide-ranging debate. A Christian church conference in the Wabash River valley, a Baptist group calling themselves the "Friends of Humanity," and Methodist ministers and circuit riders all denounced slavery as a sin; the latter assailed slavery and slaveholders so bitterly as to invite angry retorts from the conventionists.[20]

Each side attempted to turn the voice of the state's four weekly newspapers to its advantage, and here the contest was much more even. After considerable pulling and hauling, the *Illinois Gazette* of Shawneetown and the *Kaskaskia Republican* supported the convention position, while the *Edwardsville Spectator* and the *Illinois Intelligencer* of Vandalia opposed it. Both sides talked of establishing additional newspapers to bolster their cause, and some efforts were made to do so. In any case, those efforts were short-lived at best, and no contemporary copies have survived.[21]

An additional journalistic advantage enjoyed by the anticonvention forces needs to be mentioned. Morris Birkbeck, the talented and cultured Englishman who had settled in southeastern Illinois only two years before Coles came to the state, became warm friends with the Governor. With antislavery views very similar to those of Coles's, Birkbeck offered to write a series of letters pointing out the evils that would accrue to Illinois and its people should slavery be legalized within its borders. Trained in the intellectual and moral principles of human liberty and writing under the pseudonym of Jonathan Freeman, Birkbeck warned Illinois farmers of the ruin that the introduction of slavery would bring among them. In simple homespun language the Jonathan Freeman letters were able

19. Pease, *Frontier State,* p. 80; Howard, p. 136; Washburne, pp. 84–85, 117.

20. Washburne, pp. 139–41; Davidson and Stuvé, pp. 325–26; Pease, *Frontier State,* pp. 81–82; Rufus Babcock, ed., *Forty Years of Pioneer Life: Memoir of John Mason Peck* (Carbondale: Southern Illinois University Press, 1965), pp. 194–95.

21. Davidson and Stuvé, p. 325; Pease, *Frontier State,* pp. 82–83; Washburne, pp. 117, 136–37.

to inspire the small, independent farmer—often debt ridden and discouraged by hard times—to renew his faith in his ability to possess the land and develop it without calling in slaveholders. In a remarkable way, Birkbeck succeeded in fitting the arguments against slavery squarely to Illinois conditions.[22]

Both factions labored under certain severe handicaps. The conventionists could scarcely bring themselves to argue openly and directly for the legalization of slavery in the state, and yet neither could they positively deny that some alteration in that direction was intended. In an effort to obfuscate the issue, conventionists attempted to be all things to all people. One of their favorite arguments was to insist that the opposition, by resisting the convention call, was really revealing not only its lack of faith in the people but also distrust of republican institutions generally. Furthermore, they were quick to suggest the convention as a remedy for any complaint that one might have with the existing constitution or the functioning of government under it. One anticonvention writer commented sagaciously, "They avow the object [of the convention call] to be to amend the particular defect which you may imagine the constitution to have."[23] There appears to have been a kind of complacent smugness in the proconvention arguments, which may have arisen from the fact that most of the state leaders (the so-called great men of the time) were in their camp.[24] It may also have reflected a belief that the weight of numbers was on their side.

But the anticonvention forces also had problems, especially at the outset when they tended to place great faith in the antislavery provision, Article VI of the Northwest Ordinance. Some among them were quick to see, however, that the same Ordinance that carried the prohibition against slavery contained a provision in Article V guaranteeing the admission of new states "on an equal footing with the original states, in all respects whatever." Exactly half of the states in the Union at that time permitted human slavery, and it is hard to see how that privilege could be denied to any of the new states should they earnestly (and legally) demand it. To have argued that the antislavery provision of the Ordinance overrode that privilege would have cast a dark shadow over the legitimate sovereignty of a state—and the new states of the West were particularly jealous of their prerogatives. Quite wisely, those opposing the convention concentrated their energies on more practical issues.

Finally, the moment of decision arrived with the general election of August, 1824—almost a year and a half after the general assembly had approved the

---

22. Spencer, pp. 157–59; Pease, *Frontier State,* pp. 87–89; Washburne, pp. 139–54.

23. *Edwardsville Spectator,* May 25, 1824, p. 1, cols. 3–5, p. 2, col. 1.

24. Washburne, pp. 106–9; Pease, *Frontier State,* pp. 84–86; Davidson and Stuvé, pp. 326–27; Howard, pp. 136–37.

convention call. By no stretch of the imagination could the outcome be called an anticlimax, even though the results were not nearly as close as had been anticipated. The proslavery party was overwhelmed; the anticonvention forces vindicated. Of the 11,612 votes cast (only 8,606 votes had been cast at the gubernatorial election just two years before), 6,640 or 57 percent opposed the calling of the convention, while 4,972 or nearly 43 percent favored it. Illinois would continue to be numbered among the free states of the Union.[25]

There are several difficult questions about the campaign. Were positions swayed? Did people change their minds? Did logical arguments win out? In the absence of hard evidence, it is possible to offer two tentative conclusions representing quite disparate points of view. One holds that public opinion *was* swayed and that the outcome of the balloting mirrored the arguments of the antislavery party. In other words, the more ambitious and resourceful and relevant campaigning of the opponents of slavery was successful.[26] Supporting that view is the lack of vigorous campaigning by proslavery forces, apparently the result of overconfidence. After all, it was a two-thirds vote in both houses of the general assembly that underwrote the call for a constitutional convention in the first place.

Another point of view holds that the outcome was simply a matter of demographics. The population of Illinois grew fantastically during those years; the state census of 1825 showed a total of 72,817, almost double the population reported at the time of statehood in 1818. Much of the growth occurred in the middle counties and in the more distant western counties of the state as settlement pushed up the Illinois River valley. Represented in this sizeable pool of newcomers were non-slaveholding southerners, Yankees from New England and the East, and the multiple-moving neighbors from the region in between. Obviously, little sentiment for slavery would be found in any of those groups, and no one should have been surprised at the outcome. The conventionists showed their greatest strength in the river counties along the southern border of the state opposite Kentucky and Missouri, where Gallatin County returned an 82 percent majority for the convention and Jefferson County 70 percent. On the other hand, the issue was a toss-up in the transitional counties that separated the southern region from the rapidly growing central Illinois counties. In the northernmost populated area, the anticonvention forces ran up majorities that stagger the imagination: in Pike County, 90 percent; Morgan County, 91 percent; and in Edgar County, across the state on the Indiana border, 99 percent.[27]

---

25. Pease, ed., *Illinois Election Returns,* p. 27; Davidson and Stuvé, pp. 326–27; Pease, *Frontier State,* pp. 89–91. Only 8,606 votes were cast in the 1822 gubernatorial election and 4,707 in the 1824 presidential election.

26. Pease, *Frontier State,* pp. 87–90.

27. Pease, ed., *Illinois Election Returns,* pp. 27–29.

Edward Coles died in 1868 in Philadelphia. In 1953 Illinois Governor William G. Stratton authorized the National Urban League to lay a wreath on Coles's grave in that city's Woodland Cemetery. The monument praises him as "Humanist, Courageous Humanitarian, Statesman."

Following the spirited contest of 1823–1824, the slavery issue disappeared from Illinois politics but the problem did not go away. The ambivalent situation of slaves being present in Illinois remained. Longterm indenture contracts still prevailed, and it would be another twenty years before the courts would find the entire indenture system illegal. In two penetrating and insightful articles, one in this *Journal* and the other in the *Journal of the Early Republic*, Paul Finkelman has called attention to the virulence of slavery wherever it was permitted to take root, its persistence, and the great difficulty of eradicating its remaining vestiges even in Illinois.[28] The state's vicious Black Code, reenacted in 1853, was not finally repealed until very near the end of the Civil War.

28. Finkelman, "Slavery, the 'More Perfect Union,' and the Prairie State," *Illinois Historical Journal*, 80 (1987), 248–69; Finkelman, "Slavery and the Northwest Ordinance: A Study in Ambiguity," *Journal of the Early Republic*, 6 (1986), 343–70.

Coles considered the convention fight the high point of his career, and rightly so. I wish I could tell you that he rode his victory in the slavery debate to a series of electoral triumphs in the years ahead. Unfortunately, the opposite is true. The 1824 campaign was not only his finest hour, it was virtually his only hour! He was not an effective politician, least of all in the rough and tumble frontier politics of the 1820s. First, last, and always the Virginia patrician, he was referred to by one of his staunchest admirers as that "stiff little Virginia autocrat." When his term ended, Coles retired to a quiet bachelor life on his Edwardsville farm. He traveled extensively, made money from his St. Louis real estate investments, and, after a disastrous campaign for a congressional seat, left Illinois permanently in 1832 for a happier life in Philadelphia.

Coles seems to be one of those individuals who has to be rediscovered and reinterpreted by each succeeding generation. Nineteenth-century historians were almost painfully laudatory in their assessment of his role in the slavery debate, and nearer our own time Clement Eaton in his highly regarded *Mind of the Old South* makes the firm statement that Coles "emigrated from his native state to Illinois, where he led a notable fight to save the state from adopting a form of slave labor."[29] Estimates continue to vary. A recent doctoral dissertation treating the career of Edward Coles concludes that the Governor carried out his duties competently but could not be said to have saved the state from slavery. Kurt Leichtle sees Coles as a man who had "opportunities to do extraordinary things and to champion great causes, but who through human frailty [and bad timing] missed most of the opportunities."[30]

On the other hand, there are those who see Edward Coles as a kind of miniature Jefferson on the Illinois prairie. There may be a certain legitimacy in this, but it is certainly not necessary. Edward Coles is quite capable of standing on his own record and does not need to be bolstered by the Jefferson image. Though historians are extremely reluctant to indulge in sweeping generalizations (and wisely so), it is very difficult to avoid the conclusion that, save for the initial restraining influence of Article VI of the Ordinance of 1787 ("There shall be neither slavery nor involuntary servitude in the said territory") and the spirited and courageous fight of Governor Edward Coles and his supporters against the proposed call for a constitutional convention, Illinois might well have been numbered among the slave states of the nation.

---

29. The book was published by Louisiana State University Press in 1967; see p. 6.
30. Leichtle, pp. 3–4.

4. Slavery, the "More Perfect Union," and the Prairie State

PAUL FINKELMAN

IN ACCEPTING THE REPUBLICAN NOMINATION for United States senator in 1858, Abraham Lincoln told his supporters that "a house divided against itself cannot stand." He asserted that the American "government cannot endure, permanently half *slave* and half *free*." Lincoln predicted that the nation would "become *all* one thing, or *all* the other." He warned his audience that the decision was in the balance; that the outcome was uncertain; and that freedom might lose out. "We shall *lie down* pleasantly dreaming that the people of *Missouri* are on the verge of making their State *free;* and we shall *awake* to the *reality,* instead, that the *Supreme* Court has made *Illinois* a *slave* State."[1]

Lincoln spoke in the wake of the Supreme Court decision in *Dred Scott* v. *Sandford.* That case is best known for two specific holdings of the Court: that the Missouri Compromise was unconstitutional, and that free blacks could never be citizens of the United States, and thus they had no standing to sue in federal

---

PAUL FINKELMAN received the Ph.D. from the University of Chicago in 1976, and was a Fellow in Law and Humanities at Harvard Law School from 1982 to 1983. He currently is a member of the history department of the State University of New York at Binghamton. Finkelman is the author of *An Imperfect Union: Slavery, Federalism, and Comity* (1981), *Slavery in the Courtroom* (1984), and *The Law of Freedom and Bondage* (1985). He serves as editor of the forthcoming *Slavery, Race, and the American Legal System, 1700–1872* and is also writing a history of the Bill of Rights.

1. Roy P. Basler, ed., Marion Dolores Pratt and Lloyd A. Dunlap, asst. eds., *The Collected Works of Abraham Lincoln* (New Brunswick, N.J.: Rutgers University Press, 1953–1955), II, 461, 467 (hereafter cited as *Collected Works*).

Illinois Historical Journal Vol. 80, No. 4 (Winter 1987): 248–269 court. But, in upholding Scott's status as a slave, the Court also ruled on the meaning of the Illinois Constitution. Besides living north of Missouri, in what eventually became Minnesota Territory, Scott had lived in Illinois. Part of his claim to freedom, which the Court brushed aside, rested on his Illinois residency. Thus, when Lincoln warned of awakening to discover "that the *Supreme* Court has made *Illinois* a *slave* State," he was making more than simply a rhetorical point. He was certainly fearful of "another Supreme Court decision, declaring that the Constitution of the United States does not permit a *state* to exclude slavery from its limits." A case that might have led to such a decision was in fact then making its way through the New York courts.[2]

Lincoln's speech was also informed by his experiences as an attorney in Illinois, a state where tensions between slavery and freedom were often apparent. Indeed, few states better illustrate the problems of trying to maintain "a more perfect Union" of slave and free states.

From its early settlement until at least the Civil War, Illinois was in many ways as much a southern state as a northern one. Almost half of the state was geographically south of the Mason-Dixon line. Much of Illinois bordered on two slave states. The area's first European settlers were French, many of whom owned slaves. Most of the state's earliest Anglo settlers came from the South. A few masters, such as Edward Coles, came to Illinois to free their slaves. But most who came north to Illinois brought with them their pro-Southern, proslavery biases. Some hoped to create a slave state on the northern banks of the Ohio. Despite the prohibition on slavery in the Northwest Ordinance, slavery remained prevalent throughout the Illinois Territory. The Illinois Constitution of 1818 protected existing slavery in the state and allowed the limited introduction of new slaves for short periods of time. In 1823 a proslavery majority in the Illinois legislature passed a resolution calling for a state constitutional convention for the purpose of legalizing slavery throughout the state. An influx of northern settlers, vigorous campaigning by anticonventionists, and the fortuitous failure of a proconvention newspaper prevented the convention from being called. The failure of the convention movement did not end proslavery sympathies in the state, however. Nor did it change the status of slaves already in Illinois. Thus, as late as 1848 slaves were legally held in the state.[3]

---

2. *Dred Scott* v. *Sandford,* 19 Howard (U.S.) 393 (1857); *Collected Works,* II, 467; *Lemmon* v. *The People,* 20 New York 562 (1860). The case is discussed in Paul Finkelman, *An Imperfect Union: Slavery, Federalism, and Comity* (Chapel Hill: University of North Carolina Press, 1981), Chs. 9–10.

3. N. Dwight Harris, *The History of Negro Servitude in Illinois . . . 1719–1864* (Chicago: A. C. McClurg, 1904), pp. 27–49; Peter S. Onuf, "From Constitution to Higher Law: The Reinterpretation of the Northwest Ordinance," *Ohio History,* 94 (1985), 5–33; Merton L. Dillon, "The Antislavery Movement in Illinois, 1809–1844," Diss. University of Michigan 1951, pp. 73–122.

The voters' decision to reject a constitutional convention—and thus keep Illinois a free state—did not end the state's dilemma as a free jurisdiction in a house divided. On the contrary, by remaining a free state with slave-state neighbors, Illinois was inevitably drawn into the crisis of the Union that developed between 1820 and 1860. In that period Illinois' leaders were forced to make hard choices over their obligations to the United States Constitution, comity and good faith to their slave-state neighbors, and fidelity to their own constitution and free-state status. Judicial and political leaders of the state faced three slavery-related constitutional issues: interstate transit of slaves across Illinois, prevention of the kidnapping of free blacks living in Illinois, and return of fugitive slaves.

Illinois officials often went out of their way to develop smooth and harmonious relations with their slave-state neighbors. More than any other Northern state (except Indiana), Illinois cooperated with its slaveholding neighbors. Part of the tradition of cooperation developed from the state's heritage of slaveholding and its large number of citizens of southern ancestry. Also affecting Illinois' response to slavery was a profound Negrophobia, especially in the southern and central parts of the state. Illinois' support of Southern demands was not complete, however. All three branches of Illinois government, but especially the judiciary, were sometimes more sensitive to the claims of free blacks, fugitive slaves, and abolitionists.

In order to understand the role Illinois played in the crisis of the Union, it is first necessary to examine briefly how Illinois responded to the presence of slaves and free blacks. Here the position of Illinois was unique among all the free states.

SLAVERY IN EARLY ILLINOIS

Slavery was prohibited in the Illinois Territory by the Northwest Ordinance. Despite the Ordinance, slavery and other forms of involuntary servitude flourished. Territorial governors, starting with Arthur St. Clair in 1790, interpreted the Ordinance to be prospective, and to free only those slaves brought into the territory after July 13, 1787. Thus, the "French settlers" were allowed to retain their slaves throughout the territorial period and well after statehood.[4]

Settlers of the Illinois country persistently, although futilely, petitioned Congress to amend or repeal the Ordinance to allow them to bring new slaves into

---

4. Finkelman, "Slavery and the Northwest Ordinance: A Study in Ambiguity," *Journal of the Early Republic,* 6 (1986), 343–70, argues that the Ordinance did not immediately end slavery and that it was probably not meant to do so. St. Clair to George Washington, May 1, 1790, in *Territorial Papers of The United States,* ed. Clarence Edwin Carter (Washington, D.C.: GPO, 1934), 11, 248. The Illinois Supreme Court did not declare the slaves of the "old French settlers" to be free until 1845. *Jarrot* v. *Jarrot,* 2 Gilman (Ill.) 1 (1845).

the territory. The failure of those petitions led to elaborate statutes designed to evade the slavery prohibition of the Ordinance. The first was adopted by the Indiana territorial government in 1803. Reenacted in later years and supplemented by other acts designed to protect the property rights of those who held indentured "servants," the statutes allowed for the indenture of former slaves for virtually unlimited periods of time. Under those laws hundreds of slaves were brought into the territory as "indentured servants." With indentures running up to ninety-nine years, such blacks were, for all practical purposes, slaves. They could be beaten and punished by their owners, jailed for running away, and their indentures (and thus their persons) could be sold, traded away, or bequeathed.[5]

Most of the pressure for allowing slavery in the Indiana Territory had come from settlers in present-day Illinois. With the division of the two territories in 1809, Illinois residents were able to move closer to creating a slave jurisdiction in the Old Northwest. In 1809 the new territorial government adopted all of the older Indiana territorial laws, including those creating a pseudo-slavery through indentures. In 1813 the legislature set a new standard for treating free blacks by prohibiting them from coming into the territory. The following year, "An act concerning negroes and Mulattoes" explicitly allowed the hiring of slaves in Illinois. The legislature guaranteed the owners of such hired slaves that the law would "not operate in any way whatever to injure the right of property in the master, in and to the service of such slave or slaves."[6]

---

5. Clarence Walworth Alvord, ed., *Cahokia Records, 1778–1790,* Collections of the Illinois State Historical Library, Vol. 2 (Springfield: Illinois State Historical Library, 1907), p. 567; Alvord, ed., *Kaskaskia Records, 1778–1790,* Collections of the Illinois State Historical Library, Vol. 5 (Springfield: Illinois State Historical Library, 1909), pp. 488, 493; Jacob P. Dunn, *Slavery Petitions and Papers,* Indiana Historical Society Publications, Vol. 2, No. 12 (Indianapolis: Bowen-Merrill, 1895), pp. 443–529; *American State Papers, Miscellaneous,* Vol. 1 (Washington, D.C.: Gales and Seaton, 1834), pp. 155–57, 477–78. The first law adopted was "A Law concerning Servants, Adopted from the Virginia code, and published at Vincennes, the twenty-second day of September one thousand eight hundred and three . . . ," reprinted in Francis S. Philbrick, ed., *The Laws of Indiana Territory, 1801–1809,* Collections of the Illinois State Historical Library, Vol. 21 (Springfield: Illinois State Historical Library, 1930), p. 42. The law was reenacted in 1805 and 1807, along with other legislation to protect slavery (ibid., pp. 136–39, 203–4, 463–67, 523–26, 657–58). See also Nathaniel Pope, *Laws of the Territory of Illinois, Revised and Digested under the Authority of the Legislature* (Kaskaskia: Matthew Duncan, 1815), II, 467–77, 646–54.

6. Philbrick, ed., *The Laws of Illinois Territory, 1809–1818,* Collections of the Illinois State Historical Library, Vol. 25 (Springfield: Illinois State Historical Library, 1950), pp. 51, 91–92, 157–58.

"Barbarity committed on a free African, who was found on the ensuing morning, by the side of the road, dead!" is from Jesse Torrey, A Portraiture of Domestic Slavery in the United States, *printed in 1817. Engravings on pages 80 and 83 are also from that volume.*

Under the law, slaves could be brought into the territory as laborers for up to twelve months, but there was no limit on the number of twelve-month periods that a slave could work. It would have been perfectly legal to bring slaves in for twelve months, remove them from the territory for a day, and then bring them back for another twelve months. Since the law did not contain any sanction against keeping the slave longer than twelve months, the subterfuge may have been unnecessary. Continuous twelve-month contracts, without any removal from the territory, might have been legal. Since the majority of the political and legal figures in the territory were proslavery—and many, like Governor Ninian Edwards, were slaveowners themselves—it is not surprising that there is no known instance of any slave being freed during the territorial period through the intervention of any political official or judge.

Illinois entered the Union in 1818, ostensibly as a free state. Unlike every other free state, however, Illinois allowed some forms of slavery to remain within its jurisdiction and provided no mechanism for ending slavery. Between 1780 and 1804 Pennsylvania, Connecticut, Rhode Island, New York, and New Jersey had all passed gradual emancipation statutes that guaranteed an eventual end to slavery in those places. Massachusetts, New Hampshire, and the new free states of Vermont, Ohio, and Indiana had ended slavery by their constitutions. Illinois took none of those steps.[7]

The Illinois Constitutional Convention of 1818 would probably have made Illinois a slave state, except that doing so would have delayed statehood. By that time, however, the leaders in Illinois were adept at maintaining slavery while appearing to have a free jurisdiction. The Illinois Constitution of 1818 contained a clause declaring, "Neither slavery nor involuntary servitude shall hereafter be introduced into this state otherwise than for the punishment of crimes whereof the party shall have been duly convicted." By prohibiting slavery that might "*hereafter* be introduced" (emphasis added), the clause implied that slaves already in the state would not be freed.[8]

The Constitution, written in August, 1818, also preserved indentures made prior to December, 1818. In that four-month period Illinois residents were free to bring in more indentured blacks, which some Illinois whites apparently did. Finally, the 1818 Constitution allowed the limited hiring of slaves in the state until 1825. Illinois came as close to permitting slavery as possible while still being considered a free state. In 1823–1824 Illinois came within a few hundred votes of calling another constitutional convention that would have explicitly allowed slavery in the state.[9]

FREE BLACKS IN THE STATE OF ILLINOIS

Given the proslavery implications of the 1818 Constitution and the biases of many of the state's early political leaders, it is perhaps to be expected that free blacks were unwelcome in Illinois. Free blacks were the antithesis of slaves. Moreover, the presence of free blacks undermined slavery and involuntary servitude. Like the slave states of the South, Illinois restricted the immigration of free blacks and severely limited their rights in the state.

In 1819 Illinois adopted "An Act respecting Free Negroes, Mulattoes, Servants, and Slaves" designed to preserve slavery and involuntary servitude and to

---

7. The ending of slavery in other states is discussed in Arthur Zilversmit, *The First Emancipation* (Chicago: University of Chicago Press, 1967), and Finkelman, *An Imperfect Union*, Chs. 1–3.

8. Illinois Constitution of 1818, Art. VI.

9. Ibid.; Eugene H. Berwanger, *The Frontier Against Slavery* (Urbana: University of Illinois Press, 1967), p. 14. Population statistics for the period are not totally accurate, but they do indicate a rapid growth in indentured blacks from 1818 to 1820. Margaret Cross Norton, ed., *Illinois Census Returns, 1810, 1818*, Collections of the Illinois State Historical Library, Vol. 24 (Springfield: Illinois State Historical Library, 1935), pp. xxx–xxxii. See also Theodore Calvin Pease, *The Frontier State, 1818–1848*, Centennial History of Illinois, Vol. 2 (Springfield: Illinois Centennial Commission, 1918), pp. 49–50.

regulate free blacks. The act provided for the registration of slaves and servants already in the state. The law prohibited persons from bringing slaves into the state for the purpose of emancipating them. If a slave was emancipated in the state, however, the former owner was required to give a bond "in the penalty of one thousand dollars" against the ex-slave's ever seeking public assistance. It further provided that no black could settle in the state without producing a certificate of freedom.[10]

This law was supplemented by a new statute of the same title passed in 1829. It required that blacks entering the state find sureties to give bond to insure they would not become a burden to the county. Anyone hiring or harboring a black who had not fulfilled those requirements could be fined $500. Any black entering the state without a certificate of freedom from another state would, under this law, be considered a runaway slave. Such a black could be held in jail for up to a year, while the sheriff advertised for the owner. Finally, slaves who entered the state seeking employment could not sue for their freedom. The law was amended in 1831 to provide for fining free blacks who failed to comply with its provisions.[11]

Illinois passed a number of other statutes designed to regulate blacks and limit their access to the state. The government of Illinois made its policies quite clear. Existing slavery was to be preserved and the growth of a free black population was to be discouraged. Such policies would affect how Illinois dealt with slaves and slaveowners in other states during the thirty years leading to the Civil War.

INTERSTATE TRANSIT

The interstate movement of slaves raised important legal and constitutional questions for free states. Put simply, the interstate transit of slaves forced free states to choose between enforcing their own constitutions, which prohibited slavery, and granting comity—or legal force—to the laws of states that allowed slavery. How a free state dealt with visiting slaves said much about its commitment to its own ideals of freedom and its commitment to the Union. The actions of a free state also reflected attitudes towards free blacks. By the eve of the Civil War most Northern states resolved the questions in favor of freedom and against interstate harmony. A few Northern states, including Illinois, came down on the other side of the question.

The legal problems raised by the interstate transit of slaves were complicated and technical. Slavery was traditionally viewed as a local institution. By the time

---

10. *Laws of Illinois,* 1 G.A., 2 Sess. (1819), p. 355.

11. *Revised Laws of Illinois,* 6 G.A. (1828–1829), p. 109; *Laws of Illinois,* 7 G.A. (1830–1831), p. 101.

of the American Revolution the status of *slave* was considered an anomaly in Anglo American law that could be supported only by the force of positive law. Thus, in *Somerset* v. *Stewart* (1772), William Murray, Lord Mansfield freed a slave voluntarily brought to England by his master on the theory that "The state of slavery is of such a nature, that it is incapable of being introduced on any reasons, moral or political; but only by positive law, which preserves its force long after the reasons, occasion, and time itself from whence it was created, is erased from memory: it's so odious, that nothing can be suffered to support it, but positive law."[12]

Before 1836 Northern states accepted the force of the *Somerset* precedent but did not implement it because they felt an obligation to grant comity to visiting slaveowners from other states. That comity was simply one of the many compromises necessary to maintain a union of free and slave states.[13]

In the nation's first six decades, few cases involving the *Somerset* precedent were brought before Northern courts. Thus, while *Somerset* had not been adopted by Northern courts, neither had it been rejected by them. Then, starting with *Commonwealth* v. *Aves,* an 1836 Massachusetts case in which a slave in transit was freed, antislavery lawyers successfully brought into most Northern courts cases that placed *Somerset* squarely before Northern judges. Responding to shrewd antislavery activism, most Northern courts quickly adopted the *Aves* precedent. Antislavery activists were also successful in generating legislative support for statutes that declared slaves free the moment their masters brought them into free states. These laws were similar to judicial adoptions of *Somerset.* Both the laws and the court decisions simply reaffirmed what Northerners had always believed: that slavery was incompatible with a free-state constitution, and unless restricted by the United States Constitution, a state had the power to free any person within its jurisdiction. Thus, slaveowners who brought their human property into Massachusetts, New York, Pennsylvania, and other free states did so at their own peril.[14]

The situation in Illinois was different. Before the 1840s no cases involving slave transit reached courts in Illinois. Slaveowners heading for Missouri or Kentucky often traveled in Illinois, or even lived there before reaching their

---

12. *Somerset* v. *Stewart,* Court of King's Bench, 98 Eng. Rep. 499, at 510; 1 Lofft 1 (1772) at 19; Finkelman, *Imperfect Union,* pp. 34–40.

13. Finkelman, *Imperfect Union,* Chs. 1–3.

14. *Commonwealth* v. *Aves,* 18 Pickering (Mass.) 193 (1836). For developments in other states, see Finkelman, *Imperfect Union.* For an analysis of *Somerset* v. *Stewart* in American constitutional theory, see William M. Wiecek, *The Sources of Antislavery Constitutionalism, 1760–1848* (Ithaca, N.Y.: Cornell University Press, 1977).

final destination in a slave state. Kentucky and Missouri masters also used their slaves in Illinois if they owned property in both states. Some slaves were also rented out in Illinois. Such uses of slave labor were accomplished with no apparent interference from the Illinois courts. Indeed, court action may have been precluded by two statutes—one passed in 1827 and the other in 1829.

The 1827 Illinois Criminal Code provided for a $500 fine or six months in jail for anyone who harbored a slave or servant "owing service or labor to any other person or persons, whether they be residents of this state[,] of any other state, territory, or district within the limits and under the jurisdiction of the United States." The same penalties applied to those who might "hinder or prevent" an owner "from retaking or possessing" his slaves in a "lawful manner."[15] The law apparently applied to slaves in transit as well as fugitives. The law does not appear to have prevented slaves in transit from claiming their freedom, but it would seem to allow for the prosecution of any whites aiding those slaves.

An 1829 statute prohibited suits for freedom by slaves who came into Illinois and hired themselves out. Whether a court would have applied the statute to slaves "brought" into Illinois by their masters is unknown. The thrust of the statute, however, was clearly both to prevent the growth of a black population in Illinois and to protect the slave property of masters from other states.[16]

The 1829 law did not lead to any reported litigation. In 1843, however, two cases arose under the 1827 act. In Bureau County, abolitionist Owen Lovejoy was convicted of harboring a slave brought into the state by her owner. Lovejoy appealed to the circuit court, and Judge John D. Caton ruled that the moment a master voluntarily brought a slave into Illinois the slave became free under the state's constitution.[17] The decision had little precedential value because it was an unre ported circuit court case, but it did indicate that one of the most prestigious judges on the Illinois bench wished to adopt the *Somerset-Aves* line of cases.

A majority of the Illinois bench was not prepared to join Caton in bringing the jurisprudence of the Prairie State in line with the rest of the North. That same year, in *Willard* v. *The People,* the Illinois Supreme Court upheld the conviction of Julius Willard for harboring a slave who escaped after she had been brought into the state by her master.[18]

15. *Revised Laws of Illinois,* 5 G.A. (1826–1827), p. 156; *Revised Laws of Illinois,* 8 G.A. (1832–1833), p. 206.

16. *Revised Laws of Illinois,* 6 G.A. (1828–1829), pp. 109–11.

17. Harris, pp. 111–12.

18. *Willard* v. *The People,* 4 Scammon (Ill.) 461 (1843). Willard and Lovejoy were technically charged under the 1833 reenactment of the 1827 law.

The *Willard* case reveals the support given by Illinois to comity and harmony within the Union. The slave in question, Julia, had been voluntarily brought to Illinois by Sarah Liles, her owner, who was passing through Illinois on her way to Louisiana. Willard hid Julia, and for that he was convicted under the 1827 law for harboring a slave owing service or labor to someone in another state. From the arguments of counsel it appears that Willard was initially charged with aiding a fugitive slave. The Illinois Supreme Court recognized this as a transit case, however, and ultimately dealt with it in that way.[19]

There were two reasonable grounds for overturning Willard's conviction. The court might have treated it as a case involving a fugitive slave, as the initial prosecution had done. As such, the court could have declared that the 1827 law was unconstitutional because it usurped the exclusive power of Congress to regulate the rendition of fugitive slaves. Such a ruling would have been based on the United States Supreme Court's 1842 decision in *Prigg* v. *Pennsylvania,* which contained language implying that Congress had exclusive jurisdiction over the return of fugitive slaves. That position was strenuously argued by Willard's counsel. While some Northern jurists used the *Prigg* decision to avoid hearing cases involving fugitive slaves, the Illinois court, in 1843, declined to take that route.[20] While recognizing the connections between the *Willard* case and the case of a fugitive slave, the Illinois Supreme Court correctly refused to classify it as a fugitive slave case because Julia had not actually escaped into Illinois. The Illinois court might also have held that Julia became free the moment her owner voluntarily brought her into Illinois. That position would have been a simple application of the *Somerset-Aves* precedents to the facts of the case and would have followed the analysis made by Judge Caton in Lovejoy's case.

Although Caton sat on the Illinois Supreme Court, he was unable to persuade his brethren to follow his Lovejoy opinion. In rejecting a *Somerset-Aves* approach to slave transit, the majority went out of its way to support interstate harmony at the expense of Julia's freedom, reflecting the sympathies of the legislature. Both the legislature and the court placed a higher value on interstate comity and harmony than on freedom for a slave. In his opinion of the court, Judge Walter B. Scates stressed the need for interstate harmony, including accommodating the needs of citizens of slave states who visited free states. Thus, Scates asserted that Illinois "does most distinctly recognize the existence of the institution of

---

19. Ibid.

20. *Prigg* v. *Pennsylvania,* 16 Peters (U.S.) 539 (1842). For a discussion of judges using *Prigg* to overturn such laws, see Finkelman, "*Prigg* v. *Pennsylvania* and Northern State Courts: Anti-Slavery Use of a Pro-Slavery Decision," *Civil War History,* 25 (1979), 5–35.

slavery" in the United States, leading him to conclude that "the slave does not become free by the Constitution of Illinois by coming into the State for the mere purpose of passage through it."[21]

Scates believed that to rule otherwise "would be productive of great and irremediable evils, of discord, of heart burnings, and alienation of kind and fraternal feeling, which should characterize the American brotherhood, and tend greatly to weaken, if not destroy the common bond of union amongst us, and our nationality and character, interest, and feeling." Scates continued: "Thousands from Kentucky, Virginia, Maryland, Tennessee, and the Carolinas . . . have sought and found free and safe passage with their slaves" across Illinois. Unlike virtually every other Northern judge, Scates interpreted the Privileges and Immunities Clause of the United States Constitution to protect the right of transit with slaves for American citizens from other states.[22]

The *Willard* decision clearly reflected the intent of the Illinois legislature and was consistent with other proslavery decisions by the state's highest court. Nevertheless, not everyone in the state approved of the decision. The *Alton Telegraph* noted that the decision was "in direct conflict" with decisions in Massachusetts, Pennsylvania, and other Northern states. The *Telegraph* clearly tried to shame the state's court by pointing out that Illinois was out of step "with what is regarded *now* as the settled law of the land."[23]

In 1847 the Illinois court began to move in step with the rest of the North on the adoption of the *Somerset* principle. In that year Chief Justice William Wilson freed Jane Bryant and her four children, slaves owned by General Robert Matson of Kentucky. Matson also owned land in Illinois, where he had kept Jane for two years. Chief Justice Wilson ruled that "by bringing Jane" to Illinois "and domiciling" her there, Matson lost all claim to her. The case was heard while Wilson was riding circuit, and was not appealed. Nevertheless, it signaled a change in the decision-making of the Illinois court.[24]

The change was confirmed in *Hone* v. *Ammons* in 1852, when the full supreme court affirmed that in Illinois "the presumption of the law" was that all blacks were free. The only exception was fugitive slaves. Slaves in transit were not fugitives and thus were free if found in Illinois. Judge Lyman Trumbull, although ill and about to leave the court for the United States Senate, wrote a long concurring

---

21. *Willard* v. *The People*, p. 471.

22. Ibid., pp. 471–72.

23. Harris, p. 115.

24. *In re Jane*, 5 Western Law Journal 202 (1847); Matson is erroneously identified as Mateson.

opinion attacking slavery. He cited cases from New York, England, and Massachusetts, as well as the recently adopted Illinois Constitution of 1848, in arguing that slavery could not exist in Illinois.[25] Illinois had finally entered the mainstream of Northern legal thought.

The *Willard* and *Hone* decisions violated two long-standing aspects of public policy in Illinois. First, they led to an increase of the state's black population by freeing slaves in transit, with the likely result that former slaves would remain in the state. Second, the decisions undermined the interstate harmony that Illinois, the quintessential border state, wished to preserve. The legislature reaffirmed those policies in 1853 with a statute that prohibited any free black from moving into the state and also declared that masters in transit had a right to pass through the state with their slaves.[26]

The right to transit was incorporated into a comprehensive statute enacted to prevent all blacks—slaves, fugitive slaves, and free blacks—from entering the state. For the Illinois legislature a commitment to interstate harmony happily coincided with Negrophobia and racism. Antiblack attitudes made it far easier for the Illinois legislature to support comity.

Political support for a proslavery position is illustrated by Jane Bryant's suit for freedom. Her master, General Robert Matson, in seeking to retain his property right in Jane and her children, hired the best lawyer he could find. In Illinois, in 1847, that meant hiring Abraham Lincoln. Lincoln, of course, was more than just a lawyer. He was also an extremely ambitious politician at the height of his pre-presidential success. Lincoln's role in the case suggests his own ambivalence about slavery and race. His action contrasts with his future cabinet members, Salmon P. Chase and William H. Seward, who had consistently defended fugitive slaves, free blacks, and abolitionists, but would have never thought of taking the case of a slaveowner. Lincoln's willingness to represent a slaveowner is also indicative of antiblack, antiabolitionist, pro-Southern sentiments in Illinois, and the weakness of the Illinois antislavery movement in 1847. Lincoln could take the case and not worry that it would destroy his chances for future elective office. One cannot imagine a similar case being taken by a

25. *Hone* v. *Ammons*, 14 Ill. 28 (1852), at 29; Trumbull to John D. Caton, June 29, 1853, John D. Caton Papers, Box 5, Library of Congress. The theoretical position distinguishing fugitives from slaves in transit was reaffirmed in 1857, when the court asserted that "negroes within our jurisdiction are supposed to be free" (*Rodney* v. *Illinois Central Railroad*, 19 Ill. 42 [1857]). *Rodney*, however, did not actually involve the freedom of a slave but was a damage suit against the railroad for the loss of a slave. It is unclear, in view of the 1853 law, whether the Illinois court would have freed a slave in transit after 1853.

26. *Laws of Illinois*, 18 G.A. (1853), p. 57.

politician—particularly a Whig—in most of Ohio, Pennsylvania, New York, or New England.[27]

On the eve of the Civil War, Illinois was one of three Northern states that granted visiting masters a right of transit with their slaves. In the crisis of the Union, at least on that issue, Illinois clearly stood for compromise. Indeed, during the Oregon debates of 1848 Senator Sidney Breese of Illinois admitted that courts in his state "uniformily decided against . . . freedom," although in similar cases the slave states of Kentucky and Missouri would have granted freedom based on residence or transit in Illinois. Breese, described by an antislavery congressman from Ohio as a "cold-hearted, doughfaced scoundrel," clearly reflected the racist views of many of his constituents.[28] Yet the position of Illinois was not one of complete capitulation to every Southern demand. Even after the legislature specifically protected slave transit, the Illinois bench continued to maintain its recently adopted position that there was a presumption of freedom for all people m Illinois.

PERSONAL LIBERTY AND FREE BLACKS

While the Illinois court accepted a presumption of freedom on the eve of the Civil War, the state nevertheless remained generally hostile to free blacks. That hostility, as has already been noted, began in the territorial period. After statehood Illinois adopted a complex series of laws designed to make the migration of free blacks difficult and complicated. In 1848 Illinois attempted to stop black immigration entirely through a provision in the state's new constitution that required the general assembly to "pass such laws as will effectually prohibit free persons of color from immigrating to and settling in this state, and to effectually prevent the owners of slaves from bringing them into this state, for the purpose of setting them free." The laws were to be passed at the first session of the assembly after the adoption of the constitution. Not until 1853, however, did the state legislature finally pass such a law.[29]

---

27. *In re Jane,* at 202–6; John J. Duff, *A. Lincoln: Prairie Lawyer* (New York: Rinehart & Co., 1960), pp. 130–49. During the same year, Salmon P. Chase and William H. Seward were co-counsel before the Supreme Court defending an abolitionist who had helped runaway slaves; see *Jones* v. *Van Zandt,* 5 Howard (U.S.) 215 (1847).

28. The other two states allowing slave transit were Indiana and New Jersey. Breese is quoted in [Thomas Hart Benton] *Historical and Legal Examination of that Part of the Decision of the Supreme Court of the United States in the Dred Scott Case, Which Declares the Unconstitutionality of the Missouri Compromise Act* (New York: Appleton, 1857), pp. 44n–45n; Jacob Brinkerhoff to Chase, March 26, 1849, Salmon Portland Chase Papers, Historical Society of Pennsylvania, Philadelphia.

29. Illinois Constitution of 1848, Art. XIV; *Laws of Illinois,* 18 G.A. (1853), p. 57.

The Black Laws seem to have had little effect on the actual migration of blacks into Illinois, although many individuals suffered anxiety from registration procedures and fear of prosecution.[30] Between 1820 and 1860 the state's total black population increased by more than 500 percent, from 1,374 to 7,628. In 1850 half the blacks recorded by the census were born outside the state. In the decade from 1850 to 1860 the Illinois black population increased by over two thousand—a 40 percent jump. Two factors make the increase particularly notable. First, the Fugitive Slave Law of 1850 had made life difficult for runaways in the North. This was especially true in Illinois because of its close proximity to the South. Many fugitive slaves and free blacks along the Ohio River fled north to the upper Midwest, northern New York, or New England. Other blacks, fugitive and free, abandoned the United States altogether and emigrated to Canada. Second, while pressure from the 1850 federal law should have reduced the black population in Illinois, black migration was absolutely prohibited by state legislation after 1853. Nevertheless, the state's black population increased dramatically. Clearly, anti-immigration statutes did not discourage blacks from moving to the state.[31]

The ever-growing free black population created an enormous dilemma for Illinois lawmakers, judges, and politicians. On one hand, the state was firmly on record as opposing any black migration. On the other hand, the question for legislators was what to do with those blacks, and how much protection to give them. Because free blacks were often claimed as fugitive slaves, the protection of free blacks was inextricably tied to the rendition of fugitive slaves.

---

30. For one of the few examples of enforcement of the Illinois Black Laws, see J. N. Gridley, "A Case under an Illinois Black Law," *Journal of the Illinois State Historical Society,* 4 (1912), 401–25. John Jones, a black leader in Chicago, called the anti-immigration law "a dead letter." Jones, *The Black Laws of Illinois, and a Few Reasons Why They Should be Repealed* (Chicago: Tribune Book and Job Office, 1864), p. 13. The John Jones Collection at the Chicago Historical Society contains preprinted certificates of freedom from Madison County dated 1844. Such papers may have served to protect blacks from kidnapping as well as to intimidate blacks. The James Gallagher Papers at the Chicago Historical Society contain the Macoupin County record of an Alabama man who emancipated his slave there in 1837, but there is no indication that the clerk demanded a bond from the former owner or in any other way complied with the Illinois laws.

31. United States Bureau of the Census, *Negro Population, 1790–1915* (Washington, D.C.: GPO, 1918), pp. 57, 63; Robin W. Winks, *The Blacks in Canada: A History* (New Haven, Conn.: Yale University Press, 1971), pp. 234, 492. Winks avoids any final determination of how many blacks moved into Canada after passage of the 1850 law, but does indicate that the population grew substantially. Official census figures found 4,669 blacks in Canada West (Ontario) in 1851 and 11,223 in 1861.

Most Northern states passed personal liberty laws designed to prevent the kidnapping of free blacks.[32] Those laws also complicated the rendition of fugitive slaves. Some of the laws were in fact good-faith efforts to balance the need for free blacks to be protected from kidnappers with the rights of slaveowners to recover their runaway slaves. That was the purpose of Pennsylvania's 1826 act "to Give Effect to the Provisions of the Constitution of the United States Relative to Fugitives From Labour, For the Protection of Free People of Colour, and To Prevent Kidnapping."[33]

In the 1840s and 1850s a number of Northern states passed new and stronger personal liberty laws that were in fact designed to thwart the return of fugitive slaves, under the guise of preventing kidnapping. New York's 1840 act "to extend the right of trial by jury" was aimed at protecting fugitive slaves in that state. So too was Ohio's 1857 law, which prohibited the use of state facilities for the incarceration of alleged fugitive slaves.[34] The laws were a result of the growing abolitionist movement in the North, the increasing Northern hostility towards slavery expansion, and the return of fugitive slaves.

The personal liberty laws stemmed from two distinct, although interrelated, philosophies. The anti-kidnapping laws reflected a Northern commitment to due process that has been underestimated by most scholars of the period. Despite the racism of the antebellum North, most Northern states in fact did protect the liberty and basic human rights of their black neighbors. The personal liberty laws were a key component of that protection.[35]

The personal liberty laws also reflected a wide range of abolitionist, antislavery, and Christian sentiment against the rendition of fugitive slaves. Whites and blacks throughout the North opposed the enforcement of the federal fugitive slave laws through a variety of violent and nonviolent, legal, extralegal, and illegal methods. Slaves were rescued from the hands of federal marshals, slaveowners, and professional slave catchers in Massachusetts, Pennsylvania, New York, Ohio, and Wisconsin. Blacks organized vigilance committees, often with white allies, to prevent the return of fugitives. Thousands of Northerners aided fugitive slaves. A few—like James G. Birney and John VanZandt in Ohio and John Hossack

---

32. Thomas D. Morris, *Free Men All: The Personal Liberty Laws of the North, 1780–1860* (Baltimore: Johns Hopkins University Press, 1974).

33. *Pennsylvania Laws, 1826*, pp. 150–55.

34. *New York Laws, 1840*, pp. 174–77; *Ohio Laws, 1857*, pp. 186, 221–22.

35. Leon Litwack, *North of Slavery* (Chicago: University of Chicago Press, 1961); Berwanger, pp. 30–59. For an analysis that differs substantially from Litwack, see Finkelman, "Prelude to the Fourteenth Amendment: Black Legal Rights in the Antebellum North," *Rutgers Law Journal*, 17 (1986), 415–81.

and Julius Willard in Illinois—ended up caught in the meshes of the law. Many others, however, working on the "underground railroad" or operating openly above ground, helped runaway slaves without ever facing legal action.[36]

Countless citizens petitioned against the fugitive slave laws and voted against those who supported them. Many Northerners no doubt sympathized with the fictional Mary Bird of *Uncle Tom's Cabin.* When her husband, Senator Bird, asserted that there were no legal, constitutional, or political reasons for returning runaway slaves, Mary Bird responded: "Now, John, I don't know anything about politics; but I can read my Bible; and there I see that I must feed the hungry, clothe the naked, and comfort the desolate; and that Bible I mean to follow." Such religiously based sympathy for fugitive slaves helped motivate political abolitionists, who in turn worked for the passage of personal liberty laws.[37]

The history of personal liberty legislation in Illinois differs from that of most of the North. Throughout the antebellum period the Illinois legislature went out of its way to prevent free blacks from settling in the state. The legislature was far more concerned with helping masters recover fugitive slaves than with preventing the kidnapping of free blacks.

In 1825 the state passed "An Act to more effectively prevent Kidnapping," which was directed at persons taking "any negro, mulatto, or person of color" out of the state against their will in order to enslave them. Despite its title, the law was not very effective. The penalties for violation included fines, but not imprisonment.[38] There is no record that anyone was ever prosecuted under that section of the law.

---

36. *Birney* v. *The State,* 8 Ohio 230 (1837); *Jones* v. *Van Zandt,* at 215; Chase, *Reclamation of Fugitives From Service: An Argument ... in the Case of Wharton Jones vs. John Vanzandt* [sic] (Cincinnati: R. P. Donogh, 1847); *Report of the Trial of John Hossack Indicted For Rescuing a Fugitive Slave from the U.S. Deputy Marshal at Ottawa, October 20th, 1859* (Chicago: Press & Tribune, 1860); and *Willard* v. *The People,* p. 461; Harris, pp. 111–12. In Chicago, Charles Dyer singlehandedly rescued a fugitive slave from his captors who had tied him up in the Mansion House. In broad daylight Dyer entered the room where the slave was, cut his bonds, and pointed to the window. As the slave escaped and Dyer left the room, the slave's owners were "paralyzed for the moment by the audacity of the rescuer" but then gave chase. Dyer fended them off with a cane. The fugitive slave had been living with Dyer's family. "Charles Volney Dyer," *Biographical Sketches of the Leading Men of Chicago* (Chicago: Wilson & St. Clair, 1868), p. 76; clipping, *Chicago Inter Ocean,* June 17, 1883, Zebina Eastman Papers, Chicago Historical Society. By the 1850s antislavery men could openly solicit money in Chicago to aid fugitive slaves (receipt, Dec. 7, 1850, Eastman Papers).

37. Harriet Beecher Stowe, *Uncle Tom's Cabin* (1852; rpt. New York: New American Library, 1966), p. 93. For the importance of religion in Illinois antislavery, see Linda Jeanne Evans, "Abolitionism in the Illinois Churches, 1830–1865," Diss. Northwestern University 1981, and Dillon, pp. 103–5, 178–90.

38. *Laws of Illinois,* 4 G.A., 1 Sess. (1825), pp. 149–51.

Any prosecutions under the law would have been severely handicapped by an 1827 act that prohibited the testimony of any "negro, mulatto, or Indian" against a white person. Such laws were of course not uncommon. Illinois, however, remained unusual because it kept that prohibition right through the end of the Civil War. By 1860 only four Northern states—Indiana, Illinois, Oregon, and California—prohibited black testimony. The two Pacific Coast states repealed their restrictions in 1862 and 1863.[39]

The 1825 anti-kidnapping law also prohibited the removal to other states of blacks indentured for a term of years. The only penalty for such a removal was the loss of services of the indentured black, however.[40] The penalty obviously was not a deterrent, since—once out of the state—an indentured black might be treated as a slave or sold as one.

In 1855 the legislature authorized the governor to appoint agents to secure the liberty of Illinois residents kidnapped and sold as slaves in other states. The act appears to have been a bona fide attempt to help rescue free blacks taken out of the state against their will.[41]

The 1855 act was apparently a response to two controversies between Illinois and Missouri. over the alleged kidnapping of free blacks living in the Prairie State. In 1849 Governor Augustus C. French sought the extradition of three men accused of kidnapping a black named Wade. Missouri Governor Austin King asserted that Wade was in fact a fugitive slave, and thus the alleged kidnappers could not be extradited to Illinois. In a heated exchange of letters, French defended the right of Illinois to define kidnapping and to punish those who violated the law. In the end, however, the alleged kidnappers remained in Missouri.[42]

In 1852 Governor French again sought the extradition of three alleged kidnappers. The victim was Charles Bartelle, a black descendant of slaves owned by French settlers. Bartelle had been born after the adoption of the Northwest Ordinance. French argued that Bartelle was never the slave of anyone, and

39. *Revised Laws of Illinois,* 5 G.A. (1826–1827), p. 320. Iowa had prohibited black testimony, but repealed that law in 1856 *(Laws of Iowa, Passed at the Sixth General Assembly,* pp. 235–36). Iowa also prohibited black immigration, but that law was repealed in 1860 *(Revision of 1860, Containing All the Statutes of a General Nature of the State of Iowa* [Des Moines: John Teesdale, State Printer, 1860], Ch. 159, Sec. 3978). *The Code of Civil Procedure and other General Statutes of Oregon Enacted . . . September 8, A.D. 1862* (Oregon: Asahel Bush, State Printer, 1863), p. 174; *General Laws of the State of California, From 1850 to 1864, Inclusive* (San Francisco: H. H. Bancroft, 1865), Sec. 5332.

40. *Laws of Illinois,* 4 G.A., 1 Sess. (1825), pp. 149–51.

41. Ibid., 19 G.A. (1855), p. 186.

42. Evarts Boutell Greene and Charles Manfred Thompson, eds., *Governors' Letter-Books, 1840–1853,* Collections of the Illinois State Historical Library, Vol. 7 (Springfield: Illinois State Historical Library, 1911), pp. 207–9, 212–16.

therefore those who took him to Missouri were kidnappers. The Governor of Missouri, asserting that Bartelle was in fact a fugitive slave, refused to comply with the extradition requisition.[43]

The actions of Governor French suggest the limits of Illinois' interstate cooperation. Illinois would willingly capture fugitive slaves, incarcerate them, and advertise for their owners. Similarly, Illinois would punish its own citizens who helped slaves escape. But, at least in the 1840s and 1850s, Illinois would not tolerate the kidnapping of its free black residents. French's actions and the 1855 law may have stemmed in part from a sense of humanitarian obligation, but the main thrust of the issue was sovereignty. Illinois demanded the right to define for itself what constituted a crime within its jurisdiction. It was not inconsistent, therefore, for Illinois to punish people who helped slaves escape in Illinois and also to seek to punish people who kidnapped free blacks from Illinois.[44] There is no indication that the 1855 law was in fact ever used to secure the liberty of any kidnapped blacks.

FUGITIVE SLAVES AND THE OBLIGATIONS OF THE UNION

Despite the 1855 statute and Governor French's correspondence with his Missouri counterparts, Illinois' personal liberty laws were weak and relatively impotent against kidnappers. The weakness of Illinois' personal liberty legislation contrasts sharply with other states, which closed their facilities to slave catchers in the 1840s and 1850s and in other ways attempted to deter the removal of blacks from their jurisdictions. The state legislation also contrasts with actions by the city of Chicago. In 1850 the Chicago Common Council strongly urged citizens of that city, including police officers whose salaries were appropriated by the council, to refuse to participate in the enforcement of the new Fugitive Slave Law. The council condemned the law as "revolting to our moral sense and an outrage upon our feelings of justice and humanity."[45]

Few antebellum issues were as explosive as the rendition of fugitive slaves. The stakes were high for all concerned. The cases were also complicated. For the runaway a rendition meant not only an end to freedom but return to almost certain punishment. The fugitive Anthony Burns was partially crippled by the treatment he received after he was returned to Virginia. Even more than the physical pain was the mental and emotional anguish. A return to slavery signaled, for most fugitive slaves, an end to a hope and a dream. Few slaves were as

43. Ibid., pp. 244–45.

44. Ibid., pp. 65–66, 69–78.

45. Charles W. Mann, *The Chicago Common Council and the Fugitive Slave Law of 1850* (Chicago: Chicago Historical Society, 1903), p. 85.

desperate as Margaret Garner, who took the lives of her own children in order to prevent their return to servitude. Similarly, the fugitive Jerry begged a crowd to kill him, rather than allow his return to slavery. He was more fortunate than most and was rescued that same night by a mob in Syracuse, New York. At Christiana, Pennsylvania, fugitive slaves risked their lives in a gun battle with a posse led by their master and a federal deputy marshal.[46]

For a master the return of a fugitive slave was a matter of dollars—lots of them. Slaves, worth between $500 and $1,200, were extremely valuable possessions; but also at stake was an issue of constitutional right. Masters often spent more than a slave was worth to assert their rights as slaveowners under the Constitution. For masters the return of their slaves was a moral issue from which they could not back away. Burns's owner, for example, refused an offer for more than his slave was worth if he would free him. The offer was refused, at least in part, to vindicate his rights. At Christiana, Edward Gorsuch declared he would get his slaves back or "go to Hell trying." Where he ended up in the afterlife is unclear, but when the gunfire stopped, his slaves were on their way to Canada, and he was on his way to an early grave.[47]

For Northern whites the rendition of a fugitive could also be a painful experience. Abolitionists could not bear the thought of a rendition happening in their communities. Ann Phillips, wife of abolitionist Wendell Phillips, urged her cousins to agitate against the return of Burns because "if this man is allowed to go back *there is no* antislavery in Massts. —We may as well disband at once if our meetings and papers are all talk." After his conviction for violating the Fugitive Slave Law of 1850, John Hossack told the federal court in Illinois that he acted because he was "opposed to carrying out wicked and ungodly laws" and because he loved the "freedom" of his state and country. To preserve that freedom, Hossack rescued a fugitive slave, for which he paid a fine and spent a short time in jail.[48] Preventing the rendition of a fugitive slave was as much a

---

46. Burns to Richard Henry Dana, Dec. 18 [1854], Wendell Phillips Papers, Blagden Collection, Box 45, Houghton Library, Harvard University. See also Charles Emery Stevens, *Anthony Burns: A History* (Boston: John P. Jewett and Co., 1856), pp. 181–97; Eugene H. Roseboom, *A History of the State of Ohio: The Civil War Era, 1850–1873* (Columbus: Ohio Historical Society, 1944), pp. 344–45; *New York Tribune,* Oct. 8, 1851; Finkelman, "The Treason Trial of Castner Hanway," *American Political Trials,* ed. Michal Belknap (Westport, Conn.: Greenwood Press, 1981), pp. 79–100.

47. Finkelman, "The Treason Trial of Castner Hanway," pp. 79–100.

48. Ann Phillips to Anne and Deborah Weston, May 25, 1854, Weston Family Papers, Boston Public Library; *Speech of John Hossack, Convicted of a Violation of the Fugitive Slave Law, Before Judge Drummond, of the United States District Court, Chicago, Ill.,* Anti-slavery Tracts, new series, No. 11 (New York: American Anti-slavery Society, 1860), pp. 4–5; *Report of the Trial of John Hossack.*

matter of honor for abolitionists as returning the slave was a matter of honor for the slaveowner. Similarly, for politicians seeking Southern support, a successful rendition was equally one of honor.

All of those competing interests and sentiments were felt by Northern legislators and judges. For the judge hearing the case of a fugitive slave, the issue was often one between natural law and positive law. It was equally one of justice to the slave, who deserved to be free, and justice to the master, who had a constitutional right to his property. It was an issue that few judges willingly faced. Legislators faced similar dilemmas, although perhaps not as sharply. Neither the master demanding his property nor the slave pleading for his liberty ever argued their case in the state assemblies. Yet the conscientious legislator could not avoid knowing that a vote for a personal liberty law would cut one more strand of the bonds of Union, while a vote against personal liberty might bring sleepless nights and electoral defeats. In most states personal liberty won out over the Northern cries of disunion coming from the South. Illinois, however, was not with the majority of the North on this question.

In its willingness to aid in the rendition of fugitive slaves, Illinois went further than other Northern states to support the Constitution and the Union. Legislation supporting the return of fugitive slaves contrasts sharply with the paltry protections Illinois offered its own free blacks. Not until 1825 did Illinois adopt legislation to protect free blacks from kidnapping. The 1825 anti-kidnapping law provided no jail sentences for kidnappers.[49]

The Prairie State's concern with fugitive slaves began before the passage of the anti-kidnapping law and continued through the secession crisis. The 1819 act "respecting free Negroes, Mulattoes, Servants and Slaves" provided penalties for slaves and servants leaving their master's premises without a pass. The law, however, did not directly affect those who might aid a runaway slave. That "defect" was partially remedied by the 1827 criminal code, which provided a jail term and fines for anyone convicted of harboring a slave or servant owing service or labor under the laws of any American jurisdiction.[50]

The 1829 "Act Respecting Free Negroes and Mulattoes, Servants and Slaves" dealt at greater length with the problem of fugitive slaves. Section One provided a $500 fine for anyone harboring a black who had entered the state without a certificate of freedom. Of that amount, half would be paid to the informant. The clause obviously made helping a fugitive slave a risky act and at the same time may have induced some Illinois citizens to act as slave catchers. Section

---

49. *Laws of Illinois,* 4 G.A., 1 Sess. (1825), pp. 149–51.

50. Ibid., 1 G.A., 2 Sess. (1819), pp. 354–61; *Revised Laws of Illinois,* 5 G.A. (1826–1827), pp. 156–57; *Revised Laws of Illinois,* 8 G.A. (1832–1833), pp. 206–7.

Two of the law dealt directly with fugitive slaves by asserting that any black who could not prove his or her freedom "shall be deemed a runaway slave or servant." Such a legal provision was quite common in slave states, but virtually unknown in free states. In essence, Illinois adopted the Southern presumption that all blacks were slaves, unless they could prove otherwise—a rejection of the law of freedom that distinguished the North from the South. Blacks without free papers could be jailed for six weeks and then hired out "month to month, for the space of one year" while the sheriff advertised the existence of the "runaway." If no owner claimed the "runaway," the next circuit court would grant freedom papers. Finally, the law provided that any slaves coming into the state and claiming to be free would be arrested and returned to their owners. The laws of the 1820s were reenacted in later years, and were incorporated into the official revised statutes of Illinois published in 1858.[51]

The contrast between the meager protections for free blacks and assistance to slaveowners went beyond legislation. While there were no known prosecutions under the 1825 law designed to prevent kidnapping, there were a number of arrests and jailings both of blacks believed to be fugitive slaves and those accused of helping them. In 1847, for example, in the famous Matson case, a court ordered that the blacks claiming their freedom be held in jail on the ground that they were "in Illinois without certificates of freedom." Only after the court held Jane and her children to be free were they released. Had the court held that Jane was still a slave, then the whites who helped her would have been subject to prosecution. A similar situation had occurred in Bureau County in 1841, when Jonathan Holbrook was indicted for harboring an alleged fugitive slave named John Dolan (alias Black Jack). The grand jury admitted it did not know who Dolan's owner was but nevertheless approved the prosecution of Holbrook. Similarly, abolitionists Julius Willard, Owen Lovejoy, and Richard Eells were prosecuted for aiding blacks alleged to be fugitives. Both Lovejoy and Willard aided slaves brought into the state by their owners. Lovejoy's conviction was reversed by Judge Caton, while riding circuit. Willard, however, was fined $20 and court costs by Judge Samuel D. Lockwood, who was also riding circuit at

---

51. *Revised Laws of Illinois,* 6 G.A. (1828–1829), pp. 109–11, and the amendment is in *Laws of Illinois,* 7 G.A. (1830–1831), p. 101. The 1827 law was reenacted in 1833 with slight changes in the section numbers *(Revised Laws of Illinois,* 8 G.A. [1832–1833], pp. 206–7); Section 147 became 149, 148 became 150, and 150 became 152. Later prosecutions in the 1840s used the 1833 revision section numbers. The Black Laws were all reenacted as part of the revised statutes of 1845 *(Revised Laws of Illinois,* 14 G.A. [1845], pp. 387–91), and again in 1857 (Samuel H. Treat, Walter B. Scates, and Robert S. Blackwell, comps., *The Statutes of Illinois, Embracing All of the General Laws of the State, in Force December 1, 1857* [Chicago: D. B. Cooke, 1858], pp. 820–24).

the time. Willard appealed to the full Illinois Supreme Court, which affirmed the conviction.[52]

The case of Richard Eells was more correctly one involving a fugitive slave. Eells gave employment and lodging to a fugitive slave owned by a Missouri resident. For that he was indicted under the 1827 law, as Willard and Lovejoy had been.[53] Eells appealed his conviction on two separate grounds. The Illinois court's rejection of those arguments further illustrates the position of the state with regard to interstate harmony.

Eells first argued that the indictment did not charge that he knew he was harboring a fugitive slave. This defect in the indictment led to the argument that Eells in fact had no "notice" that the person he hired was a fugitive slave. Eells could legitimately state that he did not *know* that the person in his house was a slave. That argument could have provided an easy, noncontroversial, and constitutionally legitimate way for the Illinois court to overturn Eells's conviction. In a similar case in 1837 the Ohio Supreme Court had accepted such arguments, made by Salmon P. Chase, in overturning a conviction of the abolitionist James G. Birney. Unlike its Ohio counterpart, however, the Illinois court was not looking for an easy way to avoid upholding Eells's conviction. Thus, Justice James Shields dismissed the argument with the rather odd conclusion that "[t]he essence of the offence consists in the attempt to defraud the owner of his property," and not in harboring the slave. Justice Shields, of course, failed to explain how Eells could have attempted to defraud the owner of a slave when he did not know that the person in his house was a slave. However illogical Shields's point, he nevertheless made it clear that the Illinois court was intent on upholding the conviction and the interstate harmony it implied.[54]

The second objection went to a complicated constitutional question. In 1793 Congress had passed a fugitive slave law that set out methods for returning fugitive slaves and punishing those who aided them. In 1842, in *Prigg* v. *Pennsylvania*, the United States Supreme Court had not only upheld the validity of the 1793 law but also struck down a Pennsylvania personal liberty law that had added requirements to the rendition process. In his opinion of the court, Justice Joseph Story had implied that states might be precluded from legislating on fugitive slave rendition because that was exclusively the jurisdiction of Congress.[55]

---

52. *In re Jane*, pp. 202–6; Duff, pp. 130–49; "Indictment of Jonathan T. Holbrook in Bureau County for harboring a black named John Dolan, alias Black Jack, as a fugitive from slavery," copy in Eastman Papers; Dillon, pp. 333–34.

53. Dillon, pp. 331–32; *Eells* v. *The People*, 4 Scammon (Ill.) 498 (1843).

54. *Birney* v. *The State; Eells* v. *The People*, at 509.

55. *Prigg* v. *Pennsylvania*; Finkelman, "*Prigg* v. *Pennsylvania* and Northern State Courts," p. 8.

Attorneys for Eells argued that under *Prigg* only the federal government could prosecute people for helping fugitive slaves; therefore, the Illinois law was unconstitutional, and Eells had to go free. Shields responded that *Prigg* only prevented states from passing laws "which may interfere with the right of the master to the service of his fugitive slave."[56] Illinois had no such laws, and so both the statute and the conviction were sustained. Three justices—Lockwood, Thomas C. Browne, and Chief Justice William Wilson—dissented.

In *Eells* the Illinois court showed its willingness to convict citizens of the state for helping fugitive slaves. That position contrasted with virtually all other free state courts, which by that time consciously avoided aiding slaveowners and slave catchers.[57] The *Eells* opinion demonstrated that Illinois, unlike most other Northern states, placed interstate harmony and fidelity to the national Constitution far above any concepts of natural law or the pro-freedom implications of the state's own constitution.

The Eells affair indicated the distance that Illinois would go in supporting the needs of its slave-state neighbors while also illustrating the limits of that policy. While Eells was under indictment in Illinois, Governor Thomas Reynolds of Missouri sought his extradition as a fugitive from justice for harboring a fugitive slave from Missouri. Reynolds claimed that Eells had stolen the slave from Missouri, and thus he should be tried in that state. Illinois Governor Thomas Ford initially agreed to extradite Eells, but then changed his mind when he discovered that Eells had not been in Missouri for the previous two years, and therefore could not have "fled" from that state. Ford noted that Eells was a physician in Quincy and was "all the time publicly about in the city" when he allegedly committed the crime of slave stealing in Missouri. Ford told Governor Reynolds that he had been "furnished with a great mass of written testimony, too voluminous to be set forth," that convinced him that Eells was innocent of the charges against him in Missouri.[58]

Ford's refusal to extradite Eells has been ascribed to protest meetings by antislavery activists in northern Illinois. Such meetings may have affected Ford—as they might any politician—but, since Ford was totally unsympathetic to abolitionists, the meetings may not have been crucial. Ford assured Reynolds that "the fanatical and misguided Sect called Abolitionists" had "no countenance or encouragement from the people" of Illinois. Nevertheless, the "arrest, imprisonment and transportation of an innocent man" could not be allowed, even "under pretence of suppressing or punishing the excesses of a Sect."[59]

---

56. *Eells* v. *The People*, p. 510.
57. Finkelman, "*Prigg* v. *Pennsylvania* and Northern State Courts," pp. 8–14.
58. Greene and Thompson, eds., p. 71.
59. Ibid., p. 77.

"Kidnapping" from Jesse Torrey's 1817 Portraiture of Domestic Slavery

More important, no doubt, than Ford's sense of justice towards an innocent man—especially an innocent abolitionist—was his sense of state sovereignty. He asserted that "the first and highest duty of a Governor, is to the people of his own State." He argued that "State Governments were erected upon this principle."[60] Ford would not extradite Eells, because to do so would violate the sovereignty of his state. Illinois would willingly prosecute Eells for crimes committed in Illinois against the slaveowners of Missouri, but Missouri could not try a citizen of Illinois for a crime committed in Illinois. That would violate the sovereignty of Illinois.

FUGITIVE SLAVES AND THE CRISIS OF THE UNION

Throughout the 1820s, 1830s, and into the 1840s, the three branches of Illinois government generally granted comity to visitors and travelers passing through the state with slaves. The governors were willing to allow the extradition of abolitionists if they had actually gone to slave states and helped slaves escape. The policies developed out of a general concensus on two issues: that blacks should be kept out of the state, and that interstate harmony was a major political goal.

60. Ibid., p. 76.

The concensus began to break down in the 1840s. The Illinois judiciary initiated that change. In 1841, in *Kinney* v. *Cook,* the Illinois court asserted that in cases involving the status of blacks living in that state "the presumption is in favor of liberty." The burden of proof in claiming a black's labor rested with the alleged owner. The court, however, did not deny that with proper proof a claim to a black's labor as an indentured servant or slave might be sustained. Four years later, in *Jarrot* v. *Jarrot,* the Illinois high court declared that all blacks born in Illinois after the adoption of the 1818 Constitution were free, regardless of the status of their parents. In his opinion of the court, Justice Walter B. Scates also asserted that any black born in Illinois since the adoption of the Northwest Ordinance of 1787 was also free. A majority of Scates's colleagues, however, did not endorse his second conclusion.[61]

The *Kinney* and *Jarrot* decisions ran counter to legislative actions dating from 1819. They clearly undermined the concensus on the status of blacks in Illinois. The decisions reflected, at least in part, the development of a sophisticated antislavery bar. The prevailing attorney in both cases was Lyman Trumbull, who would ultimately serve on the Illinois Supreme Court. The change in attitude—and the limits of that change—were apparent in the convention that wrote the 1848 Illinois Constitution. That document finally ended all slavery and indentured servitude in the state. Yet it also prohibited free blacks from immigrating to the state.[62]

In 1852, in *Hone* v. *Ammons,* the Illinois court expanded its "presumption of freedom" to include all blacks found in the state. Two years earlier, in *Thornton's Case,* the court had struck down an 1829 law that required sheriffs to arrest and incarcerate alleged fugitive slaves. The court ruled, as it had refused to do in the cases of Willard and Eells, that Congress had exclusive jurisdiction over fugitive slaves. In *Thornton's Case,* Chief Justice Samuel Treat, citing Justice Story's decision in *Prigg* v. *Pennsylvania,* declared the Illinois statute void "because it assumes to legislate upon a subject matter over which congress has exclusive jurisdiction."[63] Taken together, the two cases put the Illinois court on the cutting edge of the legal attack on slavery. The court had asserted that it would assume all blacks in the state to be free and that it would not allow state officials to help in the capture and return of fugitive slaves.

---

61. *Kinney* v. *Cook,* 3 Scammon (Ill.) 232 (1841); similar principles of law were enunciated in *Bailey* v. *Cromwell,* 3 Scammon (Ill.) 71 (1841); *Jarrot* v. *Jarrot.*

62. Illinois Constitution of 1848, Art. XIII, Sec. 16, and Art. XIV.

63. *Hone* v. *Ammons;* the initial trial is reported as *David Howe* [sic] v. *Godfrey Ammons,* 1 Western Legal Observer 306 (1849). *Thornton's Case,* 11 Ill. 332 (1850), at 336; the appeal is reported as Dec. Term, 1849, but was not decided until 1850.

The results were unacceptable to the Illinois General Assembly. In 1853 the legislature effectively overruled the implications of *Hone* by declaring that slaves in transit were not entitled to claim their freedom. In 1857 the court reasserted that Illinois would have no part in the rendition of fugitive slaves. In *Rodney* v. *Illinois Central Railroad,* the court refused to allow a Missouri slaveowner to recover the value of a slave who had escaped by boarding an Illinois Central train at Cairo.[64] Until 1850 the state, through its courts and legislature, had readily aided masters seeking fugitive slaves and had willingly prosecuted those who helped fugitive slaves. But *Thornton* and *Rodney* signaled that the Illinois court, like most of its Northern counterparts, would not play the role of slave catcher.

The Illinois legislature was unwilling to follow the court's leadership on this issue, just as it had rejected the court's decisions on slaves in transit. Although the court emphatically declared unconstitutional Illinois' fugitive slave law, the legislature nevertheless included it as part of the 1858 revised statutes.[65] Thus, a statute declared unconstitutional in 1850 remained on the books after an official revision of the laws in 1858. On paper, at least, the state of Illinois supported harmony within the Union at the expense of liberty for all.

ILLINOIS: A HOUSE DIVIDED

By the eve of the Civil War, Illinois was truly a house divided against itself on the question of fugitive slave rendition. In southern Illinois fugitive slaves were easily captured and returned while those who helped them faced prosecution under state laws. After 1850 federal officials and slave catchers operated with little direct interference from local citizens. All fugitives captured south of Champaign were either returned to their owners by a federal court or taken back to slavery without any court hearing at all.[66]

In northern Illinois the situation was quite different. Slave catchers entered Chicago at their own risk. Citizens in that city openly aided fugitive slaves without fear of capture. In 1846, for example, Dr. Charles V. Dyer, a prominent physician, employed a fugitive slave from Kentucky in his house. When his master seized him, Dyer rescued the fugitive and beat off the Kentuckians with his cane. Dyer faced no prosecution even though he had harbored a fugitive slave in violation of Illinois law. Nor did the alleged master seek to prosecute

64. *Laws of Illinois,* 18 G.A. (1853), p. 57; *Rodney* v. *Illinois Central Railroad.*

65. *Thornton's Case;* Treat et al., comps., p. 821.

66. Analysis is based on tables listing all fugitive slave renditions in Stanley W. Campbell, *The Slave Catchers: Enforcement of the Fugitive Slave Law, 1850–1860* (Chapel Hill: University of North Carolina Press, 1970), pp. 199–207.

"The Author noting down the narratives of several freeborn people of colour who had been kidnapped," from Jesse Torrey's Portraiture of Domestic Slavery

Dyer for the battery or sue him for the value of the slave. Two years later Dyer stalled a courtroom proceeding until a crowd gathered and rescued a captured fugitive.[67]

The passage of the new fugitive slave law in 1850 led to more organized opposition. Within weeks after the passage of the 1850 law, Chicago blacks had formed the "Liberty Association," whose members were assigned to "patrol the city, each night and keep an eye out for interlopers." When slave hunters appeared in the city, they were warned that their safety could not be guaranteed. Meanwhile, as already noted, the city council went on record as opposing enforcement of the law. In the first fugitive slave case under the federal law the judge determined that the person was not a fugitive slave. In 1860 a Chicago judge had a sheriffs deputy remove a slave from federal custody on an alleged violation of a city law. The slave was then released and escaped. In nearby Ottawa, mobs rescued slaves in 1851 and 1859. While some slaves were returned from the northern part

67. Rufus Blanchard, *Discovery and Conquests of the Northwest with the History of Chicago,* Vol. 2 (Chicago: Rufus Blanchard and Co., 1900), pp. 289, 297; "Charles Volney Dyer," pp. 76–77; *Chicago Inter Ocean,* June 17, 1883; A. T. Andreas, *History of Chicago From the Earliest Period to the Present Time* (Chicago: A. T. Andreas, 1885–1886), 1, 604–8, 11, 454.

of the state, the successful returns were accomplished without legal action. In other words, slaveowners could bring slaves out of the northern part of the state only if they did so quietly and without being discovered.[68]

Illinois lawmakers were also divided on how to deal with the return of fugitive slaves. The courts chose fidelity to fundamental justice, the Constitution of Illinois, the legal trends in other free states, and a narrow and strict reading of the United States Constitution. The legislature chose fidelity to a broad reading of the United States Constitution and to a spirit of comity and interstate harmony.

Those questions, like so many other critical legal issues, ultimately became political issues. They emerged, quite appropriately, in the Lincoln-Douglas debates of 1858. Geographically, the two men seemed to be on the wrong side of the question. Douglas, a native of New England and since 1847 a resident of northern Illinois, represented a proslavery position. Lincoln, originally from Kentucky and a resident of southern Illinois, took the opposite position. Although neither man expressed it in these terms, the two debaters also reflected the division between the Illinois legislature and the Illinois Supreme Court. Oddly enough, Douglas, a former member of the state supreme court and a defender of the United States Supreme Court, took the side of the legislature. Lincoln, a former state legislator, came down on the side of the Illinois Supreme Court.

Put another way, Douglas favored the state's long-standing hostility to free blacks and sympathy for slaveowners. Lincoln took the opposite position. Douglas, Lincoln correctly told his audience in Chicago, "cares not if slavery is voted up or down."[69] Lincoln, of course, did care. Similarly, Douglas would relegate all blacks to servitude because he feared there would otherwise be interracial marriage and the destruction of white society. Lincoln was less fearful and protested "against that counterfeit logic which presumes that because I do not want a negro woman for a slave, I do necessarily want her for a wife." Lincoln understood he "need not have her for either."[70]

---

68. Mann, pp. 9; 199–207; *Chicago Inter Ocean,* June 17, 1883; Eastman to Chancellor Jenks [1874], Eastman Papers. Indicative of the geographical division in the state was the 1853 seizure in Alton of a black woman who had for two years lived in the community and married a local black resident. She thought she was free because the son of her Tennessee owner had voluntarily left her in Alton. When she was eventually seized by her owner, black and white residents raised money to purchase her freedom for $1,200. W. T. Norton, ed., *Centennial History of Madison County, Illinois and Its People* (Chicago: Lewis Pub. Co., 1912), pp. 213–17. It seems likely that a similar situation in Chicago or Ottawa would have resulted in a rescue.

69. *Collected Works,* 11, 497.

70. Ibid., p. 498.

Lincoln was also not ready to argue for total racial equality. To do so would have been political suicide. It also would have run counter to his own thoughts. The Lincoln of 1858 was clearly ambivalent about race although certainly in favor of white supremacy. In that regard he was fully in tune with his constituents, including the entire Illinois Supreme Court. But, like the court, he was unwilling to relegate blacks to the status of permanent servitude. Douglas, like the legislature, looked to the past as a model for the place of blacks in Illinois and America. At the most basic level Lincoln anticipated the future, arguing:

> There is no reason in the world why the negro is not entitled to all the rights enumerated in the Declaration of Independence—the right of life, liberty and the pursuit of happiness. I hold that he is as much entitled to these as the white man. I agree with Judge Douglas that he is not my equal in many respects, certainly not in color—perhaps not in intellectual and moral endowments; but in the right to eat the bread without leave of anybody else which his own hand earns, he is my equal and the equal of Judge Douglas, and the equal of every other man.[71]

Had the 1858 senatorial election been decided by a popular vote, Lincoln might have won. But, win or lose, the closeness of the outcome suggests the vast changes in Illinois from the 1830s to the 1850s. The debates, like the conflicting court decisions and statutes of Illinois, underscore the dilemmas of a state on the border between slavery and freedom. These problems illustrate the nature of a constitution in a house divided.

71. Ibid., III, 249.

5. "Pretty Damned Warm Times"

The 1864 Charleston Riot and "the Inalienable Right of Revolution"

ROBERT D. SAMPSON

AMID THE GUNSHOTS AND FALLING BODIES on the courthouse square in Charleston on March 28, 1864, Marcus Hill's first concern was for the safety of his horses. After he led the animals from a hitching rack on the square to the shelter of an alley, Hill was asked what he thought of the present situation. "[P]retty damned warm times," he replied.[1] The frustrations, tensions, antagonisms, and conflicting political views that provided dry tinder in Indiana, Iowa, and Illinois during the Civil War had ignited into armed confrontation all around Hill. When it was over, nine men (six Union soldiers, two Democrats, and a Republican civilian) were dead, and twelve men were wounded, likely making the event the deadliest of its type in the North except for the New York City draft riots.[2]

ROBERT D. SAMPSON received the Ph.D. in history from the University of Illinois in 1995. He is the author of "'Honest men and law-abiding citizens': The 1894 Railroad Strike in Decatur," which appeared in this *Journal* in 1992. Sampson is a communications specialist with the College of Agricultural, Consumer, and Environmental Sciences at the University of Illinois at Urbana-Champaign.

1. Deposition of Marcus Hill, April 6, 1864, Records of Draft Riots, 1864, Coles County Circuit Clerk, Charleston. Immediately after the riot, local and military authorities interviewed a number of eyewitnesses, who often provided irrelevant and hearsay testimony. The occasional gem of description, however, makes the tedious review of the documents worthwhile.

2. See Coleman and Spence, "The Charleston Riot, March 28, 1864," *Journal of the Illinois State Historical Society,* 33 (1940), 7–56 (the article was reprinted in *Eastern Illinois University Bulletin,* April, 1961, pp. 78–112). William F. Hanna, in "The Boston Draft Riot," *Civil War History,* 36 (1990), places the death toll in the July 14, 1863, event at eight (see pp. 268–69).

Illinois Historical Journal Vol. 89, No. 2 (Summer 1996): 99–116

Although the level of violence and the location—in the heart of Abraham Lincoln's central Illinois—make it one of the most intriguing incidents on the Civil War home front, the Charleston Riot largely has been ignored. Fifty years ago, Charles Hubert Coleman and Paul H. Spence carefully sifted through the conflicting stories and legends to assemble the only published, scholarly treatment of the incident. They made clear many but not all of the contributing factors—previous armed confrontations, street beatings, physical and mental harassment and abuse, and an abundant supply of whiskey. That situation exploded into gunfire when David Nelson Wells, a young Edgar County Democrat, or Copperhead—as those Democrats' whose opinions ranged from anti-Lincoln administration to antiwar to pro-South were commonly known in east central Illinois—and Union soldier Oliver Sallee encountered each other on the courthouse square.

Gathered around the square on March 28, 1864, were the two main bodies of contention—members of Companies C and G of the Fifty-fourth Illinois Infantry, who were to assemble later that day in Mattoon after a furlough, and Democrats from Coles and Edgar counties, some of whom had previously clashed with the troops. Added to the lure for both groups was the presence of three leading Democrats—United States Representative John Rice Eden, Judge Charles Henry Constable, and Coles County Sheriff John Hardwicke O'Hair. Democrats feared that the soldiers might attempt to humiliate those leaders with forced loyalty oath takings, and some saw this as the time and place to take a stand against military bullying. As the day wore on, the groups moved about the square, eyeing each other and engaging in threatening conversations.

Sallee was not intimidated by the Democratic farmers—whom he referred to as "butternuts"—as they poured into town. He bragged that should the Democrats start any trouble, "the soldiers could whip any of the butternuts if that was what they came for." John Elsberry Hanks, a Democrat, was equally determined, vowing of the soldiers that "the butternuts would make them sup sorrow . . . before we leave town."[3]

Wells was in a party headed for the goldfields of California, and he had stopped in Charleston only for the day. He was particularly vocal and confrontational, according to witnesses, who recalled the young man in his dark clothing and yellow, low-crowned hat. On the west side of the courthouse, outside the courtroom where Judge Constable was presiding, Wells and Sallee came in contact. Neither the exact sequence of events nor the roles of aggressor and defender can be conclusively established. Within seconds, however, shots rang out. Sallee sunk to the ground, firing as he fell. Wells staggered away, fatally

3. Deposition of W. W. Goodrich, April 1, 1864, Records of Draft Riots, 1864.

wounded, and died in the doorway of a grocery store. Almost immediately firing became general.[4]

Democrats ran to their wagons, producing weapons from under loads of hay and other goods. Some pulled sidearms out of their pockets and coats. Although the soldiers had left their rifles stacked at the railroad depot, several of them apparently carried pistols and joined in the fray. Inside Constable's courtroom, former congressman and prominent local Democrat Orlando Bell Ficklin had "no serious concern" at the first shot, perhaps thinking it an accidental discharge. Sheriff O'Hair, who was fulfilling his official duties in the courtroom during the trial of an alleged hog thief, felt the sting of a bullet nicking his chin. Simultaneously, a "terrible kicking and thumping" commenced against the west door to the courtroom. As the door gave way, Greenville M. Mitchell of Charleston, commander of the troops, and Robert Winkler, a local Democrat, came tumbling into the room, "engaged in a struggle for life or death, each having a revolver and striking or shooting at the other."[5]

Rushing to Mitchell's assistance was Major Shubal York, the Fifty-fourth's surgeon, an outspoken Republican and abolitionist and father of a man who had seriously wounded a Democrat weeks earlier in Paris, Illinois. Before York could complete his mission, he was fatally wounded. George W. Parker, who came to his side, was urged by York to "get the Doctor, I am shot all to pieces." O'Hair escorted Congressman Eden, who was in the courtroom, to the west door of the courthouse, where he threw open the door and was greeted with gunfire from three men. Though the shots penetrated his coat, he was not hit, and he returned the fire. Eden dashed across the square and rapidly moved to the east. As Eden fled, O'Hair plunged into the heart of the fray—the area outside the courtroom on the west side of the courthouse.[6]

While the bloody contest played out in the courthouse, a larger choreography of violence filled the square. On the east and south sides of the courthouse lawn, Democrats fired at Union soldiers, ducked behind trees and a small outbuilding on the courthouse lawn to reload, and they then sought out new targets. Sheriff O'Hair did not join them, however. He stood beside a firing line of several Democrats, aligned perhaps in a defensive formation in front of the

4. Deposition of Noah G. Calhoun, April 2, 1864, ibid.; Coleman and Spence, pp. 22–24.

5. Depositions of Orlando B. Ficklin, April 1, 1864, and George W. Parker, April 1, 1864, both in Records of Draft Riots, 1864; "Memoirs of Frank T. O'Hair (son of John Hardwicke O'Hair) dictated to Adin Baber, Kansas, Ill., May 13, 1932, based on conversations with Uncle Berry Hanks and his mother, Evaline O'Hair," "Charleston Riot—Newspaper Items" Folder, Charles Coleman Papers, Eastern Illinois University Archives, Charleston; Coleman and Spence, pp. 24–27, 25n.

6. Deposition of George W. Parker; "Memoirs of Frank T. O'Hair"; Coleman and Spence, pp. 24–26.

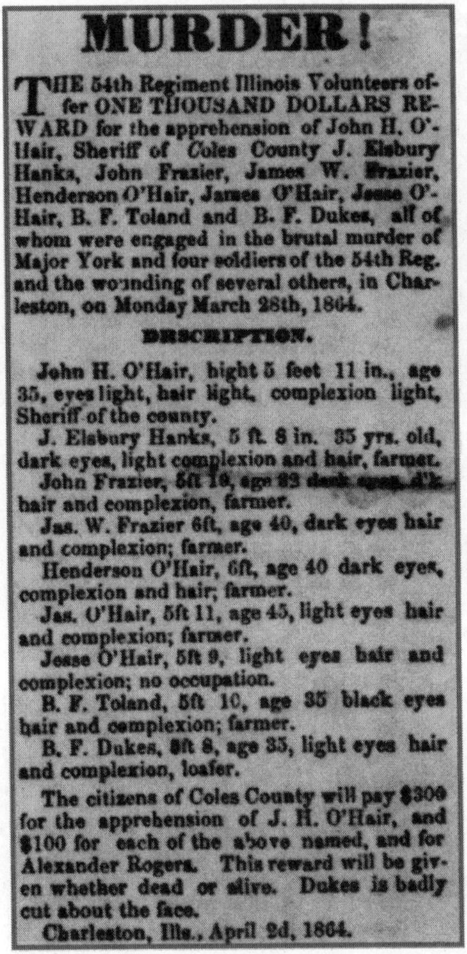

MURDER!

THE 54th Regiment Illinois Volunteers offer ONE THOUSAND DOLLARS REWARD for the apprehension of John H. O'-Hair, Sheriff of Coles County J. Elsbury Hanks, John Frazier, James W. Frazier, Henderson O'Hair, James O'Hair, Jesse O'-Hair, B. F. Toland and B. F. Dukes, all of whom were engaged in the brutal murder of Major York and four soldiers of the 54th Reg. and the wounding of several others, in Charleston, on Monday March 28th, 1864.

DESCRIPTION.

John H. O'Hair, hight 5 feet 11 in., age 35, eyes light, hair light, complexion light, Sheriff of the county.

J. Elsbury Hanks, 5 ft. 8 in. 35 yrs. old, dark eyes, light complexion and hair, farmer.

John Frazier, 5ft 10, age 23 dark eyes, d'k hair and complexion, farmer.

Jas. W. Frazier 6ft, age 40, dark eyes hair and complexion; farmer.

Henderson O'Hair, 6ft, age 40 dark eyes, complexion and hair; farmer.

Jas. O'Hair, 5ft 11, age 45, light eyes hair and complexion; farmer.

Jesse O'Hair, 5ft 9, light eyes hair and complexion; no occupation.

B. F. Toland, 5ft 10, age 35 black eyes hair and complexion; farmer.

B. F. Dukes, 5ft 8, age 35, light eyes hair and complexion, loafer.

The citizens of Coles County will pay $300 for the apprehension of J. H. O'Hair, and $100 for each of the above named, and for Alexander Rogers. This reward will be given whether dead or alive. Dukes is badly cut about the face.

Charleston, Ills., April 2d, 1864.

This wanted notice appeared in the April 6, 1864, issue of the Mattoon Independent Gazette.

building's west door. Farmer John Frazier rode his horse back and forth in the street through the cross fire, urging the Democrats to the fight and emerging unscathed. The firing from all groups—soldiers and Democrats—became so intense that it stripped the bark off trees in the courthouse yard. "Boys, this is bad," an excited Jesse O'Hair reportedly said, as he ducked into a store during the battle. "Just look at the dead men." The duration of the firefight was probably only a few minutes. The event known as the Charleston Riot ended as Sheriff O'Hair rallied the Democrats at the southeast corner of the square and marched them east on Jackson Street out of town.[7]

7. Deposition of Stephen E. Guthrie, April 1, 1864, Records of Draft Riots, 1864; Coleman and Spence, pp. 25–27.

After the firing had ended and the main body of Democrats had left town, the last casualties occurred. A tardy Democrat seized by the troops was shot to death when he attempted to break free. The same shots killed a Republican storekeeper caught in the line of fire.[8]

Historical interpretations of Copperheadism in the decades following the Charleston Riot tend to view it as "tainted with treason," as Iver Bernstein observed of the Northern Democratic antiwar movement as a whole. That approach was overturned three decades ago by the work of Frank Ludwig Klement.[9]

Historian Mark E. Neely, Jr., credits Klement with proving "beyond any reasonable doubt, that no systematic, organized disloyal opposition to the war existed in the North." Neely concluded, however, that Democratic accusations of political motivation in the civilian arrests were wrong, that the Democrats had no special tradition of civil liberty protection, and that after a short time they abandoned attempts to paint Lincoln as a dictator by use of the arrests issue. Yet, Neely acknowledges that the Democrats' most persistent use of the civil liberty issue coincides with the crucial months preceding the Charleston Riot.[10]

---

8. Coleman and Spence, p. 27.

9. Bernstein, *The New York City Draft Riots: Their Significance for American Society and Politics in the Age of the Civil War* (New York: Oxford University Press, 1990), p. vii. For pre-Klement views of Copperheads and the Charleston Riot, see Arthur Charles Cole, *The Era of the Civil War, 1848–1870,* Centennial History of Illinois, Vol. 3 (Springfield: Illinois Centennial Commission, 1919), pp. 290–311; [Isaac Funk], *Copperheads under the Heel of an Illinois Farmer* (n.p. [1863]), p. 3. The most extreme denunciations of Copperheads by a twentieth-century author can be found in Wood Gray, *The Hidden Civil War: The Story of the Copperheads* (New York: Viking, 1942). For a historiographical view, see John T. Hubbell, "Politics as Usual: The Northern Democracy and Party Survival, 1860–61," *Illinois Quarterly,* Sept., 1973, p. 24. Coleman and Spence prove Hubbell's point about Lincoln-influenced interpretations (see pp. 42–43). For Klement's main works addressing Copperheadism and relevant citations, see "Middle Western Copperheadism and the Genesis of the Granger Movement," *Mississippi Valley Historical Review,* 38 (1951–1952), 680, 694; "Economic Aspects of Middle Western Copperheadism," *The Historian,* 14 (1951–1952), 27, 42; *The Copperheads in the Middle West* (Chicago: University of Chicago Press, 1960), pp. 33–34. Also important in the reassessment of Copperheadism are works by Richard Orr Curry, "The Civil War and Reconstruction, 1861–1877: A Critical Overview of Recent Trends and Interpretations," *Civil War History,* 20 (1974), 216, and "A Note on the Origins and Usage of the Term 'Butternut' During the Civil War," *Mid-America: An Historical Review,* 44 (1962), 125. For an opposing view, see David E. Long, *The Jewel of Liberty: Abraham Lincoln's Re-Election and the End of Slavery* (Mechanicsburg, Pa.: Stackpole Books, 1994). One historian who has examined Civil War confrontations in Indiana between Union supporters and Democrats indicates that violent incidents like Charleston's were not sudden, unexplainable outbursts (see G. R. Tredway, *Democratic Opposition to the Lincoln Administration in Indiana,* Indiana Historical Collections, Vol. 48 [Indianapolis: Indiana Historical Bureau, 1973], p. 72).

10. See Neely, *The Fate of Liberty: Abraham Lincoln and Civil Liberties* (New York: Oxford University Press, 1991), pp. xii, 202, 207–8. For examples of "bottom-up" and activist

Jean Harvey Baker contends that "considerable evidence" exists that nineteenth-century Americans paid close attention to politics and had a "broader, deeper understanding of issues" than later generations. At the heart of Baker's argument lies an activist republican ideology rooted in the Democratic party and passed on to new generations by both education and experience. Antebellum American history texts, she notes, "focused on the revolution." Taken to Democratic rallies by their parents, youngsters "began to absorb the community's self-perpetuating partisan culture," which included a "suspicion of power, a fear of human motives, [and] an expectation of conspiracy." That culture provided guideposts for a "logic of rebellion"—a set of conditions that in extreme cases could justify taking up arms against perceived oppressors, just as the men of 1776 had done. Democrats incorporated that "logic of rebellion" in their view of the proper role and conduct of government. "Behind every set of Northern Democratic messages rested an accumulation of symbols and traditions, a kind of switchboard on which languages, themes, and modes of expression connected belief and believer, past and present, perception and reality."[11]

A key word on this "switchboard" was "corruption," a term seen by Democrats as a "replacement of public instincts of virtue and prudence by exclusive interests affiliated with a centralized government." The term resonates in classical republican theory, calling to mind an "organic cancer, eating at the vitals of the body politic and working a progressive dissolution." Essential to the concept was a steady progression of abuses that proved intractable to electoral or judicial control, indicating the existence of a conspiracy to usurp liberty. Such a perspective gives added meaning to the complaint that a Charleston Democrat addressed to the *Chicago Times* on January 25, 1863. The author prayed for divine protection for New York Governor Horatio Seymour in his efforts to "defend the rights of the citizen from the oppressors who now rule the people with a rod of iron from the Capitol at Washington. *History does not produce a more damnable and corrupt set of tyrants.*"[12]

It is likely that the letter writer, as well as other local Democrats using the same language, came of age imbibing Democratic and republican ideology in

---

republican ideology approaches, see Bernstein; Jean H. Baker, *Affairs of Party: The Political Culture of Northern Democrats in the Mid-Nineteenth Century* (Ithaca, N.Y.: Cornell University Press, 1983); Sean Wilentz, *Chants Democratic: New York City & the Rise of the American Working Class, 1788–1850* (New York: Oxford University Press, 1984).

11. Baker, pp. 23, 52, 82, 147–48; Bernard Bailyn, *The Ideological Origins of the American Revolution* (Cambridge, Mass.: Harvard University Press, 1967), p. 94.

12. Baker, pp. 147, 157; *The Record of Hon. C. L. Vallandigham* (Columbus, Ohio: J. Walter, 1863), p. 68; Lance Banning, *The Jeffersonian Persuasion: Evolution of a Party Ideology* (Ithaca, N.Y: Cornell University Press, 1978), p. 47; *Mattoon Independent Gazette*, Jan. 24 [Feb. 1], 1863, p. 2, col. 4.

the atmosphere described by Baker. To such a person, use of the word corruption goes deeper than the general twentieth-century meaning of financial improprieties and payoffs. Seen from that perspective, the letter writer's closing warning, "Our people [here] are now a good deal like a magazine,—it will take but little more to produce an explosion that will shake this Union from centre to circumference," takes on meaning beyond idle threat. Combined with a series of physical attacks and the suppression of free speech that increasingly frustrated Coles and Edgar County Democrats, the letter adds a new interpretation to the Charleston Riot.[13]

Fearful of centralizing trends in the government and economy, shocked by Lincoln's emancipation policy, feeling unsafe on the streets of their own communities, and being told by one congressman that the battle, if necessary, would be taken beyond the normal electoral and legal tactics and by another congressman that there was a government plot to deny them access to the ballot, the Democrats at Charleston who took aim and fired were convinced that the preconditions—the "logic of rebellion"—justified their actions.

Former United States Senator George Ellis Pugh of Ohio, whose law partner, former United States Representative Clement Laird Vallandigham of Ohio, had been arrested and spirited from his home in the dead of night by troops, articulated the "logic of rebellion" when he asserted: "The best security to people for their liberty, is the conviction that they will defend it."[14] Such convictions were not limited to Ohio nor to the streets of Charleston. Over the last twenty years, a number of studies of Indiana and Iowa Civil War–era Democrats indicate that frequent violent confrontations with Republicans and soldiers occurred. For example, a "grave danger of a spontaneous revolt existed" in Indiana, concludes G. R. Tredway, a student of the state's Civil War Democracy. By the spring of 1863, opposition to emancipation, resentment of political coercion, and Northern military failure created the "potential for an outbreak of massive resistance." The same year as the Charleston Riot, a "spectacular gun battle" occurred in Noblesville, Indiana, when a Democratic political meeting was held too close to a Republican agricultural fair. Other Hoosier hot spots were Fort Wayne, Greensburg, Danville, and Brown and Sullivan counties.[15]

An incident in Sullivan County—though occurring after the Charleston Riot—was typical of the confrontations. In July of 1864, soldiers and local Republicans invaded a picnic and attempted to force young men present to

---

13. *Mattoon Independent Gazette,* Jan. 24 [Feb. 1], 1863, p. 2, col. 4.

14. Bailyn, p. 94; "Speech of George Pugh," *Papers from the Society for the Diffusion of Political Knowledge,* No. 9, p. 4.

15. Tredway, pp. 78–79, 81–82, 85, 89, 99–100, 104–6, 280–81.

take loyalty oaths. Some resisted, and the soldiers left, only to return armed. One soldier knocked a boy down, and another soldier—Matt Brown—shot the youth when he started to flee. Nine hours later, the young man died. Brown had already killed one Democrat—a Terre Haute physician—for which he was never arrested or tried. That such incidents never escalated to the level of Charleston is attributed by Tredway "as much to chance as to management." As in Illinois, Tredway found that Union soldiers stationed or on leave in Indiana were likely to wreck Democratic newspapers, disrupt party meetings, and attack Lincoln administration opponents. He contends that "soldiers were above the law as far as offenses with political connotations were concerned, regardless of their magnitude." Victims of such crimes, if they were Democrats, enjoyed "little hope of redress."[16]

Democrats fared no better in Iowa, according to recent scholars and at least one contemporary observer, J. D. Nelson, who wrote to future Illinois Representative John Francis Snyder: "God damn there [*sic*] administration I wish I could sink some of them in hell." Bordering insurgent-racked Missouri and home to a Democratic minority, Iowa saw a number of violent clashes and acts of intimidation against Democrats.[17] As in Indiana, Iowa Democrats found them selves outside of the law. "[N]o man's personal safety can be assured for one moment after the conclusion shall have been clearly arrived at that he is a traitor," lamented the *Burlington Weekly Hawk-Eye*.[18] Hubert H. Wubben notes that on a number of occasions, Democratic editors called upon citizens to organize and put an end to political harassment, but "nothing happened." David L. Lendt, who also studied Iowa's Civil War Democracy, believes that Democrats were a "victimized minority" and that "no evidence" exists linking them to the incidents of violence against marshals. He adds, however, that "sufficient evidence" can be found that many Democrats, particularly editors, "were systematically persecuted for political purposes."[19]

For a short time, the *Coles County Ledger* provided an editorial voice for Democrats opposed to the Lincoln administration's war policies. It acknowledged the burden of dissent. "An eye of suspicion is turned upon every Democrat who does

---

16. Ibid., pp. 103–6, 280–81.

17. Nelson to Snyder, Aug. 31, Oct. 4, and Nov. 22, 1863, Box 3, Folder 4, John Francis Snyder Papers, Illinois State Historical Library, Springfield.

18. For examples of Iowa clashes, see Hubert H. Wubben, *Civil War Iowa and the Copperhead Movement* (Ames: Iowa State University Press, 1980), pp. 113–14; *Burlington* (Iowa) *Weekly Hawk-Eye*, Aug. 24, 1861, p. 2, col. 2.

19. Wubben, p. 120; Lendt, *Demise of the Democracy: The Copperhead Press in Iowa, 1856–1870* (Ames: Iowa State University Press, 1973), pp. 133, 135.

not bellow himself hoarse over this terrible war," editor J. M. Eastin observed.[20] Illinois Democrats who took issue with the administration escaped neither the label Copperhead nor the spontaneous and official forms of repression inflicted upon their Iowa and Indiana neighbors. Some two thousand Illinoisans were arrested in an effort to "suppress propaganda and opposition." Fifty-two citizens were indicted for "harboring, concealing, or employing" deserters or helping them to escape, thirty of those indictments coming in the two months preceding the Charleston Riot. Almost any citizen, it seemed, was subject to accusation, provided it was structured in terms of loyalty. William Shane, who cheered for Jefferson Davis and "god damned Lincoln to hell," found himself the object of two complaints. Such a climate, observed Illinois historian Donald F. Tingley, was ripe for a massive outbreak of "[n]ame-calling and witch-hunting" aimed at Democrats, despite the fact that they too "paid their taxes, served in the army, and hoped to preserve the Union."[21]

Early in the war, prominent Illinois Democrats, and United States Representatives William Alexander Richardson of Quincy, James Carroll Robinson of Marshall, and William Joshua Allen of Marion joined Vallandigham in a protest of the administration's initial arbitrary arrests. Within a year, Allen was one of forty people arrested in southern Illinois—all sharing the common traits of "devotion to the Democratic Party" and criticism of the Lincoln administration. The threat of large-scale violence in Williamson County necessitated placing it under martial law in order to complete the draft enrollment in 1864. Olney, the county seat of Richland County, was allegedly besieged for three days by men vowing to destroy the local enrollment lists. Yet, that may have been a case of wartime exaggeration. An account written long after the war by Bryant Higgins, who "guarded" the Richland County Courthouse, indicates that no shots were fired, nor were any attempts made to cut off the town or seize the records.[22]

---

20. *Coles County Ledger* (Charleston), Jan. 30, 1862, p. 2, col. 2. A major problem in studying central Illinois Democratic attitudes towards the Civil War is the lack of newspapers reflecting those views. Only scattered copies of key Democratic newspapers in Charleston and Paris survive.

21. J. M. Hofer, "Development of the Peace Movement in Illinois During the Civil War," *Journal of the Illinois State Historical Society,* 24 (1931–1932), 110; Kellee Green Blake, "Aiding and Abetting: Disloyalty Prosecutions in the Federal Civil Courts of Southern Illinois, 1861–1866," *Illinois Historical Journal,* 87 (1994), 104; "Depositions of Abigail M. Kinney, Elen Greening, and Kate Redman, March 6 and May 29, 1863," Kate Redman Papers (SC 1248), Illinois State Historical Library; Tingley, "The Clingman Raid," *Journal of the Illinois State Historical Society,* 56 (1963), 362–63.

22. Klement, *Copperheads in the Middle West,* pp. 18–19; Blake, pp. 103–5; Edward Conrad Smith, *The Borderland in the Civil War* (1927; rpt. New York: AMS Press, 1970), p. 340; Higgins, "Reminiscent Sketch of Richland County," in *Biographical and Reminiscent History of Richland, Clay and Marion Counties Illinois* (Indianapolis: B. F. Bowen & Co., 1909), pp. 422–23.

The *Chicago Tribune* and Illinois Governor Richard Yates jointly employed Joseph King Cummins Forrest to stir up public fears from time to time with anxious reports of Copperheads armed to the teeth and on the march. Rather than accuracy, Forrest's guiding journalistic principle was the potential that his sometimes fanciful creations had for advancing the Yates and Lincoln administrations. A good example of his style is the "Great excitement" reported in Fulton County. Local opposition to draft enrollment existed there, but it was inflated by the *Tribune* to tales of Copperhead fortifications and six hundred to one thousand "insurgents" running through the streets. Klement studied the incident and concluded that the confrontation, labeled a "war" by the *Tribune,* was "largely the fault of an arrogant enrolling officer." Republicans were "anxious to use the incident to benefit their party." Behind the scare campaign, Klement found the experienced hand of Forrest.[23]

Even before the Fulton County incident, Illinois Democrats sought relief at the ballot box. During the 1862 elections, the party called on voters to reject "the reign of terror" and "the policy of intimidation and arrest." While it was not the only issue in that election, it was clearly an important one, given the chilled climate for free speech in Illinois and other states. Illinois voters responded in 1862, returning a Democratic state legislature, increasing the size of the party's share of the state's congressional delegation, and putting Democrats into office at the county level. Among the beneficiaries of that rebuke to the Lincoln administration were Eden—a Sullivan attorney, Douglas Democrat, and former prosecutor, who took the new Seventh District congressional seat—and O'Hair, who gained the office of Coles County Sheriff.[24]

The combination of events that left Illinois Democrats with little or no relief despite their electoral triumph is composed of Democratic incompetence and poor leadership, Republican intelligence and skill, and simply bad luck. From a new state constitution to efforts to bridle Yates to attempts to nudge the Lincoln administration towards peace negotiations, the Democrats met failure and frustration on every front.[25] The importance of those developments in the context of the Charleston Riot is the inability of the ballot box to end what many Democrats viewed as misguided, even oppressive, policies.

Weeks before the Charleston Riot, Eden rose in Congress to denounce the trend of Republican policy. He asked his opponents: "If you are not for the Union

---

23. Klement, *Copperheads in the Middle West,* pp. 79, 143–44, 285n; *Chicago Tribune,* Aug. 15 (p. 1, col. 3), Aug. 18 (p. 1, col. 3), Aug. 19 (p. 1, col. 2), Aug. 22 (p. 1, col. 4), 1863.

24. *Illinois State Register* (Springfield), Sept. 9, 1862, p. 2, col. 1; Klement, *Copperheads in the Middle West,* p. 21; Coleman and Spence, pp. 7–9.

25. For an account of the Democratic-controlled state legislature's attempts to best Yates in the battle over the proposed 1862 state constitution, see Cole, pp. 266–72.

as it was, what sort of Union are you for? . . . A Union without States, without *habeas corpus,* without trial by jury, without free speech or free press, without a free ballot?" Rather than the Union he and others had come to maturity under, the Republicans were aiming for a configuration not unlike a tax-oppressed, liberties-denied European dictatorship. He feared, if not already in place, that "tyranny" was not too far away.[26]

What led to such conclusions? Why would Eden invoke the charged language of activist republican ideology? The answer lies in events, as well as statements by Eden and Robinson, indicating a steady progression through the "logic of rebellion."

Many Coles County residents were either Southern immigrants or descendants of Southern-born parents. That alone would provide an explanation for some of the peace sentiment in the county. Others may have been repelled by the bloody toll of battle. A number clearly indicated their deep-seated opposition to emancipation and the specter of former slaves migrating to Illinois.[27] Whatever their particular motivations, Coles County Democrats, as early as January, 1863, were reaching out to fellow citizens in search of an end to the killing.

One group of distinguished and contentious citizens met in the Coles County Courthouse the evening of January 17, 1863, to seek a peaceful end to the Civil War. "The people have not only lost all heart in the war, but they loathe and detest it . . . as the greatest and basest fraud that was ever practiced upon the patriotic impulses of a loyal and devoted people," they contended.[28] Ficklin, described by the *Mattoon Independent Gazette* as the "great He-snake of the Copperheads of this County," presided. Also on hand were a number of "unconditional Union men" ready to "assist in overruling any disloyal proceedings which might be attempted." According to the *Gazette,* Ficklin's opening address was filled with familiar Democratic charges: "abolition," "Government bastiles [*sic*]," "habeas corpus," and "constitution."

Preliminaries complete, the meeting moved to a debate over a resolution calling for an immediate armistice and protesting the taxes being levied to support

---

26. John R. Eden, *Speech of the Honorable John R. Eden of Illinois, Delivered in the House of Representatives, February 27, 1864* (Washington, D.C.: Constitutional Union, 1864), pp. 5, 12 (copy in Moultrie County Historical Society Library, Sullivan, Ill.). See also *Congressional Globe,* 38 Cong., 1 Sess., Vol. 34, Pt. 53, pp. 860, 862.

27. Bailyn, p. 94; Coleman and Spence, p. 9; *Coles County Ledger,* Jan. 30, 1862, p. 2, col. 2; *Mattoon Independent Gazette,* Jan. 24 [Feb. 1], 1863, p. 2, col. 4. For examples of the effects of racism on the election of 1862, see Bruce Tap, "Race, Rhetoric, and Emancipation: The Election of 1862 in Illinois," *Civil War History,* 39 (1993), 101–25.

28. *Charleston Courier,* quoted in the *Mattoon Independent Gazette,* Jan. 24 [Feb. 1], 1863, p. 2, col. 2.

the war. At that point, the *Charleston Courier* contended, "all the malignant spirits and rowdies" from the area were brought in by the Republicans to either break up the meeting, or override its proceedings." It is not clear if the resolution labeling the war a "fraud" was actually adopted. Surviving newspaper accounts leave the impression that the attempt to talk peace degenerated into confusion and disorder. It is clear that the Democrats were not satisfied. The *Gazette's* account of the January 17 meeting also featured the previously quoted letter to the *Chicago Times* from a Coles County Democrat announcing a second peace meeting.[29]

The *Gazette* charged that the letter was written by Jacob I. Brown. In the Republican newspaper's opinion, Brown's missive was "more damnable treason than we have ever before seen in the same space of print, from a citizen of Coles County." Jefferson Davis could, no doubt, be warmed by Brown's sentiments, the *Gazette* assured readers.[30] Brown had informed the *Chicago Times* that the "democracy of Old Coles are wide awake" and "clamorous" for peace. "If ever done, it [peace] must be accomplished by the democratic party," Brown asserted. Yet, he added, the party's "mouth has been sealed so long by the suspension of the writ of *habeas corpus* and the thousand and one worse than French Bastiles." He concluded by comparing the citizens of Coles County to an ammunition dump ready to explode at the next spark.[31]

Apparently, only Democrats were allowed to attend the second peace meeting, held on January 31. Ficklin again presided, and Eden was on hand to deliver a two-hour speech. "He showed to the entire satisfaction of the little Copper-snakes, that the Administration is meaner than the Devil, and corrupt as hell, and that it is the duty of every 'Democrat' in the county to help (Jeff. Davis) put it out of power," the *Gazette* caustically observed. That time the organizers succeeded in offering and passing resolutions that, according to the *Gazette,* called for an armistice, opposed paying taxes for the purpose of compensated emancipation, and opposed the unconditional emancipation of slaves in the Rebel states. Of the meeting's resolution declaring that habeas corpus "must and shall be maintained," the *Gazette* professed outrage: "This is an actual threat to resist the authorities."[32]

Even with the *Gazette's* attempt to hang the traitor label on the Democrats, there were apparently Republicans who saw the need to at least talk with the

---

29. *Mattoon Independent Gazette,* Jan. 24 [Feb. 1], 1863, p. 2, cols. 1–2; *Charleston Courier,* quoted in ibid., col. 2.

30 *Mattoon Independent Gazette,* Jan. 24 [Feb. 1], 1863, p. 2, col. 3.

31. Ibid., col. 4.

32. Ibid., Feb. 7, 1863, p. 2, col. 1.

John Rice Eden

opposition. In early February, a meeting was held in Mattoon between "members of the unconditional Union church and the *habeas corpus*, 'political bastille' organization" that included open discussion and a "pledge [of] personal friendship to prevent any violence which might grow out of the present combustible state of the Government affairs." A committee was appointed to address the county's citizens, urging them to "keep cool." Attacking the meeting, the *Gazette* dismissed it as of little value. Events would prove, however, the validity of the participants' concern over violence.[33]

Within weeks, the "*habeas corpus* 'political bastille'" party had a bold example of civil authority's erosion to contemplate. Judge Constable, while presiding in Charleston, had refused to allow Union troops based in Indiana to take four deserters that they had captured in the city back to Indiana. He not only released the four men but also ordered the arrest of two of the army officers as "kidnappers." Aroused by that action, Oliver Hazard Perry Throck Morton, Indiana's Republican governor, ordered military officials in his state to proceed to Illinois, arrest Constable, and return with him. The troops completed one part of the mission—arresting Constable—but the jurist was ordered released by a federal judge before he could be transported to Indiana. Clearly, state boundaries and

33. Ibid., col. 3.

the supposed superiority of civil over military authority provided no protection when one defied high-ranking Republican officials.[34]

Within months, mounting anger led to a mass Democratic demonstration in Mattoon. One of the signs boldly held aloft by determined Democrats that day reflected the logic of rebellion. "The plea of military necessity," the placard proclaimed, "is the plea of tyrants."[35]

Throughout the summer of 1863, Mattoon achieved notoriety among Illinois Democrats as a place where they could be "continually insulted, mobbed, and stigmatized as copperheads, secessionists, & c." Coles County was split geographically as well as ideologically with the Republican vote heaviest in the western part of the county, the area dominated by Mattoon. Democratic strength tended to center in Charleston and the rural areas to the east. Concerned about the ability to hold and exercise opinions without fear of harassment in what the *Chicago Times* described as the "most fanatical, intolerant, mobocratic hole of abolitionism in this part of the State," Democrats decided on a show of force.[36]

Early on August 1, Democrats began arriving in Mattoon by train, wagon, and on foot, determined to "maintain the rights of free speech and personal liberty." Armed with "shotguns, rifles, and muskets," the Democrats' procession stretched three miles through the city, filled by some eight thousand to twelve thousand people—a number disputed by the *Gazette,* which insisted upon three thousand, still an impressive number. Held proudly aloft were banners proclaiming "Free Speech, Free Press, and an Independent Judiciary," and "For President, Horatio Seymour, for Vice President, C. L. Vallandigham."[37]

Robinson and Eden addressed the assembled Democrats. They delivered "[g]ood, sound democratic doctrines," the *Chicago Times* reported, including "strict and implicit obedience to and enforcement of the laws, and the maintenance of the rights of free speech, free press, and personal liberty, at all hazards, even to the bitter end." The newspaper warned Republicans that the rally clearly indicated that the Democrats "are as well able to protect themselves as others are to oppress them." Continued frustration of legitimate grievances and harassment on the streets would be met with action at the "ballot-box." Democrats were ready to achieve their rights "forcibly with the cartridge-box. . . . [W]hen all peaceful means fail, the democracy are ready and armed to maintain those rights as their fathers won them." Eden, according to the *Gazette,* made a similar

---

34. Ibid.; Coleman and Spence, pp. 13–14.

35. *Mattoon Independent Gazette,* Aug. 5, 1863, p. 2, cols. 1–2.

36. *Chicago Times,* Aug. 6, 1863, p. 1, col. 5; Coleman and Spence, pp. 8–9.

37. *Chicago Times,* Aug. 6, 1863, p. 1, col. 5; *Mattoon Independent Gazette,* Aug. 5, 1863, p. 2, cols. 1–2; Coleman and Spence, pp. 15–16.

Orlando Bell Ficklin

point about Democratic opposition to tyrannical actions, vowing to "fight these measures through the courts, and if we fail will fight them through the Supreme Courts, and Congress, and if we fail there also, we will *still fight them in another way.*"[38]

For some Coles County residents, the display of strength and fiery words had the desired effect. Several days later, the *Gazette* was grousing about a call for a "Peace at Home" meeting to be held on August 17. Rejecting the call, the newspaper condemned it as a mere attempt to "inveigle loyal men into a compromise of duty and principle. . . . We want no local peace based upon the undermining of the American Union."[39] A warning had again been received, an effort to lower the level of tension made and contemptuously rejected by the Republican newspaper in that party's Coles County stronghold.

Others were also convinced that the time for peaceful accommodation was long past. In September, Congressman Robinson addressed a Democratic rally

38. *Chicago Times,* Aug. 6, 1863, p. 1, col. 5; *Mattoon Independent Gazette,* Aug. 5, 1863, p. 2, cols. 1–2. The author's attention was called to Eden's previously unnoticed remarks in Barbara L. Biehl, "The Charleston Riot," TS, Department of History, Eastern Illinois University, Charleston.

39. *Mattoon Independent Gazette,* Aug. 12, 1863, p. 2, cols. 1–2.

in Casey, charging that there was a government conspiracy to keep Democrats from the polls. It was their duty, he emphasized, to resist and even, if necessary, to "*wade through blood knee deep* to the ballot box." A few days later, the *Shelby County Leader* made the message even clearer for those who felt their rights were being trampled upon by would-be tyrants. If the people concluded that the "government [had] become destructive of the ends for which it was created, there will remain that INALIENABLE RIGHT OF REVOLUTION."[40]

To many Republicans and soldiers, particularly those who had faced Confederate fire, such talk was treasonous and required strong measures. One way of publicly converting antiwar citizens was a loyalty oath, usually administered in the public streets to a kneeling Democrat. "I do solemnly swear to support the Administration, Abraham Lincoln, all proclamations now issued and all that may hereafter be issued, so help me God." A polarized political climate, charged by the blood of battle and casualty lists, widened the gulf between citizens of opposing views.[41]

"Butternut Britches and Hickory Poles, Democrats, Democrats Damn their souls" was a popular jingle with Coles County Republicans as 1863 passed into 1864.[42] Coleman and Spence attribute some of the sentiment to "increased activity by the Sons of Liberty," though without offering any solid evidence about the existence of the allegedly pro-Southern secret society. Democrats, however, were engaging in what the authors termed "loose talk" about draft resistance and defying the government. In early 1864 another element was added to the volatile mixture in Coles County that assured eventual violence when members of the Fifty-fourth Illinois Infantry began their leave in Mattoon. The soldiers received the furlough as a reenlistment bonus. Like idle soldiers in Indiana and Iowa, those men—many of them from the area—enjoyed nothing more than several good drinks and a bout of their "favorite sport"—forcing Democrats to their knees to take an "oath of allegiance."[43]

Democratic farmers venturing into Mattoon ran the risk of being pulled from their wagons and forced to kneel in a muddy street to take the loyalty oath. Neither wealth nor professional status provided immunity. Judge Constable, a

---

40. Ibid., Sept. 9, 1863, p. 2, col. 2; *Shelby County Leader* (Shelbyville), quoted in ibid., Sept. 16, 1863, p. 2, col. 1.

41. See Coleman and Spence, p. 15.

42. Ibid. In *Dark Lanterns: Secret Political Societies, Conspiracies, and Treason Trials in the Civil War* (Baton Rouge: Louisiana State University Press, 1984), Klement raises serious questions concerning the existence of groups like the Sons of Liberty and Knights of the Golden Circle. In some cases, they were the work of deluded enthusiasts whose unrealistic schemes *were* taken seriously by Republican propagandists and officials, sometimes with devastating results.

43. Coleman and Spence, pp. 15–16.

prominent target due to his earlier confrontation with Indiana civil and military authorities, was waylaid by soldiers in Mattoon on January 29, 1864, and forced to take the loyalty oath. Also humiliated that day was physician J. W. Dora, a Democrat. Dora's harassment, however, did not end on January 29. On February 17 the *Gazette* contained both what was surely a desperate yet embarrassing plea from Dora and a condescending endorsement by Colonel James True, who appears to have functioned as a sort of political orthodoxy enforcer in addition to his military duties.[44] "Colonel . . . you will do me the justice to make known my true position to your political friends, or any persons who may heretofore or may hereafter impugn my motives for having entertained the peculiar political tenets which I from early education had imbibed," wrote the physician in an exchange of correspondence given to the newspaper by True. The letter suggests that Dora continued to be harassed by soldiers and Republicans for his views, and he sought, by repudiating those opinions, to gain relief. Grudgingly, True granted it, noting that the physician had "formerly been looked upon by some with suspicion, and probably not without cause," but now he "comes up heartily for the maintenance of the Union."[45]

Retaliation, rather than supplication, was the best cure for such "outrages," counseled the *Chicago Times*. "If the law will not protect Democrats from insults and outrage, they must protect themselves," the newspaper warned. Incidents like the assault upon Constable should be "dealt with by 'lynch law.' . . . Democrats must retaliate upon abolitionists who counsel such lawlessness."[46] Blood had already been shed by the time the Chicago newspaper's warning was reprinted in Mattoon. On January 30 a drunken soldier in Mattoon shot in the back and killed a Democrat who attempted to flee rather than take the loyalty oath. The *Gazette* made much of the victim's alleged poor character, even asserting that his wife and children were pleased to learn of his death.[47]

Edgar County was also heating up. Milton York, son of Shubal York—the surgeon who was killed on March 28—was involved in an altercation on February 16 in Paris that left a Democrat severely wounded. Six days later, a larger confrontation occurred when six soldiers and fourteen Democrats engaged in a gun battle. A Democrat was fatally shot, and two soldiers were wounded. Some reports indicate that the incident stemmed from a rumored attempt by the soldiers to destroy the local Democratic newspaper's office.[48]

---

44. Ibid.; *Mattoon Independent Gazette*, Feb. 17, 1864, p. 2, col. 4.

45. *Mattoon Independent Gazette*, Feb. 17, 1864, p. 2, col. 3.

46. *Chicago Times*, Feb. 2, 1864, p. 2, col. 2.

47. Coleman and Spence, p. 16. See also *Mattoon Independent Gazette*, Feb. 3 (p. 2, cols. 1, 2, 5), April 6 (p. 2, col. 1), 1864.

48. Coleman and Spence, pp. 16–17.

The Coles County Courthouse was the site of the confrontation between members of Companies C and G of the Fifty-fourth Illinois Infantry and Coles and Edgar County Democrats that resulted in the Charleston Riot.

By early March, the focus shifted back to Charleston, where two Democrats—including Benjamin Franklin Dukes, later identified as one of the leading participants in the Charleston Riot—were "severely beaten" by soldiers on the city's streets. Two days before the Charleston Riot, soldiers attacked and disarmed two Copperheads—James O'Hair, Sr., and Benjamin Franklin Toland—who also took part in the March 28 riot.[49]

Since the war began, a climate of repression, harassment, and physical attack steadily spread throughout Coles and Edgar counties. Rumors took on the appearance of fact in such an atmosphere, as citizens were ready to believe the worst of their opponents. When the normal remedies of the ballot box and the courts failed, a few were willing to emulate the founders of the Republic and take up arms to protect their rights.

Reports that soldiers would attempt to attack and humiliate Eden, Constable, and other Democrats in Charleston on March 28 during court day and a scheduled Democratic rally sharpened the appetite for revenge. Democrats from Coles and Edgar counties made plans to be on the courthouse square that day ready to defend their rights. David Nelson Wells was one. "By God," he said, "we have taken all we are going to take from the soldiers."[50]

Young E. Winkler, a Coles County Democrat, had a question for Robert Stricklin when the pair met a few days before the riot. What authority, Winkler asked, did the soldiers furloughed in the area have to "take up a man and whip

49. Ibid., p. 18.
50. Deposition of H. G. Green, April 2, 1864, Records of Draft Riots, 1864.

him to death?" Indicating that he was already convinced of the answer, Winkler added that he "could get up a squad of men in two days and go down and clean Charleston out."[51] Early on March 28, Robert McClain rode by the home of B. M. Dice in rural Coles County and inquired if he wanted to accompany him to Charleston. McClain had heard that "abolitionists" would attempt to break up Eden's scheduled speech, and he wanted to lend a hand in preventing such an action. On the way into town, the pair overtook a soldier, and McClain proposed that they "halloo for Valandigham [*sic*]." Dice counseled against such action to no avail. McClain went on to curse the soldier, call him a "damn thief, a son of a bitch," and after Dice refused to ride further with him, McClain condemned his friend as a "damned abolitionist son of a bitch."[52]

On Sunday, March 27, Joseph Nesbit was among a group discussing Eden's planned speech and the possibility of interference by soldiers. John Toland said that "all had best go prepared (meaning to go armed) as he thought there might be some trouble."[53] Others shared that concern. Moving about the courthouse square on March 28, Jacob Daisey said that he heard rumors that soldiers would attempt to stop Eden's speech, which was countered by Democratic promises to see that it was delivered.[54]

Some Democrats arriving in Charleston the morning of March 28 had more in mind than speeches. In Pritchard's store, several boasted that they "had come into town to see if the soldiers would make them take the Oath," and they grumbled about the attack two days earlier on James O'Hair, Sr., and Benjamin Toland.[55] O'Hair, Sr., urged his fellow Democrats not to "return many words with them [soldiers] we will give them hell in the outcome." He said that if it came to shooting, "he would be satisfied" if he could get Shubal York in his sights.[56]

The potential for trouble was clear to nearly everyone. Eden cancelled his speech, and with Ficklin, he circulated around the square urging Democrats to return peaceably to their homes. Others were intent on the Democrats remaining. Henderson O'Hair said, "[D]on't one of you Democrats leave for we come here to attend to this thing, and we must stick together." For too long, he complained, the "soldiers had been running over the citizens." Robert Leitch tried to play peacemaker, but he was told by Wells and Benjamin Toland that "they had been badly treated by them (the soldiers) and were going to have revenge." Not

51. Deposition of Robert Stricklin, April 2, 1864, ibid.
52. Deposition of B. M. Dice, April 3, 1864, ibid.
53. Deposition of Joseph Nesbit, April 6, 1864, ibid.
54. Deposition of Jacob Daisey, n.d., ibid.
55. Deposition of V. K. Curd, April 1, 1864, ibid.
56. Deposition of M. C. McLain, April 1, 1864, ibid.

only were soldiers likely targets for their rage, but also citizens "who pointed men out to the soldiers as Democrats" as well.[57]

One soldier claimed that before the riot began he observed one Democrat stalking about the square, a pistol in each hand, saying that "he would kill any Abolitionist that spoke to him." And moments before Wells encountered Sallee, Wells was heard to say, "By God we have taken all we are going to take from these soldiers . . . if soldiers did not quit their cutting up that Hell would be to pay."[58] Once the shooting began, it became clear that anyone resembling a soldier was fair game for the Democrats. At least four eyewitness accounts indicate that civilians wearing an article of military clothing were subject to attack.[59]

After the riot, Sheriff O'Hair and others gathered at Harrington's blacksmith shop in rural Coles County. Someone in the crowd asked if they were "taking up arms against the Government." No, said O'Hair, they were fighting a mob. It was "the Democrats that were in danger . . . no man was safe who bore the name of Democrat."[60]

The aftermath of the riot—the mass arrests, imprisonment without charge in the federal prisons, waves of rumors, the flight of the O'Hairs and other leading participants, and the failure to gain convictions for those finally brought to trial in connection with the incident—is covered in detail in the Coleman and Spence article.[61] Initial Democratic newspaper reaction, while regretting the violence, expressed neither surprise nor condemnation, seeing the Charleston Riot as a

---

57. Depositions of David Johnson, n.d., and Robert Leitch, April 2, 1864, both in ibid.; Coleman and Spence, pp. 20–21.

58. Depositions of Henry Touraw, April 4, 1864, and H. G. Green, both in Records of Draft Riots, 1864.

59. For accounts of civilians in articles of military clothing coming under attack, see Depositions of Charles Fleming, April 2, 1864, Enos Mullen, April 2, 1864, W. A. Braselton, April 1, 1864, and W. D. Wyeth, April 1, 1864, all in ibid.

60. Deposition of Willie Clapp, April 6, 1864, ibid.

61. For the aftermath of the riot, see Coleman and Spence, pp. 27–56. Colonel Mitchell survived the war and served as warden of the Chester state prison under Governor Richard James Oglesby. Eventually, he returned to Charleston, where he died on May 21, 1895, while working in his garden, located within earshot of the courthouse square. Until his death, Mitchell reportedly carried a heavy pocket watch, its case creased by a bullet from the riot. Sheriff John Hardwicke O'Hair, after a brief exile in Canada, returned to Illinois and settled in Edgar County, where he died on October 7, 1872. Members of the O'Hair family continued to seek and win public offices in Edgar County. Sheriff O'Hair's son, Frank Trimble O'Hair, defeated Joseph Gurney Cannon for a seat in Congress in 1912, and he was likely headed for another term when he died on May 13, 1932 (see *Chicago Tribune*, June 16, 1895, p. 46, cols. 1–3; "Memoirs of Frank T. O'Hair"; "Home of John H. O'Hair and Birthplace of John H. O'Hair," "Charleston Riot Materials Used" Folder, Coleman Papers). For more on the O'Hair family, see Mrs. C. Gerald Brann, *The Michael O'Hair Family* ([Bloomington, Ind.]. 1957), copies at the Edgar County Historical Society, Paris, Ill., and the Illinois State Historical Library.

potentially valuable object lesson for Republicans. "Hereafter, when democrats are assaulted by soldiers, our advice is that after disposing of their assailants, they ascertain, if possible, who it was that incited the attack and retaliate upon that man sharply in kind."[62]

Coleman and Spence concluded that the incident was triggered by "personal hostility rather than a particular issue," and they placed the bulk of the blame "on the shoulders of the more extreme Copperheads."[63] While correct, that explanation falls short in light of the protracted and steadily escalating pattern of harassment that preceded the riot, as well as the political climate faced by those in the Midwest who were critical of the Lincoln administration.

Democratic rhetoric and newspaper comment in the months before the riot strongly suggest that historian Baker's theoretical "switchboard" was buzzing, that existing conditions posed a clear and present danger to liberty, and that institutions for the redress of grievances were dysfunctional. Social, racial, and political resentments could not help but be inflamed by the fiery language of Eden and Robinson—leading citizens and members of Congress—and the *Chicago Times*'s recommendation for retaliatory violence after the Judge Constable oath-taking incident. Rather than wonder how the Charleston Riot occurred, a review of incidents in Iowa, Indiana, and elsewhere in Illinois leaves one wondering why there were not more incidents such as Charleston's.

By concentrating on arrest records, Neely may have missed the significance of numerous violent confrontations in creating an atmosphere of politically motivated intimidation on the streets. In light of the clashes in Indiana, Iowa, and Illinois, Coles County Democrats may have believed, with good reason, that their civil liberties were threatened, even if a dispassionate examination of arrest records 130 years later reveals few purely political arrests.

An exercise in counterhistory would likely devise a scenario in which bloodshed was avoided on March 28, 1864. To do so, however, the calls for "Peace at Home" had to gain more support from the leading Republican newspaper, more control had to be exercised by those commanding the soldiers, and Republicans had to be more tolerant of opposing views and Democrats less insistent on voicing theirs. But none of these things happened, and the pent-up tensions exploded on the courthouse square.

Given one praiseworthy outcome of the Civil War—the abolition of slavery—combined with the Democrats' vociferous and interminable agitation of antiblack prejudice for political gain, it is easy, by focusing on that part of their message, to enthusiastically consign those men and women and their ideas to

62. *Illinois State Register,* April 2, 1864, p. 2, col. 1.
63. Coleman and Spence, pp. 52, 56.

history's refuse pile. But the Midwest of the 1860s was not the Midwest of the late twentieth century in terms of racial views, and the abuses of power and suppression of opinion inflicted upon the Democrats were real and not easily dismissed.

Writing off the Copperheads as "traitors or quasi-secessionists," Richard Orr Curry believes, "tends to obscure the depths of racism and conservatism in American society, the continued existence of which still poisons our efforts to create a just and humane society." Consignment of Eden to traitor status makes it possible to avoid grappling with the questions he raised in Congress a few weeks before the riot. "The men now in power," he charged, "undertake to restore union and harmony . . . by the most intolerant proscription of all who differ with them in opinion. . . . Can the Union ever be restored in that way?" Both the sincerity and legitimacy of Eden's question have to be accepted. As Curry notes, to hide an important part of history—a once-vibrant activist republican tradition—behind a curtain of shame puts our history askew.[64]

On March 28, Coles and Edgar County Democrats could reflect upon a pattern of harassment, disrupted peace meetings, numerous similar examples in nearby states as well as Illinois, rumors that their access to the ballot box would be denied, and an attempt made on that day to attack one of their leading spokesmen. In their eyes, March 28 was the time to take a stand, to rebuke the oppressor.

There can be no apology for the violence that day on Charleston's square nor for the attacks upon dissenting civilians, which provided one of its direct causes. Yet in a country that has experienced widespread dissent from an unpopular and arguably ruinous war in recent generations, sympathy may be readily found for the Democrats' predicament. "The noblest use of free speech in this or any free country," contended Ohio Democratic Congressman Samuel Sullivan Cox during the days of repression, "is to criticise closely the political conduct of our agents. . . . A healthy state of the body-politic requires a party at all times, standing upon the fundamental law as the basis of its existence, and fearlessly vigilant against the encroachments of power."[65]

---

64. Curry, "Civil War and Reconstruction," p. 217; Eden, p. 12. See also *Congressional Globe,* 38 Cong., 1 Sess., Vol. 34, Pt. 53, p. 862.

65. *Congressional Globe,* 37 Cong., 3 Sess., Vol. 33, Pt. 80, pp. 1267–68.

6. “Honest Men and Law Abiding Citizens”

The 1894 Railroad Strike in Decatur

ROBERT D. SAMPSON

WITHOUT WARNING IN THE EARLY EVENING of June 30, 1894, crews of incoming Wabash Railway Company passenger trains in Decatur, Illinois, brought their locomotives to a halt near Union Depot and silently walked away. Eventually, a massive logjam of railcars snarled not only the depot area but the adjacent rail yards as well. Passengers pleaded, fumed, and one even threatened to shoot, but the trains did not move—the Pullman Strike had arrived in Decatur.

The Pullman Strike, which began in Chicago, tied up railroad traffic nationwide, sparking a decisive confrontation between the federal government and the fledgling American Railway Union (ARU). In Decatur, the Wabash became the ARU's strike target. By Sunday morning, July 1, strikers and their families, as well as crowds of onlookers, gathered about Union Depot and halted the movement of Wabash trains with their bodies and angry words. Bombarded with complaints from stranded passengers, Wabash officials attempted to move the trains, turning to the few remaining workers who had not joined in the walkout. The company also placed railroad detective William Ballard at their head.

Ballard, a man of authoritarian manner and seemingly eager to provoke confrontation, walked ahead of a locomotive that slowly pulled away from the depot. Vigorously swinging an iron bar in a wide arc before him, he intended to

---

Decatur resident ROBERT D. SAMPSON, a former newspaper reporter and congressional aide, is a Ph.D. candidate in history at the University of Illinois. Sampson's main interest is Jacksonian America, and his proposed dissertation is on John L. O'Sullivan and the *Democratic Review* magazine. This paper was presented at the Eleventh Annual Illinois History Symposium in December of 1990.

Illinois Historical Journal Vol. 85, No. 2 (Summer 1992): 74–88

clear the human blockade confronting him. "Get out of the way, you ——— or I'll brain you," he yelled amid the noise of the locomotive and the crowd, parting those who stood in his way with a torrent of flashing iron and profanity. His progress was suddenly halted by a man who broke from the crowd and pulled a gun, leveling it at Ballard. The railroad detective quickly reached for his own gun as others in the crowd interceded, pulled the assailant's arm down, and hustled him away. Only cool heads, timely action, and the determination of the strikers had averted bloodshed. An incident that might have ignited violence in Chicago, Spring Valley, or Danville—communities where confrontations led to loss of life—became just another bit of colorful trivia for the newspapers' summaries of the day's events.[1]

While general accounts provide a survey of the Pullman Strike and its effects on workers' lives, the Decatur experience presents numerous examples of the price exacted for defying corporate and government power. Decatur railroad workers were among thousands throughout Illinois participating in the strike, and their conduct was marked by strenuous efforts to maintain nonviolence, build union solidarity, and develop community support. The nonviolent tactics of Decatur strikers provide a practical example of that commitment as reflected in testimony before the United States Strike Commission by ARU President Eugene Victor Debs and both military and journalistic witnesses. The factors

---

1. *Decatur City and Macon County Directory, 1893* (Terre Haute, Ind.: Charles Ebel & Co., 1893), p. 95; *Herald-Despatch* (Decatur), July 2, 1894.

leading to the men's decision to break ranks and to the failure of the Decatur strike correspond to the actions described in general accounts. Also, Governor John Peter Altgeld's decision to dispatch state troops to the city and his refusal to remove them long after it appeared there was little danger of violence remains a mystery. Examination of Altgeld's correspondence and appointment calendar for both the strike period and a year earlier at the time of the lynching of an African American in Decatur suggest that he may have harbored doubts about Macon County Sheriff Peter Perl's ability to control crowds.[2]

Of the five railroads crossing through Decatur in 1894, the Wabash was the largest. With two separate lines entering and leaving the city, Decatur was a major switching point for the Wabash, and its passenger depot sold more tickets than any other on the system, including Chicago and St. Louis. The Wabash employed some seven hundred local workers at its $2 million facility, and its payroll pumped some $50,000 per month into the local economy.[3] Clearly, any disruption of service would not only tie up the entire system but also would have significant effects on the local economy.

Described as a "year of fast-moving drama," 1894 presented a unique "spectacle of greater despair" and "more serious labor disturbances" than had ever been seen before. "Pent-up bitterness" engendered by a changing society led railroad workers around the country to participate in that class warfare, and their strikes in the century's closing decades inspired other workers to engage in struggles with corporate power.[4] In Illinois alone, strikes idled 16 percent of the labor force at the height of a depression.[5] As June ended, Decatur's three dailies—the *Decatur Daily Review*, the *Daily Republican*, and the *Herald-Despatch*—were filled with accounts of the final gasps of the local coal miners' unsuccessful action from April to July as part of the national coal strike.[6] Those stories were mixed with reports of the growing likelihood of a railroad strike called by Debs's new ARU on behalf of workers at the Pullman Palace Car Company near Chicago.

---

2. For other accounts of the Pullman Strike in downstate Illinois, see Harry Jebsen, Jr., "The Role of Blue Island in the Pullman Strike of 1894," *Journal of the Illinois State Historical Society*, 67 (1974), 275–93; Stephen Freedman, "Organizing the Workers in a Steel Company Town: The Union Movement in Joliet, Illinois, 1870–1920," *Illinois Historical Journal*, 79 (1986), 3–18.

3. *Plat Book of Macon County, Illinois* (Chicago: Alden, Ogle & Co., 1891), p. 15; *The City of Decatur* (Dixon, Ill.: B. F. Shaw Printing Co., 1892), pp. 10–11.

4. Almont Lindsey, *The Pullman Strike: The Story of a Unique Experiment and of a Great Labor Upheaval* (Chicago: University of Chicago Press, 1942), p. 1; see also Shelton Stromquist, *A Generation of Boomers: The Pattern of Railroad Labor Conflict in Nineteenth-Century America* (Urbana: University of Illinois Press, 1987), p. 267.

5. Lindsey, p. 12.

6. For details of the Decatur coal strike, see the *Decatur Daily Review, Daily Republican* (Decatur), and *Herald-Despatch*, April–June, 1894.

While local news reports did not predict the Decatur strike, there had been evidence as early as April that some Wabash workers were dissatisfied. New wage scales (revised downward) and layoffs in the shops were among the factors that led the *Herald-Despatch* to report on the local strike's eve that Decatur's Wabash workers had experienced "their share of the burden" in the company's response to the economic downturn.[7]

As the Pullman Strike spread, a group of Decatur Wabash workers gathered on June 30 in Engineers' Hall, a meeting place only a few blocks away from Union Depot, apparently to discuss rumors that they would be forced to travel to St. Louis to replace striking workers there. A few hours later, all the switchmen in the Wabash yards walked off the job. The strike quickly spread to engineers and firemen, and by 7 P.M. the railroad yards had, reported the *Daily Republican,* the appearance of a "deserted race track." In those opening hours, the reason for the Decatur strike was not clear. Some of the men insisted that it was not an American Railway Union-related action, but instead it was based on long-standing grievances with the Wabash, particularly wage cuts. Though the strikers later claimed affiliation with the ARU and took orders from Debs, H. W. Shimer, president of the short-lived ARU local, attributed the strike to the engineers' dissatisfaction with their wages.[8]

News of the strike spread quickly that Saturday, and crowds began gathering at the depot. In a meeting during the strike's first hours, the workers agreed unanimously, the *Review* reported, that "an act of violence was the enemy of the strikers."[9] On Sunday, July 1, the strike drew the curious much as if it were an entertainment spectacle rather than a struggle between capital and labor. Ladies in their Sunday finest strolled amid the stranded freight and passenger cars, and the milling throng in its holiday mood gave the Wabash yards the "appearance of a parade ground." Eventually, an estimated five thousand persons gathered along the Wabash line from the depot to the Jasper Avenue crossing, the eastern edge of the switching yards. The prime danger, the *Herald-Despatch* observed, was not of violence to person and property but to the ladies' "dainty gowns and white kid shoes which suffered in the cinders." Within a few days, it was estimated that the Wabash was losing $40,000 a day in revenue, and the east-west ends of the system were "wholly tied-up." Eventually some six hundred workers went out at Decatur.[10]

---

7. *Herald-Despatch,* June 29, 1894; see also *Decatur Daily Review,* May 2 (p. 4, col. 2), June 12 (p. 2, col. 3, p. 7, col. 4), June 21 (p. 5, col. 2), June 22 (p. 1, col. 2, p. 6, cols. 4–5), June 26 (p. 6, col. 4), June 28 (p. 6, cols. 4–5), June 29 (p. 6, cols. 3–4), 1894.

8. *Herald-Despatch,* July 1, 1894; *Daily Republican,* July 2, 1894, p. 1, cols. 2–3, p. 4, col. 3.

9. *Decatur Daily Review,* July 1, 1894, p. 2, col. 1.

10. *Herald-Despatch,* July 1, 2, 1894; *Decatur Daily Review,* July 1 (p. 2, col. 3), July 3 (p. 2, col. 4), July 4 (p. 2, col. 4), July 5 (p. 2, cols. 1–2), 1894.

Union Depot (above) became the focal point of Wabash railroad workers when they joined the Pullman Strike. At one time, an estimated five thousand people gathered around the depot to observe the progress of the strike.

Curiously, the strike was limited to the Wabash. The city's other rail lines, including the two lines of the Illinois Central, continued to function. There is no indication why workers on the other railroads did not join nor any sign in the news accounts that they were pressured by strikers.[11] Perhaps the Wabash strikers were distracted by more immediate concerns, for despite the holiday atmosphere around Union Depot and early successes in verbally persuading arriving train crews to join them, the strikers knew that local company officials were determined to meet the challenge and to do everything possible to keep the system open. In the predawn hours of July 1, three Wabash officials rested atop a pile of ties in the congested switching yard and "wondered what they would do next." Within hours, whether or not by their direction, a telegram signed by "500 Sufferers" demanding immediate assistance to end their forced stay in Decatur was sent to Governor Altgeld. In effect, the telegram's author or authors, purporting to be rail passengers, wanted the governor to dispatch troops to aid their departure.[12]

11. *Herald-Despatch,* July 4, 8, 1894; *Decatur Daily Review,* July 4, 1894, p. 2, col. 3.

12. *Herald-Despatch,* July 1, 1894; "500 Sufferers" to Altgeld, July 1, 1894, Record Group 101.22, File 88-126, No. 105, John Peter Altgeld Correspondence, Illinois State Archives, Springfield (hereafter cited as Altgeld Correspondence).

As in similar cases, Altgeld was torn between private sympathies and public duty. During the coal strike, he had demonstrated his concern over the tendency of employers to seek state militia as a cheap method of strikebreaking by issuing General Orders No. 7, which explicitly declared that troops were not to be used as "custodians or guards of private property." Yet, he insisted that his sympathy for laboring men and women could not stand in the way of protecting the public. When faced with allegations that the public safety was endangered, Altgeld, after satisfying himself as to the accuracy of the complaint, was prone to thrust aside doubts and respond with troops. Upon receiving the plea of the "500 Sufferers," Altgeld telegraphed Macon County Sheriff Perl that he had a request for assistance "purporting to come from five hundred passengers now detained at the depot." He asked Perl for a full report as well as assurances that the sheriff could protect the "traveling public" and "enforce the laws." Perl replied that he had been able to maintain order but could do so no longer. Within a matter of hours, Altgeld dispatched troops to Decatur and ordered the sheriff to see that "all trains unlawfully held are released at once."[13]

Why did Altgeld respond so quickly? In his first telegram, use of the word "purporting" indicated that the governor may have had suspicions about the legitimacy of the telegram. Also, as a friend of labor he was surely aware that the presence of troops often produced an inflammatory effect upon a dispute. Unlike some communities also requesting troops, Decatur had suffered no violence during the coal strike. Beyond Perl's response, the answer might lie in events that occurred more than a year before when an African American accused of rape and confined in Perl's jail was dragged from his cell by a mob and lynched across the street from the courthouse. Altgeld not only had news accounts and editorials decrying Perl's handling of the situation (amid rumors of the mob's imminent arrival, the sheriff had conveniently decided to visit the World's Columbian Exposition at Chicago), but also the governor's records indicate he may have received personal testimony critical of Perl's conduct.[14]

---

13. "Altgeld to Adjutant General, May 25, 1894, Correspondence Book, p. 656, Altgeld Correspondence; Altgeld to Perl, July 1, 1894, Correspondence Book, pp. 112, 113, ibid.; see also Harry Barnard, *Eagle Forgotten: The Life of John Peter Altgeld* (1938; rpt. Secaucus, N.J.: Lyle Stuart, 1973), pp. 277–78, 290–91; Lindsey, p. 15. Perl's reply to Altgeld's first telegram has apparently been lost. In a speech in New York two years later, Altgeld said that Perl requested help. A newspaper editorial at the time refers to Perl's message (see Altgeld, "Address on Labor Unrest and the Pullman Strike," in *The Mind and Spirit of John Peter Altgeld: Selected Writings and Addresses,* ed. Henry M. Christman [Urbana: University of Illinois Press, 1960], p. 131; *Decatur Daily Review,* July 3, 1894, p. 4, col. 1).

14. Sundiata Keita Cha-Jua, "'Join hands and hearts with law and order': The 1893 Lynching of Samuel J. Bush and the Response of Decatur's African American Community," *Illinois Historical Journal* 83 (1990), 187–200.

John Peter Altgeld

Altgeld had legitimate reason to believe that if a crisis arose, Perl would be unable to handle it. The governor's inclination to put the public safety above his own sympathies and suspicions and Perl's demonstrated incompetence may have led Altgeld to the conclusion that he had no choice but to dispatch troops to Decatur.

Stunned by Altgeld's decision, Decatur residents viewed it as an insult to the city. The news, the *Herald-Despatch* related, broke like a "thunderclap from a clear sky, more especially when there had been no rioting here." The same account hinted at the Perl connection, noting that the dispatch of troops was yet another event that had made the sheriff's term in office a "long series of surprises." The sheriff was on the scene at Union Depot adding a new trade to his resume. The mortician-turned-sheriff was reported to be helping Wabash officials switch cars. The Democratic *Review* gave Altgeld lukewarm editorial support for his decision but noted that he was "pretty generally damned if he does and damned if he does not" in the present climate.[15]

Transporting some of the troops to Decatur proved to be a problem. Difficulties obtaining an engineer delayed one trainload of troops from leaving

15. *Herald-Despatch*, July 2, 1894; *Decatur Daily Review*, July 3, 1894, p. 4, col. 1.

Springfield, and the trip to Decatur was apparently so difficult and the city's reputation for persuasion so great that Altgeld advised Colonel J. S. Culver, a commander of a subsequent troop train bound for Danville, that if he reached Decatur to proceed at once to Danville. "Keep your engineer in hand and if necessary promise him any sum of money up to a couple of hundred dollars to take you through," Altgeld insisted. Unless the officer took care to get out of Decatur quickly, he and his troops might face being stranded "for want of an engineer."[16]

Fortunately for Altgeld, there were some troops in Decatur already—the local unit and its commander Lieutenant Colonel Frank P. Wells, who operated Morehouse & Wells Company, a local wholesale-retail hardware store. By Sunday, July 1, crowds were swarming around the depot. Any attempt to move a train provoked the crowd to surround the engine and halt its progress. Several women in the crowd jeered at those workers refusing to join the strike. Around the depot area, the throng surged back and forth between the arguments that were breaking out. At one point, a working engineer's wife pushed her way through the crowd and unsuccessfully pleaded with her husband to join the strike.[17] Ordered by Perl "to do everything possible to aid the Wabash Co. to move trains which were unlawfully held," Wells marched one of his units through the depot area, clearing the crowd at bayonet point. As the bottled up trains began moving, a detachment of state militia accompanied each out of the yards.[18]

Among those stranded by the strike was a group of Chicago labor organizers traveling to a state labor convention in Springfield. The arrival of the group—which included the pardoned Haymarket defendants Michael Schwab and Oscar Neebe—provided another potential spark to upset the nonviolent commitment of the Decatur strikers. One account placed the party's size at ninety, and its leaders decided to lend their efforts to the local strike by holding a public meeting. Their attempt to secure Central Park in downtown Decatur was repulsed by Mayor David C. Moffitt, who later defended his action in the *Review*: "When I want Chicago agitators here to address the people in a crisis like this I will send for them."[19]

---

16. *Report of the Adjutant General of Illinois . . . 1893 and 1894* (Springfield, Ill.: Ed. F. Hartman, Printer and Binder, 1895), pp. 92–93; Altgeld to Culver, July 2, 1894, Calendar of Correspondence, No. 120, Altgeld Correspondence.

17. *Past and Present of the City of Decatur and Macon County, Illinois* (Chicago: S. J. Clarke Pub. Co., 1903), p. 814; *Daily Republican,* July 2, 1894, p. 4, col. 2; *Decatur Daily Review,* July 3, 1894, p. 2, cols. 5–6.

18. *Report of the Adjutant General,* p. 100.

19. *Daily Republican,* July 3, 1894, p. 4, col. 5; *Decatur Daily Review,* July 4, 1894, p. 2, col. 4.

This drawing depicts the military helping to move a train out of Chicago. A similar event occurred in Decatur when Lieutenant Colonel Frank P. Wells ordered his men to move Wabash trains as they cleared the crowd at bayonet point.

On July 2, the group met at Engineers' Hall, where several of them addressed the strikers. William Howard, an official in the Chicago local of the National Longshoremen's Association—described in a *Republican* account as "evidently of African descent" and in the *Herald-Despatch* as "a large, fine looking mulatto with a wonderfully strong voice"—stunned the crowd. He expressed a desire to "throttle George Pullman with his left hand and beat him to death with his right." He said that if a rattlesnake should bite Pullman's poisonous heart the reptile would die. As his audience sat in shocked silence, Howard said that rights that could not be won with ballots and strikes might have to be won with bullets. If that proved to be the case, he would be found where the bullets were the "thickest," and to prove his sincerity, he bragged of scars from bullets on his head and knees.[20]

Thomas J. Morgan, another member of the group and identified as a "veteran labor agitator," quickly jumped up and condemned his colleague, begging the audience's understanding. Sensing the crowd's negative reaction, Morgan

20. *Daily Republican,* July 3, 1894, p. 3, cols. 3–4; *Herald-Despatch,* July 3, 1894.

insisted that Howard had lost his head and compared him to Samuel Fielden, who said things at the 1886 Haymarket Square rally that he did not mean and later regretted. According to the *Review*, Morgan urged the strikers, "Do not let your passions run away from you, for if you do you divorce public sympathy from you." Noting the reporters who had busily scribbled down Howard's remarks, Morgan criticized them for focusing on the inflammatory comments and not the "sensible things." During all this, Schwab sat quietly in a dark corner. The next day, the group "suddenly" boarded an Illinois Central passenger train bound for Clinton.[21]

If the strikers were not receptive to the confrontational message of Howard, they were already irritated by the actions of local officials. At the same meeting, Mayor Moffitt attempted to counter his denial of the Central Park meeting permit with a criticism of Altgeld's dispatch of troops, an action he "could see no cause for." The military presence, he said, was "an insult to the citizens of Decatur." Moffitt also commended the strikers for their nonviolent conduct. Following the mayor, Sheriff Perl took the rostrum and attempted to defend his conduct. The audience questioned him with such "considerable force" that the chairman of the meeting had to call for order.[22]

Engineers' Hall quickly became the strikers' focal point for building solidarity, coordinating efforts to maintain nonviolence, and reaching out to the community for support. Located on the second floor of a building a few blocks from Union Depot and the Wabash yards, the hall was home to three of Decatur's twenty-two unions. The key railroad trades—engineers, firemen, and switchmen—normally met there. During the strike, the room might have been more accurately labeled ARU Hall. When news came that the national Brotherhood of Locomotive Engineers not only refused to sanction the strike but threatened expulsion for members who participated, the Decatur local defied the hierarchy.[23]

In the opening hours of the strike, Engineers' Hall was the scene of numerous meetings. At one gathering an anonymous committee of three—a switchman, a conductor, and a fireman—was appointed to prepare and issue public statements on behalf of the strikers. Believing, perhaps, that anonymity would protect them from Wabash retaliation should the strike fail (an erroneous assumption as events proved), only H. W. Shimer, the local president, was quoted by name. An initial action of the committee dealt with self-control. "Any man who commits

---

21. *Daily Republican*, July 3, 1894, p. 3, col. 3; *Herald-Despatch*, July 3, 1894; *Decatur Daily Review*, July 3, p. 6, col. 3.

22. *Decatur Daily Review*, July 3, 1894, p. 2, col. 3.

23. *Decatur City and Macon County Directory, 1893*, pp. 47–49; *Herald-Despatch*, July 3, 1894.

a breach of the peace will be considered an enemy to the cause," the committee warned. "It is intended that the strike shall be orderly throughout."[24]

After the state troops arrived, and especially once the federal injunction banning activity around Union Depot and the switchyard was posted, Engineers' Hall took on even greater importance. Men occupied there were not likely to become involved in altercations with the ever-aggressive Ballard and the special deputies Perl created from the ranks of railroad detectives imported by the Wabash from St. Louis. Meetings—business and social—were in session all day. Recitations, singing, and public speaking were on the entertainment portion of the program. "The uncertainty of the situation did not prevent the men from enjoying themselves," the *Herald-Despatch* reported. Like revival meetings, the sessions also occasionally featured the testimony of a converted "sinner" who had seen the light. One such man was a strikebreaker who was "won over to the cause" and decided to remain among his new, "true-hearted, noble friends."[25]

Seeking public support, the strikers may have written letters to the editor. One such letter, signed "One of Them," decried the fact that "property rights are closely defended and followed and property protected right or wrong, while human rights are left to the tender mercies of human selfishness. The working man is admonished to live if you can, die if you must." The writer condemned Perl's increasingly pro-Wabash actions as "an insult to our citizens . . . an outrage on the public." While no violence had yet occurred, the letter writer was sure where at least partial blame belonged if it did. "Anarchy and lawlessness among the rich and powerful are largely responsible for the same result among the working classes."[26]

Prostrike sentiment was spreading throughout the community, even in the most unlikely places. Addie L. Davis, a widow who was stenographer to A. H. Landers, the Wabash master of transportation, let slip a remark one day in the office expressing her sympathy with the strikers. As a result, "some few remarks passed" between Davis and Landers, ending when the woman quit. Later, she was publicly sworn into the ARU at an Engineers' Hall rally.[27]

Considerable evidence suggests that the strikers enjoyed widespread community support. A study of the Pullman Strike in Blue Island notes that merchants there refused to sell food and beverages to federal marshals, special deputies, and soldiers, thereby making that location different from others involved by showing "its unity in support of its workers."[28] But contemporary accounts of

---

24. *Decatur Daily Review,* July 1, 1894, p. 2, cols. 2–3.

25. *Herald-Despatch,* July 6, 1894; *Decatur Daily Review,* July 6, 1894, p. 2, cols. 1–2.

26. *Decatur Daily Review,* July 8, 1894, p. 5, col. 3.

27. *Decatur City and Macon County Directory, 1893,* p. 158; *Decatur Daily Review,* July 11, 1894, p. 2, col. 4.

28. Jebsen, p. 293.

the Decatur strike provide numerous examples of similar actions that go beyond that level of support for the workers' cause.

Barbers in the blocks adjacent to Union Depot refused to shave strikebreakers. Waitresses at nearby hotels and lunch counters pledged not to serve the "new men." The ARU called for a boycott of the Union Depot hotel and restaurant, which was heavily patronized by the strikebreakers, who were usually under guard since the Wabash feared exposing them to the entreaties of the strikers. The boycott was averted when the owner of the hotel appeared at Engineers' Hall to plead for withdrawal of the action, explaining that under the terms of his lease he had no choice but to serve railroad employees. Other unions supported the strikers, notably the printers at the *Review,* who appointed a delegation to attend an Engineers' Hall meeting and offer their support.[29]

Newspaper readers seemed to enjoy stories of the strikebreakers' incompetence. The *Review* reported a near miss between a scab-operated Wabash switch engine and another railroad's engine at the crossing where the two lines intersected. A one-armed switchman with the Illinois Central, who was not on strike but was sympathetic, allowed that he was taking out a $3,000 accident policy since he was forced to work near the "new" men and had "no desire to have a Wabash engine piled on top of the one arm he [had] remaining."[30]

About midway through the strike, a committee of strikers visited local businessmen, seeking funds to support the strike and were, according to reports, "well-received" and collected "a considerable amount of money."[31] Attorney David Hutchison, a speaker at a Fourth of July celebration, used his remarks to show support, "without qualification," for the strikers. He skewered Perl with sarcasm, using both a play on words and racist slang to remind his audience of the sheriff's lack of fortitude during the lynching. Recounting a recent trip to Union Depot, he confessed that he had been led to believe he would find trouble and possibly violence. But when he arrived, Hutchison said, "I had to elbow my way through crowds of nice young men and pretty girls."[32] A Wabash engineer summed up the feelings of the strikers for the *Herald-Despatch*: "We want to win but we want to do so as honest men and to sustain our reputation as law-abiding citizens."[33]

The following Sunday, July 8, Rev. D. F. Howe of the First Methodist Church defended the cause of labor from the pulpit. "Let railroads have a greater interest

29. *Decatur Daily Review,* July 4 (p. 2, col. 2), July 10 (p. 2, cols. 4–5), July 12 (p. 2, col. 5), 1894; *Herald-Despatch*, July 4, 1894.

30. *Decatur Daily Review,* July 11, 1894, p. 2, cols. 4–5.

31. Ibid., July 6, 1894, p. 2, col. 3; *Daily Republican,* July 9 (p. 1, cols. 2–3), July 11 (p. 4, col. 2), 1894.

32. *Daily Republican,* July 5, 1894, p. 3, col. 5; *Decatur Daily Review,* July 5, p. 1, cols. 2–3.

33. *Herald-Despatch*, July 5, 1894.

in their men personally. Discharge no man without cause," he urged. Labor unions, he preached, were essential to defend the individual worker. "It is downright meanness to see how little you can get a man to work for."[34]

Another manifestation of support blossomed in the streets. Faced with a hostile national press, leaders of the ARU hit upon a means for citizens to support their cause by wearing white ribbons that indicated their sympathy with the strike. It succeeded, and by July 4 an American Federation of Labor organizer in Chicago reported to his chief, Samuel Gompers, that "you cannot go a block without you see some people wearing a white ribbon."[35] On July 7, the Decatur strikers asked the public to take up the white ribbon, and by the next day the badge was a common site around Union Depot.[36]

The *Review*, the most prostrike of Decatur's newspapers, represented the high point of public support in its July 11 editorial on the national strike: "When 150,000 men decide cheerfully to give up work for sympathy with fellow working men it is time to conclude these men have something that looks much like justice on their side." Evidence of public support in Decatur bolsters Herbert Gutman's thesis, which is cited by Harry Jebsen, Jr., to account for similar actions in Blue Island. Jebsen observes that the "affluent middle class" of smaller communities like Blue Island and Decatur were "almost exclusively" merchants who were reliant on the support of working people.[37]

There were others in Decatur, however, who were not as supportive of the strike. The most prominent example of public support for the Wabash's position is found in a telegram sent to Altgeld appointee and possible confidant Bradford K. Durfee of Decatur that was likely intended for the governor. Signed by several prominent citizens, including banker and land speculator James Millikin, the telegram voiced fear that without the militia the Wabash would be paralyzed. Rumors circulating on July 4 and 5 that the militia might be withdrawn raised the specter of trouble, the citizens argued. Railroad officials had also been sending Altgeld messages that opposed the rumored withdrawal.[38]

Opposition also came from those who supported President Grover Cleveland's repression of the strike. The aged members of Dunham Post No. 141,

34. *Decatur Daily Review*, July 10, 1894, p. 5, col. 2.

35. Philip S. Foner, *History of the Labor Movement in the United States* (New York: International Pub., 1947–1987), II, 264. For the national scope of the ribbon campaign, see also Lindsey, p. 317; Sidney Lens, *The Labor Wars: From the Molly Maguires to the Sitdowns* (Garden City, N.Y.: Doubleday, 1973), pp. 95, 105.

36. *Herald-Despatch*, July 8, 1894; *Daily Republican*, July 9, 1894, p. 1, col. 3.

37. *Decatur Daily Review*, July 11, 1894, p. 4, col. 1; Jebsen, p. 283.

38. Millikin et al. to Durfee, July 5, 1894, Correspondence Book, No. 119, Perl to Altgeld, July 3, 1894, Correspondence Book, No. 129, and Charles M. Hayes to Altgeld, July 3, 1894, Correspondence Book, No. 124, all in Altgeld Correspondence.

the local chapter of the Grand Army of the Republic, offered to assist in putting down "with relentless hands the spirit of anarchy or rebellion." The post's resolution called for supporters of Cleveland, and by implication the railroads, to wear American flags in their lapels and praised the conduct of Sheriff Perl. The strikers responded by regretting that the GAR had "seen fit to arraign itself upon the side of the plutocracy" but down played its impact given the "weak and declining strength" of its members who were "in their dotage." Later, when Sheriff Perl's conduct cost him one of the three bondsmen necessary to hold his office, the GAR members indicated that they could provide "500 men" who would replace the bondsman.[39]

Bondsman Hieronymous Mueller, who was to become a leading Decatur industrialist, was prompted to withdraw his bond because of Perl's illegal deputization of several nonresidents provided by the Wabash. Illinois had enacted a law in 1893 forbidding the appointment of special deputies if such individuals had not been a resident of the county for at least one year previous. Once federal authorities intervened, those men took on the added power of deputy federal marshals. Attempts by the strikers to gain prosecution of Perl for that violation proved futile, however.[40]

Testimony before the United States Strike Commission and various subsequent accounts of the Pullman Strike are consistent in their criticism of the use of such special deputies and of their conduct, which in some instances promoted violence.[41] They were described by reporter Harold I. Cleveland of the *Chicago Herald* as "a very low, contemptible set of men."[42] In addition, Perl began performing railroad switching duties within the first twenty-four hours of the strike and became, in effect, a railroad employee. The conduct of railroad detective Ballard was equally frustrating to the strikers and more damaging in the long run. His iron bar and profanity-assisted movement of a train on the first day was condemned by the *Review* as inflammatory. The *Republican* of July 13 later credited the railroad detective with giving the strike "its death blow by

---

39. *Daily Republican,* July 11, 1894, p. 3, col. 3; *Decatur Daily Review,* July 12 (p. 2, col. 5, p. 3, col. 3), July 15 (p. 1, col. 3), 1894.

40. *Daily Republican,* July 6 (p. 8, col. 3), July 7 (p. 8, cols. 3–4), 1894; *Decatur Daily Review,* July 7, 1894, p. 2, cols. 1–2; John H. Keiser, *Building for the Centuries: Illinois, 1865–1898,* Sesquicentennial History of Illinois, Vol. 4 (Urbana: University of Illinois Press, 1977), pp. 242–43.

41. U.S. Strike Commission, *Report on the Chicago Strike of June–July, 1894,* Senate Executive Document, No.7, 53 Cong., 3 Sess. (Washington, D.C.: GPO, 1895), pp. 368–71, 379–80, 396–99; Lens, p. 99; Jerry M. Cooper, *The Army and Civil Disorder: Federal Military Intervention in Labor Disputes, 1877–1900* (Westport, Conn.: Greenwood, 1980), pp. 8–9; Gerald G. Eggert, *Railroad Labor Disputes: The Beginnings of Federal Strike Policy* (Ann Arbor: University of Michigan Press, 1967), p. 159; Lindsey, pp. 166–67, 243–44; Foner, II, 269.

42. U.S. Strike Commission, p. 371.

a clever trick." That trick consisted of employing a spy who infiltrated the ranks at Engineers' Hall and kept Ballard informed of all plans. One poststrike job applicant was surprised when Ballard produced a piece of paper and quoted, according to the *Review* of July 14, an "accurate and complete account" of the striker's remarks at Engineers' Hall.[43]

Despite frustrations stemming from the illegal actions of Perl and the bullying of Ballard, the Decatur strikers held firm in their commitment to nonviolence. Two strikers—Fred Young and F. M. Wiley—intervened quickly on July 2 to break up a heated dispute at Union Depot, telling their fellow strikers that no fights would be allowed. When Clarence Kelso, a local bartender, tried repeatedly to start fights allegedly on behalf of the strikers, the railroaders disavowed and condemned his actions.[44] The most violent incident of the Decatur strike occurred on July 9 when an engineer was struck and slightly injured by a large object thrown into the cab of his engine as it slowly rounded the curve at the Mercer Street crossing. Ballard and two special deputies rushed to the scene, apparently got into a dispute with two bystanders—Joe Brewster, a plumber, and Charles Munea, a painter—and arrested them. The men were later released, and eventually sixteen-year-old Frank Floyd was arrested for the attack.[45]

No striker was ever charged in Decatur. United States Marshal William B. Brinton of Springfield told the *Review* that Decatur had been "comparatively quiet and peaceable. . . . If we had had only railroad men to deal with[,] this strike would have been an easy matter to handle." Similar sentiments fill the pages of the Strike Commission's report.[46]

The generosity of the victors was easily afforded as the defeat of the ARU nationally and in Decatur was a crushing blow. The turning point of the strike was July 4, the day before a federal injunction "placed the full legal power of the government at the discretion of the [railroad] association."[47] In Decatur, the placards placed around Union Depot on July 5 made clear the consequences of interfering with the Wabash's operations. Any attempt to talk with strikebreakers was prohibited on or near railroad property. After Debs's arrest and

43. *Daily Republican,* July 2 (p. 4, cols. 1–3), July 3 (p. 4, col. 1), July 5 (p. 1, col. 2), July 13 (p. 1, col. 2), 1894; *Decatur Daily Review,* July 3 (p. 2, cols. 2, 6), July 14 (p. 2, cols. 1–2), 1894.

44. *Decatur Daily Review,* July 3 (p. 2, col. 5), July 12 (p. 2, col. 4), 1894; *Daily Republican,* July 9 (p. 1, col. 2), July 11 (p. 4, col. 2), 1894.

45. *Decatur Daily Review,* July 10 (p. 3, col. 2), July 11 (p. 2, col. 5), July 12 (p. 2, col. 4), 1894; *Daily Republican,* July 10, 1894, p. 4, col. 2; *Herald-Despatch,* July 10, 1894.

46. *Decatur Daily Review,* July 13, 1894, p. 2, col. 2; U.S. Strike Commission, pp. 383–85, 402–8.

47. Nick Salvatore, *Eugene V. Debs: Citizen and Socialist* (Urbana: University of Illinois Press, 1982), p. 133.

Harper's Weekly *of July 14, 1894, depicted special deputies hired by federal marshals during the Pullman Strike as they lined up for badges and weapons.*

his subsequent communications problems with the union locals, the Decatur portion of the railroad strike ended as suddenly as it had begun. Around midnight on July 11, seven strikers applied for their old jobs, and within two hours a dozen more followed. According to the *Republican*, by 10 A.M. the next morning, men were reporting to the Wabash offices in groups of a "half-dozen or more" seeking reemployment, "should the company see fit." Among those who remained out, the break in the ranks created "universal dismay," and all efforts to preserve solidarity proved "fruitless." By July 12, Wabash officials could confidently declare that their line was now "in apple pie order."[48]

Amid the scramble for jobs, the days of singing, speeches, and solidarity at Engineers' Hall were forgotten. For many, bitterness replaced brotherhood. "From now on," declared one unemployed engineer, "I'm my own grand chief," implying that in his future, the railroad union leaders would have little say. Another former striker described the situation as every man for himself, and in order to survive, he was adopting a "dog eat dog policy. . . . Yes sir, I am looking for a job, and I want one bad." According to an engineer, he and his fellows had now placed themselves "literally at the disposal of the company and if I should

48. *Decatur Daily Review,* July 6 (p. 2, col. 3), July 12 (p. 2, col. 4), July 13 (p. 2, col. 1), 1894; *Daily Republican,* July 12, 1894, p. 1, col. 2.

live one thousand years I would never be caught in another labor strike."[49] The Decatur comments reflected the national sentiment that the social solidarity that had developed in many communities had been disrupted. What followed was for many "a personal calamity, often entailing the sacrifice of a home and community ties."[50]

Just as the Wabash had used a spy to identify labor activists in Decatur, other railroads used similar tactics around the nation. In the weeks that followed, the Illinois Central took back only two-thirds of its strikers, but the Rock Island rehired all but 450 of 4,500. Thousands of workers were blacklisted as railroads shared information. Decatur was no exception; a "great many" men stood to lose their homes. On July 13, the day Debs admitted the inevitable and declared the Pullman Strike over, the Wabash had 275 to three hundred applications from former strikers on file in Decatur. A number of strikers were simply told it would be "useless and a waste of time" to apply. Nearly half of the men were estimated to be out of work. 'This is the time to help them out," the *Review* declared. At Engineers' Hall, a remnant gathered awaiting the final word from Debs. Those present were for the most part "men who do not expect to ever re-enter the railroad service in Decatur." The Wabash was expected to make things as difficult as possible for those strikers rehired in order to discourage future strikes.[51]

The day after the Decatur strike was broken, the once bustling Union Depot platform provided a "very mournful sight" as the defeated strikers stood in small groups "discussing each other's prospects for returning to work." Local businessmen once canvassed for funds to support the strike were now asked to sign petitions in efforts to "secure jobs for their favorites." The white ribbons that once boldly asserted support for the strike had become a thing of the past. At the Wabash carshops, 140 of the two hundred strikers were rehired. The remaining sixty, all reported to be ARU members, were told "to go elsewhere." All striking trackmen were reportedly "out for good," and several switchmen were told not even to bother applying.[52]

After the strike, Addie L. Davis, the plucky stenographer who quit her job on principle, was reported to be seeking work in Chicago. Ballard, the Wabash's point man, was "just now as big a chief as Sitting Bull was in his palmiest days," reported the *Review*. "He is eagerly sought for and followed up by a few of the

---

49. *Herald-Despatch*, July 21, 1894; *Daily Republican*, July 12 (p. 1, col. 2), July 13 (p. 1, col. 2), 1894.

50. Stromquist, pp. 221–22.

51. Lindsey, pp. 337–38; *Herald-Despatch*, July 15, 1894; *Decatur Daily Review*, July 14, 1894, p. 2, cols. 1, 3.

52. *Daily Republican*, July 13 (p. 1, cols. 2–3), July 16 (p. 4, col. 2), 1894.

ex-strikers who want him to put in a few good words for them at headquarters. . . . It is tacitly understood that his endorsement is right now worth considerable." Such a fact was, conceded the *Republican*—the newspaper most consistently critical of the strike—"a humiliation which cuts some of the men to the quick." Sheriff Perl—no longer needed to supervise the now-departed militia nor tend to his railroad duties—was reported to be holding his "usual popular reception" afternoons in his office.[53]

Some strikers may well have taken the attitude of Tom Burke, a painter in the Wabash shops. "Particularly marked for decapitation," Burke was preparing to leave the city for Cincinnati. A "leading spirit" of the ARU and "glad of it," he had no regrets. "No one dragged me into this affair. I went in with my eyes open and knew just what to expect if we lost. It was either win or lose and I'm ready to take my medicine. My only regret is that I'll probably have to leave Decatur. I have come to like the town as a place to live."[54]

Despite doing everything they were supposed to do—maintaining nonviolence, seeking and gaining community support, building a sense of solidarity through meetings and associations—Burke and his fellow workers lost. They were defeated not through their own failings but by the intervention of the federal government aggravated by the willingness of one local official—Perl—to do the Wabash's bidding. Perl exceeded his instructions by using state troops to keep people away from strikebreakers. Even a governor reluctant to provide state troops for use as strikebreakers proved powerless against the combination of federal, local, and corporate power that confronted the Decatur strikers.

To the striking men it may have seemed ironic that the officials controlling the federal and local forces of that powerful trio had been elected by workingmen. Certainly, those men learned the lesson that historian Shelton Stromquist contends was taught by the strike: "Workers' struggles take place in a political context." Controlling the instruments of state power "is ultimately decisive."[55] The question that the strikers had to face and the question that Tom Burke perhaps struggled with on his way to Cincinnati was: How do workers gain such control or at least a measure sufficient to counterbalance corporations?

• • •

AUTHOR'S NOTE: The author thanks James Barrett for his encouragement and counsel and Robert W. Johannsen for his helpful editing advice.

---

53. *Herald-Despatch,* July 21, 1894; *Decatur Daily Review,* July 14, 1894, p. 2, col. 1; *Daily Republican,* July 13, 1894, p. 1, col. 3, p. 4, col. 1.

54. *Decatur City and Macon County Directory, 1893,* p. 127; *Decatur Daily Review,* July 17, 1894, p. 2, col. 1; *Herald-Despatch,* July 15, 1894.

55. Stromquist, p. 274.

7. The Alton School Case and African American Community Consciousness, 1897–1908

SHIRLEY J. PORTWOOD

IN 1892 AFRICAN AMERICANS IN ALTON, ILLINOIS, looked back at the postemancipation years with considerable satisfaction and pride. They boasted of their many individual and collective accomplishments in that small river city, and they anticipated that even greater successes would follow. Henry B. Hunter, a local black leader and the Alton correspondent for the Springfield *State Capital,* a weekly black newspaper, noted some of those victories in his column: "Messrs. Wilson and Carter have opened a blacksmith shop on second street: good for them; let other colored men come to the front."[1] Hunter, who was very active in the United Brothers of Friendship (UBF)—an international black fraternal order—and president of the Alton Lovejoy Club, later wrote: "Onr [our] farmers of Woodriver pay taxrs [taxes] [in the amount of] $77.900. These men have made rapid progress since 1863. Let our people press forward, we are coming to the front."[2] Hunter

---

SHIRLEY J. PORTWOOD received a B.A. in history from Southern Illinois University at Edwardsville and an M.A. and the Ph.D. from Washington University. She is the author of "Black Migration to Pulaski County, Illinois, 1860–1900," which appeared in this *Journal* in 1987. She has also published articles in the *International Journal of Sociology of the Family* (1988) and the *Journal of Negro History* (1992). Portwood is a professor in the Department of Historical Studies at Southern Illinois University at Edwardsville.

1. *State Capital* (Springfield), March 5, 1892, p. 1, col. 5.

2. Ibid., Feb. 27 (p. 1, col. 3), May 14 (p. 4, col. 5), Aug. 13 (p. 4, col. 2), 1892, Nov. 12, 1898, p. 3, cols. 1–2; *Alton Evening Telegraph,* Jan. 24, 1898, p. 3, col. 4. Woodriver is a neighboring area east of Alton. In an earlier article, Hunter indicated that African Americans had first moved to the Alton area in larger numbers beginning in 1863.

Illinois Historical Journal Vol. 91, No. 1 (Spring 1998): 414–437

Alton's riverfront, circa 1903

also observed: "To-day our colored citizens are paying taxes on $75,000 worth of property in the city of Alton, and we are pressing onward."[3] Hunter was a central figure in the Colored Republican Club, and he would later become president of that organization. He expressed the sentiments of many African Americans in Alton and elsewhere when he suggested that the Republican party deserved considerable credit for blacks' improved socioeconomic condition. He also added that "we are pressing onward and never shall forget Lovejoy, Lincoln, Grant and the Republican party."[4] Viewed from Hunter's perspective, then, one clearly discerns both race consciousness and Republican party loyalty within Alton's African American community of 1892.

Five years later, Hunter and many other black Altonians were reconsidering their support of the Republican party amid charges that the party's commitment to them and to equalitarian principles had waned. That reassessment was precipitated by an 1896–1897 decision by Alton Mayor Henry Brueggemann, the city council, and the board of education—most of whom were Republicans—to segregate the public school system, which had been desegregated since the early 1870s. Within months of the new policy, Alton became racially polarized. White residents who publicly expressed their views—regardless of their political affiliation—supported the new policy of segregated schools, although there were often bitter factional disputes within the Grand Old Party (GOP) and between

3. *State Capital,* Jan. 16, 1892, p. 1, col. 4.

4. Ibid., Jan. 16 (p. 1, col. 4), Feb. 27 (p. 1, col. 3), Aug. 13 (p. 4, col. 2), Aug. 20 (p. 1, col. 5), 1892; *Illinois Record* (Springfield), Dec. 24, 1898, p. 3, col. 2.

the Republicans and Democrats on other issues. African Americans, with few exceptions, favored integrated schools.[5]

Alton blacks, numbering 943 in a total population of 13,647 by 1898, used their ties of kinship, friendship, and community as a base for resisting the Republican city leadership on the school question. They organized the Alton Citizens Committee, which drew both its leadership and its rank and file from black institutions, including churches, benevolent and fraternal societies, sororities, and the press. While ministers played only a limited role, church members were numerous within the movement.[6] Indeed, the strength of black institutions and the black community network is one of the most striking features of the confrontation in which African Americans used self-help and racial solidarity to resist segregated schools.

---

5. Numerous articles in the *Illinois Record* indicate blacks' growing dissatisfaction with the Republican party. Virtually every issue contains information about the Alton School Case. Further, black Democratic newspapers like Springfield's *Messenger* and the Salt Lake City and Chicago *Broad Ax* (1895–1927) reinforced the point. The *St. Louis Star,* Sept. 26, 1897, p. 4, cols. 4–7, contains a feature story on Alton Mayor Henry Brueggemann and the school segregation issue. For Alton's segregated schools from 1859 to the early 1870s, see Alton, Illinois, Board of Education, "Minutes, August, 1859–December, 1897," Aug. 25, 1859, pp. 6–7, Sept. 1, 1859, p. 9, and Alton, Illinois, Superintendent of Schools, "Superintendent's Records, 1869–70," pp. 26, 30–35, 46–47, both at Alton Community Unit School District No. 11 Office, Alton, Ill.; *Illinois Record,* March 26, 1898, p. 3, col. 2. The secondary literature on the Alton School Case is limited. See August Meier and Elliott M. Rudwick, "Early Boycotts of Segregated Schools: The Alton, Illinois Case, 1897–1908," *Journal of Negro Education,* 36 (1967), 394–402; Amy Hildebrand, "A Comparative Study of Bias in Newspaper Coverage of Race-Related Events Regarding Education," Thesis Southern Illinois University at Edwardsville 1995; W. T. Norton, ed. and comp., *Centennial History of Madison County, Illinois and Its People, 1812 to 1912* (Chicago: Lewis Pub. Co., 1912), pp. 301–12. In *The Black Struggle for Public Schooling in Nineteenth-Century Illinois* (Carbondale: Southern Illinois University Press, 1987), Robert L. McCaul presents the larger historical context of black education in Illinois. See also *Alton Evening Telegraph,* April 20 (p. 3, col. 4), Aug. 10 (p. 2, cols. 3–4), Sept. 3 (p. 4, cols. 3–4), Sept. 14 (p. 2, cols. 2–3), Oct. 10 (p. 3, col. 5), Oct. 12 (p. 2, cols. 2–3), 1898, Feb. 10 (p. 3, col. 4), March 6 (p. 3, col. 4), March 17 (p. 3, col. 5), March 30 (p. 3, col. 5), 1899; *Edwardsville Intelligencer,* May 17 (p. 1, cols. 1–4), May 20 (p. 1, col. 7), Sept. 2 (p. 1, col. 4), Sept. 9 (p. 1, cols. 1–4}, 1898; *Illinois Record,* May 21, 1898, p. 3, cols. 1–2; Alton City Council, "Proceedings, 1896–1908," Alton City Clerk's Office, Alton, Ill.

6. The *Alton Evening Telegraph,* March 3, 1898, p. 3, col. 5, reports the results of the special school census. United States Department of Commerce, Bureau of the Census, *Negro Population, 1790–1915* (Washington, D.C.: GPO, 1918), p. 96, gives the 1900 black population of Alton as 896. Meier and Rudwick note the near absence of black clergy (see p. 396). Wood River Baptist Association, "Minutes, 1890–1910," lists members of the Union Baptist Church who, according to newspaper accounts and other data, were leaders in the citizens committee. The *Alton Evening Telegraph,* Nov. 20, 1897, p. 5, col. 5, identifies one black minister from Alton who was involved. See also *Illinois Record,* April 9 (p. 3, col. 1), June 18 (p. 3, col. 1), 1898.

Alton blacks challenged separate schools for eleven years, from 1897 to 1908, employing sit-ins, a boycott, and litigation. The latter included a petition to the Illinois Supreme Court for a writ of mandamus to compel the admission of African Americans to all public schools in Alton. That action developed into a lawsuit, *The People of the State of Illinois, ex rel., Scott Bibb* v. *The Mayor and Common Council of the City of Alton*—popularly known as "The Alton School Case," "The Alton School Fight," and "The Alton School Question"—which went through seven jury trials and five appeals to the Illinois Supreme Court.[7] African Americans argued their right to integrated schools based upon the Illinois School Laws of 1872 and 1874, which, as the Illinois Supreme Court had affirmed in earlier cases, had outlawed segregated schools. Arguing for the plaintiff in the Alton case, attorney John J. Brenholt quoted the School Law in a brief presented before the Illinois Supreme Court: "[A]ll Boards of School Directors, Boards of Education or school officers, whose duty it now is or may hereafter be to provide, in their respective jurisdictions, schools for the education of the children between the ages of six and twenty-one years, are *prohibited* from excluding, *directly* or *indirectly,* any such child from such school on account of the color of such child."[8]

The Alton School Case placed blacks in opposition to most leaders of the Republican party in Alton and Madison County during the period that historian Rayford W. Logan has described as the "nadir" of race relations in the United States. The conflict also mirrored the entire state of Illinois and the nation, where growing tensions between African Americans and whites within the Republican party threatened the solidarity of the GOP. Republican sway over the black vote became increasingly tenuous as more African Americans lost confidence in the party. The historical scholarship on issues of race within the Republican party during the post-Reconstruction era focuses primarily upon the South, incorporating only limited information about the northern front of the battle.[9] Yet the primary sources, especially those from within the African American

---

7. The *Illinois Record* has information on the case in virtually every extant copy. The *Alton Evening Telegraph* also extensively covered the case.

8. Brief of John J. Brenholt, for Relator, p. 2, *The People of the State of Illinois, ex rel., Scott Bibb* v. *The Mayor and Common Council of the City of Alton,* Case File No. 11726, Supreme Court of Illinois, Record Series 901.001, Illinois State Archives, Springfield (hereafter cited as *People* v. *City of Alton* Case File).

9. Logan, *The Betrayal of the Negro, From Rutherford B. Hayes to Woodrow Wilson* (New York: Collier, 1965). For Carbondale, see *Illinois Record,* June 4, 1898, p. 3, col. 2. For Bloomington, see ibid., Feb. 25, 1899, p. 1, cols. 1–2, p. 3, col. 6. For Jacksonville, see ibid., April 30, 1898, p. 3, col. 2. For Peoria, see ibid., March 11, 1899, p. 3, col. 4. For a brief sketch on African Americans and the Republican party in Illinois, see Roger D. Bridges, "Blacks in a White Society," in *Illinois: Its History & Legacy,* ed. Bridges and Rodney O. Davis (St. Louis: River City Publishers, Ltd., 1984), pp. 90–99.

community, clearly reveal widespread dissatisfaction with GOP policies among blacks in Illinois and many other venues.

Within their own state, black citizens in Alton found ample precedent for resisting separate schools. During the Civil War, Chicago's black community had successfully resisted a segregated education system through a combination of peaceful strategies, including sit-ins, boycotts, and political activism. In the 1880s and 1890s, blacks in Du Quoin, Bloomington, Quincy, Centralia, and Upper Alton had taken their grievances to court when white Republican city and school officials had persisted in maintaining dual school systems.[10]

In Upper Alton, contiguous to Alton, the Republican school board and city council had long neglected to provide any education for blacks. African Americans' protests had ultimately secured public education in 1870, but in segregated schools. Pressing for full equality in 1889, African Americans in that small city sued for the right to attend all public schools. Although they won the case on appeal to the Illinois Supreme Court, city officials flatly refused to integrate the schools.[11]

Upper Alton's success in maintaining separate schools, despite the supreme court ruling, may have been one of the factors that prompted Alton city officials to segregate their schools. The 1896 United States Supreme Court's landmark decision in *Plessy* v. *Ferguson* also may have encouraged separate schools in Alton. Further, Upper Alton's and other contiguous communities' continued interest in annexation to Alton provided an additional incentive for the city council and board of education to segregate the schools. August Meier and Elliott Rudwick in their article on the Alton School Case suggest that the desire to attract more white residents from Saint Louis and other areas with segregated schools was a likely consideration.[12]

---

10. Michael W. Homel, *Down From Equality: Black Chicagoans and the Public Schools, 1920–41* (Urbana: University of Illinois Press, 1984), pp. 1–26; Meier and Rudwick, pp. 394–95; *Illinois Record,* Nov. 20 (p. 2, col. 3), Dec. 4 (p. 4, col. 2), Dec. 18 (p. 3, col. 3), 1897, Jan. 15, 1898, p. 1, cols. 3–4; *Alton Evening Telegraph,* Nov. 20, 1897, p. 5, col. 5. McCaul discusses some of these cases (see pp. 127–42).

11. Board of Education, Upper Alton, Illinois, "Minutes, August 1868–December 1885," April 2, 1870, p. 40, June 16, 1870, p. 42, June 20, 1870, p. 42, June 27, 1870, p. 47, Alton Community Unit School District No. 11 Office. McCaul discusses the Quincy school case at some length, the Alton and Upper Alton cases briefly, and notes the other two (see pp. 127–42). For the Upper Alton case, see *The People, ex rel., John Peair* v. *The Board of Education of Upper Alton School District,* in Norman L. Freeman, *Reports of Cases at Law and in Chancery Argued and Determined in the Supreme Court of Illinois* (Springfield, Ill.: n.p., 1889), pp. 613–26. See also *Forum* (Springfield), May 11, 1907, p. 1, cols. 1–2.

12. Hildebrand notes the importance of *Plessy* v. *Ferguson* (see pp. 7, 89). See also Meier and Rudwick, p. 395.

This sketch of Alton Mayor Henry Brueggeman was published in the Saint Louis Star *on September 26, 1897.*

Alton blacks charged that Mayor Henry Brueggemann's personal racial animus had prompted the segregation. Some witnesses in the Alton lawsuit testified that the mayor had referred to blacks as "niggers" and indicated: "The colored children must attend the school houses that were built for them if it takes the whole police [force] of the City of Alton to do it." Further, Brueggemann used the school case to gain support for his next mayoral bid. Frequently under attack, even by members of his own party, the mayor found that the school issue united many whites.[13]

The reason that Alton city and school officials segregated their schools remains conjectural in the final analysis. Written sources contain limited information about the officials' thoughts and actions as they usually avoided making

13. Brief of Louis J. Palmer, for Relator, pp. 6–7, Brief of John J. Brenholt, pp. 6–7, and Abstract of the Record and Index, pp. 69–70, 78, 90, all in *People* v. *City of Alton* Case File; *Alton Evening Telegraph,* March 31, 1896, p. 3, col. 5, Feb. 9 (p. 2, cols. 2–3), April 23 (p. 4, col. 2), Aug. 10 (p. 2, cols. 3–4), Nov. 9 (p. 3, col. 5), Nov. 23 (p. 2, cols. 2–3), Dec. 14 (p. 2, col. 2), 1898, March 15 (p. 2, col. 2), Dec. 5 (p. 3, col. 5), 1899; *Edwardsville Intelligencer,* May 17 (p. 1, cols. 1–4), Sept. 6 (p. 4, col. 4), 1898; *Illinois Record,* May 21, 1898, p. 3, col. 1, March 25, 1899, p. 2, col. 1.

direct references to the dual school system. Their reticence was in all likelihood prompted by the lawsuit against them. Further, the defense strategy was to deny that the Alton school system was racially segregated.[14] During the Madison County Circuit Court trials, most evidence revealing a pattern of segregation was excluded by the judges upon the request of the defense. Thus, Alton officials were spared explaining that all children assigned to the Lovejoy and Douglass schools were black, while all assigned to the other five schools were white. The desegregated high school remains a mystery. Even black newspapers, usually forthcoming in discussing the Alton School Case, did not address the high school situation.

The Alton School Case was one of many confrontations between black and white Republicans in post-Reconstruction Illinois. African Americans in Decatur, for example, sharply criticized the GOP, due in part to issues surrounding the 1893 lynching of Samuel J. Bush. Bush, an itinerant black who had spent a brief time in the Decatur area, had been arrested on a charge of raping a white woman.[15] While awaiting trial in the Macon County Jail, a white mob lynched him. Angry blacks held public meetings and other protests in which they articulated their race consciousness and resistance to white hegemony. The following year, they successfully organized to prevent the lynching of another black man. In the 1898 elections, many Decatur blacks expressed bitter rage and growing political independence by threatening to bolt the GOP because they blamed two candidates, Isaac R. Mills and Henry Midkiff, for their failure to prevent Bush's lynching six years earlier. Mills, the candidate for Congress, had been state's attorney in 1893, and Midkiff, the candidate for Macon County sheriff, had been a deputy sheriff. Lacking viable alternatives, most Decatur blacks ultimately supported the GOP in the election, but meanwhile they had registered their dissatisfaction in unmistakable terms.

African Americans in Alexander and Pulaski counties in extreme southern Illinois, in Chicago, Springfield, and other areas throughout the state challenged

---

14. Brief and Argument of Respondents (L. D. Yager, E. B. Glass, Bradshaw & Hilskoetter), pp. 4–8, and Brief and Argument of John F. McGinnis and Henry S. Baker, Attorneys for Respondents, pp. 16–18, both in *People* v. *City of Alton* Case File; *Alton Evening Telegraph,* Dec. 5 (p. 3, col. 5), Dec. 6 (p. 3, col. 6), 1899, March 31, 1900, p. 7, col. 5; *Alton Weekly Telegraph,* Dec. 16, 1897, p. 5, col. 3.

15. Sundiata Keita Cha-Jua, in "'Join hands and hearts with law and order': The 1893 Lynching of Samuel J. Bush and the Response of Decatur's African American Community," *Illinois Historical Journal,* 83 (1990), 187–200, discusses the Bush lynching, although the author does not emphasize the role of Republican party politics. In a later, as yet unpublished piece in the author's possession, "'A Warlike Demonstration': Legalism, Violent Self-help and Electoral Politics in Decatur, Illinois, 1894–1898," Cha-Jua discusses the political impact of the Bush lynching. See also issues of the *Illinois Record* from Sept. 24 through Nov. 5, 1898.

GOP policies and demanded greater hegemony within the Republican party. Beginning in 1880, Pulaski County voters elected blacks to such city and county offices as county commissioner, county coroner, and city attorney of Mound City, the county seat. In Cairo, the Alexander County seat, African Americans scored impressive electoral victories as early as the 1870s, serving as Cairo police magistrate, county coroner, and in other county and city positions. During the 1890s, as many as three blacks simultaneously sat on the Cairo Board of Aldermen. Chicago blacks gained posts as Cook County commissioner and Illinois state representative, and they also held other local and state positions. After other Chicago blacks had run unsuccessfully for alderman, Oscar Stanton DePriest was elected to that post in 1915, largely as a result of the uncompromising stance of the women of the Alpha Suffrage Club and other black activists. Otis B. Duncan, a Springfield black, captured the Republican nomination for alderman in the 1898 primary, but he lost to the Democratic candidate in the general election. Blacks attributed his defeat to the defection of white Republicans.[16] Despite those victories at the ballot box, Illinois blacks were quick to point out that they were woefully underrepresented in political positions and in party decision making. Thus, they demanded increasingly more and higher appointive and elective offices, boldly threatening to bolt the party.

Further criticism of the Republican party came from such black leaders of national repute as William Edward Burghardt Du Bois, Ida Bell Wells-Barnett, and James Milton Turner. Wells-Barnett's challenges came in assorted speeches and writings, including her autobiography. Du Bois wrote numerous articles in which he, like the Alpha Suffrage Club five years later, urged African Americans to use their votes for the benefit of their race, rather than automatically

---

16. City Council, Mound City, Illinois, "Minutes," Vol. I, pp. 73, 500–505, 524, 553–58, and Vol. II, pp. 37, 184–85, 198, 206–7, 219, 325, Mound City Public Utilities Building; Secretary of State, Election Returns, Petitions, and Papers, 1882–1905, Vol. VI, pp. 39, 190, 215, 293, 328, 347, 364, 390, 403, 456, 483, 495–500, 576, Vol. VII, pp. 41, 130, Record Series 103.032, Illinois State Archives; Pulaski County, Illinois, Commissioners, "County Commissioners Records," Vol. II, pp. 455, 457, 493, and Vol. III, pp. 298–99, Pulaski County Courthouse, Mound City. Joanne Wheeler discusses, with some questionable interpretations, Cairo race relations in "Together in Egypt: A Pattern of Race Relations in Cairo, Illinois, 1865–1915," in *Toward a New South? Studies in Post-Civil War Southern Communities,* ed. Orville Vernon Burton and Robert C. McMath, Jr. (Westport, Conn.: Greenwood, 1982), pp. 103–34. See also City Council, Cairo, Illinois, "Minutes," Book G, pp. 87, 376, Book H, pp. 5, 18, 21, 27, 32, 38, 54, 56, 65, 83, Book I, pp. 28, 34, Book O, pp. 50, 168, 171, 190, 216, 223–35, 246–47, 310–11, Cairo City Clerk's Office, City Hall, Cairo; *Cairo City Directory, 1895–96* (Cairo, Ill.: Daily Telegram, 1895), p. 29; Wanda A. Hendricks, "'Vote for the advantage of ourselves and our race': The Election of the First Black Alderman in Chicago," *Illinois Historical Journal* 87 (1994), 171–84; *Illinois Record,* April 9 (p. 1, cols. 3–4), Aug. 20 (p. 2, col. 1), 1898.

consigning them to the GOP. After bitter struggles with white Republicans, Turner eventually abandoned the party altogether and became a Democrat.[17] In the face of an increasingly insensitive Republican party, African Americans in Illinois and the nation turned to their own preexisting social institutions—and created new ones—to address their own needs and to protest their declining status within both the larger society and the GOP.

In the Alton School Case, the UBF and the Sisters of the Mysterious Ten (SMT)—a black sorority with chapters throughout the United States, the Caribbean, and Africa—provided much of the leadership for the struggle. The UBF hall became the headquarters for the black citizens committee that directed the opposition to the segregation plan, and UBF leaders were prominent within the organization. The all-male citizens committee held weekly meetings to discuss strategy, raise funds, and unify the black community. An autonomous women's council also met at the hall and in private homes. Both groups held numerous "entertainments" to raise money and to build and maintain community support for their fight.[18] Dances, banquets, picnics, concerts, grand receptions, and other social activities, always popular among African Americans in Alton, became even more numerous and raised hundreds of dollars in the period from 1897 through 1908.

Mayor Brueggemann, the school board, and the city council moved quickly to implement the new policy after making their May, 1897, decision to build segregated schools. After construction delays, which prompted officials to defer by two weeks the beginning of the school year, Lovejoy and Douglass became the city's two "colored" schools. From the purchase of building sites in early June to the start of school in mid-September, the construction of separate schools had taken only three and one-half months. The total cost of the two schools had been relatively modest—approximately $11,000, of which $3,250, or nearly 30 percent,

---

17. *Illinois Record,* May 7, 1898, p. 3, col. 1; Alfreda M. Duster, ed., *Crusade fur Justice: The Autobiography of Ida B. Wells* (Chicago: University of Chicago Press, 1970). The *Broad Ax* (Chicago), March 1, 1902, p. 1, col. 2, reports the cancellation of a scheduled presentation by Wells-Barnett. See also *The Horizon: A Journal of the Color Line,* Feb., 1908, pp. 17–18, June, 1908, pp. 2–5, July, 1908, pp. 5–7, Aug., 1908, pp. 1–8, Sept., 1908, pp. 4–8; Gary R Kremer, *James Milton Turner and the Promise of America: The Public Life of a Post-Civil War Black Leader* (Columbia: University of Missouri Press, 1991).

18. W. H. Gibson, *History of the United Brothers of Friendship and Sisters of the Mysterious Ten . . .* (Louisville, Ky.: Bradley & Gilbert, 1897). See also *Illinois Record,* Jan. 15 (p. 3, cols. 1–2), Feb. 26 (p. 3, col. 1), March 12 (p. 3, col. 1), March 19 (p. 3, cols. 1–2), March 26 (p. 3, col. 1), April 2 (p. 3, col. 2), June 4 (p. 3, col. 1), June 11 (p. 3, col. 1), June 18 (p. 3, col. 1), June 25 (p. 3, col. 1), July 30 (p. 3, col. 1), Aug. 6 (p. 3, col. 2), Dec. 10 (p. 3, cols. 1–2), 1898; *Palladium* (St. Louis), March 7, 1903, p. 1, col. 4.

had gone to purchase the two lots.[19] The final figure was less than half that of the recently constructed Washington School—designated for whites only—built in 1895–1896. The black schools were smaller in size than the white schools. Further, all-white schools employed at least four teachers, each of whom taught a maximum of two grades, while the black schools had two teachers who each taught three or four grades. Court testimony by Florence Barbour, a black teacher at Lovejoy, indicated another disparity between the black and white schools: "There are two rooms in the Lovejoy school and six grades are taught there."[20] Thus, Barbour indicated that Lovejoy did not include all eight grades, as did all white schools. Additionally, black teachers earned less than their white counterparts. Those disparities prompted Harry B. Coats, a boycott leader, to argue that the black schools "are not as good as any of the other schools in Alton by one-half."[21]

When the 1897–1898 school year began on September 20, 1897, school officials barred the entry of black children to the five previously existing schools and directed them to the new, segregated Lovejoy and Douglass schools. The entire fourteen-man Alton police force was deployed, with two patrolmen at each of the five white schools. Scott Bibb's children, Ambrose and Minnie, were among

---

19. Alton, Illinois, Board of Education, "Minutes, August 1859–December 1897," May 4, 1897, p. 382, June 7, 1897, p. 387, June 11, 1897, p. 387, Sept. 14, 1897, p. 394; Alton City Council, "Proceedings," May 11, 1897, p. 287; *St. Louis Star,* Sept. 26, 1897, p. 4, cols. 4–7. The Alton City Council, "Proceedings," Aug. 10, 1897, p. 344, notes that $3,350 was paid for the lots, but this figure appears to be in error by $100. The proceedings entry for Nov. 2, 1897, p. 397, gives the total cost of the two schools as $11,100.01. The Alton Board of Education, "Financial Journal, August 1873–December 1907," Sept.–Nov., 1897, pp. 225–29, and the "Douglass and Lovejoy Schools, Account Number 68," both in Alton Community Unit School District No. 11 Office, indicate that a total of $7,701.15 was expended on the schoolhouses. This figure does not include the $3,250 cost of the lots. Another board source gives slightly different figures. The Alton Board of Education, "Ledger, January 1874–1922," in ibid., indicates that the "New School Houses Special Fund" contained "$7,698.15" (seep. 68) and that $3,250 had been spent on the lots in June (seep. 58) for a total of $10,948.15. H. B. Starr's court testimony placed the figure "in the neighborhood of $11,000" (see Abstract of the Record and Index, p. 169).

20. Board of Education, "Financial Journal, August 1873–December 1907," June 1895–Nov. 1896, pp. 196–214; Abstract of the Record and Index, p. 11; Board of Education, Alton, Illinois, "Minutes, August 1859–December 1897," May 12, 1897, pp. 382–83; "Minutes, Board of Education, Alton, Illinois, January 1898–January 1909," May 3, 1898, pp. 6–7, May 7, 1900, pp. 75–76, May 11, 1900, pp. 52–54, June 5, 1902, pp. 112–13, May 4, 1904, pp. 166–68, July 5, 1905, pp. 212–13, Alton Community Unit School District No. 11 Office. Even after the board adopted a pay scale based on the grade level taught, black teachers still were paid less than white. See Superintendent of Schools, Alton, Illinois, "Record of Teachers' Meetings, October 2, 1875–March 21, 1901," Dec. 10, 1900, and Dec. 13, 1900, p. 140, ibid. See also Abstract of the Record and Index, pp. 91–92.

21. *Alton Evening Telegraph,* Oct. 14, 1897, p. 2, col. 3.

In 1897, the City of Alton moved to segregate its public elementary schools. Shown above are Alton's public schools, circa 1895: (from the center and then clockwise from the upper left) Washington, Irving, Garfield, Humbolt, and Lincoln.

the black children turned away from the Washington School, where they had previously gone, and school authorities reassigned them to Lovejoy.[22] With the assistance and encouragement of other Alton blacks, Bibb would soon bring legal action.

Refusing to accept segregation, Bibb and other African American parents accompanied their children to school and insisted that they take their places alongside the white children. The white teachers, acting on instructions from the school board, Mayor Brueggemann, and the city council, separated white students from black students and ignored the latter while teaching the former.[23]

22. Witnesses at the 1900 trial agreed that the police were present, but disagreed over who had called them and what their role was. Clearly, black children were permitted to attend only Lovejoy and Douglass schools, and officers used physical force to attain that end. See Abstract of the Record and Index, pp. 26–91; *Alton Evening Telegraph,* Sept. 23 (p. 3, col. 5), Oct. 5 (p. 3, col. 3), 1897; *Illinois Record,* Dec. 3, 1898, p. 3, col. 1. The Alton City Council, "Proceedings," Sept. 14, 1897, p. 357, reveals that the mayor had anticipated a need for force by appointing four "special police" to serve "without pay to be assigned to duty at the Alton public schools and the vicinity." All thirteen aldermen present voted "aye." See also Abstract of the Record and Index, pp. 143–47.

23. Abstract of the Record and Index, pp. 27–30, 40–41, 43–44, 47–48, 52–53, 77; *St. Louis Post-Dispatch,* Sept. 23 (p. 13, cols. 5–6), Sept. 24 (p. 3, col. 3), 1897; *St. Louis Star,* Sept. 26, 1897, p. 4, cols. 4–7; *Alton Evening Telegraph,* Sept. 20, 1897, p. 3, col. 6.

Bibb well exemplifies the interplay of family, friendship, and community that represented a theme in the school fight. Born a slave in Missouri, Bibb and his family had moved to Alton in 1863. In 1897 he worked at the Illinois Glass Works as a fireman—a well-paid, semi-skilled position. His brother, Allen, was a laborer. Scott and Allen lived with their families within a few doors of each other, allowing them to raise their children in an extended family network. By the 1890s the Bibb families had become prominent socially and economically, as numerous references to them in the social columns of newspapers attest. Both Scott and Allen were members of the UBF and other black organizations. Minnie Bibb, Scott's wife, was also a noted figure within the black community. In 1907, for example, she was president of the Helping Hand Club, a black self-help organization.[24] During their thirty-five-year residency in Alton, the Bibbs had improved both their social and their economic status markedly, and, no doubt, they expected still greater advances. The segregation of the once integrated Alton school system represented a threat to their status and signaled that further decline might follow.

Meanwhile, the citizens committee formed to spearhead the campaign against segregated schools retained John J. Brenholt, a prominent local Republican leader and a former mayor of Alton, as legal counsel. Brenholt represented the Forty-seventh District in the Illinois Senate from 1899 to 1902, and in 1900 he ran unsuccessfully for Congress. Brenholt served as attorney to Scott Bibb and the school committee for the next eleven years. The *Edwardsville Intelligencer,* a Democratic newspaper, attempted to induce Brenholt to publicly address the reasons for his participation in the case. Although the newspaper editorialized that the "voters should compel the wiley Colonel to speak out," Brenholt remained silent on the issue.[25]

Brenholt's service to the school committee, together with his appearance at public meetings within the black community, and his profuse praise of blacks' service in the Spanish-American War convinced blacks that he was "very sensitive" and "a wise selection for the Senate,"[26] as well as a "true Republican."[27]

---

24. Abstract of the Record and Index, pp. 26–27; *W. H. McCoy's Alton City Directory for 1902–1903* (Keokuk, Iowa: W. H. McCoy, n.d.), p. 40. See also *Forum,* June 8, 1907, p. 1, cols. 1–2; *Alton Evening Telegraph,* Nov. 22 (p. 3, col. 6), Nov. 23 (p. 3, col. 6), 1899; *Illinois Record,* April 2 (p. 3, col. 1), Oct. 29 (p. 3 col. 1), 1898, March 11, 1899, p. 3, col. 1.

25. For Brenholt, see Norton, ed. and comp., p. 427; Alton City Council, "Proceedings, April 25, 1893–April 25, 1895," pp. 125–474, Alton City Clerk's Office; John Clayton, *The Illinois Fact Book and Historical Almanac, 1673–1968* (Carbondale: Southern Illinois University Press, 1970), pp. 256, 258; *Alton Evening Telegraph,* Jan. 9, 1899, p. 2, col. 2, March 10, 1900, p. 4, cols. 2–3; *Edwardsville Intelligencer,* Oct. 11, 1898, p. 2, col. 1.

26. *Illinois Record,* Dec. 3, 1898, p. 3, col. 2.

27. Ibid., Oct. 8 (p. 3, col. 1), Nov. 12 (p. 3, cots. 1–2), 1898.

African Americans correctly presumed that Brenholt assisted them because he believed in the justness of their cause. Brenholt's commitment to the Alton School Case allowed African Americans to view the school segregation issue as a part of the factionalism that permeated the Republican party, rather than as an issue on which virtually all Republicans agreed. In that view, they were wrong, however, as Brenholt's public championing of integrated education was a stance that he shared with few, if any, whites in late-nineteenth- and early twentieth-century Alton. Indeed, Republican Alderman George Burton, the only other local white who had reportedly empathized with the black cause in a public setting, later denied under oath that he had done so.[28]

John McAuley Palmer, the Civil War general who had served first as Illinois governor while a Republican and later as United States senator after becoming a Democrat, was co-counsel for Bibb and the black citizens committee. Reportedly, Palmer had agreed to serve *pro bono,* pursuant to a visit by Bibb, Coats, Eugene Drew, and Lee Jackson. Palmer had successfully represented several black clients seeking integrated education, thereby enhancing his reputation as a "friend of the Negro."[29] It is significant, however, that those victories were nullified by the refusal of school boards and city officials to comply with the court decisions. Palmer also acted from principle. His actual involvement in the case was limited, however, due to his advanced age and declining health, but he did induce his son, Louis James Palmer, to take his place in the legal proceedings.[30]

Within two weeks of the beginning of the 1897–1898 school year, African Americans in Alton began a boycott of all public schools that would last eleven years. The aforementioned boycott in Chicago in the 1860s, credited by some with desegregating that city's schools, may have served as a model. Another in Buffalo, New York, in 1867 failed to end that city's segregated schools.[31] The Alton boycott was effective in minimizing black attendance in the city's

---

28. See ibid., May 21 (p. 3, col. 1), May 28 (p. 3, col. 1), 1898. See also Abstract of the Record and Index, pp. 62, 164–66.

29. *Alton Evening Telegraph,* Sept. 24, 1897, p. 3, col. 5; *Alton Weekly Telegraph,* Sept. 30, 1897, p. 5, col. 1; *St. Louis Post-Dispatch,* Sept. 23, 1897, p. 13, col. 3; *Illinois Record,* Jan. 28, 1899, p. 2, col. 1; Meier and Rudwick, pp. 397–98; *Broad Ax* (Chicago), Feb. 2 (p. 1, cols. 3–4), Nov. 23 (p. 1, cots. 2–4), 1901.

30. McCaul, pp. 128–42; Thomas Dean Hamblin, "Drive the Last Nail: John M. Palmer and the Blacks in Illinois and Kentucky," Thesis Southern Illinois University at Carbondale 1976; *Alton Evening Telegraph,* Oct. 22, 1897, p. 2, col. 3, Feb. 15 (p. 3, col. 3), May 7 (p. 3, col. 1), 1898; *Illinois Record,* April 9 (p. 3, col. 3), Nov. 5 (p. 3, col. 1), 1898; Brief of Louis J. Palmer.

31. Meier and Rudwick is the best secondary source on the Alton boycott. They also briefly discuss other boycotts. Homel discusses black education in Chicago before 1920 (see pp. 1–26).

grade schools, but it did not achieve its ultimate goal of ending the dual school system.

On October 1, 1897, two weeks into the segregation battle, only ten students out of nearly three hundred eligible to attend—and about 180 or so who were likely to have attended without a boycott—had enrolled in the Lovejoy and Douglass schools. By the end of November, fourteen had enrolled but only ten attended. At the conclusion of the school year, the number enrolled had increased to seventeen. Although black enrollments and attendance increased in the second year, they remained substantially less than the 272 for which school officials had planned. Forty-four students were enrolled and about forty-two attended the two schools by the end of the second year. At the end of the 1903–1904 school year, eighty-eight blacks were in school. Throughout the eleven-year boycott, black enrollments fluctuated dramatically from one month to the next, but in the final years as many as 75 to 80 percent of the preboycott numbers were enrolled, signaling a weakening of the boycott. By the end of the 1907–1908 school year, there were 144 black children enrolled in Alton's public schools.[32]

The school board and city council immediately proposed to end the boycott by employing a truant officer. A "well known colored man," probably Hunter or Drew, responded immediately that blacks were not intimidated by the truant officer and that they would not send their children to school, according to the *Alton Evening Telegraph*. The newspaper indicated that the man had argued: "If the truant officer should arrest colored people because their children do not attend Douglas and Lovejoy schools, the burden of proof will rest entirely with the Board of Education."[33] Although periodic references to the truant officer were made in school board minutes and the press, there is little, if any, evidence that the truant officer significantly increased black enrollments. At the October 3, 1905, meeting of the Alton School Board, the "committee to secure [a] truant

32. Alton Superintendent of Schools, "Teachers' Reports," Oct. 1, 1897, pp. 104–5, Alton Community Unit School District No. 11 Office. An 1898 special school census showed that there were three hundred blacks of school age—between the ages of six and twenty-one—but little more than half were likely to attend schools, as few Altonians, black or white, continued their education beyond the age of about fourteen. For the school census, see *Alton Telegraph*, March 3, 1898, p. 3, col. 5. See also "Teachers' Reports," Nov. 27, 1897, p. 109, June 18, 1898, pp. 122–23; Alton City Council, "Proceedings," July 12, 1898, pp. 525–26. The school board purchased 276 desks—four of them for teachers—for the two black schools. See Alton Board of Education, "Minutes," Aug. 20, 1897, p. 391. See also "Teachers' Reports," June 16, 1899, pp. 142–43, June 10, 1904, p. 245, June 12, 1908, p. 41, June 18, 1908, p. 61.

33. *Alton Evening Telegraph*, Oct. 6 (p. 3, col. 4), Oct. 16 (p. 5, col. 4), Oct. 18 (p. 3, col. 4), 1897. In a signed letter published in the Oct. 18, issue, Drew indicated: "The colored people have no fear of the proposed truant officer" (see p. 2, col. 3).

officer" issued its strongest report, noting that Thomas O'Leary, the truant officer, "has been at work with good results."[34] Yet, the board supplied no further details to validate its point.

The school board, with the approval of the mayor and city council, had selected a total of four schoolteachers—three black and one white—for the two black schools, two at each building. Frances (Fannie) Barbour and Florence Barbour, sisters who were popular and socially prominent within Alton's African American community, were among the new teachers. Due to their cooperation with the school board and city officials and despite their earlier popularity, some blacks perceived the Barbours as race traitors whose self-interest had superseded racial solidarity. Florence's testimony at the 1899 trial probably undermined her credibility within the black community as her attempts to obscure a number of points weakened the case. For example, while she indicated that she had taught at the Lovejoy School since September, 1897, she claimed not to know that it was a "colored" school: "I don't know what school that is with reference to color."[35] The sisters and their mother, also named Frances, alienated some blacks still further when they reportedly tried to induce black parents to send their children to the separate schools. In a sharply worded and crude commentary, Drew warned Fannie and her mother that the school committee was well aware of their activities. He gratuitously reminded the Barbours that they were black, implying that their loyalties should have been with the school committee and the boycott: "She and her poor old mother should go to the mirror and take a look at themselves, for they must have forgotten that they are Negroes by birth. Now we can heartily reccomend [*sic*] them as a part of the worse Niggers in Alton."[36] Other black supporters of segregated schools were similarly ridiculed by Drew and other school committee members.[37] Thus, the threat of social isolation and public scorn became a very important means of enforcing the boycott within the African American community.

---

34. Board of Education, Alton, Illinois, "Minutes, August 1859–December 1897," Dec. 7, 1897, p. 399; Board of Education, Alton, Illinois, "Minutes, January 1898–January 1909," July 18, 1905, p. 214, Oct. 3, 1905, p. 227, Oct. 2, 1906, p. 262, Oct. 2, 1907, p. 309, Dec. 4, 1907, p. 317, Nov. 4, 1908, pp. 389–90.

35. See *Illinois Record,* Nov. 6, 1897, p. 2, cols. 4–5, Feb. 5 (p. 3, col. 1), Feb. 12 (p. 3, cols. 1–2), March 26 (p. 3, col. 1), 1898. In *What a Woman Ought to Be and to Do: Black Professional Women Workers During the Jim Crow Era* (Chicago: University of Chicago Press, 1996), Stephanie J. Shaw discusses the high value that blacks placed upon "mutual obligation," and "community consciousness," or, concern for the black community (see pp. 2, 41–67). See also Abstract of the Record and Index, pp. 91–92.

36. *Illinois Record,* Feb. 5, 1898, p. 3, col. 1.

37. See ibid., March 26 (p. 3, col. 2), April 2 (p. 3, col. 2), July 16 (p. 3, cols. 1–2), Nov. 12 (p. 3, col. 2), 1898.

Although information about the schooling of black children during the boycott is fragmentary and inconclusive, the education of Alton's black grade-school children undoubtedly suffered. Some black children received alternative schooling. For example, some parents sent their children to live with relatives and friends in other districts. Other African American children received private instruction in Alton, as had Minnie and Ambrose Bibb and William H. Joiner's two children. Nettie Poindexter may have been the teacher for some of those children as she established a private school in her home. Census data for 1900 indicates that many school-age black boys worked outside of the home. Thus, if they received formal education, it was only part-time. Many children received no formal education for years at a time, as was the case with Lilah Giles's and Harriet Pitts's children.[38]

During their fight with Alton officials, African Americans felt betrayed by the GOP and complained bitterly about both the segregated schools and the party itself. Drew—chairman of the citizens committee and the Alton correspondent for Springfield's *Illinois Record,* an African American newspaper that extensively covered the Alton school fight—sharply criticized the Republican municipal leadership. In a letter dated February 19, 1898, Drew spoke of Alton as "the home of E. P. Lovejoy and the foundation of a base discrimination against the Negro race under a Republican administration."[39] Later, Drew charged that a "Republican, a Caucasian leader of Alton" had shown greater concern and financial support for the Cubans in their struggle for independence from Spain than for African Americans in their fight against racism. The Republican politician reportedly had helped to raise $500 for Cubans, but had donated only a token amount to the school fight, declaring: "Uncle, you boys are in a bad predicament about your children going to school, and here is fifty cents to help you boys fight the school officials, but don't use my name publicly." Although this anecdote may well have been apocryphal, it nonetheless revealed Drew's perception of white Republicans as being disinterested in their black political allies, patronizing in addressing black men as "Uncle" and "boys," and unwilling to take a public stand in behalf of black rights.[40]

Drew, who served as corresponding secretary to the citizens committee after his tenure as chairman, remained a central figure in the school struggle for years. His involvement well illustrates the importance of kinship, friendship, and community ties within the fight against segregated schools. A stonecutter

38. Ibid., Sept. 17, 1898, p. 3, col. 1; Abstract of the Record and Index, pp. 32–34, 44–45, 49–51, 88–89; *Alton Evening Telegraph,* Sept. 14, 1908, p. 1, col. 4; Population Schedules of the Twelfth Census of the United States, 1900: Madison County, Illinois, Reel 325 (microfilm in the Illinois State Archives) (hereafter cited as 1900 Madison County Population Schedules).

39. *Illinois Record,* Feb. 19, 1898, p. 3, col. 1.

40. Ibid., Jan. 8, 1898, p. 1, col. 5, p. 3, col. 3.

whose investments in real estate had made him one of the wealthiest members of the Alton black community, Drew was also an active member of both the UBF and the Union Baptist Church, traditional black institutions that provided numerous members to the school fight. In 1899, Drew was elected chairman of a black citizens' group that honored local African Americans returning from the Spanish-American War with a reception and a "grand banquet."[41]

Drew's column in the *Illinois Record* provided invaluable information to the black community not only about the school case but also about other social and political developments. His wife, Laura, also a noted figure within the black community, served on the Ladies School Committee and as president of the Ladies Sewing Circle of the Union Baptist Church.[42] Drew was a product of the Alton public school system, which he had attended for ten years, starting in about 1868, when the schools were still racially segregated. During his matriculation, he had forged relations that would later assist him and the citizens committee in the school fight. For example, one of Drew's first teachers had been James Henry Magee, who later became prominent in Chicago's black community where he published a "race Journal," *The Brotherhood*.[43] Magee also led that city's fund-raising effort on behalf of the Alton Citizens Committee. By 1906 Magee held a position in the state printer's office in Springfield, and still later he became president of a private trade school, Ambidexter Institute, in that city.[44] Magee maintained communication with the Alton black community, assisting in the school case.

While a grade-school student in the early 1870s, Drew had resisted the segregated schools. Years later, he recalled: "I shed my blood twenty-five years ago while helping to mix the schools in this city; I'll never forget it."[45] After completing eight years in grade school, Drew studied at Alton High School for two years, leaving the school in 1878, one year shy of graduation. Ambrose Bibb, an African American classmate of Drew's, completed the rigorous high school program and

41. Ibid., Jan. 8 (p. 1, col. 5, p. 3, col. 3), Feb. 26 (p. 3, col. 1), April 2 (p. 3, col. 1), 1898, March 11 (p. 3, col. 1), April 1 (p. 3, col. 2), April 15 (p. 3, col. 1), 1899; Abstract of the Record and Index, p. 83; 1900 Madison County Population Schedules.

42. *Illinois Record,* May 7 (p. 3, col. 1), May 21 (p. 3, col. 1), 1898.

43. Ibid., March 26, 1898, p. 3, col. 2; Alton Board of Education, "Superintendent's Records, 1869–70," pp. 9–11, 30–35, 46–47; Alton Board of Education, "Teachers' Reports to the Superintendent, Alton Illinois High School, 1876–78," Alton Community Unit School District No. 11 Office; Magee, *The Night of Affliction and Morning of Recovery: An Autobiography* (1873; rpt. Miami, Fla.: Mnemosyne Pub. Co., 1969), pp. 143–44; *State Capital,* March 28, 1891, p. 1, col. 4.

44. *Alton Telegraph,* Sept. 23, 1897, p. 3, col. 3; *Illinois Record,* Nov. 6 (p. 3, col. 1), Nov. 13 (p. 1, col. 2), 1897, Feb. 19 (p. 2, col. 3), Dec. 10 (p. 3, col. 1), 1898. See also Magee, *High Thoughts and Aims Reach High and Noble Things* (Springfield, Ill.: n.p. [1906]). This work can be dated to 1906 based on an advertisement for it in the *Forum* (see June 9 [p. 1, col. 4], Sept. 22 [p. 7, col. 2], Dec. 22 [p. 5, cols. 1–2, p. 6, cols. 1–2], 1906).

45. *Illinois Record,* March 26, 1898, p. 3, col. 2.

Attorney John J. Brenholt represented Scott Bibb in Bibb's 1900 Illinois Supreme Court case against Mayor Henry Brueggemann and the City of Alton. The Alton building shown here housed Brenholt's law offices.

graduated in 1879.[46] Bibb and Drew maintained their ties over the years, sharing many of the same community activities, including membership in the UBF.

When Scott Bibb, Ambrose's brother, sued city officials for their refusal to permit his son, named after his uncle, and his daughter, Minnie, named after her mother, to continue attendance at the Washington School, Drew, their old friend and longtime associate, joined in the battle.

Harry B. Coats, only twenty-four when the school fight began, was another key figure in the citizens committee. Working variously as a hotel waiter, janitor at city hall, and coatroom clerk for the Illinois General Assembly, he was a spirited and outspoken leader. After being elected to the presidency of the citizens committee in March of 1898, he publicly expressed his disappointment in "the action of the Republican School Board and administration."[47] In

---

46. Alton Public Schools, "Graduates of Alton High School, 1871–1913," and "Alton High School Scholarship, Punctuality, Attendance, and Deportment Records," Book 1 (1876–1879), pp. 33, 72, Book 2 (1878–1880), pp. 17, 49, both in Alton Community Unit School District No. 11 Office.

47. 1900 Madison County Population Schedules. Biographical data on H. B. Coats can be found in the city directory, census records, city council proceedings, and newspapers. Personality traits can be gleaned from Coats's court testimony and letters in newspapers. See *W. H. McCoy's Alton City Directory for 1902–1903*, p. 62; *Illinois Record*, April 2, 1898, p. 3, col. 1; *Alton Evening Telegraph*, Oct. 14 (p. 2, col. 3), Oct. 22 (p. 2, col. 3), 1897; Abstract of the Record and Index, p. 58. The Alton City Council, "Proceedings," June 11, 1901, p. 550, indicates that Coats was a janitor at city hall. The entry on May 9, 1903, p. 233, is the last reference to Coats in that capacity.

a letter to the editor of the *Alton Evening Telegraph,* Coats was chagrined: "We feel somewhat surprised over the matter to think that this affair has occurred when the city is under a Republican administration." Alluding to the greater importance of racial over party solidarity, he continued: "But politics enter only for a small consideration in this matter."[48] In a second letter to the newspaper several weeks later, Coats continued his criticism of the city government, arguing that although the Civil War and Elijah Parish Lovejoy's death should have obviated race as an issue, race relations and racism remained problematic in Alton. One week later, Coats noted that the city of Alton was experiencing difficulty in attracting speakers of national repute to give the major address at the forthcoming dedication of the new Lovejoy Monument. He saw the reluctance of prestigious figures to participate as an indication of their disapproval of the new segregationist policy of Mayor Henry Brueggemann, the school board, and the city council: "In view of the action of the Republican School Board and administration no wonder not one of the noted men of the nation wish[es] to go on record with a speech for such an occasion at such a time."[49]

Coats—often addressed as H. B.—maintained strong familial, friendship, and community relationships that sustained him in the school fight. His brother, Edward J. Coats, served as recording secretary of the citizens committee. The Coats brothers were both members of the UBF. Edward lived next door to his brother and shared a residence with their widowed mother, their two younger brothers, and Edward's wife. The Coats family, like many of those active in the school fight, were members of the Union Baptist Church, where H. B. served as clerk in 1903 and again from 1906 to 1908. Mary Coats, H. B.'s wife, was also enmeshed in community activities. In 1908 she served on the eight-person Temperance Committee for the Wood River Baptist Association, a regional organization that included black Baptist churches from central and southern Illinois.[50]

The community network of Alton blacks extended beyond the immediate environs of the city and into the entire state of Illinois and throughout the country. That pipeline provided letters of encouragement as well as donations to Alton blacks in their fight with the Republican government of Alton. The

48. *Alton Evening Telegraph,* Sept. 21, 1897, p. 3, col. 5.

49. Ibid., Oct. 14 (p. 2, col. 3) , Oct. 22 (p. 2, col. 3) , 1897.

50. Ibid., Sept. 25, 1897, p. 5, col. 5; *St. Louis PostDispatch,* Sept. 24, 1897, p. 1, cols. 1–2; *Illinois Record,* April 2, 1898, p. 3, col. 1; *W. H. McCoy's Alton City Directory for 1902–1903,* p. 62; 1900 Madison County Population Schedules; *Minutes of the Wood River Baptist Association and Ministers' and Deacons' Union* (Monmouth, Ill.: Review Printing Co., 1903), p. 46; *Minutes of the 68th Annual Session [of the] Wood River Baptist Association* (Monmouth, Ill.: Review Printing Co. [1906?]), p. 26; *Minutes of the 69th Annual Session [of the] Wood River Baptist Association* (n.p. [1907?]), p. 33; *Minutes of the 71st [70th] Annual Session [of the] Wood River Baptist Association* (n.p. [1908?]), pp. 24, 46.

James Henry Magee

Edwardsville Intelligencer claimed that black churches in Chicago had raised $600. Although that figure is not corroborated elsewhere, there is ample evidence that African Americans in Chicago raised funds for the school fight. The Young People's Mutual Improvement Society of Decatur also donated money. W. R. Bond from Austin, Illinois, made a contribution, as did blacks from other Illinois towns. A group donation came from as far as Saint Paul, Minnesota.[51]

The *Illinois Record* printed a number of letters to the editor that supported the school case. S. T. Archer of Venice, Illinois, wrote: "We hope to be of some benefit to the citizens of Alton though the conflict does not reach us directly as individuals, but it does indirectly as a nation."[52] Another encouraging letter from Samuel G. Hicks, a Clay City man, appeared in the March 26, 1898, edition. In its February 22, 1908, edition, Springfield's *Forum* reported having received eleven letters "commenting upon the Alton and Chicago school troubles."[53] The Illinois Colored Historical Society of Springfield, with Magee as president and Jennie McClain as secretary, extended its congratulations to the school committee in a 1908 resolution.[54]

---

51. *Illinois Record,* Nov. 6 (p. 1, col. 6, p. 3, col. 1), Nov. 13 (p. 1, cols. 1–2), Nov. 27 (p. 3, col. 2), 1897, Jan. 8 (p. 1, col. 5, p. 3, col. 3), Jan. 22 (p. 3, col. 2), Feb. 5 (p. 3, col. 3), Feb. 12 (p. 3, col. 2), March 19 (p. 3, col. 3), March 26 (p. 3, cols. 1, 3), April 16 (p. 3, col. 1), Dec. 10 (p. 3, col. 1), 1898; *Edwardsville Intelligencer,* Oct. 5, 1897, p. 1, col. 6.

52. *Illinois Record,* Feb. 5, 1898, p. 3, col. 3.

53. Ibid., March 26, 1898, p. 3, col. 3; *Forum,* Feb. 22, 1908, p. 8, col. 1.

54. *Forum,* May 9, 1908, p. 1, cols. 2–3.

The African American press editorialized about the Alton School Case, often noting the apostasy of the Republican party. In 1897, the Salt Lake City *Broad Ax,* which relocated to Chicago in 1899, wrote disparagingly of "all the Republican city officials of Alton, Illinois."[55] The following year, James H. Porter, the editor of the *Illinois Record,* excoriated the Republican party for its failure to appoint blacks to prestigious political patronage jobs and to enforce the Illinois School Law.[56] Ida Bell Wells-Barnett, hailed by her peers as the "princess of the Negro press," denounced the Alton municipal government as well as the board of education.[57] Springfield's *Forum* ran an editorial praising Bibb and declaring the final "Supreme Court's Decision Sweeping."[58]

The Afro-American Protective League of Illinois—the state branch of the National Equal Rights League, a black self-help organization—added its support and encouragement in the Alton School Case at the league's November 19–20, 1897, and September 27–28, 1898, conferences in Springfield. Both Drew and Coats attended in 1897, and Drew went again in 1898. Drew and other delegates spoke on the school cases of Alton, Centralia, and Du Quoin at an 1897 session. At the second Springfield conference, Drew was elected second vice president of the league. Later, in an open letter to league members, M. A. Majors and Hugh Singleton, the state secretary and state treasurer, respectively, argued that the "school affairs" were "objects of interest, concerning which the entire race should direct their attention, and give sparingly of their means to aid them." They added a warning to African Americans, cautioning them against unconditional support of the Republican party: "As a race, we are too loyal which fact is alas! to[o] well known by the party of which we form a part."[59]

The Illinois Supreme Court in its final judgment in the Bibb case ordered the integration of the Alton schools. The court harshly admonished the circuit court for racism on the part of both the judge and the jury. The mayor and city council of Alton undermined the decision by holding that it applied only to Minnie and Ambrose Bibb. Even their younger siblings were barred from the white schools. Ambrose reportedly had taken a job out of state and promised to return

---

55. *Broad Ax* (Salt Lake City, Utah), Oct. 2, 1897, p. 1, col. 1.

56. *Illinois Record,* Jan. 15, 1898, p. 1, cols. 3–4.

57. Ibid., April 23 (p. 3, col. 1), May 7 (p. 3, col. 1), 1898. In her autobiography, Wells-Barnett discussed her opposition to segregated schools, although without specifically addressing the Alton situation (see Duster, ed., pp. 274–78).

58. *Forum,* May 2, 1908, p. 2, cols. 1–2.

59. *Alton Evening Telegraph,* Nov. 20, 1897, p. 5, col. 5; *Alton Weekly Telegraph,* Nov. 25, 1897, p. 5, col. 1; *Illinois Record,* Nov. 13 (p. 1, col. 3), Dec. 4 (p. 1, cols. 1–2), Dec. 18 (p. 3, col. 3), 1897. The word "sparingly" here is undoubtedly either a misprint or simply the wrong choice of a word; the word here should have been "generously."

to Alton in January in order to complete his schooling. Minnie was assigned to the Washington School where she was placed in third grade alongside children barely half her age because the superintendent of schools contended that she could not function at the high school level that the Bibbs had claimed for her. After a few weeks at Washington, where she was the only black student, Minnie withdrew from school.[60]

Meanwhile, it had become clear that the mayor, the city council, and the school board had no intention of allowing other blacks into the white schools, the supreme court decision notwithstanding. Scott Bibb threatened another lawsuit to compel the admission of his three other children, but the suit never materialized.[61]

Having failed in their attempts to integrate the Alton schools through peaceful resistance and legalistic means, African Americans, no doubt, considered other options. They might have attempted to change the composition of the city council and the school board through the electoral process, but this would have had a remote chance for success as blacks constituted less than 6 percent of the population of Alton. Economic measures such as a boycott of white businesses would have been unlikely to succeed for the same reason. Had they employed more radical means of resistance, they would have risked violent retaliation.

In Alton, as elsewhere, race relations had become increasingly strained during the late nineteenth and early twentieth centuries. Such racially motivated terrorism as severe beatings, lynchings, and race riots were rampant at the time. As many scholars have shown, whites used violence and the threat of violence to reassert and maintain their hegemony. Mob attacks against blacks in Illinois included one lynching in Decatur in 1893, an attempted one in the same city in 1894, one in Belleville in 1903, and nearly two dozen others. Additionally, blacks viewed the murders and other physical attacks upon African American strikebreakers in the Virden and Pana mine wars of 1898 as racial terrorism. Race riots in Springfield during August, 1908, underscored the fact that Illinois whites were willing to use racially based terrorism for social control. Reportedly, whites in Alton and vicinity began to speak of using physical violence against blacks

60. *The People, ex rel., Scott Bibb* v. *The Mayor and Common Council of Alton,* in Isaac Newton Phillips, *Reports of Cases at Law and in Chancery Argued and Determined in the Supreme Court of Illinois* (Springfield, Ill.: n.p., 1899), pp. 615–33; *St. Louis Post-Dispatch,* Sept. 14 (p. 1, col. 7), Sept. 20 (p. 2, col. 2), Sept. 29 (p. 2, col. 7), 1908; *Alton Evening Telegraph,* Sept. 14 (p. 1, col. 4), Sept. 15 (p. 1, col. 4), Sept. 25 (p. 1, col. 1), Sept. 29 (p. 1, col. 3), 1908.

61. For the beginning of the 1908–1909 school year, see *Alton Evening Telegraph,* Sept 8 (p. 1, col. 1), Sept. 9 (p. 1, col. 2), Sept. 10 (p. 1, col. 6), Sept. 12 (p. 5, col. 4), Sept. 14 (p. 1, col. 4), Sept. 17 (p. 1, col. 4), Sept. 18 (p. 1, col. 5), Sept. 19 (p. 1, col. 1), Sept. 25 (p. 1, col. 1), Oct. 3 (p. 1, col. 4), 1908.

in the wake of the Springfield riots.[62] Given the atmosphere in Alton, the state, and the nation, those comments were taken seriously by African Americans.

Alton blacks, no doubt, reassessed the boycott for another reason: Additional delays in educating their children would have been even more devastating to the educational level of the black community than had the past eleven years. When the 1908–1909 school year began, only a few African American children attended, but their numbers increased steadily over the ensuing weeks. By the end of the first semester, most black children had enrolled in the "colored" grade schools, signaling African Americans' acknowledgment that the Alton schools would remain segregated. It would take another fifty years before the educational system in that city would be desegregated once again.

The school fight had ended after eleven years, but its legacy remained. The racism of the Republican school and city officials had undermined the credibility of the GOP within the black community. Although most Alton blacks remained within the Republican party after 1908, many seriously questioned the party's commitment to equalitarian principles. In subsequent years, their disaffection for the party intensified, as did that of other blacks in Illinois and the nation. Continuing within the party, then, did not indicate that African Americans found Republican policies acceptable, only that they saw no viable alternative to it, as the Democrats offered them even less.

---

62. Cha-Jua, "'A Warlike Demonstration,'" p. 2, and "'Join hands and hearts with law and order'"; *Palladium,* March 7 (p. 1, col. 4), June 20 (p. 4, col. 2), 1903. For the Pana and Virden mine wars, see Victor Hicken, "The Virden and Pana Mine Wars of 1898," *Journal of the Illinois State Historical Society,* 52 (1959), 263–78; John H. Keiser, "Black Strikebreakers and Racism in Illinois, 1865–1900," ibid., 65 (1972), 313–26; *Alton Evening Telegraph,* Oct. 10, 1898, p. 3, col. 4; *Illinois Record,* Oct. 22 (p. 3, col. 3), Oct. 29 (p. 2, col. 2), Nov. 12 (p. 2, col. 2), 1898, March 25, 1899, p. 2, col. 1. Roberta Senechal's *The Sociogenesis of a Race Riot: Springfield, Illinois, in 1908* (Urbana: University of Illinois Press, 1990) is the best secondary source on the Springfield riot. See also James Krohe, Jr., *Summer of Rage: The Springfield Race Riot of 1908* (Springfield, Ill.: Sangamon County Historical Society [1973]). Meier and Rudwick's contention that a speaker at the Wood River Baptist Association's Annual Conference in Alton discouraged continuing the fight for integrated schools cannot be accepted, however. Their sources are the *Alton Evening Telegraph* and the *St. Louis Post-Dispatch,* which were biased against blacks. Further, the 1908 annual meeting did not begin until September 3, one day *after* the *Telegraph* ran the story. The Minutes of the Wood River Baptist Association give no indication that the school case had been discussed by the body. The newspapers may have quoted a single person who had expressed a personal opinion on the eve of the conference. It is also possible that the story was a fabrication, as were others printed by the two newspapers. A story in the *St. Louis Globe-Democrat* on Aug. 19, 1908, claimed that a Saint Louis white mob pursued two blacks, yelling, "Give him Springfield. We will give it to him" (see p. 1, col. 6).

Alton blacks had displayed considerable political sophistication and race consciousness in placing their own community interests ahead of those of the Republican party. In so doing, they had shown tremendous commitment to the racial self-help and resistance to oppression emphasized by many African Americans throughout the country. Further, they had demonstrated that their voices would be raised not only in their own communities, but also within the larger society. Subsequent generations would use the same modes of resistance—sit-ins, boycotts, and litigation—to desegregate schools and other public facilities. Alton blacks' tremendous respect for using legal remedies was also evident. Party and city officials, by their refusal to obey the supreme court decision, had demonstrated that they had the political clout needed to deprive African Americans of their legal victory and to establish their own hegemony. The Republican party leadership and city officials had also revealed the importance of race over all other considerations, including respect for the law.

8. The Dry Machine

The Formation of the Anti-Saloon League of Illinois

THOMAS R. PEGRAM

"THIS MAN BROWN, FROM PESOTUM, has surprised me some," wrote a Champaign County Republican official to gubernatorial hopeful Frank O. Lowden's campaign manager at the close of 1915. "He is so dry that you can see him sizzle when you talk to him and I have had more trouble . . . trying to educate him that we are not voting on the wet and dry proposition [but] for Republican candidates." From all parts of Illinois troubling evidence poured into Lowden headquarters, indicating that a new generation of grassroots activists like Brown were yoking their political loyalty to the vexing question of liquor regulation.[1]

The Illinois General Assembly had felt that influence for more than a decade. In the 1907 legislative session alone, thirty-two separate bills pertaining to the regulation of alcohol were introduced. By 1911 the wet and dry forces in the

---

THOMAS R. PEGRAM was awarded the Ph.D. from Brandeis University. He is currently assistant professor of history at Loyola College in Maryland and has also taught at Ohio State University. A specialist in modem American political and social institutions, Pegram has written on business lobbyists and agricultural reform in Illinois. His book *Progressives and Partisans: Private Interest and Public Policy in Illinois, 1870–1922,* will be published soon. The author thanks the staff of the Special Collections at Regenstein Library of the University of Chicago and the manuscript staff at the Illinois State Historical Library. He also thanks Morton Keller and James Matthew Gallman for their comments.

1. C. N. Clark to W. H. Stead, Dec. 4, 1915, Series 3, Box 21, Frank O. Lowden Papers, Regenstein Library, University of Chicago.

Illinois Historical Journal Vol. 83, No. 3 (Autumn 1990): 173–186

This cartoon illustrates the Anti-Saloon League's successful manipulation of public opinion through publicity, in this case through its magazine, Illinois Issue.

lower house had organized Liberal and Temperance committees, and attitudes toward saloon regulation determined the outcome of several contested elections in that session. Ten thousand supporters of the Anti-Saloon League of Illinois journeyed to Springfield on February 14 to demand a county option law. On February 16 a *Chicago Tribune* reporter predicted, "The wet and dry row will become the supreme issue of the legislature." By 1913 divisions over liquor helped delay for three months the selection of a Speaker.[2]

Saloon regulation also disturbed the political equilibrium in large and small communities across the state. Divisions sparked by a state law that required Chicago saloons to close on Sundays over whelmed the 1907 city charter that was meant to modernize governmental administration of the metropolis. In the tiny Bureau County towns of Sheffield and Buda, the contest over saloons

2. *Chicago Tribune,* Feb. 3 (p. 6, cols. 1–2), Feb. 14 (p. 4, col. 5), Feb. 16 (p. 7, col. 1), 1911; *Champion of Fair Play,* May 11, 1907, p. 1; John D. Buenker, "The Illinois Legislature and Prohibition, 1907–1919," *Journal of the Illinois State Historical Society,* 62 (1969), 372.

not only upset long-standing arrangements of township government but also split local residents into License and No-License parties that determined political allegiances long after the matter of licensing saloons had been settled. The powerful appeal of the crusade disrupted reform coalitions and splintered party regularity.[3]

Regulation of alcoholic beverages was probably the most divisive issue in state and local politics between the turn of the century and American entry into the First World War. In Illinois, the insistent demands of the Anti-Saloon League (ASL) forced lawmakers to determine the propriety of licensing saloons. Professional politicians, reformers, urbanites, and rural folk all felt the special power of the issue. Some embraced it, others sought to overcome its appeal when it threatened to eclipse their own concerns, but everyone had to adjust to its peculiar dynamism. By the end of the Progressive period, Illinois joined in the national decision to dismantle the liquor industry through constitutional amendment. The development of the ASL "dry machine" in Illinois brought a new political sophistication to the temperance cause as the League pioneered the mechanics of single-issue lobbying that have become central components of moral reform movements in modern American life.

Political turmoil over liquor regulation was not unique to the Progressive era. Grassroots partisans of temperance and associated pietist values had successfully asserted themselves against the professional elite of the Republican party in several northeastern and midwestern states during the 1880s. The result of that "onslaught by ethnoreligious imperialists" was the fragmentation of the carefully built Republican coalition and a rash of electoral defeats. Memories of those past experiences provoked the strong resistance of many politicians to a renewed effort to place temperance reform at the center of public policy.[4] Party professionals at the turn of the century wanted to prevent the return of that uncontrollable and potentially disastrous sentiment.

Although the resurgent political movement to exterminate the liquor traffic resonated with a moral fervor inherited from past campaigns, the organization, tactics, and strategy were crucially different. The key to those differences was the Anti-Saloon League of America. Founded in Ohio in 1893 as part of the extraordinary explosion of disciplined, limited-interest political pressure groups, the ASL seized control of the movement when its most important rivals for leadership—the Prohibition party and the Woman's Christian Temperance

3. Maureen A. Flanagan, *Charter Reform in Chicago* (Carbondale: Southern Illinois University Press, 1987); *Sheffield Times*, April 5, 1912, p. 1, cols. 1–2, 5, and Jan. 28, 1916, p. 4, col. 1.

4. Paul Kleppner, *The Third Electoral System, 1853–1892: Parties, Voters, and Political Cultures* (Chapel Hill: University of North Carolina Press, 1979), p. 303.

Our Anti-Saloon League Creed

I believe in the supremacy of law.

I believe in the divine authority of civil government.

I believe in right laws and the righteous execution of law.

I believe in the nomination and election of the right kind of men.

I believe in the impeachment of officials who will not enforce the law.

I believe in the freedom of the state from the political domination of the liquor traffic.

I believe in the freedom of the national government from complicity with the liquor traffic.

I believe in the ultimate redemption of the world from the power and dominion of strong drink.

I believe in the final absolute annihilation of the saloon in every nation of the world.

The Anti-Saloon League advocated the closing of saloons through legislation. The League's creed illustrates its single-mindedness in freeing the world from "the power and dominion of strong drink."

Union—were at their weakest. The Prohibition party, never much of a force in American politics, split in 1896 over the issue of a broad reform plank and thereafter declined from the modest strength exhibited in 1888 and 1892. Although still a powerful and active temperance organization, the WCTU was wracked by internal dissension through the 1890s and suffered an irreplaceable loss when its dynamic leader, Frances Willard, died in 1898.[5]

The Anti-Saloon League emphasized sound organization, realistic goals, and tough practical politics. Its focused assault on the saloon—the institutional symbol of the liquor traffic—diverted attention from the moral failings of the individual drinker. That dogged opposition to the saloon would win respect from politicians. ASL officials took pains to inculcate among their followers a

---

5. Jack S. Blocker, Jr., *Retreat from Reform: The Prohibition Movement in the United States, 1890–1913* (Westport, Conn.: Greenwood Press, 1976), pp. 45, 100–47; Ruth Bordin, *Woman and Temperance: The Quest for Power and Liberty, 1873–1900* (Philadelphia: Temple University Press, 1981), pp. 140–55.

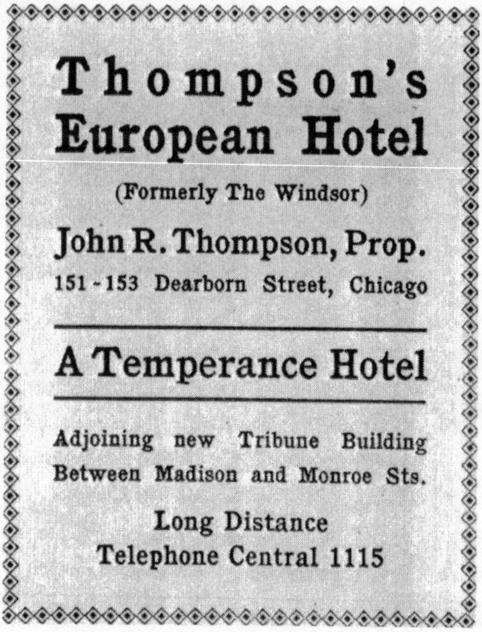

In this August 26, 1906, advertisement in Illinois Issue, *Thompson's European Hotel of Chicago proclaimed itself for temperance. Chicago, unlike most cities in the state, however, never conducted a local option referendum.*

willingness to "forsake their party in at least one campaign, and vote for a man who is personally distasteful to them, who does not belong to their church and their lodge, and who stands right, instead of a man on their own party ticket who perhaps belongs to their church, belongs, perhaps, to all their lodges, and who is a personal friend, but who stands wrong."[6] Devotion to a single issue maintained the potency of the ASL as a pressure group, but its measured, incremental legislative program was grounded in realistic political compromises. "Temperance people everywhere should take conditions, not as they ought to be," insisted the ASL, "but as they are."[7] Local option legislation was the ASL's device for extending prohibition into states unwilling to go completely dry. Local option elections—referenda in which voters decided whether saloons should be licensed—could be held at the county, municipal, or even precinct level. The ASL found local option the most flexible legislative method for attacking the saloon wherever it was vulnerable. The adoption of Anti-Saloon League tactics

6. W. M. Burke, "The Anti-Saloon League as a Political Force," *Annals of the American Academy of Political and Social Science,* 32 (1908), 31.

7. *Anti-Saloon League Year Book, 1909* (Columbus: Anti-Saloon League of America, 1909), p. 171.

transformed the Illinois temperance movement from a blundering nativist crusade to an efficient political machine.[8]

The temperance movement faced one of its sturdiest challenges in Illinois. Chicago, the dominant city of the Midwest and the key to commercial and industrial fortunes, contained the largest inland concentration of alcohol consumers. Most of the city's large immigrant population—reared in a tradition that valued the tavern and the moderate use of alcohol—exerted its substantial political influence in defense of the license-paying saloon. But Chicago was not the only major stronghold of liquor interests in Illinois. Peoria, with abundant grain and fresh water ideal for distilling liquor, was home to several plants of the American Spirits Manufacturing Company, popularly known as the Whiskey Trust. The full political strength of the liquor industry and its supporters opposed temperance advocates in the Prairie State.[9]

Local control of liquor regulation was the preeminent theme in the late-nineteenth-century anti-saloon fight in Illinois. The Cities and Villages Act of 1872 confirmed the licensing power of city councils, village presidents, and boards of trustees. The same year, however, temperance pressure led to passage of the Dramshop Act, which provided for Sunday closing and made saloon owners and bartenders responsible for damages wrought by drunken patrons. Eleven years later, with the Harper High License Act, the general assembly set the minimum cost of a license at $500 for a saloon that served hard liquor and $150 for one in which only beer and malt liquors were available. Those acts established that saloons were responsible for the drunkenness and subsequent behavior of their customers, that the number of saloons should be controlled (in this case through high license fees), and—most important—that the general assembly could provide guidelines for local regulation. The Anti-Saloon League

8. For a history of the national organization, see K. Austin Kerr, *Organized for Prohibition: A New History of the Anti-Saloon League* (New Haven, Conn.: Yale University Press, 1985), and Peter H. Odegard, *Pressure Politics: The Story of the Anti-Saloon League* (New York: Columbia University Press, 1928). Antiforeign sentiment maintained a disturbing, if understated, presence. Despite the League's claim to represent the Christian church, old stock Protestant denominations appeared to make up the true constituency. Beyond a few token representatives in highly visible positions, Catholics, Episcopalians, and Lutherans generally remained outside the fold. ASL devotees tried not to attack the churches that resisted their efforts, but nativist assaults on "foreign" churches and their immigrant communicants regularly cropped up in the ASL press (*American Issue,* April 11, 1908, p. 11, and Aug. 15, 1908, pp. 8–9).

9. See Perry R. Duis, *The Saloon: Public Drinking in Chicago and Boston, 1880–1920* (Urbana: University of Illinois Press, 1983); Anti-Saloon League of America, *Proceedings of the Annual Convention of the Anti-Saloon League of America, 1907* (Westerville, Ohio: American Issue Pub. Co., 1907), p. 91.

later built upon those foundations, but it was not yet strong enough to sustain the temperance movement.[10]

Before the Anti-Saloon League appeared, temperance sentiment was hampered by a lack of centralized leadership, divisive companion issues, and a diffusion of effort. The experience of the movement in Rockford—a growing industrial city of about 25,000 with a large Swedish population—during the 1890s reveals both the fervor and the many weaknesses of temperance crusades. Rockford had outlawed saloons in 1881 and 1888 but could not enforce the ban. The city council turned instead to a policy of high license fees and a limit of twenty saloons. By 1892, thirty-seven saloons flourished, each paying $1,000 for a license.[11]

Despite enthusiasm and active support from local Protestant churches, Rockford foes of the saloon failed to build an organized, disciplined political movement. The conflict centered on the city council, where members divided between those willing to issue more licenses and those wishing to restrict them. In 1892, a majority of no-license candidates, running under four separate labels, were elected to the city council. Factional rivalries split the no-license council vote, however, and pre vented that majority from controlling the council. Even worse, temperance advocates allowed the outside issue of nativism to poison the appeal of anti-saloon sentiment. The virulent, antiforeign American Protective Association (APA) gained momentum steadily. Officials of the Rockford Citizens' Association, the largest no-license organization, kept silent when a temperance speaker suggested that sacramental wines were a conduit to drunkenness; they did not rebuke the public suggestion of one of their followers in 1892 "to shut the gates at Castle Garden [New York] and exterminate a few of the pests that Europe has poured out from her jails and poor-houses." Having cut itself off from many Swedish Protestants who opposed saloons, the Citizens' Association formally allied itself with the APA in 1893 and elected a nativist mayor. For the next two years, no-license voters complained that the mayor paid more attention to nativism than to the danger of saloons. Divided into tangled, amateurish factions, the Rockford temperance organizations were incapable of directing the powerful no-license sentiment into a united political movement. In fact, by 1895 Rockford still received more than $38,000 in saloon

10. Duis, p. 12; Ernest Ludlow Bogart and John Mabry Mathews, *The Modern Commonwealth, 1893–1918,* Centennial History of Illinois, Vol. 5 (Springfield: Illinois Centennial Commission, 1920), p. 386; Bogart and Charles Manfred Thompson, *The Industrial State, 1870–1893,* Centennial History of Illinois, Vol. 4 (Springfield: Illinois Centennial Commission, 1920), pp. 43–47, 140.

11. *Rockford Register-Gazette,* April 9 (p. 2, col. 2), April 16 (p. 2, cols. 4–5), 1892.

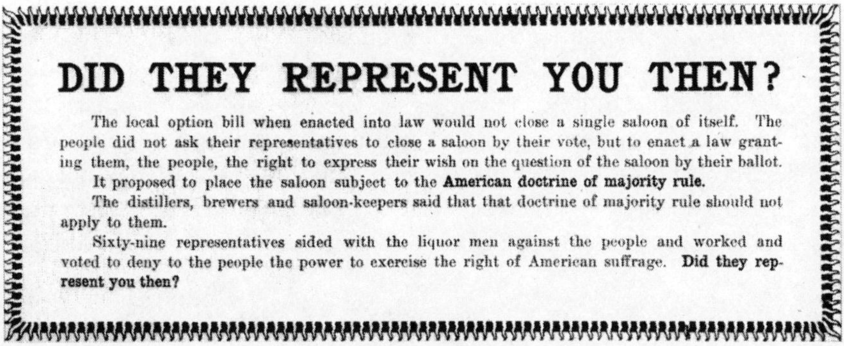

DID THEY REPRESENT YOU THEN?

The local option bill when enacted into law would not close a single saloon of itself. The people did not ask their representatives to close a saloon by their vote, but to enact a law granting them, the people, the right to express their wish on the question of the saloon by their ballot.

It proposed to place the saloon subject to the **American doctrine of majority rule.**

The distillers, brewers and saloon-keepers said that that doctrine of majority rule should not apply to them.

Sixty-nine representatives sided with the liquor men against the people and worked and voted to deny to the people the power to exercise the right of American suffrage. **Did they represent you then?**

The Anti-Saloon League called for the defeat of members of the Illinois General Assembly who voted against the option bill. The final victory came during the 1907 session.

license fees. Moreover, unlicensed "blind pigs" prospered, and arrests for liquor law violations and gambling mounted.[12]

Rockford did not eliminate saloons until the Anti-Saloon League of Illinois pushed a local option bill through the general assembly in 1907. By that time the city of nearly 45,000 was far more difficult to dry up. But armed with the local option referendum, voters temporarily closed saloons in 1908 and made the ban permanent in 1912. Mayor William W. Bennett credited the ASL for the triumph: "They have taught us to fight together," he enthused. "They have taught us to believe in ourselves. They have taught us to play practical politics."[13] Anti-Saloon League methods transformed Rockford from a city with a substantial yet divided and ineffective temperance sentiment into one of the largest saloonless cities in the nation.

The Anti-Saloon League of Illinois rose to preeminence among Illinois temperance organizations between 1900 and 1907 through single-mindedness, precise organization, and a practical legislative agenda that produced an effective statewide local option law. But success was not instantaneous. Encouraged by the outpouring of Illinois temperance sentiment in the 1890s, the national ASL launched a state organization in 1898 that was intended to work through youth societies of Protestant churches. Despite high expectations, the Illinois ASL floundered for two years under incompetent and lackadaisical leadership,

12. Ibid., April, 1892–April, 1895; quotation is from ibid., April 18, 1892, p. 4, col. 3. See also *Reports of the City Officers of the City of Rockford, Illinois, for the Fiscal Year 1895* (Rockford: Clavert Bros., 1895), pp. 10, 14, 51.

13. Anti-Saloon League of America, *Proceedings, 1913*. p. 104.

haphazard organization, and foolish promises. When twenty-six-year-old attorney William Hamilton Anderson became superintendent of the League in November of 1900, it was in tatters. Anderson's clergyman predecessor—after an eleven-month tenure marked by listless effort and an unquestionably careless, probably deceitful, management of finances—had resigned suddenly and fled to St. Louis. Only $150 remained in the League's bank account to cover outstanding checks and a stack of unpaid debts (not even the office desk and

Attorney-Prohibitionist William Hamilton Anderson was born in Carlinville, Illinois, on August 8, 1874. After graduating from Blackburn College in 1892, he entered the University of Michigan at Ann Arbor, where he received a law degree in 1896. Anderson married Clarice Otwell of Carlinville in 1901. His strong support of the temperance movement led to employment as attorney of the Anti-Saloon League of Illinois in 1900. That same year he became superintendent of the League. During his tenure, Anderson not only transformed the League into one of the most powerful lobbies in Illinois but also constructed a politically devastating bloc of temperance voters. Those efforts led to passage of the local option bill in 1907. Anderson continued to serve the temperance cause nationwide throughout his life. He died September 4, 1959, and was buried in Carlinville.

chair were paid for). Of the six district ASL superintendents, one was ineffective, three did not even reside in the state, and Dr. M. M. Parkhurst of the Chicago district had set up a private temperance fiefdom, giving neither recognition nor money to the state League. One League trustee was unaware of his position, and he refused to serve when asked to do so by Anderson. Pastors and businessmen in Jacksonville, Danville, Freeport, and other towns complained that ASL officials had reneged on pledges to funnel community contributions back into local work, provide matching grants, and furnish detectives to enforce saloon regulations. The League stood in dire need of reconstruction.[14]

As was the case with other emerging pressure groups at the turn of the century, talented and dedicated leadership stabilized the state ASL, tailored it to fit its natural constituency, and launched an aggressive and focused campaign to win specific goals. Anderson overhauled League finances, installed a more effective bookkeeping system, and then hired accountants to oversee it. He repaired the League's strained relations with local pastors and businessmen, delivered money that had been promised but never distributed, then ensured that such problems would not recur by centralizing authority in his office. Most important, Anderson fused existing anti-saloon sentiment behind a specific piece of legislation—a binding local option referendum law—for which the ASL would be principal lobbyist. The official endorsement of that bill by the Protestant churches of Illinois and their designation of the ASL as their legislative agent became the key to the vitality of the organization and the source of future temperance victories.[15]

Anderson's talents as a tough politician, a blunt speaker, and a persistent lobbyist augmented his administrative abilities. His prickly, acerbic language and confrontational style made many enemies—so many that at times he carried a gun—but he also influenced lawmakers. "Who rules Illinois," demanded the Chicago liquor trade journal, *Champion of Fair Play*, "the Governor, the Legislature or Blustering Anderson?" Years later, Anderson's assault on newspapers and politicians in New York led to a criminal conviction for third degree forgery and a short term in Sing Sing. But between 1900 and 1905, when he left to join

---

14. W. A. Smith, *A History of the Anti-Saloon League of Illinois* (Chicago: Anti-Saloon League of Illinois, 1925), pp. 9, 11; Anderson to the Headquarters Committee of the Board of Trustees of the Illinois Anti-Saloon League, Nov. 20, 1900, and Anderson to the State Board of Trustees of Illinois ASL, May 1, 1901, both in Box 2, William H. Anderson Papers, Regenstein Library, University of Chicago.

15. Anderson to Trustees, May 1, 1901, May 27, 1902, and Anderson to Illinois ASL Directors, 1904, Box 2, Anderson Papers; Anti-Saloon League of Illinois, *Report, 1905* (Chicago: Anti-Saloon League of Illinois, 1905), p. 7.

the New York ASL, Anderson built a model organization in Illinois, one that would provide superintendents to eleven other states.[16]

"In order to conduct a campaign we must have an issue," exclaimed Anderson. To that end, he helped draft a model local option bill that ASL supporters introduced in each session of the general assembly between 1901 and 1907. The League's bill provided for a local option election at either the county, township, city, town, village, ward, or precinct level upon petition by 25 percent of the voters. Local option took exclusive saloon-licensing power away from city councils and village boards and gave it to the public. The bill also declared that a no-license vote of a larger district would invalidate a license majority in any smaller unit of that district, but that a smaller unit's no-license vote could stand within a larger license unit. Anderson did not expect quick passage, but he used the model bill as "the means of receiving a large amount of advertising" to attract support from Protestant churches.[17]

Over the next four years Anderson built the Illinois ASL into an official church federation. The League mailed sample copies of publications and the text of the model bill to Illinois ministers, especially before autumn meetings of the major religious conventions in 1901. The Illinois and Rock River Methodist conferences, which included Chicago congregations, not only endorsed the model bill but recommended the formation of voter committees in each church to assist the ASL. One month later pastors in Springfield issued a call for all Illinois ministers to work for local option through the League. By 1905 the state board of directors was redrawn, and legal control of the organization was transferred to the spokesmen of supporting religious denominations. Actual authority, however, was centralized in the hands of the superintendent. Anderson subdued rivals and hired competent, dedicated workers to run the five revamped state districts. Ten fieldworkers roamed the state spreading the local option message and raising money, which went directly to Anderson's headquarters for disbursement.[18]

---

16. *Champion of Fair Play,* March 18, 1905, p. 1; Norman Harding Dohn, "The History of the Anti-Saloon League," Diss. Ohio State University 1959, p. 88; Anderson to the Constituency of the Anti-Saloon League of Illinois, Nov. 14, 1905, Box 2, Anderson Papers; Odegard, pp. 228–40; Smith, p. 14.

17. Anderson to Trustees, May 1, 1901. For the model bill, see *The New Local Option Bill* (Chicago: Anti-Saloon League of Illinois, 1905). Township option gave rural areas some power to influence the license question in adjoining municipalities. For the seventeen counties not organized under the township system, the local option bill divided those counties into election precincts that functioned as townships for local option elections; see Walter F. Dodd and Sue H. Dodd, *Government in Illinois* (Chicago: University of Chicago Press, 1923), pp. 20–21.

18. Anti-Saloon League of America, *Proceedings, 1904,* pp. 52–53; Anderson to Trustees, May 27, 1902, "Annual Meeting of the Board of the Anti-Saloon League, July 2, 1903," and

While the church federation furnished neither leadership nor control over strategy, it provided something more valuable: an organized constituency that placed money, voters, and the makings of a grassroots political machine at the disposal of the Anti-Saloon League. The central feature of the alliance between the League and Illinois Protestantism was the Anti-Saloon Field Day, an annual event in which cooperating churches devoted one regular Sunday service to the work of the ASL. In place of the sermon, an Illinois League field-worker reported on the progress of ASL activity and solicited donations in the form of cash or subscription cards. The program enabled field-workers to cover their own salaries and traveling expenses for weekday agitation, while winning additional converts to the fight. League revenue increased from $2,500 in 1900 to $40,000 in pledges in 1905; by 1908, $60,000 was raised, and Field Day addresses were made in an average of twenty-five pulpits every Sunday. That support allowed League workers to take on the appearance of efficient, unsleeping fanatics in the frightened imaginations of liquor men. "There is not a hole or corner in the State where they will not go," wailed the *Champion of Fair Play*.[19]

The League insisted on full control over fund raising and lobbying. As an "invariable rule," ASL speakers refused to enter churches that offered a pulpit but declined a subscription for League work. It likewise rejected church offerings in lieu of entertaining Field Day speakers. The national ASL even refused the requests of some churches that a percentage of money raised be set aside for local projects. Nor did the ASL allow churches free rein in supporting legislation. League officials requested that pastors preach sermons supporting the local option bill on the first Sunday following its introduction in the general assembly for three consecutive legislative sessions. ASL pamphlets instructed clergymen to interrupt revivals if necessary to preach in favor of the bill, gave tips on dealing with newspapers, warned against statements "so beautifully indefinite that the people will take this for a regular temperance sermon," and insisted that the Anti-Saloon League be mentioned by name. In 1903, one thousand ministers complied; in 1905 the number grew to two thousand; and in 1907—the year local option was finally enacted—some 2,500 Illinois pastors pressed the legislature to pass the bill.[20]

By 1905, the church federation furnished the Illinois ASL with a large constituency—the nearly one million members of affiliated churches and temperance

---

Anderson to Directors, 1904, all in Box 2, Anderson Papers; Anti-Saloon League of Illinois, *Report, 1905*, p. 3. For Anderson's vision of the church federation, see Anderson, *The Church in Action Against the Saloon* (n.p.: Anti-Saloon League of America, 1906).

19. *Champion of Fair Play,* March 31, 1906, p. 1; Anderson to Directors, 1904; Anti-Saloon League of America, *Proceedings, 1905*, p. 64; *American Issue,* May 9, 1908, p. 12.

20. Quotation is from *New Local Option Bill,* p. 4; Anderson, p. 49; Anti-Saloon League of America, *Proceedings, 1905* (p. 63), *1907* (p. 92); *American Issue,* Feb. 15, 1907, p. 12.

Field Day at Springfield

Sunday, January 28th, was League Field Day at Springfield. Ten of our representatives spent the day in that city and the cause was presented in twenty different churches. Congregations were good and a deeper interest was manifested than ever before in the history of our work. The material support was also much greater than at any previous Field Day the League has had in that city.

The most important events of the occasion were the afternoon meetings in the Assembly Hall of the Capitol. At 2:30 p. m. Mr. Curtis, our district man at Springfield, addressed a company of three hundred boys. At 3:30 a large mass-meeting of between four hundred and five hundred men was addressed by James K. Shields, State Superintendent, and J. F. Burke, Attorney and Legislative Superintendent. The audience manifested the warmest sympathy for the cause and it was almost 6 p. m. before the meeting adjourned. Splendid service was rendered at the mass-meeting by a Male Quartette and at both meetings by the High School Orchestra.

These meetings were held under the auspices of the Y. M. C. A. and will prove of great benefit for the cause represented by the League. The day's work was under the supervision of Mr. Curtis of the Springfield district and the results reflect great credit upon his effort. He is an energetict man and knows how to bring things to pass.

groups—and an existing infrastructure that facilitated thorough community organization. Voter committees drawn from Protestant youth societies canvassed their congregations and neighborhoods on behalf of League-endorsed political candidates. They forwarded to League offices detailed lists of voters, indicating such items as party preference, attitudes toward particular candidates, and names of influential sympathizers.[21] The church federation built the Illinois League into a powerful, thoroughly organized political hybrid that included a party machine that mustered large numbers of disciplined voters and a pressure group that focused exclusively on a single concern and pursued it with every resource that came to hand. Explicit in its desires, ever watchful, ready to commit its significant bloc of voters to any candidate who chose to stand with its policies or against any who opposed them, the Anti-Saloon League of Illinois was undoubtedly the most effective temperance organization ever active in Illinois and one of the most powerful lobbying associations in the Progressive era.

In pursuit of an effective local option law, the ASL patiently built up pressure on lawmakers over several sessions of the general assembly. In 1903 Anderson spurned a quick compromise, explaining that "a fragmentary measure is

21. *New Local Option Bill*, p. 9; Anti-Saloon League of Illinois, *Report, 1905*, p. 8.

no stronger a vote-getter than a comprehensive one" and that by cultivating intransigent opposition from legislators the popular pressure for local option would grow more intense. Indeed, the legislature's bipartisan "organization" tied to Chicago Republican boss William Lorimer managed to kill the bill, which spurred greater ASL efforts in the 1904 elections. The League concentrated its resources on a symbolic contest in Peoria, "the World's Whiskey Center," and against a few selected enemies from the 1903 session. Through careful application of the three-vote electoral system for Illinois House seats, ASL votes elected a Prohibition party candidate in Peoria, defeated a pro-license incumbent and a saloonkeeper for the other district seats, and beat down the nomination of the special representative of the Liquor Dealers' Protective Association. In 1905, Anderson's enemies crafted a counterfeit local option bill subject to a statewide referendum that would allow the pro-license majority in Chicago to scuttle the initiative. Anderson boldly endorsed the bill and forced his nervous opponents to backtrack. The next year the League defeated the committee chairman whose amendment killed local option in 1905. Opportunistic lawmakers such as Cicero J. Lindly of Bond County and John Gillett Oglesby of Logan County began to reverse their opposition to local option.[22]

The Anti-Saloon League accompanied its legislative efforts with a steady hum of publicity against the liquor industry's weakest point, the saloon itself. The League attacked the saloon's principal public justification—that it was a major financial contributor to local government through the payment of license fees—by chronicling the public cost of crime, poverty, and disease attributable to the saloon. Figures showed that despite $177,000 from liquor licenses, East St. Louis struggled under a net indebtedness of nearly $1,500,000. ASL publicists grimly observed that "the vast sum of money paid to the city of Chicago by the liquor traffic does not begin to cover the actual annual expenses of the city which are made necessary largely by the existence of the liquor traffic."[23] On the other hand, the ASL pointed to the prosperous, saloon-free town of Hoopeston as enjoying low taxes, serene local politics, and the business patronage of seven manufacturing plants attracted by the local no-license policy. After Galesburg and Rockford voted out the saloon, the ASL compared the decline in arrests

---

22. Anderson to Directors, July 2, 1903, Box 2, Anderson Papers; *New Local Option Bill,* pp. 12–14; Anti-Saloon League of America, *Proceedings, 1904,* p. 53; *Champion of Fair Play,* Jan. 28 (p. 1), Feb. 4 (p. 4), Feb. 11 (p. 1), May 6 (p. 1), 1905, and Nov. 3 (pp. 1–2), 1906; Smith, p. 15; *Mendon* (Ill.) *Dispatch,* April 19, 1905, Insert, p. 1, cols. 1–2; *American Issue,* Aug. 24, 1906, pp. 8–9; E. H. Curtis to Oglesby, March 19, 1906, M. J. McCarthy to Oglesby, Jan. 29, 1906, and penciled reply on back, Feb. 13, 1906, Box 30, Oglesby Family Papers, Illinois State Historical Library, a division of the Illinois Historic Preservation Agency, Springfield.

23. *Anti-Saloon League Year Book, 1913,* p. 70.

This poster is an example of the promotional literature supplied by the Anti-Saloon League to local option crusaders.

and the subsequent increase in bank savings to the less-favorable conditions of the license period. In Carbondale, the tax rate dropped after the city abolished its ten saloons. Anti-saloonists insisted that temperance and good government went hand in hand.[24]

By 1907 the League movement in Illinois was at flood tide, and the time for practical politics had arrived. Anderson's departure for New York in 1905 had rendered those lawmakers who had developed a personal dislike of the brusque superintendent more amenable. The model local option bill was again bogged down in the House of Representatives, but the bill for a new Chicago city charter was also caught up in legislative thickets. Capitalizing on the situation, ASL officials drew up a compromise local option bill that removed the county and

24. *American Issue,* May 18, 1906, p. 6, and Jan. 18 (p. 2), March 1 (p. 8), July 5 (p. 13), 1907; Anti-Saloon League of America, *Proceedings, 1913,* p. 106.

And We Have Only Begun To Fight!

Counties Made Anti-Saloon Territory To Date Under Local Option Law

Johnson	Boone	Cumberland	Fayette	Macon	Shelby
Massac	Brown	De Witt	Gallatin	Mercer	Saline
Scott	Champaign	Douglas	Greene	Moultrie	Washington
Union	Clark	Winnebago	Hamilton	Piatt	Wayne
Williamson	Coles	Edgar	Jefferson	Richland	White

The April 10, 1908, Illinois Issue *listed counties that had gone dry after passage of the local option law.*

ward option features. They then constructed an agreement with friends of the beleaguered Chicago charter bill to trade support on the two measures. On May 7, 1907, an unlikely alliance of rural temperance advocates and Cook County representatives combined to pass the Chicago charter and local option bills in tandem.[25]

The 1907 local option bill remained the greatest triumph of the League until 1919, when Illinois became the twenty-sixth state to ratify the Eighteenth Amendment. Although the ASL repelled a strong assault on the township option law in 1909 and steered several minor liquor bans through the legislature, the League failed to enact county option legislation. Chicago remained obdurate; no citywide local option referendum ever got on the Chicago ballot. But with the assistance of the ASL's law enforcement branch, the township option law of 1907 proved sufficiently powerful to dry up most of the state.[26]

In the first election under the new law, precincts and municipalities in the seventeen (mostly southern) Illinois counties not under township organization banished some 250 of the 339 saloons within their confines. The initial statewide

25. *The Illinois Local Option Law* (Chicago: Anti-Saloon League of Illinois, 1907); *Laws of Illinois,* 45 G.A. (1907–1908), p. 297; Smith, pp. 15–16; *Champion of Fair Play,* May 11, 1907, pp. 1, 4; *American Issue,* May 31, 1907, p. 5; *Illinois House Journal,* 45 G.A. (1907–1908), pp. 812–13, 843, 986–87; *Merulon Dispatch,* May 15, 1907, p. 2, col. 5. The Chicago charter bill passed the House by a 93–47 vote—forty-one representatives endorsed by the Illinois ASL voted for the bill. The local option bill passed the House by an 83–65 vote—eighteen Cook County representatives provided the margin of victory *(House Journal,* 45 G.A. [1907–1908], pp. 843, 986–87).

26. Smith, pp. 18–19; Anti-Saloon League of America, *Proceedings, 1913,* p. 380; *Illinois Local Option Law,* p. 38. For an example of League preparations for a local option election, see *American Issue,* Dec. 7, 1907, p. 12.

Cover of the May 1, 1908, Illinois Issue. *The map shows the results of the battle to close saloons after one year of local option.*

test of the law came on April 7, 1908, with similar results; in the eighty-four counties participating in the election, 1,052 townships voted dry and fifteen hundred saloons went out of business. The dry surge peaked around 1910, when forty of the state's 102 counties and 1,059 of its nearly 1,500 townships and precincts were entirely without saloons. When Illinois ratified the Prohibition Amendment in 1919, fifty-five counties and 1,425 townships had already voted out the saloon under the terms of the 1907 local option law.[27]

The dry machine demonstrated the power—and the drawbacks—of organized interest groups in the new "regulatory polity" of the twentieth century. Whether it was a symbolic crusade to reestablish the dominance of middle-class Protestantism in law if not in fact or a clear-eyed response to the material threat posed by the saloon, the temperance movement that produced the Anti-Saloon League of Illinois added another contestant to the jumble of interest groups whose demands complicated the formation of public policy during the Progressive

27. *American Issue,* Nov. 16, 1907, p. 9; *Champion of Fair Play,* Oct. 19, 1907, p. 8; Anti-Saloon League of America, *Proceedings, 1909,* p. 97; *Anti-Saloon League Year Book, 1910* (p. 65), *1913* (p. 29), *1919* (p. 112).

era. The liquor question was not a shadow issue or a sideshow. The emotional intensity displayed by both the ASL and its enemies and the general assembly's failure to prevent the saloon issue from seeping into other legislative concerns suggest the powerful hold of temperance on the public consciousness. Yet, the structure of the League magnified not the public commitment to the eradication of saloons but its obsessive fidelity to that issue above all others. Concerned citizens could support the League without abandoning their political parties or other commitments. League officers, the professionals who actually determined policy and interacted with lawmakers, brought a different sensibility to the work. Because they viewed abolition of the liquor traffic as the most vital social reform of the age, ASL leaders either ignored other social problems or insisted that their cause must take precedence.

The mechanics of interest-group pressure reinforced the demands of ideology. In order to influence the general assembly, the Illinois League concentrated its resources on a single issue and judged legislators by that simple standard. Composed of the loose church federation, a highly motivated leadership cadre, and a streamlined legislative program, the dry machine was both more influential and narrower in interest than the sum of its parts.

Gifted with organizational skill and political acumen, the leaders of the Anti-Saloon League of Illinois nevertheless failed to appreciate the limited appeal of their creed. They considered their movement a great engine of the public interest, and scornfully rebuked opponents as defenders of a corrupt, socially destructive status quo. Few of the church federation voters—however critical they might have been of saloons, immigrants, and "Chicago politics"—shared in the unrelenting harshness of that judgment. Enactment of local option in 1907 satisfied enough of them to deflate the further effectiveness of ASL campaigns. Promises of fair treatment from politicians, such as the one Frank Lowden eventually issued in 1916, smoothed the ruffled feathers of partisan anti-saloonists and kept them among the party faithful. The saloon problem continued to trouble many Illinois voters after 1907, but not so exclusively as to blot out partisan loyalties or divert attention from other public concerns. By the 1920s, the Illinois League was grimly hanging on, losing the battle for hearts and minds. In the twentieth century, interest groups found that they could influence laws, but they could not govern.

9. Chicago Working Women's Struggle for a Shorter Day, 1908–1911

SUELLEN HOY

> If Agnes Nestor and her fellow workers had not been on the job continuously, forcing the men to do what they had promised . . . daily and hourly watching every turn of that bill, we would have been defeated long ago.
>
> —Margaret Dreier Robins, President, Chicago Women's Trade Union League, June 2, 1909[1]

IN 1909, FOUR WORKING WOMEN from Chicago attracted widespread notice for their success in securing passage of a law that made ten hours the maximum legal working day for a large number of Illinois women. The four who led the effort, according to the local press, not only "ran a legislature" but also "put the lobby of the Illinois Manufacturers' Association to rout." These "girls," representing their unions of glove makers, laundresses, and waitresses, were active members of the Chicago Women's Trade Union League (CWTUL) and committed to improving in essential ways the lives of women workers. Although young (in their late twenties and thirties), all four—Agnes Nestor, Elizabeth Maloney, Anna Willard, and Lulu M. Holley—were earnest, determined, and tenacious. They bore little resemblance to the anarchists involved in the 1886

SUELLEN HOY is guest professor of history at University of Notre Dame. Her current research focuses on the social and political activism of members of the Chicago Women's Trade Union League. Hoy's most recent publications are *Ellen Gates Starr: Her Later Years* (2010); "The Irish Girls' Rising: Building the Women's Labor Movement in Progressive-Era Chicago," *Labor* 9 (Spring 2012), 77–100; and "Sideline Suffragists [women trade unionists and the ballot]," *Chicago History* 39 (Summer 2013), 4–27.

1. Margaret Dreier Robins to Irene Osgood, June 2, 1909, Margaret Dreier Robins [MDR] Papers, Reel 21 (microfilm ed., National Women's Trade Union League [hereafter NWTUL] Papers), Chicago History Museum [hereafter CHM].

Journal of the Illinois State Historical Society Vol. 107, No. 1 (Spring 2014): 9–44

Four Girl Lobbyists Who Ran a Legislature

Agnes Nestor

Lulu Holley

Anna Willard

Elizabeth Maloney

THE CHICAGO SUNDAY TRIBUNE.

"*Four Girls Who Ran A Legislature.*" Chicago Tribune, *July 25, 1909*

Haymarket bombing, which for decades had made it possible—even patriotic—to "denounce all those connected with a demand for shorter hours." But their class consciousness and their experience as industrial workers set them apart from middle-class reformers. A Chicago contemporary described the trade unionists as "industrial feminists." Practical activists, they wanted shorter hours, higher wages, and safer working conditions: in short, a fuller and more secure life.[2]

The "girl" lobbyists achieved a significant, although incomplete, victory in 1909. They failed to obtain the eight-hour law they sought, and the new ten-hour law covered only those employed in factories, laundries, or mechanical establishments—women who worked in a gendered ghetto of unskilled, low-paying, dead-end jobs. Waitresses, who had helped spearhead the legislative effort, were not included. But, two years later, Maloney and Willard, officers of the Chicago Waitresses' Union (Local 484), returned to Springfield as part of Nestor's advance guard to broaden the scope of the law to cover workers like themselves and to limit a full workweek to fifty-four hours. Once again in 1911, their victory was only partial. To win protection for nearly all the state's women workers, they sacrificed the fifty-four-hour restriction. And so it would remain for over a quarter of a century. Not until 1937 did the Illinois state legislature pass an eight-hour-day law.[3]

The efforts of these trade unionists to obtain an eight-hour day have received scant attention from historians of labor or women. The success of thousands of male skilled workers in securing the eight-hour day for themselves "through organization and combination" during the 1890s seems to have rendered the fewer, less skilled female workers invisible. Yet they—regularly referred to as "girls" since most were young, unmarried, and first- or second-generation immigrants—were

---

2. Quoted in *Chicago Tribune*, July 25, 1909; *Chicago Record-Herald*, February 13, 1911; and Josephine Goldmark, *Impatient Crusader: Florence Kelley's Life Story* (Urbana: University of Illinois Press, 1953), 28. The first use of the phrase "new industrial feminism" appeared in Mildred Moore, "A History of the Women's Trade Union League of Chicago" (M.A. thesis, University of Chicago, 1915), 3; organization, education, and legislation (including the ballot) were the industrial feminists' tools (see Moore, 17). See also Diane Kirkby, "'The Wage-Earning Woman and the State': The National Women's Trade Union League and Protective Labor Legislation, 1903–1923," *Labor History* 28 (Winter 1987), 65; and Annelise Orleck, *Common Sense and a Little Fire: Women and Working-Class Politics in the United States, 1900–1965* (Chapel Hill: University of North Carolina Press, 1995), 6.

3. Alice Henry, "The Campaign in Illinois for the Ten-Hour Law," *American Federationist* 17 (August 1910), 671; *Chicago Tribune*, March 21, 1909; and *Chicago Record-Herald*, February 13, 1911. On the law's partial success, see Joseph L. Candela, Jr., "The Struggle to Limit the Hours and Raise the Wages of Working Women in Illinois, 1893–1917," *Social Service Review* 53 (March 1979), 23.

among the least powerful in the labor market. They continued to toil long, arduous days of between twelve and fourteen hours. As late as 1908 and 1909, in candy factories, a six-day-week was the rule and, during the busiest seasons, many women worked eighty or ninety hours a week. The same hourly practices governed other jobs in laundries, restaurants and hotels, factories, elevated roads, and department stores. And the attitude of employers was frequently contemptuous—like that of Clarence A. Knight, president of the Oak Park Elevated Road, who boasted that "we give our girls no vacations . . . [and] if the hours of their labor are shortened they are likely to get a permanent vacation."[4]

Knight's callousness regarding women workers was not unusual. It was remarkably similar, in fact, to the general attitude of the Illinois Manufacturers' Association, which since its founding in the 1890s had successfully blocked a series of progressive labor reforms. While claiming that he was "for women," the association's secretary, John M. Glenn, stated that his members stood firmly against any legislation "restricting the privilege of women to sell their labor." Illinois manufacturers did not intend to overwork women or "grind them down," he insisted; they simply wanted their female employees available for "overtime" when there was work to do. Comments like these did not surprise the four trade unionists advocating the eight-hour day in Springfield. Although looked upon as "girls," they were not inexperienced in dealing with the demands of employers who favored "a law with no limit on hours." They knew what they were up against in the Illinois Manufacturers' Association. What proved equally troublesome were the sometimes confusing and often capricious workings of the state legislature. After nine exhausting weeks of lobbying at the capitol, Nestor and her colleagues came to understand that there were "more ways of killing a bill than by defeating it on a roll call."[5]

Although it had been an enormous challenge for the trade unionists who led the fight and the women who supported it, all agreed that the new law provided "a necessary step toward the eight-hour day." Almost immediately, it improved the daily lives of thousands of wage-earning women in Illinois. Nestor, who exhibited "a rare capacity" for lobbying, stood out as an able leader of women workers; and the CWTUL demonstrated that it could be an effective partner in the local labor movement. What follows weaves together these symbiotic elements in the history of working-class women's political activism: the winning of the ten-hour

4. Quoted in *Chicago Record-Herald*, February 27 and June 29, 1911.

5. Earl R. Beckner, *A History of Labor Legislation in Illinois* (Chicago: University of Chicago Press, 1929), 188–89; quoted in *Chicago Record-Herald*, February 23, 1911; *Chicago Tribune*, May 20, 1913; and "The Girls Who Did the Work," *The Eight Hour Fight in Illinois* (1909), NWTUL Publications, Reel 9 (microfilm ed.), 14.

day in Illinois and the prominence of Nestor and the CWTUL in the trade union movement.[6]

AN EIGHT-HOUR DAY

The United States Supreme Court's ruling in the *Muller* v. *Oregon* case in February 1908 triggered the onset of a vigorous campaign in Illinois for the eight-hour day. The court upheld Oregon's constitutional right to limit the workday for women to ten hours. Weeks after learning of the *Muller* decision, members of the Chicago Waitresses' Union, which had already secured a ten-hour day through negotiation, instigated discussions among CWTUL members on how they might win an eight-hour day. Most of the trade unionists were too young to have experienced a brief period from 1893 into 1895 when Illinois women had worked only eight hours under a new law. Yet, through their Hull-House acquaintances, few of them were unaware of it and thus were eager to try again. Early on, CWTUL manifested its support for such protective legislation, and unionists were among the most enthusiastic.[7]

Agnes Nestor and Elizabeth Maloney, recognized for having organized Chicago's glove makers and waitresses, understood the need for organization. But they were also practical and readily recognized the advantages of legislation. State laws for shorter days, safer job sites, or better wages would improve the working conditions and lives of large numbers of women, most of whom lacked the organizational strength to negotiate with their employers. In 1907, the CWTUL cooperated with the Chicago Federation of Labor in sponsoring a conference and an industrial exhibit that generated "widespread interest among unionists and the general public." At its end, both groups urged adoption of industrial legislation for women, especially an eight-hour day. Then, in winter 1908, the Supreme Court's Oregon ruling "put new heart" in CWTUL members, prompting them to consider actions to shorten their workdays. That spring, its Legislative Committee organized two more conferences (one for sympathetic

6. "The Girls," *Eight Hour Fight*, 16; Beckner, *History of Labor Legislation*, 194–95, 206; Mary E. McDowell, "The Girls' Bill: A Human Proposition," *Survey* 22 (July 3, 1909), 510; and Susan E. Hirsch, "Nestor, Agnes," in *Women Building Chicago: A Biographical Dictionary*, ed. Rima Lunin Schultz and Adele Hast (Bloomington, IN: Indiana University Press, 2001), 623–26. The CWTUL was also effective during the 1910 garment workers' strike.

7. "The Girls," *Eight Hour Fight*, 3–4; Olive Sullivan to Mary Dreier, March 9, 1908, MDR Papers, Reel 20; S. M. Franklin, "Elizabeth Maloney and the High Calling of the Waitress," *Life and Labor* 3 (February 1913), 36; and Kirkby, "'The Wage-Earning Woman and the State,'" 56. As Kirkby pointed out, unlike the New York branch of the WTUL, the Chicago organization "turned to legislation long before 1913."

members of local women's clubs and another for trade unionists) to build support for new labor laws.[8]

In the face of this enthusiasm, John R. Commons, the University of Wisconsin economist and secretary of the American Association for Labor Legislation, feared that CWTUL members were overreaching and urged caution. Illinois was in a "peculiar" situation, he instructed. In 1895, the state's Supreme Court had overturned the eight-hour law enacted in 1893. It had been drafted by Florence Kelley (then living at Hull-House) and supported by Chicago's leading women reformers, including Jane Addams, Ellen Gates Starr, and members of the short-lived Illinois Woman's Alliance. City and state labor leaders had backed the legislation as well as women unionists, who would directly benefit from the law. Most notable among them was Mary Kenney, a bookbinder and labor organizer also residing at Hull-House. When the bill passed in May 1893, Kelley became Illinois' chief factory inspector and Kenney one of her assistants.[9]

Women and girls who typically spent six days every week and most of their waking hours in poorly paid industrial jobs realized that they were being shortchanged wages as well as a decent life. What Kelley's factory inspections had discovered in Chicago's sweatshops in the 1890s remained unaltered fifteen years later for a majority of female employees. Even those few who feared shorter hours because of the threat of reduced earnings would not have disputed the common belief that their lives felt like a living death. Since most of them were "unfit for almost anything else" at the end of the day, bookbinder Mary McEnerney said there was hardly "a girl who wouldn't rather have the extra time than the extra money." But in March 1895, the Illinois Supreme Court sided with W. C. Ritchie and Company, a paper box manufacturer in Chicago, and unanimously rejected what the majority of the state's women workers preferred.[10]

---

8. On the industrial exhibit and conference, see *The Women's Trade Union League of Illinois* (1908), NWTUL Publications, Reel 9, 10–11; and Agnes Nestor, *Woman's Labor Leader: An Autobiography of Agnes Nestor* (Rockford, IL: Bellevue Books Publishing Co., 1954), 88–90. See also "The Industrial Conference: An Eight Hour Programme," *Union Labor Advocate* 8 (June 1908), 15; "The Eight-Hour Day," (July 1908), 23; and Robin Miller Jacoby, *The British and American Women's Trade Union Leagues, 1890–1925: A Case Study of Feminism and Class* (Brooklyn: Carlson Publishing, 1994), 122.

9. J. R. Commons to Margaret D. Robins, April 8, 1908, MDR Papers, Reel 20. For a full discussion of the 1893 eight-hour-day legislative campaign, see Kathryn Kish Sklar, *Florence Kelley & the Nation's Work: The Rise of Women's Political Culture, 1830–1900* (New Haven: Yale University Press, 1995), 234–39, 255–63, and 280–85. On the Illinois Woman's Alliance, see Meredith Tax, *The Rising of the Women: Feminist Solidarity and Class Conflict, 1880–1917* (New York: Monthly Review Press, 1980), 86–87.

10. Quoted in *Chicago Tribune*, September 26, 1908 and May 31, 1909. See also Beckner, *History of Labor Legislation*, 189.

Although wage-earning women found protection in the eight-hour law, the Illinois Supreme Court judged it discriminatory. In *Ritchie* v. *People*, the court took a familiar, unprogressive position very much in accord with the laissez-faire philosophy of the times. Rather than protecting citizens, the judges chose to uphold their celebrated but spurious freedom of contract, ruling that the eight-hour law restricted a citizen's basic right "to control his or her own time." Deciding to support Illinois' employers over workers, the judges insinuated that working women and girls were at liberty to choose their schedules or had freely agreed to toil twelve or fourteen hours each day.[11]

Despite the court's decided lack of understanding or interest in their plight, female workers accelerated their organizing during the late 1890s to secure what protections they could. By 1904, over 35,000 of them had joined unions (most in locals composed entirely of women), which made Chicago one of the best organized cities for working women. While the manners and methods of their leaders differed, they generally displayed "executive ability, endurance, and self-control." John Fitzpatrick, president of the Chicago Federation of Labor, had dealings with them and remarked that they were "on the square, and dead game, too." In addition to local labor's backing, female trade unionists were welcomed in the city's leading settlement houses (Hull-House on the West Side and the University of Chicago Settlement near the stockyards on the South Side), where they regularly held meetings.[12]

In November 1903, at the annual meeting of the American Federation of Labor in Boston, a group of delegates and settlement workers established the national Women's Trade Union League (WTUL). It was unique as the first national body committed to organizing women workers and cooperating with them as allies. In some ways, it resembled the defunct Illinois Woman's Alliance of the early 1890s, but WTUL's goals—similar to those of a British organization of the same name—were broader in scope. Since it proposed to assist the nation's working women in forming trade unions, the league's executive board clearly recognized the urgent need to involve actual workers in its leadership as well as in its ranks. Hence the board decided to create branches in Boston, New York, and Chicago, where large numbers of women worked in factories and where the settlement movement was strong. Addams and Mary McDowell of the University Settlement, both WTUL board members, wasted little time in establishing a Chicago branch. In January 1904, twenty-five individuals assembled at Hull-House for

11. Ibid, 189. Quoted in 90. Like employers, the judges' ideal was "an unregulated market." Candela, "Struggle to Limit the Hours," 24.

12. Quoted in *Chicago Tribune*, February 21, 1904; Tax, *Rising of the Women*, 91; and Eleanor Flexner, *Century of Struggle: The Woman's Rights Movement in the United States* (Cambridge: Harvard University Press, 1996 [1959]), 204–5.

the inaugural meeting, where they elected McDowell as president and a trade unionist from the stockyards, Maud Sutter, as vice president. During the following months, the branch met informally either at Hull-House or the University Settlement.[13]

In September 1904, at the end of a disappointing stockyard strike that had for weeks involved Chicago's labor leaders and social reformers, Addams and McDowell hosted a reception at Hull-House for the city's female workers. Its purpose was twofold: to honor members of the stockyards' first women's union who had actively participated in the recent strike; and to explain WTUL's objectives in the hope of recruiting a corps of dedicated unionists to the Chicago branch. Among those in attendance was Agnes Nestor, a young glove maker of Irish-Catholic parentage from the North Side. "Quiet & shy as a little mouse," she was just over five feet tall, slightly built, and appeared much younger than her twenty-four years. Had she not been invited "to say something" at the reception, she would likely have gone unnoticed. Years later, she recalled that occasion and how anxious she had been, having had to speak publicly in the presence of McDowell, Addams, and Starr. But "we liked them tremendously," she wrote. Before leaving, she and her union friends eagerly applied for membership.[14]

In many respects, Nestor was quite ordinary. Like large numbers of other working-class girls, she had left school after eighth grade to work. She got a job at the Eisendrath Glove Company at Elston and Armitage, not far from where she lived with her parents and siblings. As revealed in a diary she kept in 1900, Nestor enjoyed her friends and family, especially her sister, with whom she liked to shop, see plays downtown, and attend church. She also read newspapers, particularly coverage of local strikes and layoffs, and admitted to having

---

13. See Philip S. Foner, *Women and the American Labor Movement: From the First Trade Unions to the Present* (New York: Free Press, 1982), 128–31; Ellen Lindstrom, "National Women's Trade Union League," *Union Labor Advocate* 5 (February 6, 1904), 28; and Alice Henry, "Service Is Their Watchword," *Life and Labor* 11 (July 1921), 206. Henry mistakenly referred to the Illinois Woman's Alliance as the Women's Protective Union. See also *Chicago Tribune*, January 5, 1904; and Agnes Nestor, "Women Workers Marching On," *Life and Labor* 11 (June 1921), 1. For more on CWTUL's origins, see Suellen Hoy, "The Irish Girls' Rising: Building the Women's Labor Movement in Progressive-Era Chicago," *Labor* 9 (Spring 2012), 77–100.

14. Anna Nicholes, "Reception Tendered to Union Girls," *Union Labor Advocate* 5 (November 1904), 25–26; quoted in Margaret D. Robins to Mary Dreier, July 23, 1907, MDR Papers, Reel 20; and quoted in Nestor, *Woman's Labor Leader*, 64. I have also relied on three biographical essays of Agnes Nestor in narrating her early life: Hirsch, "Nestor," in *Women Building Chicago*, 623–26; David Brody, "Nestor, Agnes," in *Dictionary of American Biography, 1946–1950* (Supplement Four), ed. John A. Garraty and Edward T. James (New York: Charles Scribner's Sons, 1974), 625–27; and Clarke A. Chambers, "Nestor, Agnes," in *Notable American Women: A Biographical Dictionary*, ed. Edward T. James, Janet Wilson James, and Paul S. Boyer, no. 3 (Cambridge MA: Harvard University Press, 1971), 615–17.

become something of a "hero-worshipper" of a young organizer, Sophie Becker, a member of the Boot and Shoe Makers' Union and a delegate to the Chicago Federation of Labor's Organization Committee.[15]

Never in robust health, Nestor found piecework exhausting. She complained often of being so tired that "she could hardly work." She was routinely frustrated that on some days there was not enough to do but on many others too much. Then she and her co-workers labored long hours—"like rats in a trap"—while forced to pay for the power that ran their machines as well as for broken needles and oil. The oil was expensive, and machine operators were required "to go to certain out-of-the-way places to obtain it." In 1898, at the age of eighteen, she led a strike of fed-up female employees. After ten days, they won their demands and subsequently formed a union separate from the men's. In 1902, Nestor's co-workers chose her for president. That year, she went as a delegate to the founding convention of the International Glove Workers' Union of America (IGWU) in Washington, D.C.; and the year after, she became a national vice president and member of its executive board. Having learned the principles of trade unionism from her father, an ardent unionist and also a practiced parliamentarian, she held her own and spoke competently and convincingly on issues important to glove workers.[16]

Nestor's physical appearance belied her natural ability. As one of only a few women who were national leaders of a trade union, her life had begun to change. In 1906, it was altered permanently. After nine years as a glove maker, she was elected to a salaried position as the IGWU's secretary-treasurer and never returned to Eisendrath's. In 1908, following a meeting between employers and several IGWU members, a lawyer who had been present found Nestor impressive, having "a mind like a trip-hammer." (He also commented that, although she looked "just American," she was "Irish all the way through.") By then, Nestor had been involved in the CWTUL for four years and was a member of its national board. She was also supplementing her earnings as an IGWU official by working

15. Nestor was born on June 24, 1880 in Grand Rapids, Michigan, where she attended both parochial and public schools until the eighth grade. See the biographical essays cited above; Nestor, *Woman's Labor Leader*, 3–26; and entries in Agnes Nestor's handwritten diary, June 1900–June 1901. A copy is in the Agnes Nestor Papers, Box 1, Folder 1, CHM. On Sophie Becker, see *Chicago Tribune*, August 6, 1901; Dorothy Richardson, "Trades-Unions in Petticoats," *Leslie's Monthly Magazine* 57 (March 1904), 493; and Nestor, *Woman's Labor Leader*, 34.

16. Nestor's old glove-making friend, Israel Solon, remembered them as "rats" in a letter to her, August 18, 1931, Nestor Papers, Reel 3. Quoted in Agnes Nestor, entry dated June 24, 1900, and May 23, 1901. See also Nestor, *Woman's Labor Leader*, 27–44. Quoted in 29, 42–44. Nestor recalled, "long talks about labor problems" (44) with her father, a former member of the Knights of Labor, and an "excellent parliamentarian" (42).

as a CWTUL organizer. She had found her calling and, as it would turn out, something more—a career as a professional trade-union leader.[17]

Before leaving Eisendrath's, however, Nestor was merely one of several hundred thousand women workers in Illinois weighed down with the drudgery and insecurities that accompanied long hours and low pay. Among them were a sizeable number of women (over 30,000 in Chicago by 1910) who lived away from families and were frequently said to be "adrift." Most were migrants who had moved from the country to the city in search of better-paying jobs and found lodging with women like themselves. Others continued to live at home and bore the double burden of unskilled industrial work and routine domestic chores. One such factory worker who kept house for her father and brothers remarked: "they don't work any harder than I do, but when I get home, I've got to do housework."[18]

For all of them, a shorter working day held the promise of a fuller life—"time to see and learn things." Maloney, who was Nestor's age and whose Irish-Catholic parents also depended on her wages, knew firsthand the frustration of not being able to enjoy "the store of beauty, of books and pictures and music that this world contains." Impatient for an "eight-hour day" and a "living wage," which were both emblazoned on the league's emblem, Maloney, Nestor, and their unionized co-workers recoiled at Commons' cautionary advice to seek "the simple ten-hour day" first. He believed, as he told Margaret Dreier Robins, CWTUL president, that the chance of success would be greater. He insisted that "the essential thing" in Illinois was to establish the principle that "the legislature has the power under the constitution to regulate the hours of women workers."[19]

Had Robins not been committed to creating a democratic organization that reflected the desires of those it represented, she might have taken Commons' advice and overruled the trade unionists. But that was not generally her manner,

---

17. On Nestor, see William Hard and Rheta Childe Dorr, "The Woman's Invasion," *Everybody's Magazine* XIX (November 1908), 805. Nestor said she consulted her father about her future when she was "old enough to think of settling on a career." See Nestor, *Woman's Labor Leader*, 43. See also Tax, *Rising of the Women*, 121–22, on careers for women in the labor movement, which became possible because of the WTUL.

18. See Joanne J. Meyerowitz, *Women Adrift: Independent Wage Earners in Chicago, 1880–1930* (Chicago: University of Chicago Press, 1988), 1–20, 75–83. Quoted in Consumers' League, *The Forty Eight Hour Law: Do Working Women Want It?* (New York: Consumers' League, 1927), 34.

19. Elizabeth Maloney, "Chicago Waitresses' Union Local 484," *Life and Labor* 1 (November 1911), 1; and Commons to Robins, April 8, 1908. See League's emblem, adapted to Chicago, in "The Women's Trade Union League of Chicago, 1908–1909" (1910), NWTUL Publications, Reel 9.

even though it was her family's fortune that underwrote most of the league's initiatives and programs. Convinced that WTUL's future depended on the leadership of able rank-and-file members, Robins placed her "bets on the girls." She knew unorganized workers would not be "led from the outside" but by other women workers informed on labor issues, trained in organizational practices, and capable of handling large problems. None of CWTUL's founders disputed this goal, but the ways of reaching it were far from clear.[20]

After succeeding McDowell as CWTUL president in January 1907, Robins also became president of the national league, now headquartered in Chicago under her leadership. She continued the practice of holding monthly meetings on Sunday afternoons in Bowen Hall at Hull-House. By year's end, however, she was eager to position the CWTUL more centrally within the city's labor movement. In November, she wrote to her sister, Mary Dreier, that she was "very quietly" orchestrating a move from Hull-House to Federation Hall on La Salle Street, where the Chicago Federation of Labor held its monthly meetings and the league had office space. On February 9, 1908, when members voted on the proposed move, Robins was not disappointed in the results: 51–20 in favor. From then on, CWTUL meetings were held in "a place closer to the heart of unionism"—despite protests from "the conservative element," some of whom Robins was aware considered her "a disturber of the peace" and "a most unfortunate troublemaker."[21]

---

20. Margaret D. Robins' father, Theodor Dreier, a German immigrant who became partner in the New York branch of an English iron firm, left Robins a substantial inheritance when he died in 1898. See Elizabeth Anne Payne, *Reform, Labor, and Feminism: Margaret Dreier Robins and the Women's Trade Union League* (Urbana: University of Illinois Press, 1988), 8, 14, 58, 70. Quoted in Margaret D. Robins to Raymond Robins, April 15, 1918; and Margaret D. Robins to Mrs. Shaw, July 1920, MDR Papers, Reels 55 and 26.

21. Margaret D. Robins to Mary Dreier, Nov. 4, 1907 and Februrary 19, 1908, MDR Papers, Reel 20. For more on CWTUL's move from Hull-House, see Payne, *Reform, Labor, and Feminism*, 61–69. Three newspapers (the *Chicago Examiner*, *Chicago Record-Herald*, and *Chicago Tribune*) carried accounts of the incident on February 10, 1908. All the trade unionists and Robins—plus two "allies," Corinne Brown and Alice Post—voted to move to Federation Hall. McDowell was present; Addams was not. In May 1907, shortly after becoming president, Robins led some 4,000 workers in a Chicago parade on behalf of Charles Moyer and Big Bill Haywood of the Western Federation of Miners, who had been accused (falsely, it would turn out) of murder. She was outraged by the violation of their civil liberties and also wanted to show her loyalty to organized labor. Many of CWTUL's middle-class allies (i.e. Addams, Louise de Koven Bowen, Ellen Henrotin, and others) were opposed to this "radical" action, even though "the working girls expressed themselves frankly and unanimously in favor." After the parade, the Chicago Woman's Club blackballed Robins; for her part, Robins continued to view these women as "conservative." See, for example, two letters: Margaret D. Robins to Louise Bowen, May 20, 1907, and to Mary Dreier, May 22, 1907, MDR Papers, Reel 20. See also Payne, *Reform, Labor, and Feminism*, 77–78.

Most of Chicago's "allies"—the name given to the league's middle-class members, many of them settlement house residents and their "conservative" friends—regarded the WTUL as an extension of the labor movement within the woman's movement. Robins held the opposite view, arguing that the WTUL represented "the woman's movement within the labor movement." And trade union members, who saw themselves as women and workers, tended to agree. Thus, once the spirited discussion over the move from Hull-House had ended and the votes were tallied, Nestor's comments to the press reflected that tension but were not surprising. Pleased with the result, she said that Federation Hall "suit[ed]" her, even though the "surroundings are more beautiful" in Bowen Hall. She also remarked that "the Halsted Street car service is awful"—a point of some consequence to workers.[22]

The CWTUL's relocation to Federation Hall, according to Robins' biographer, "gave the trade unionists a greater sense of involvement and solidarity with the labor movement." It also made Robins "a leading figure in Chicago labor circles." Seven months later, in September 1908, she was elected to the Chicago Federation of Labor's executive board—a unique achievement for a woman and one of her class. But Robins recognized that her financial independence was a "stronghold," which enabled her to act boldly in support of labor reform. Thus, in conversations on whether or not "to quit Hull House," she had not been dissuaded when warned that "a few of Miss Addams' friends" might discontinue their donations to the league.[23]

During the spring and summer of 1908, as CWTUL members engaged in informal and formal discussions about legislative action, the allies and trade unionists alike appeared willing, even eager, to shift their focus. Rather than organizing unions, they would direct their attention and resources to securing an hours' law that would cover all of Illinois' wage-earning women. In upholding Oregon's right to restrict working hours for women, the Supreme Court had provided CWTUL members with a genuine opportunity, and they were determined to act. But would they seek Commons' "simple ten-hour day" or the long-sought eight-hour day? Some like Anna Nicholes, first secretary of CWTUL and resident of Neighborhood House Settlement in the Englewood neighborhood, agreed with Commons and favored the former. The unionists

---

22. Payne, *Reform, Labor, and Feminism*, 61; Robins to Shaw, July 1920; and *Chicago Tribune*, February 10, 1908. Nestor explained that "whenever she asked girls to join the league they objected to meeting at Hull House because of the Halsted street car service." See *Chicago Examiner*, February 10, 1908. Hull-House was located at Polk and Halsted streets, more than a mile south and west of the downtown business district.

23. Payne, *Reform, Labor, and Feminism*, 69. Payne stated that Robins was "the only middle-class woman to be so honored by a city labor federation." On Robins' election, see *Chicago Tribune*, September 21, 1908. See also Robins to Dreier, February 19, 1908, MDR Papers.

generally preferred the latter but were ambivalent, fearing the possibility of failing altogether and securing neither. By fall 1908, however, they had become more resolute.[24]

Robins' opening remarks to the delegates at the league's interstate conference in Chicago that September reflected this resolve. She stressed the necessity of an eight-hour day, stating that working women's "health and happiness" depended on it and underscoring its importance to "the home, the family, and all future generations." The next day, a large audience of some 500 trade unionists met in the Central YMCA Auditorium and initiated a "talking campaign" for a shorter day; their weapon, as the *Chicago Tribune* reported, was "a feminine verbal flood." McDowell, CWTUL vice president and a veteran of legislative campaigns in Illinois, urged them to talk "until legislators become so tired they will be forced to grant the demand from sheer exhaustion." On Sunday morning, the last day of the conference, religious services were held in two downtown churches. At St. Mary's Catholic Church, Reverend P. J. O'Callaghan, parish pastor and superior of the Paulists, delivered what Robins (not a Catholic) described as "one of the greatest labor addresses." He was warm in his welcome and respectful of what the trade unionists hoped to do: "get justice from the strong arm of capital." Instead of encouraging caution, he pressed them to "join hands" and "say to those that are making money out of blood . . . that every one laboring to create the great properties of commerce should have a share in the millions that are earned."[25]

Maloney, a fervent Catholic, was likely encouraged by Father O'Callaghan's words. She and Anna Willard, officers of the Waitresses' Local 484, had grown impatient with the ongoing deliberations and wanted action. Thus, early in 1909, they struck out on their own. They drafted an eight-hour version of the Oregon law, traveled to Springfield, and in their union's name placed it with "one of the least influential and most irresponsible members of the house," Nestor recalled. There it languished. Later in March, Robins was convinced that she had broad

---

24. "The Girls," *Eight Hour Fight*, 3–4; McDowell, "The Girls' Bill," 509–10; Steven M. Buechler, *The Transformation of the Woman Suffrage Movement: The Case of Illinois, 1850–1920* (New Brunswick, NJ: Rutgers University Press, 1986), 160; Sullivan to Dreier, March 9, 1908; Commons to Robins, April 8, 1908; "The Industrial Conference: An Eight Hour Programme," 15; and "The Eight Hour Day," 23.

25. The Episcopal Cathedral of St. Peter and St. Paul was the site of the other service. Quoted in *Chicago Tribune*, September 26 and 27, 1908; "Convention of the National Women's Trade Union League: The Chicago Conference"; Margaret D. Robins to Raymond Robins, September 28, 1908, MDR Papers, Reel 52; and "Sermon by Father O'Callaghan," *Union Labor Advocate* 8 (December 1908), 32 and 47. Both Robinses were Protestant and committed to the Social Gospel, as was Mary McDowell.

support for eight hours and asked the league's attorney, Harold L. Ickes, to draft a bill. She then stepped back and allowed "the girls" to take the lead.[26]

On March 30, 1909, Senator W. Clyde Jones of Illinois' Fifth District (in Chicago), whom Ickes had interested in the eight-hour bill, introduced it in the state legislature. The bill was promptly referred to the Committee on Labor, Mines, and Mining and given the number 343. Soon afterwards legislators christened Senate Bill No. 343 "the girls' bill," a name that endured throughout the session. It stipulated that "no female should be employed in any manufacturing, mercantile, or mechanical establishment, laundry, hotel, or restaurant in the state more than eight hours during any day of twenty-four hours, nor more than forty-eight hours in any one week of six calendar days."[27]

SETTING LIMITS

The legislative campaign in Springfield began in earnest with the bill's introduction on March 30 and lasted until the end of May 1909. The trade unionists, committed to nothing short of eight hours, knew they faced a difficult challenge and resolved to be present in some fashion at every hearing or conference at which the bill was discussed. Within a week, "the girls' bill" had its first hearing and was reported out favorably. What began in a relatively simple and straightforward manner, however, quickly became far more complicated and menacing when the Illinois Manufacturers' Association (IMA) finally took notice. Despite the publicity given the first hearing, it had escaped the IMA's attention. But, when a second hearing appeared on the senate's calendar, IMA Secretary John M. Glenn issued a call to arms to defeat an "unfair measure" that would "work an injustice to all ambitious females."[28]

Glenn had become the IMA's first permanent secretary in 1898 and remained in that position until his death in 1928. Under his leadership, the association's membership grew from less than a hundred firms to nearly 3,000. He was an

26. Maloney was known for her devotion to the Madonna. See Franklin, "Elizabeth Maloney," 37. Elizabeth Maloney, "Towards the Eight-Hour Day," *Life and Labor*, 1 (November 1911), 1; Nestor, *Woman's Labor Leader*, 91–93; and Harold L. Ickes to Margaret D. Robins, March 19, 1909, MDR Papers, Reel 21. Harold L. Ickes, in 1909, was in the early stage of a long career of progressive advocacy. He would become secretary of the interior under Franklin D. Roosevelt.

27. "The Girls," *Eight Hour Fight*, 4; McDowell, "The Girls' Bill," 510; and Beckner, *History of Labor Legislation*, 190–91.

28. "The Girls," *Eight Hour Fight*, 4. Quoted in John M. Glenn, "An Unfair Measure" [circular], April 17, 1909; and John M. Glenn to William J. Brown, April 17, 1909, both in Illinois Manufacturers' Association Papers, CHM [hereafter IMA Papers]. I am grateful to Christina A. Reynen for directing me to this collection.

energetic organizer and a fervent advocate of manufacturers' interests. He, like them, believed uncompromisingly in the rightness of a laissez-faire economy, viewed all social legislation as unnecessary, despised labor unions, and considered their leaders agitators and troublemakers. He remarked before the Chicago Culture Club in 1915 that "they carry a banner labeled for humanity, but are found in the struggling procession of the mob and the picket." As for settlement houses, Glenn charged that most large ones were "in the hands of talented and able women who [were] misdirecting their efforts and spending most of their time scolding." That union leaders and settlement workers were "supported by a misguided public sentiment" distressed him.[29]

Glenn was "caught napping" when Senate Bill No. 343 had its favorable first hearing and, as Robins delightedly remarked, the trade unionists "actually stole a march on the Illinois Manufacturers' Association." When Glenn awoke, however, he was alarmed and acted promptly, informing IMA members of the situation's seriousness. Describing the bill as "unconstitutional" and "dangerous," he complained that it was "being rushed through the General Assembly" without giving those opposed a chance to be heard. He exhorted members to appear in Springfield on April 14 to demand a rehearing. The trade unionists, aware of what they would face, still believed they could give the manufacturers "a good run for their money." And, as luck would have it, they did.[30]

April 14 proved to be a day of hearings in Springfield. In the early afternoon, before the trade unionists and manufacturers met for an informal rehearing of Senate Bill No. 343, house and senate committees held several scheduled hearings on suffrage bills. To demonstrate support, a delegation of about 200 women had traveled to Springfield on seven special trains the previous day. They were particularly interested in two measures: one that granted women statewide suffrage; and, should it fail, another that gave Chicago women the right to vote in municipal elections. At stops along the way, some in this "army of suffragists," as the press referred to them, addressed local audiences (mostly female), which were eager to see and hear them. Nestor, who spoke in Joliet on the working

29. John M. Glenn's obituary, *Chicago Tribune*, April 23, 1928; Alfred H. Kelly, "History of Illinois Manufacturers' Association," 7, 24, copy in IMA Papers, Box 129, Folder 1; and *Illinois Industries: Remarks of John M. Glenn . . . before the Members of the Chicago Culture Club, Schiller Hall, Chicago, Nov. 15, 1915* [pamphlet], 7, 8, IMA Papers. The IMA followed the National Association of Manufacturers' lead, which after 1902 showed a "new and unfriendly spirit toward organized labor." See Albion Guilford Taylor, *Labor Policies of the National Association of Manufacturers* (Urbana: University of Illinois Press, 1928), 15.

30. Quoted in Margaret D. Robins to Mary Dreier, April 16, 1909, MDR Papers, Reel 21; John M. Glenn, "This Is the Way They Moved," *Legislative Bulletin No. 11* (April 10, 1909), 1–2; John M. Glenn, "An Unconstitutional Bill," *Legislative Bulletin No. 12* (April 17, 1909), 1, both in IMA Papers, Box 199, Folder 6; and Kelly, "History [of IMA]," 13.

woman's need for the ballot, was one of the first to speak; while Addams, who appeared where the crowds were largest (in the smaller towns of Bloomington and Lincoln), was among the last.[31]

The next day, with the suffrage hearings concluded, the Chicago delegation moved to the senate chamber to observe the eight-hour-day hearing and sat (or stood) among the trade unionists who had also traveled to the capitol. The manufacturers continued to insist that they had been denied an opportunity to be heard and asked that Senate Bill No. 343 be recommitted. Senator Jones refused their request. During the hearing, which began late in the afternoon, the manufacturers argued that, if the bill passed, "all present conditions would be upset"—production costs would increase by 20 percent and wages would automatically decline. Addams, when called on, stated that any reduction in wages would not be permanent. In almost every case, she explained, "they soon are adjusted to the new conditions and return to the former scale." In her remarks, Nestor emphasized the toll that long hours took on the health and well-being of working women.[32]

Fearful that they were in danger of losing the legislative fight, some manufacturers appeared willing to support an amended bill limiting women's workday to ten hours. The trade unionists refused to consider such a bill, but they were gratified to have had Addams and Anna Nicholes speak on their bill's behalf. Robins, who had remained in Chicago because of illness, also appreciated their open support. "As they are looked upon as the conservative wing of our group," she told her sister, "it has meant a great deal to have had them publicly declare themselves." And, much to Glenn's dismay, their declarations seemed to have prompted several IMA representatives to alter their positions.[33]

In the weeks that followed, in circulars and letters, Glenn repeatedly maintained that "a compromise would be foolish." He contended that if such a law was "unconstitutional as to eight hours, it is unconstitutional as to nine or ten hours." Three days after the hearing, in an update to members, he quoted E. S. Hobbs of the Aurora Cotton Mills, who had been present in Springfield. Hobbs reported that "there was such a little, small representation of the manufacturers and employers . . . as compared with the delegation of women from 'Hull House' and the woman's [*sic*] trade unions of Chicago, that the Senators said

31. Ella S. Stewart and Catharine W. McCulloch of the Illinois Equal Suffrage Association to Agnes Nestor, April 1909, Agnes Nestor Papers, CHM. Nestor's topic was "The Lack of the Ballot: The Handicap of the Working Girls." See also newspaper coverage in *Inter Ocean*, April 4, 5, 12, 13, 1909; *Chicago Tribune*, April 9 and 15, 1909; and *Chicago Record-Herald*, April 13 and 14, 1909.

32. "The Girls," *Eight Hour Fight*, 4–6; and *Chicago Tribune*, April 15, 1909.

33. Beckner, *History of Labor Legislation*, 191; "The Girls," *Eight Hour Fight*, 6; and *Chicago Tribune*, April 15, 1909. See also Robins to Dreier, April 16, 1909, MDR Papers.

the manufacturers evidently were not enough interested in the bill to come to Springfield to oppose it." Glenn, obviously exasperated, prodded IMA members to attend the next hearing on April 21. He warned that Addams might be present "with 75 or 100 women" from Chicago "willing to spend a little money and time, and put up a big fight, while they who would sustain the loss won't so much as show their faces in Springfield." To avoid possible defeat, he told IMA members that they would have to put forth a large, united effort.[34]

Addams was not in Springfield on April 21, but a contingent of nine unionists were, plus Robins and McDowell, who traveled together from Chicago. They found themselves greatly outnumbered by some 500 manufacturers—many from the Chicago Laundrymen's Association—who packed the senate chamber in opposition to an eight-hour law. During the hearing, three individuals representing each side had an opportunity to speak. Attorneys William D. Haynie, the IMA's general counsel, and Ickes, representing the CWTUL, discussed the bill's constitutionality. Two businessmen, both IMA members, followed and argued that an eight-hour law would prompt some manufacturers to move their businesses out of state, while others would likely replace women workers with men.[35]

When it was Nestor's turn, she stood on a stool so that she could be seen and heard, and then spoke from personal experience. She explained that she had "worked nine years at a machine in a glove factory" where manufacturing was "specialized" and machines "speeded up" until she and her co-workers found it nearly impossible to "keep their health." After three or four years, she continued, "our strength and vitality are gone." In the long run, she insisted, these same employees could "turn out as much work in eight hours as in nine and a half or ten" because they would not be suffering from exhaustion. Maloney used a portion of her time to report that federal investigators had recently gathered statistics on the work of waitresses and concluded that they "walk ten miles in ten hours' work." But for men in skilled trades, she noted, "eight hours a day is enough." With a bit of asperity, she then remarked: "Now you'll have to admit that eight miles a day is about enough for any waitress to walk." At the hearing's end, one senator asked if a compromise might be possible. Neither side was willing.[36]

Following the eight-hour bill's introduction in late March, at least two or three CWTUL members were present in Springfield on each legislative day. They were compensated for their expenses (largely railroad fares and meals) and received

---

34. Glenn, "An Unconstitutional Bill," 2.

35. John M. Glenn to IMA Members, "An Unfair Measure," April 17, 1909, IMA Papers. After passing a resolution denouncing the Jones bill, the Chicago Laundrymen's Association organized a committee to go to Springfield on April 21. See also *Chicago Tribune*, April 20, 1909; *Chicago Record-Herald*, April 21, 1909; and "The Girls," *Eight Hour Fight*, 6.

36. Nestor and Maloney, quoted in *Chicago Record-Herald*, April 21, 1909; and *Chicago Tribune*, April 22, 1909. See also McDowell, "The Girls' Bill," 512.

a per diem fee of three dollars. At night, they stayed in the home of sympathetic allies, Mr. and Mrs. George Lee, and returned to Chicago on weekends. During the day, the unionists spent their time at the capitol canvassing senate and house members, while overseeing a volatile situation that changed with little or no notice. After a few weeks, Nestor and Maloney were familiar faces to doorkeepers, pages, and legislators; and newspaper coverage of "the girls' bill" had created an unusual amount of interest in Chicago and other parts of the state. It was unprecedented that a small group of young women workers would take the lead in lobbying for a bill, especially in the face of such "fierce opposition."[37]

Glenn, now in full battle gear, was not pleased with the April 21 hearing. Three days later, he sent IMA members a "legislative bulletin" explaining how unfairly they had been treated. Since their representatives had been given less than an hour to speak, he proposed "a full hearing before the Committee" with no talk of compromises. He urged as many members as possible to return to Springfield the following week and "maintain a solid front." He also wrote directly to the Liquor Dealers Association, warning of the danger before them: "if the bill is enacted into a law no woman can sell her services to exceed eight hours a day." Whom to blame? Glenn had a ready answer. The bill was promoted by "certain social settlement people in Chicago and union labor agitators." Thus, when Nestor, Maloney, and Willard arrived in Springfield on April 27, they were startled to see and hear several hundred manufacturers, all claiming that they had been denied sufficient time to make clear how the proposed law would interfere with their businesses. When they requested a rehearing, the senate, acting as a committee of the whole, acceded to their demand.[38]

Once under way, the hearing soon focused on the origins of the petitions stacked before the senators. S. H. Shoninger, president of the Chicago Garment

---

37. On the worker-lobbyists' uniqueness, see Jacoby, *The British and American Women's Trade Union Leagues*, 123. Nestor was present during the entire nine weeks, and Maloney for most of them. Other unionists went to Springfield when they could (Willard and Holley) or when asked (Mary McEnerney, Elisabeth Christman, Anna Hurley, Mae Nihil, Emma Steghagen, Stella Franklin, and Lena Buchweitz). See Margaret D. Robins to Irene Osgood, June 2, 1909, MDR Papers, Reel 21. This pattern would be repeated in 1911, for which there are receipts of expenditures. See "Receipted Legislative Bills, Agnes & Elizabeth Maloney," February 22–May 20, 1911, Agnes Nestor Papers (microfilm ed., NWTUL Papers), Reel 1. On the Lees, see Agnes Nestor, "Mrs. George E. Lee: An Appreciation," *Life and Labor* 10 (March 1920), 95; and Nestor, *Woman's Labor Leader*, 118–19. See also Octavia Roberts, "Agnes Nestor," *American Magazine* 73 (February 1912), 422; and McDowell, "The Girls' Bill," 513.

38. Quoted in IMA Papers: John M. Glenn, "Defeat the Eight-Hour Bill," *Legislative Bulletin No. 13* (April 24, 1909), 1–2, Box 199, Folder 6; and John M. Glenn Liquor Dealers Association, April 24, 1909, Box 161, Folder 1. See also Beckner, *History of Labor Legislation*, 192. Willard, who was sporadically present in Springfield, had been elected a vice president of the Illinois Bartenders' and Waitresses' Union in 1908. See *Chicago Tribune*, Dec. 12, 1908.

Manufacturers' Association, stated that the petitions were from women workers opposed to an eight-hour law, which he believed proved that the eight-hour bill had not come from actual working girls but from organized ones. In her response, Nestor ignored Shoninger's anti-union bias and turned the senators' attention back to the petitions, which she argued, were "not worth the ink they are written with." She made clear that they were doubtlessly signed during noon-hour breaks after foremen warned "the girls that men would take their place, or that their wages would be cut, or their right of contract would be abrogated." The senators followed up with questions about the petitions' preparation, and the manufacturers admitted initiating many of them. Before the hearing ended, Maloney explained in simple terms "the right of contract" and what it offered a working woman: "She can take what her employer wants to give her or she can leave it." When each side had been heard, the senate adjourned without taking action on the measure.[39]

During the following days, after a few attempts at compromise failed, it became evident that the eight-hour bill could not pass. But Senator Jones considered it possible to secure a ten-hour law. Thus, on May 4, he introduced as an amendment a duplicate of Oregon's ten-hour law, which had recognized a state's right to regulate the hours of employment for women workers and which the United States Supreme Court had sustained the previous year. If his amended bill passed, he thought it likely that the Illinois Supreme Court would follow suit. Several senators requested that action on Jones' amendment be deferred for a day. When the amendment came up the next day, it was eventually tabled after a series of legislative maneuvers. That prompted Senator Jones to introduce an entirely new bill (No. 497)—a duplicate of the one that had been tabled. As a result, at week's end, two bills were left pending.[40]

During a hectic week that was both confusing and exhilarating, Nestor kept Robins informed of the ever-changing situation through letters and a telegram. She said that they had conferred twice with Senator Jones and had had a brief meeting with Governor Charles S. Deneen. Jones explained to the trade unionists that since an eight-hour bill could not pass in the current legislative session it had become "a question of establishing limitation" on the number of hours Illinois women worked. Nestor wrote to Robins that Senator Jones "seemed most pleased" that they agreed not to oppose his amendment, while he also understood why they "could not officially stand for it." However, he cautioned them that even passage of a ten-hour law was problematic and uncertain. The governor was

---

39. Nestor and Maloney, quoted in *Inter Ocean*, April 28, 1909. See also Beckner, *History of Labor Legislation*, 192; and "The Girls," *Eight Hour Fight*, 8.

40. See *Chicago Tribune*, May 6, 1909; Beckner, *History of Labor Legislation*, 193; and "The Girls," *Eight Hour Fight*, 10.

far more reassuring. He told the unionists that the manufacturers were "really frightened at the headway" they had made. He also promised that he would talk to Senator Jones and they would "get the very best they can for us."[41]

Back in Chicago for the weekend, it is all but certain that Nestor's father met her at the door on Friday night, May 7. Each week, she told friends, when she returned from Springfield, he would be "waiting for a full account of everything that had happened." A former Democratic politician in Grand Rapids in the 1880s and (in her words) a "radical" trade unionist, he enjoyed coaching his daughter by "talking over the work that he was so much interested in." By asking her to recount weekly events and offering his comments and suggestions, he helped Nestor develop her natural abilities and grow in self-confidence. Until his death in 1917, Nestor's father remained involved in her work and encouraged her in "everything that [she] was trying to do."[42]

While in Chicago on May 8 and 9, Nestor and Maloney met first with the CWTUL's executive board on Saturday and on Sunday afternoon with members at their regular monthly meeting. To an unusually large gathering of over 400 women, mostly trade unionists, Nestor explained the situation in Springfield. She admitted that, seeing there was no hope of passing their eight-hour bill, she had become convinced that a ten-hour law was more realistic. Although disappointed, she insisted it was important "to get some kind of a law passed in order that we may carry it to the Supreme Court of the state for a test." After a short discussion, Maloney presented a resolution, which the executive board had prepared the previous day, endorsing Jones' substitute bill and encouraging "all friends of labor and social welfare" to do likewise. It passed unanimously.[43]

While Nestor and Maloney held meetings in Chicago, Glenn was hard at work urging the IMA not to support Jones' ten-hour bill. Glenn informed members in a "legislative bulletin" that, despite repeated statements that the employers had "agreed to a ten-hour amendment," it was not true. Still on May 19, despite

---

41. Agnes Nestor to Margaret D. Robins, May 4, 1909, MDR Papers, Reel 21. Nestor wrote Robins twice (morning and night) on May 4; Nestor said that, although there was still some support for the eight-hour bill, even nine hours might not be possible. The unionists' position by the day's end was: "We told the Senators we will be glad to get our 8 hours but what we are trying to prevent is there [*sic*] killing our entire Bill."

42. Agnes Nestor to Marie Obenauer, February 28, 1918; and Agnes Nestor to Mrs. Frances N. Noel, February 23, 1918, both in Agnes Nestor Papers, Reel 2. Thomas Nestor died July 31, 1917. See *Chicago Tribune*, August 1, 1917. Besides working as a machinist and owning a small grocery store, Thomas Nestor was active in Grand Rapids' politics, serving as an alderman, marshal, and treasurer. When he lost a bid for sheriff and was unable to find work, he moved his family to Chicago in 1897. There he again worked as a machinist. See Nestor, *Woman's Labor Leader*, 27–44; and Grand Rapids' *Polk City Directory*, 1875–1897. I thank Marcie Beck, Grand Rapids Public Library, for her research services.

43. See *Inter Ocean*, May 10, 1909; and "The Girls," *Eight Hour Fight*, 10–11.

more than a week of political jockeying, only Senator Jones' substitute ten-hour bill remained under consideration in the senate; and on the following day, it passed unanimously and was sent to the house of representatives. In yet another "legislative bulletin" on May 21, Glenn advised IMA members of the "grave situation at Springfield" and told those who remained complacent "not to rest on their oars." For, "if the Supreme Court should reverse itself and hold [that] the legislature has the right to restrict hours a female shall work," he warned, "it will not be long before it will . . . curtail the hours a male shall work."[44]

Nestor and Maloney, while pleased with the senate's action, remained anxious and returned early to Springfield on Monday, May 24. They immediately noticed a large delegation of manufacturers, most of whom had not been present for over a week. With the general assembly scheduled to adjourn on Saturday, May 29, both sides knew that time was running out and the ten-hour bill, affecting women workers in factories and laundries, had "a good chance of passing." Focused on the house and its deliberations, Nestor and Maloney spent the week canvassing representatives and tracking the Jones bill to prevent it from "getting stuck any place." On Friday, May 28, legislators friendly to the IMA (especially laundry owners) made a last, unsuccessful attempt to amend the bill by changing the ten hours back to eight or including mercantile establishments along with factories and laundries. With so little time remaining, either modification would have ensured the bill's defeat.[45]

Having run out of opportunities to kill the measure, the manufacturers left Springfield that Friday evening. Nestor and Maloney stayed on guard in Springfield. Late Saturday afternoon, May 29, shortly after six o'clock, Rep. Burnett M. Chiperfield of Canton called "the girls' bill" up for a vote. During the roll call, Nestor and Maloney stood together clutching the brass railing that surrounded the legislators' desks until they heard shouts that "the girls have won." The bill passed (87 to 9) with more votes than needed. After nine weeks of "worry and work" battling the manufacturers, they were victorious at last. Even more, according to Robins, they had introduced discussions of "the possibilities of the eight-hour day into every factory in Illinois."[46]

Governor Deneen signed the ten-hour bill on June 15, despite pressure from the IMA to veto it. The new law went into effect on July 1 and, almost immediately,

---

44. See IMA Papers, Box 199, Folder 6: John M. Glenn, "Female Eight-Hour Measure," *Legislative Bulletin No. 15* (May 8, 1909), 1; and John M. Glenn, "Grave Situation at Springfield," *Legislative Bulletin No. 17* (May 21, 1909), 1–2. See also "The Girls," *Eight Hour Fight*, 12. On May 20, when the senators voted in favor of "the girls' bill," they voted against the woman suffrage amendment, also introduced in late March. *Inter Ocean*, May 21, 1909.

45. See *Chicago Daily Journal*, May 28, 1909; "The Girls," *Eight Hour Fight*, 12, 14.

46. *Chicago Tribune*, July 25, 1909. See "The Girls," *Eight Hour Fight*, 14–16; and Robins to Osgood, June 2, 1909.

the state's chief factory inspector began enforcing its provisions. Mary McEnerney of the Bindery Women's Union in Chicago, who had championed a shorter day from the beginning, understood what it meant. Thousands of women and girls "formerly at the mercy of grasping employers," she told the *Chicago Tribune*, would have "more leisure and consequently healthier and happier lives."[47]

And so it was, until September 11, 1909, when Judge Richard S. Tuthill of Cook County's Circuit Court issued an injunction prohibiting further enforcement of the law. His action resulted from a bill of complaint filed by the IMA's general counsel on behalf of the Chicago-based W. C. Ritchie and Company, the same firm that had successfully contested the 1893 shorter-day law. Since women were denied their right "to make individual contracts and work as many hours as they pleased," Tuthill stated that the 1909 law was unconstitutional. In his words, it "virtually relegate[d] women back to dependence."[48]

EMBATTLED AND EMBOLDENED

Howls of indignation and protest erupted following news of Judge Tuthill's injunction. It immediately halted the chief of the state department of factory inspection, Edgar T. Davies, from enforcing the ten-hour law and restrained the state's attorney, John E. Warren, from prosecuting cases in violation of it. Tuthill, a Republican who was born in 1841 in southern Illinois (Vergennes), moved to Chicago in 1873 and was twice elected its city attorney in 1875 and 1877. He then served as United States district attorney from 1884 to 1887, when he was elected to Cook County's Circuit Court. The day after he issued the injunction, the CWTUL passed a resolution deploring it as "a backward step" and urging "proper officials [to] carry this question to the [Illinois] Supreme Court without delay." That same day, Davies telephoned Robins to tell her that the injunction would be appealed. In a letter to her husband, Robins commented confidently that the Ritchie case had brought them "so much nearer the Supreme Court" and a decision on the law's constitutionality.[49]

---

47. See John M. Glenn, "Wire Governor Deneen at Once," *Legislative Bulletin No. 18* (June 2, 1909), IMA Papers; *Chicago Daily Journal*, June 30, 1909; and *Chicago Tribune*, May 31, 1909. On Deneen's career, see Roy O. West and William C. Walton, "Charles S. Deneen, 1863–1940," *Journal of the Illinois State Historical Society* 34 (March 1941), 7–20.

48. Chicago newspapers gave widespread coverage to Judge Tuthill's decision and reaction to it. *Chicago Record-Herald*, September 12, 1909; and *Chicago Tribune*, September 12, 1909. See also John M. Glenn to "Members," "Ten Hour Injunction Proceedings," September 10, 1909, IMA Papers, Box 161, Folder: March 1909–1911.

49. *Chicago Record-Herald*, September 12, 1909; *Chicago Tribune*, September 13, 1909, and Margaret D. Robins to Raymond Robins, September 11, 1909, MDR Papers, Reel 52. See also "Richard S. Tuthill," *Bench and Bar of Chicago: Biographical Sketches* (Chicago: American Biographical Publishing Company, 1905), 140–44; and *Chicago Tribune*, April 11, 1920.

Like Robins, the trade unionists were eager to have the ten-hour law tested in the Illinois Supreme Court. Having given up on securing passage of an eight-hour law, they had little choice but to follow Commons' advice: establish the principle that the state legislature had the power to regulate their working hours. In fall 1909, that became their goal, and they were quick to upbraid anyone who criticized them for having accepted less. "In the great struggle of labor," they argued, "it has ever been the shrewd device of the exploiters of labor to defeat a possible good by demanding an impossible best." The previous spring, they had chosen to accept the "possible good" over the "impossible best." And now that the IMA had seemingly played into their hands, they felt fairly certain that the ten-hour law, like Oregon's, would be upheld. Nevertheless, they set out to arouse public opinion in its favor.[50]

Nestor, Maloney, Willard, and Holley—all veterans of the legislative battle in Springfield—agreed to participate in a statewide speaking tour. They intended to describe their experiences as wage earners and explain how a shorter day would benefit "the lives and health of women workers" in Illinois. Several other unionists, strong advocates of the new law, also volunteered. Josephine Casey, an organizer for the Elevated Railway Employees' Union who had been working in Boston, declared that she was "glad to be back in Chicago in the midst of the fight." This time, however, that fight would be waged in the court of public opinion, where almost immediately Judge Tuthill and the injunction became the prime focus.[51]

Willard of the waitresses' union was among the first to openly criticize Tuthill. Speaking for working women, she said that the injunction was "enough to keep [them] awake nights" trying to understand how a single judge could prevent "the state's attorney from prosecuting violators of the law." If he could, she reasoned, "we might be able to get along well enough with fewer judges of the Tuthill stripe." Robins stepped into the fray in support of Willard, remarking that if women "had the ballot perhaps [they] would have more just laws and fewer decisions of the kind given by Judge Tuthill." Robins vehemently objected to his statements on the right of free contract. In her opinion, they verged on the ridiculous: "Everybody who knows what is going on in the world, except judges and lawyers, knows that freedom of contract can exist only between parties on an economic equality." Or as *The Public*, a journal of progressive opinion, commented: "No one would *voluntarily* contract to work ten hours a day for less than a bare living."[52]

---

50. "The Girls," *Eight Hour Fight*, 18.

51. On CWTUL's Legislative Campaign Committee, see Margaret D. Robins to Mary Dreier, October 22, 1910, MDR Papers, Reel 21. See also "The Eight-Hour Fight and What Is Coming of It," *Union Labor Advocate* 5 (September 1909), 26; *Chicago Tribune*, September 13 and October 3, 1909. See also *Chicago Tribune*, November 25 and December 9, 1909.

52. *Chicago Record-Herald*, September 13, 1909; "Illinois Ten-Hour Law Nullified," *Woman's Journal* 40 (September 25, 1909), 154; and *The Public* 12 (September 20, 1909), 890.

The CWTUL was not alone in asking for demonstrations of support for the ten-hour law. The Chicago Federation of Labor joined in and, for the first time, included religious groups in its appeal. Throughout October, the press, public-spirited organizations, and numerous charities responded and overwhelmingly denounced Tuthill's decision. Perhaps the harshest press rebuke came from the *Chicago Evening Post*, which called attention to "the judge's intellectual measure." In its opinion, he had "indulged in old-fashioned legal metaphysics that showed how unfamiliar he [was] with the evolution of social legislation and the new attitude of the courts thereto." Not only had Illinois' law been carefully modeled on Oregon's, but by 1909 there existed a solid body of evidence demonstrating the value and reasonableness of such legislation.[53]

The progressive American Association for Labor Legislation issued a statement signed by influential Chicagoans, including Robins and Addams. It reminded Illinois citizens that in enlightened communities "knowledge and appreciation of social needs determine judicial decisions." The minister of Chicago's Sixth Presbyterian Church promised "to defend the law in public word and in private influence," while Baptists at their state convention in Galesburg passed a resolution pledging cooperation in this "noble fight for shorter hours of toil." An editorial in the Catholic *New World* saw "no justice in making a woman work ten hours when only eight are exacted of a man."[54]

Resentful of such harsh criticism, Tuthill publicly defended himself in late October against what he called "intemperate harangues." He believed his decision had been misunderstood, admitting to having made it "almost *pro forma*" in order that the case would "speedily be brought before the Supreme Court." He charged his detractors with misrepresenting him "to create so great a clamor" that the supreme court might be influenced into reversing its previous judgment in the "well-considered" Ritchie case. Should there be such a reversal, he promised to accept it "loyally and unhesitatingly" since he had "the broadest and truest sympathy with women and their cause." Yet, as many of his critics noted, it was on them that he had placed the burden of the appeal. Instead of leaving the ten-hour law in force while an appeal was made, he chose not to.[55]

At this point, Judge Tuthill may have realized his error in judgment and the likelihood that the state court would reverse the 1895 Ritchie decision. If he

---

53. *Chicago Record Herald* and *Chicago Tribune*, October 18, 1909; and *Chicago Evening Post*, September 15, 1909.

54. American Association for Labor Legislation, October 15, 1909, copy in MDR Papers, Reel 21; William P. Merrill, October 19, 1909, copy in Chicago Federation of Labor "Minutes," November 7, 1909; *Chicago Record-Herald*, October 20, 1909; and *New World*, October 9, 1909. See also *Chicago Tribune*, December 10, 1909.

55. *Chicago Record-Herald*, October 23, 1909. See also *Chicago Evening Post*, October 23, 1909; and Graham Taylor, "Illinois Ten-Hour Law," *Survey* 23 (November 6, 1909), 205–6.

had, he was correct. On April 22, 1910, the supreme court upheld the ten-hour law in its entirety. In early February, when the case was heard, the IMA lawyer's only argument against the law's constitutionality was one of precedent. Louis D. Brandeis of Boston, who had successfully argued the constitutionality of the Oregon law before the United States Supreme Court, had volunteered his services and was among a team of lawyers in Springfield who prepared and presented the counter arguments. Most of them related to women's health—the deleterious effects of overwork and of long days of routine work, especially when machinery determined the pace. In its ruling, the court underscored "the physical strain placed on women" and also indicated that because of their "maternal functions" women deserved protection. The state's attorney had shrewdly pointed out that Illinois laws already protected various classes of people, even quail and other game birds.[56]

Emboldened by the Illinois Supreme Court's decision, CWTUL members began strategizing on ways to extend the law's coverage to include women who worked in department stores, hotels, and restaurants. Nestor called the court's ruling "a great victory" and, more importantly, "a great step toward an eight-hour day working day for women." She pledged that the CWTUL would "begin a fight for that." Glenn had little to say to IMA members; he notified them of the decision and provided them with a copy of the law. To assist in its enforcement, the CWTUL distributed a leaflet (available in several languages) to women workers so they would know, according to Robins, "who & what are protected by this law." Since trade unionists generally believed that enforcement was "best secured through organized workers," the link between organization and legislation became evident. And the judicial rulings of 1909 and 1910 demonstrated clearly why the ballot was a "practical necessity" for working women.[57]

In fall 1910, the CWTUL switched gears as it became involved in the garment industry's Chicago strike. Nestor again took the lead in directing activities on behalf of the female strikers. The CWTUL organized women activists—most notably Ellen Gates Starr—on picket lines and established commissary stations for relief. Once the strike ended in early 1911, the unionists turned their attention

56. *Chicago Record-Herald* and *Inter Ocean*, April 22, 1910. See also Beckner, *History of Labor Legislation*, 199–206; "The Ten-Hour Brief," *Woman's Journal* 41 (January 22, 1910), 13; *Chicago Record-Herald*, February 10, 1910; "Court Hears Ten Hour Case," *Survey* 23 (February 19, 1910), 758–59; and Goldmark, *Impatient Crusader*, 160–62.

57. *Inter Ocean*, April 22, 1910. See also John M. Glenn to "Members," April 28, 1910, IMA Papers, Box 161, Folder March 1909–1911; Margaret D. Robins to Agnes Nestor, May 8, 1910, Nestor Papers, Reel 1; *Inter Ocean*, May 9, 1910; Margaret D. Robins to Raymond Robins, June 13, 1911, MDR Papers, Reel 52; and Margaret D. Robins, "Legislation," September 27, 1909 (at Second Biennial Conference), MDR Papers, Reel 8.

back to their legislative concerns and made preparations for introducing an amendment to the ten-hour law in the 1911 session. On February 21, Nestor, Maloney, and Willard headed once more to Springfield. This time they hoped to limit working hours to fifty-four a week, while retaining the ten-hour day, and to include most women under the law's protection.[58]

What happened at the state capitol that spring was essentially a replay of what took place two years earlier. On February 23, Sen. Charles F. Harburgh of Galesburg introduced the "girls' bill" (No. 241), and it was immediately referred to the Committee on Labor, Mines, and Mining. During the weeks that followed, the committee held hearings at which an array of individuals presented their arguments for or against the measure. Nestor was among a handful of trade unionists who spoke on its behalf. Restating the need for shorter workdays and weeks, she again explained how "the incessant, monotonous grind of the factory" stripped women workers of "their life and vitality." A report of the U.S. Department of Commerce and Labor, recently released, reinforced that position. In 1908 and 1909, it had conducted an investigation of the working hours of Chicago's female wage earners and found that elevated railroad employees, candy makers, laundresses, and department store clerks were egregiously overworked.[59]

Despite this report and the court's ruling in the Ritchie case, Glenn and the state's manufacturers were not ready to give up. Convinced of the "drastic" nature of Senate Bill No. 241, Glenn warned IMA members that another success by the trade unionists would accelerate "a move for the eight-hour day all around," including "farm help as well as domestic." In response, several businessmen pressured some female employees to write their legislators and insist that their "rights [not] be restricted"; others traveled to Springfield to personally voice their complaints. Angry over the possibility of a fifty-four-hour week, they argued that such a reduction so soon after passage of the ten-hour law would "work a great hardship on them."[60]

---

58. On strike, see *Life and Labor* 1 (January–May 1911); Zelie P. Emerson and Katharine Coman, "Co-Operative Philanthropy," *Survey* 25 (March 4, 1911), 942–48; on Nestor, *Chicago Tribune*, Oct. 28, 1910; and N. Sue Weiler, "Walkout: The Chicago Men's Garment Workers' Strike: 1910–1911," *Chicago History* 8 (Winter 1979–1980), 238–49. See also *Chicago Tribune*, February 13, 21, 1911; and *Chicago Record-Herald*, February 13, 1911.

59. See *Chicago Record-Herald*, February 23, 27, 1911; *Chicago Tribune*, February 24, 1911; and *Life and Labor*, 1 (March and April 1911), 93 and 126.

60. John M. Glenn to "Members," "Woman Ten Hour Bill," March 3, 1911; John M. Glenn, "The Eight Hour Move," *Legislative Bulletin No. 7* (March 4, 1911), 1; copy of general letter to "Honorable [name omitted], Senate Chamber, Springfield, Ill., Dear Sir," March 1911, IMA Papers, Box 161, Folder 3 and 4; and Box 199, Folder 6; and Agnes Nestor to Margaret D. Robins, March 15, 1911, MDR Papers, Reel 22.

Nestor, Maloney, and Willard met "more opposition than they had expected." By mid-March, Nestor sensed that they would again be forced to sacrifice "the impossible best" for "the possible good." On March 15, in a letter to Robins, Nestor described a conversation she had had with Senator Jones. He told her that he had been inundated with letters from manufacturers complaining of the "great hardship" a shorter workweek would impose on them. And "of course," Nestor wrote, "he believes them." Jones also made it clear that "if [they] insisted upon a 54 hour week that he [would] not be with us." Although again disappointed, they resisted any compromise, until it appeared that without one all might be lost. In late April, Nestor sent a copy of the compromise bill to Josephine Casey, who was in St. Louis organizing garment workers. Casey reassured her friend, saying it was "much better to have more occupations included even at the sacrifice of a few hours of the week." Many workers, Casey pointed out, would be "spared the torture of hearing when they are tired, the forelady in a sweet impersonal tone, 'Another hour overtime tonight, girls.'"[61]

On May 19, during the final hour of the legislative session, the house passed the amended ten-hour bill (88 to 55), which extended coverage to all women wage earners except agricultural and domestic workers. Even though it carried a sixty-hour-week provision (instead of fifty-four), the trade unionists were thrilled or, as the *Chicago Tribune* reported, "about the happiest bunch of women that ever sat around the legislative chambers." They had reason to be proud and relieved. With only two days left in the season, in an attempt to kill the measure, Rep. Edward D. Shurtleff of Marengo added an amendment—which passed by one vote—to remove the ten-hour clause. At that "most critical stage," according to John H. Walker of the United Mine Workers, "Agnes did everything she could for the Bill." Most of the lobbyists had left the capitol, thinking that the ten-hour law had been defeated; "the girls [were] alone to make the fight." They "[went] out into the air," Nestor recalled several weeks later, and at Lincoln's tomb formulated a plan. Back at the capitol, she and the others spoke individually to nearly all the senators, asking them to reject the amended, "battered" bill. The senators complied. They refused to accept Shurtleff's amendment and returned the bill to the house without it. Shortly before midnight, that bill passed. Nestor had gambled but admitted that they would rather have lost the bill "than have any joker in it at all."[62]

---

61. Olive Sullivan to Mary Dreier, March 17, 1911, MDR Papers, Reel 22; "The Girls," *Eight-Hour Fight*, 18; Nestor to Robins, March 15, 1911; and Josephine Casey to Agnes Nestor, April 26, 1911, Nestor Papers.

62. *Chicago Record-Herald*, June 29, 1911. Quoted in *Chicago Record-Herald*, May 20, 1911; John H. Walker to Margaret D. Robins, May 26, 1911, MDR Papers, Reel 22; and Mary Isabel Brush, "Most Sweeping Woman Labor Law the Work of Two Chicago Women [Nestor and Maloney]," *Chicago Tribune*, June 18, 1911.

Displeased with the general assembly's actions, IMA members pressed Governor Deneen to veto the bill. Instead he granted them a hearing on June 3, at which individuals on both sides again spoke. Against the bill was Mrs. Mary Healion, who represented employees of the elevated railroads in Chicago. She was widowed and worked twelve-hour days. She and her coworkers were afraid because they had already received "official notice that [their] places will be taken by men," if the bill became law. But it was Lulu Holley, a member of the Laundry Workers and the CWTUL, who made the most gripping appeal on the bill's behalf. She had been one of four "girl" lobbyists in the 1909 session but, due to illness, was unable to accompany Nestor, Maloney, and Willard in 1911. She appeared at the hearing, however, and expressed herself with "deep feeling." She admitted at the outset that she was "broken in health and happiness" from two decades of hard labor, which began when she was fourteen. Like others in "the ranks of the workers," Holley explained why she desired the law's protection: "when an employer placed long, terrible hours before a girl who needs the money she can do nothing but accept them." Nine days after the hearing, the governor approved the measure.[63]

The statute became law on July 1. It was "another victory for the lobby of women laborers" in what the *Chicago Tribune* characterized as "one of the bitterest contests" in the legislature. The amended law prohibited employing women more than ten hours out of any twenty-four hour period and extended its protection to nearly all of the state's female workers. Finally, a provision required employers to keep a record of the hours each woman worked. Violators could be fined twenty-five to a hundred dollars. In early 1912, a hotel manager convicted of such a violation appealed to the state's supreme court, which upheld the law several months later.[64]

OVER THE LONG HAUL

About two weeks after the amended ten-hour law went into effect on July 1, 1911, Nestor heard from a friend that store clerks in Springfield and Peoria were happy, a few "madly excited," with their shorter shifts. Even a male clerk, who left his job at ten o'clock that Saturday evening, admitted being pleased that he

---

63. *Chicago Record-Herald*, June 3, 1911. See also *Chicago Tribune*, June 3, 1911; *Chicago Record-Herald*, June 12, 1911; and "Women of the Hour: Lulu M. Holley," *La Follette's Weekly Magazine* I (August 7, 1909), 3. Deneen, a Republican, served as governor from 1905 to 1913 and succeeded in placing Illinois "among the foremost of American states in progressive legislation." Quoted in West and Walton, "Charles S. Deneen," 11.

64. *Chicago Tribune*, June 12, 1911. See also Beckner, *History of Labor Legislation*, 208–9; *Chicago Record-Herald*, Feb. 18 and June 23, 1912; and Edith Wyatt, "The Illinois Ten-Hour Law," *Survey* 28 (July 6, 1912), 490–91.

worked with women—it was "the first time in years" that he had gone home so early. When CWTUL members celebrated their legislative achievement at a Halloween cotillion, women ticket agents on Chicago's elevated railroads attended in a body. By then, they could agree with Maloney that there was "every reason for and no reason against short working hours." Few, if any, of them had been replaced by men. Nestor, however, promised not to give up until there was "an eight-hour law as binding and as sweeping as this one."[65]

Although the CWTUL legislative campaign exhausted the organization's funds, Robins was satisfied with what the trade unionists had accomplished. She had placed "her bets on the girls," and they had delivered. In fact, they proved what she and other Chicago reformers had long thought: that "the right arm . . . is union organization and the left arm is social and industrial legislation." Florence Kelley's investigations of sweated work in the garment industry during the 1890s had convinced her of the need for both organization and legislation to abolish industrial evil. A decade later, she and Josephine Goldmark persuaded Louis D. Brandeis to argue the Oregon and Ritchie cases. They also provided him with evidence on the harmful effects of overwork on women and with arguments that their biological difference from men required protection.[66]

In 1910, when the Illinois Supreme Court upheld the ten-hour law, Kelley felt especially gratified. The court had reversed the 1895 Ritchie decision, which had effectively ended her work as the state's chief factory inspector and halted social progress for fifteen years. Kelley considered the court's reversal "the most important event of the year," making it possible to move forward "with new hope and assurance." The trade unionists' "great victory" immediately benefited thousands of women and girls in Illinois and a good many more in numerous other states by the 1920s. Laws regulating women's hours also served to bolster the widely held view of progressive reformers and labor activists that government could and should protect society's most vulnerable. With the state's assistance, they believed that women workers would become more equal to men in the workplace and thus strengthen their bargaining power to secure better jobs

---

65. Harriett Reid to Agnes Nestor, July 12, 1911, Nestor Papers. See also *Chicago Record-Herald*, October 29, 1911; and Maloney, "Towards the Eight-Hour Day," 1.

66. Balance of funds at CWTUL headquarters on July 1, 1911 was $10.00. See "Financing a Campaign," *Life and Labor* 1 (August 1911), 253; and Margaret D. Robins, "Women in American Industry," *Life and Labor* 1 (November 1911), 325. See also Susan Lehrer, *Origins of Protective Labor Legislation for Women, 1905–1925* (Albany: State University of New York Press, 1987), 34–36.

and more economic independence. And, in time, the state would enact further reforms to serve the needs of the entire working class and humanize industrial society.[67]

In championing the cause of protective legislation, the CWTUL did not reject union organizing, as their involvement in the 1910 garment workers' strike demonstrated. But it supported protective legislation earlier and more enthusiastically than any other league branch, having concluded that only government could give women workers the security they wanted. In 1912, Mary Dreier told Robins that none of New York's members had attended a hearing in Albany on a shorter workweek. "Our eastern girls are awfully queer about legislation," she wrote, and "not having a legislative genius like Agnes Nestor we are heavily handicapped." By then, Nestor's legislative and organizing abilities had distinguished her from her coworkers. Despite their teasing about her small size and the document-filled bag always at her side, she had won their admiration and respect. In 1913, Nestor became CWTUL's president and held that position until she died in 1948. She was one of organized labor's most recognized leaders.[68]

Nestor never reneged on her pledge to work for a binding and sweeping eight-hour law, but CWTUL's cause failed to advance any further until 1937 (one year before the federal Fair Labor Standards Act that mandated a forty-hour week). Prior to 1937, vigorous fights regularly occurred in the Illinois legislature. Over time, while Chicago merchants and manufacturers showed much less resistance, downstate factory owners and small-town shopkeepers continued to insist that an eight-hour law would severely disadvantage or ruin them. A few close calls stoked the trade unionists' hope. In 1918, Nestor and Maloney had served on a commission, appointed by Governor Frank O. Lowden, to study the problems of women in industry. The majority report recommended shorter workdays and,

---

67. On Kelley, see Goldmark, *Impatient Crusader*, 162. For a table on industrial legislation for women in the United States in 1923, see Alice Henry, *Women and the Labor Movement* (New York: George H. Doran Company), 132–33. On Progressives and on hours legislation as an "entering wedge" to lead to further reform, see Sklar, *Florence Kelley*, 259–62; Shelton Stromquist, *Reinventing "The People": The Progressive Movement, the Class Problem, and the Origins of Modern Liberalism* (Urbana: University of Illinois Press, 2006), 3–7, 121–22; and Beckner, *History of Labor Legislation*, 206.

68. Mary Dreier to Margaret D. Robins, February 29, 1912, MDR Papers, Reel 22; Harriett Reid to Agnes Nestor, September 20, 1911 and February 15, 1912, Nestor Papers; David Thoreau Wieck, *Woman from Spillertown: A Memoir of Agnes Burns Wieck* (Carbondale: Southern Illinois University Press, 1992), 61; and photo of Nestor with bag in Roberts, "Agnes Nestor," 423.

on that basis, the governor urged legislators in 1919 to further restrict women's hours. They did not.[69]

In 1937, as house members voted on the women's eight-hour bill, Nestor watched from the gallery. When it passed, she appeared jubilant as the membership cheered her. But she later confessed that moment was not nearly as "thrilling as . . . passage of the women's Ten Hour Day Law more than twenty-five years before." There had been too many disappointments in the intervening years. In addition to the legislative defeats, an insurmountable rift had erupted during the 1920s on the national front between defenders of protective legislation and advocates of the Equal Rights Amendment who wanted it overturned; they believed maximum-hours laws denied them the promotions and higher pay available to male workers. Veterans of the endless battles wearied, although few changed their views; and old friendships, like Nestor and Casey's, often broke. The "belated victory" of 1937 also brought to Nestor's mind those young friends, especially Maloney, "who had begun the fight" and died at forty-one without witnessing passage of the eight-hour law. Yet their long struggle had not been in vain. By defending the particular needs of working women, Nestor had been faithful to their belief that protecting women at the bottom was "as important as opening up jobs for those near the top."[70]

• • •

AUTHOR'S NOTE: I am grateful to Susan E. Hirsch, Ann Durkin Keating, Walter Nugent, Christina A. Reynen, and Ellen Skerrett for their comments and suggestions.

---

69. Beckner, *History of Labor Legislation*, 210–19; CWTUL, "Industrial Survey Recommends Eight Hours for Women Workers," *Bulletin on the Eight Hour Day* (Spring 1919), 1–8, copy in NWTUL Publications, Reel 9; and William T. Hutchinson, *Lowden of Illinois: The Life of Frank O. Lowden* 2 (Chicago: University of Chicago Press), 342–43.

70. See *Chicago Tribune*, June 10, 16, 1937; Nestor, *Woman's Labor Leader*, 277; and Dorothy Sue Cobble, *The Other Women's Movement: Workplace Justice and Social Rights in Modern America* (Princeton: Princeton University Press, 2004), 228. Labor historian Dorothy Sue Cobble would not see Nestor as conservative or backward for her persistent championing of the needs of working women into the 1940s. Cobble contends that in postwar America "labor feminists" wanted "full industrial citizenship," which meant "gaining the right to market work for all women . . . and securing social rights, or the social supports necessary for a life apart from wage work" (4). See also Cobble, *The Other Women's Movement*, 139–44 and 227–28.

10. "I Too Serve America"

African American Women War Workers in Chicago, 1940–1945

LIONEL KIMBLE, JR.

Negroes,
Denounced and Deprived of Democracy
Insulted and inveighed in Industry,
Shunned and Shamed in Society,
Murdered and mangled,
On the very land for which they must fight!
They shall have some of it!
—Rhonda Walker, "I believe in Democracy So Much"[1]

THROUGHOUT THE COURSE OF UNITED STATES HISTORY, African Americans have used their labor in civilian life and the military as justification for gaining equal citizenship, dating back as early as the colonial era when African American men and women made demands for equal justice through demonstrations of patriotism. This was indeed the case during World War II, as the status of African Americans, the ability of the American military to wage war, and the idea of freedom became inexplicably linked. The changing power relationship between African Americans, business, and the federal government that occurred during World War II set the tone for the Civil Rights Movement of the 1950s

---

LIONEL KIMBLE, JR. is a Ph.D. Candidate at the University of Iowa. His dissertation, "Combating the City of Neighborhood: Employment, Housing, and Civil Rights in Chicago, 1940–1955," looks at the connections that exist between African Americans, community and workplace activism, and politics during the World War II and the beginning of the Cold War. "I Too Serve America . . ." was part of his Master's Degree essay at Iowa.

1. Poem published in September 1942, *The Crisis Magazine*, p. 1.

Journal of the Illinois State Historical Society Vol. 93, No. 4 (Winter 2000): 415–434 and 1960s. The historian Richard Dalfuime called the 1940s the "forgotten years of the Civil Rights Revolution"[2] in which African Americans began in earnest to cement their views that their participation in the war effort would lead to equal protection under the law. In reaction, many white Americans resisted the increased participation of African Americans in the military and the workplace. Active racial discrimination perpetrated by white Americans supplied "a rationale for denying this group its full rights of citizenship."[3]

African American women responded to the increased discrimination by invoking the language of work and patriotic duty. The history of black women has constantly been defined by hard work, and "black women shared with black men a desire for economic improvements and security."[4] As a result, black women as well as men began to view themselves as vital cogs in the United States war machine, bringing rising levels of black working class militancy. During the 1940s African Americans seriously questioned the relationship between the state and the individual, and how this relationship shaped race relations. In addition, the Second World War also helped change prevailing gender roles for African American women. As we shall see, black women often invoked the rhetoric of their men's military service as justification for inclusion into the army of homefront production.

This essay examines the manner in which African American women realized the Second World War would present opportunities for developing new strategies to obtain civil rights. Black women drew upon the idea of basic protection of civil rights outlined in the constitution and reiterated in the Four Freedoms by the federal government as a way of defining their citizenship. By examining the intersection between race and gender in the shadow of the changing economic and social conditions that blacks faced on Chicago's South Side during the war, one can discern the ways in which African American women reshaped the existing ideas of civil right. Nowhere was this strategy more revealing than in the fight for employment and housing that occurred in Bronzeville during the Second World War.

Recently scholars have begun to examine the connections between citizenship rights for women and the obligations citizens have to the state. Through these

---

2. Richard Dalfuime. *Desegregation of the U.S. Armed Force: Fighting on Two Fronts, 1939–1953* (Columbia, Mo.: University of Missouri Press, 1969), p. 1.

3. Ibid., p. 2.

4. Darlene Clark Hine, "Black Migration to the Urban Midwest: The Gender Dimension, 1915–1945." In Joe William Trotter ed., *The Great Migration in Historical Perspective: New Dimensions of Race, Class, & Gender* (Bloomington and Indianapolis, Ind.: Indiana University Press, 1991), p. 139.

studies we see that by denying women the claim that they were obliged to serve the state they could be denied citizenship rights.[5] But scholars have yet to fully examine the racial dimension of this theory adequately during the 1940s.[6] This essay examines the employment and housing conditions in Bronzeville during World War II when black women looked to their participation in the war effort as a means of claiming their citizenship rights.[7]

Three issues make Chicago a valuable case study during this period. Chicago experienced the largest influx of black migrants during the Great Migration and the subsequent wartime expansion during the 1940s resulted in one of the largest African American populations in the United States. Secondly, Chicago's diversified industrial setting provided an atmosphere for increased activism for civil rights on the shop-floor and in organizations such as the National Association for the Advancement of Colored People (NAACP), the Congress of Racial Equality (CORE), the Congress of Industrial Organizations (CIO), the National Negro Congress (NNC) and the Chicago Urban League. Finally, the concentration of African Americans in Chicago afforded the chance to develop a political culture inside the "Democratic machine." Additionally through the rhetoric of the Four Freedoms and the creation of the Fair Employment Practices Commission (FEPC), the Federal Government proclaimed itself willing (though in practice often reluctant), to protect African American rights, especially in the workplace.

---

5. The best examination of the phenomena is Linda Kerber's *No Constitutional Right to be Ladies: Women and the Obligations of Citizenship* (New York: Hill and Wang, 1998), Jacqueline Jones, *Labor of Love, Labor of Sorrow: Black Women, Work and the Family, From Slavery to the Present* (New York: Vintage Books, 1985), Karen Tucker Anderson, "Last Hired, First Fired: Black Women Workers during World War II." *The Journal of American History* 69:1 (1982): 83–97.

6. Several works have addressed the issue of changing roles of race, region and gender as related to African American women's history: Elizabeth Clark Lewis, *Living in Living Out,* Tera Hunter, *To 'Joy My Freedom: Southern Black Women's Lives and Labor After the Civil War* (Cambridge, Mass.: Harvard University Press, 1997), James R. Grossman, *Land of Hope: Chicago, Black Southerners, and the Great Migration* (Chicago: University of Chicago Press, 1989), and Wanda Hendrick, *Gender, Race, and Politics: Black Club Women in Illinois* (Bloomington and Indianapolis, Ind.: Indiana University Press, 1998), Nancy Gabin, *Feminism in the Labor Movement: Women and the United Auto Workers, 1935–1975* (Ithaca, N.Y.: Cornell University Press, 1990), and Ruth Milkman, *Gender at Work: The Dynamics of Job Segregation by Sex During World War II* (Urbana: University of Illinois Press, 1987).

7. Although recent work by Thomas J. Sugrue in *The Origin of the Urban Crisis: Race and Inequality in Postwar Detroit* (Princeton, N.J.: Princeton University Press, 1996) comes the closest to fully understanding the connecting between home and work within the African American community, Sugrue does not fully explore the gender issues involved in this relationship.

Chicago's old and new African Americans faced rapidly changing employment situations, and ever more acute housing shortages in Bronzeville during the early 1940s. They soon realized they would have to exert pressure to bring about change. African Americans enjoyed limited political and economic benefits during the administrations of mayors William Hale "Big Bill" Thompson, and Edward Kelly, and had won some standing in the Chicago Democratic machine of the 1930s. But during the 1940s African Americans shaped a new political activism, which differed from those of the established political arena. Employment and housing became political issues, and African Americans attempted to bring about social and economic change by means of a new grassroots political activism in Chicago.

Mayor Kelly, boss of the Democratic machine, helped African Americans gain access to political power in the 1930s and early 1940s. According to Roger Biles, "Kelly accelerated the process of constructing a black Democratic organization . . . by making available more patronage jobs than the number previously offered by the beloved Big Bill Thompson."[8] In addition to patronage positions, Kelly appointed African Americans to high posts in municipal government highlighted for example by the appointment of Robert Taylor to the chairmanship of the Chicago Housing Authority. In addition, Kelly's creation of the Mayor's Commission on Race Relations, the first organization of its kind in the nation, to avoid the level of racial violence that occurred in Detroit demonstrated the Kelly's administration proactive posture in regards to issues of race relations during the war.

Mayor Kelly's support for African Americans did not end once the war was over. During the post-war period, Kelly pushed for racially integrated housing developments, as evidenced by the Airport Homes controversy. Kelly strongly supported African American veteran organizations such as the United Negro and Allied Veterans of America (UNAVA) and American Veterans Committee. He fostered a political culture which functioned regardless of race and was unmatched anywhere in the United States.[9]

African American workers also gained access to jobs after President Franklin Roosevelt signed Executive Order 8802 which forbade discrimination against race, creed, color, or national origin in industries deemed vital for the war

---

8. Roger Biles, *Big City Boss in Depression and War: Mayor Edward J. Kelly of Chicago* (DeKalb, Ill.: Northern Illinois University Press, 1984), p. 91.

9. Information about the relationship between African American veteran organizations and the Kelly administration was noted in an unpublished paper "From Foxholes to Ratholes: African American Veterans in Postwar Chicago and the Search for Employment" by Lionel Kimble presented at the 1999 North American Labor History Conference at Wayne State University in Detroit, Michigan. Also see Robert F. Jefferson's "'Making the Men of the 93rd': African American Servicemen in the Years of the Great Depression and the Second World War, 1935–1947." Ph.D. dissertation, University of Michigan, 1995.

effort. The signing of the executive order and the creation of the FEPC was principally due to the efforts of labor leader A. Philip Randolph, president of the Brotherhood of Sleeping Car Porters (BSCP) and his March on Washington Movement. It was Randolph's and Walter White's, of the NAACP, threat in 1941 of a march on Washington D.C. by 100,000 African Americans which forced President Roosevelt to enact the order. In addition, this initiative was important because it marked the first time since Reconstruction in which the federal government actively supported non-discriminatory actions in the private sector.

For many African Americans, the Executive Order and the formation of the Committee were important victories, demonstrating the principle that the federal government would no longer condone discrimination.[10] Although the FEPC had relatively little power to force employers to end the practice of discrimination in the private sector, it was relatively effective in policing discrimination in northern industries deemed vital for wartime production.[11] In Chicago, the public support of FEPC policies grew quickly. According to historian Andrew E. Kersten "Chicago had a tradition of civil rights activism that came from the black community and the labor movement" which continued the long rhetorical legacy of black militancy dating back to the 19th century.[12] To further strengthen the ties between Chicago and the FEPC, two members of the first Committee were from Chicago: Milton Webster, vice-president of the BSCP, and Earl Dickerson,

---

10. For additional information about the FEPC in Chicago see Mary Watters' *Illinois and the Second World War, Volume II: The Production Front* (Springfield, Ill.: Illinois State Historical Library, 1952), pp. 258–286, and Andrew E. Kersten, *Race, Jobs, and the War: The FEPC in the Midwest, 1941–1945* (Urbana: University of Illinois Press, 2000).

11. It is important to note that Chicago served as the Regional office for the FEPC. Complaints would be filed in major cities which served as regional offices and catalogued until investigators could arrive from the National office in Washington D.C and hold hearings to look into the charges. By issuing an executive order that said discrimination based on race, creed, religion or national origin was wrong, the Federal government initiated steps that helped bring about racial equality in the workplace. Companies that discriminated against African Americans workers now had a legal obligation not to discriminate against them—even though many continued this practice—and African Americans used this opportunity to combat racial discrimination in the workplace. For African Americans in Chicago, the creation of the FEPC "seemed absolutely essential with more than 40 percent of the black workforce engaged in economic activities outside domestic and service employment." It also cleared the way for increased African American employment in the food processing, iron and steel, retail and manufacturing industries. For further information on this, consult Christopher Robert Reed, *The Chicago NAACP and the Rise of Professional Leadership, 1910–1966* (Bloomington, Ind.: University of Indiana Press, 1997), p. 119.

12. A recent book that offers the first regional examination of the effectiveness of the FEPC in the Midwest is Andrew Edmund Kersten's *Race, Jobs, and the War: The FEPC in the Midwest, 1941–1946* (Urbana, IL: University of Illinois Press, 2000), p. 24.

Democratic Alderman of the 2nd Ward. Dickerson was also a member of the Chicago NAACP and the president of the Chicago Urban League. As a result, with the protection of an executive order and the motivation of an already established political militancy, African American workers had real weapons with which to fight resistance to their presence in the new wartime economy.

However, not even federal policy could prevent all cases of employment discrimination. In many Northern urban areas, unemployment ran as high as 42.8% for black women.[13] In 1943, African Americans comprised 6.7% of the over 14,000,000 workers in 16,000 industries. This number was up sharply from July of 1942 (5.8%). Despite this, African American participation in wartime industries was not "commensurate with their proportion of the labor force."[14] The reason for this disparity can be attributed to several different factors, among them, racial segregation in occupational training, despite the fact that segregated job training was prohibited under earlier federal policy.

By the start of World War II, the War Manpower Commission designated Chicago a "Group One" city or one that experienced a labor shortage, but for black residents and new migrants who ventured to Chicago in search of work during the Second Great Migration the wait continued for available jobs.[15] By 1940—still a depression year—24% of black women worked in private industry while 12% were seeking work. Although this number may seem relatively low, when compared to that of foreign and native born whites, the underemployment was a serious problem among African Americans.[16] There are several reasons for these high levels of unemployment. African Americans were located in jobs that felt the effects of the economic crisis first and were excluded from additional job training programs. They were often dropped from their jobs while whites kept their jobs longer. And finally, as African Americans continued to migrate employers were unwilling to place them as new positions became available.[17]

---

13. These are totals for persons totally unemployed or on Public Emergency work as Percent of the Labor Force (15–74 years of age) by section, size of community, age, sex and color, November, 1937. Urban area is defined here as any community with a population greater than 350,000. Cited from Richard Sterner's *The Negro Share.* Originally printed in Calvert L. Dedrick and Morris H. Hanson's *Final Report on Total and Partial Unemployment, 1937.*

14. "Negroes Only 6.7% in Jobs Uses Reveals." *Chicago Bee* (July 4, 1943), p. 4. This information becomes clearer when compared with whites during the same time. The percentages of native born white men and women in the labor market were 71% and 34% respectively with 12% and 4% seeking work. For foreign-born men and women 73% and 19% in the labor market and 10% and 2% seeking employment.

15. Biles, p. 135.

16. St. Clair Drake and Horace Cayton, *Black Metropolis: A Study of Negro Life in a Northern City* (New York: Harper Torchbooks), p. 215.

17. For a fuller explanation of this see Robert C. Weaver, *Negro Labor: A National Problem* (New York: Harcourt, Brace and Howe, 1946).

To assist with this transition, organizations such as the South Parkway YWCA took an active role in wartime industrial training for African American women. The Industrial Committee of the South Parkway YWCA sent girls to summer school in Wisconsin in order to receive training to better prepare them for war work. Not only did these camps provide job training, but they also assisted the participants in "developing initiative and leadership qualities."[18] Nonetheless, race prejudice had profound consequences for African American workers' ability to find employment.

African Americans realized that for the most part their presence was unwelcome in the workplace by whites. For some whites, the increased presence of black workers threatened long established racial divisions in the workplace that had existed since the end of the Civil War. As a result, African Americans had to demonstrate that they were both better workers and better citizens than whites.[19] Newspaper such as the *Chicago Bee* urged African Americans to do ". . . all in their power to demonstrate to the man at the top that the Negro worker is just as good as the white worker."[20]

For example, a 1943 letter to the editor told workers: "Since they [whites] have been forced to hire Colored help in order to enjoy government contracts and their share in the nation's prosperity this does not mean that they for most part are satisfied with having colored employees in their plants."[21]

This person saw that while the war was being fought, Black workers were more likely to keep their jobs. But the gains made during the war were precarious. He continued: "Colored defense workers should bear in mind while they are now employed on defense jobs, and earning living wages, that these plants will tum back to their owners after the war and the FEPC may not help to keep their jobs."[22]

This letter nevertheless pointed to the hope that if African Americans proved themselves during the war their labor would not be scorned as it had been following earlier wars. Many African American demonstrated the belief that if ". . . you stick to your jobs now, and prove yourself equal and even better in conduct, work and efficiency than many white employees you will have a better

18. Letter to Claude A. Barnett from Estelle McNeal. Claude A. Barnett Papers: The Associated Negro Press, 1918–1967. Part 3: Subjects Files on Black Americans, 1918–1967, Series F: Military, Reel 3.

19. For more on the conflation of whiteness and labor, see David Roediger's *Wages of Whiteness: Race and the Making of the American Working Class* (New York: Verso, 1991).

20. "Negroes Warned to Watch Conduct on Defense Jobs." *Chicago Bee* (January 1, 1943), p. 22.

21. "Colored Defense Workers Stick to your Jobs," *Chicago Bee* (October 24, 1943), p. 19.

22. Ibid.

chance of remaining with the company after the war."[23] It would come as no surprise that when the war was over that "industry may tell government, as a private right to hire whoever we want to work."[24]

For black women on the other hand, the stakes were indeed higher during the war. Not only did their inclusion in the workplace challenge the prevailing notions of race, but they often faced the added burden of gender discrimination in their job searches.

Nationally between 1940 and 1945 married and older white women did join the labor force in increasing numbers (14.8 million to 19.5 million) and many did take blue-collar "men's jobs" for the first time. Their increased rate of employment was hardly unusual because 75% of these women had toiled before 1941 and many sought to continue working after. While many white women *could* work during this period, many black women *had* to work and had to fight doubly hard to keep the jobs they won during the war. By 1944, 40% of black women worked.[25] Of the 1,410,069 women in Chicago in 1940, 118,333 were African American of which 27,472 were employed.[26] The workplace seemed especially hostile to black women, who faced persistent racial and gender discrimination from whites, male and female, as well as black men.

The Armour Meatpacking Company was one company unfriendly to African American women seeking employment. During the 1940s, Armour often discriminated against black women workers. For example, in July 1942, fifty African American women sought work at Armour, and were refused applications. As a result, twenty-five of the women present that day filed complaints against the company stating that they were refused consideration based on their race. This event prompted the *Chicago Defender*, the National Urban League, and the FEPC to conduct an investigation in the stockyards on the Southwest side of Chicago.[27] The *Defender* reported that African American women who filled out applications for employment were refused the opportunity to submit those applications even while white women were allowed to fill out the employment blanks.[28] In response to these complaints, the editors of the *Chicago Defender*,

23. Ibid.

24. Ibid.

25. Jacqueline Jones. *Labor of Love, Labor of Sorrow, Black Women, Work and Family from Slavery to the Present* (New York: Basic Books, Inc., 1985), pp. 235–235.

26. According to 1940 census data, the three largest occupations for African American women at this time were domestic workers (10,418), service workers (7,060) and operative and kindred works (5,596)—which includes occupations such as manufacturing (2,119) and apparel (929).

27. "Begins Probe at Armour," *Chicago Defender*, July 18, 1942, p. 1.

28. *Chicago Defender*, July 11, 1942, p. 1.

the Chicago Urban League and the FEPC all met with officers in the meatpacking industry to try and compel the industry to comply with federal law.

Sophie Brown was among the twenty-five women who went to the Armour plant in search of work.[29] According to Brown's report, she was standing outside of the employment office waiting to go in to inquire about work. While she waited, white women were being allowed in the office while the black women were told to wait outside. Brown quickly spoke up and told them that "I don't think it was right for the white girls to go in and the colored girls to wait out."[30] When approached by a white male employee who tried to force the women to leave Brown told the man she was "speaking up for our rights"[31] and blocked the entrance of the office so that no other white person could be brought in. When asked by one of the white men there, "Do you think you have as many rights as these other white girls?" Brown replied "Yes I do. Every time they draft a white man they draft a colored man, so wouldn't you think I have as much right to get a job as the white girl."[32] As a response, the man pushed Brown to the ground, and called the police and had her arrested. Upon Brown's arrest, five other black women who were standing in line demanded that they be arrested along with Brown to show solidarity. This act also served as an example of how strongly African American women believed that if black men were capable of fighting for democracy in the armed services, they were capable of performing in industry.

In addition, this arrest is significant, because it epitomized A. Philip Randolph's call that "a citizen is morally bound to disobey an unjust law." According to Randolph, "all Negroes [had] to join the movement for non-violent civil disobedience" and he challenged "if Negroes [are to] secure their goals . . . they must win them . . . they must fight, sacrifice, suffer, go to jail, and, if need be, die for them. These rights will not be given. They must be taken."[33] Additionally, this incident was important because of Brown's insistence that black women's participation in the wartime economy was as important as blacks men's participation in the military. Black women saw themselves as soldiers on the homefront who were performing a duty as important as black soldiers on the battlefield.

---

29. I first became aware of this case involving Sophie Brown in an article from 1942. *Chicago Defender,* August 1, 1942, p. 3 and again in the FEPC files. She filed a complaint with the Committee in May 1944. *Records of the FEPC,* U.S. Committee on Fair Employment Practices (1941–1945), Reel 75FRA.

30. *Records of the FEPC,* U.S. Committee on Fair Employment Practices (1941–1945), Reel 75FRA.

31. Ibid.

32. Ibid.

33. *Chicago Defender,* January 24, 1943, p. 2 and Philip S. Foner, ed., *The Voices of Black America.* (New York: Capricorn Books, 1975), p. 208.

The sentiment relayed by Brown in the previous example were reiterated by another black woman—Nellie Jackson. After she was unable to find an employer willing to hire black women to essential jobs to "help the war," Jackson wrote a letter to President Roosevelt in 1943. She believed, like Brown, that discriminatory hiring practices were unfair because if black men were to be held accountable to defend democracy, black women should have the opportunity to find employment.[34]

Grace C. Estelle also wrote a letter of appeal to President Roosevelt, asking him to use his power to end workplace discrimination and "make real to us the democratic principles for which we are fighting for others."[35] Like Jackson, Estelle questioned why African Americans were continuously excluded from employment opportunities even as African American men were serving and dying in the military. For these three women, it was clear that they saw their labor as vital for securing democracy. The inability to find employment robbed these women of the ability to make claims upon the equal citizenship they desired because many of them, like Estelle and Jackson, believed that it was their duty to support the war effort at home.

Once employed in war work, African American women encountered various forms of white resistance. White men and women workers used different strategies to protest job integration which were presented in gendered terms. White men were more apt to protest over the expansion of job opportunities to black men, which whites saw as a threat to their traditional economic advantage over black men. While white men launched hate strikes and initiated workplace violence when African American men were upgraded or entered skilled jobs generally reserved for white men, white women were more prone to protest shared space, facilities, or other violations of social distance between themselves and black women.[36] For example, an incident at the Maremont Automobile Company occurred when 15 black women were refused employment because, according to personnel manager Charles Smiley "white women objected to sharing toilet facilities with [black women]."[37] This played an important role in

34. *Records of the FEPC*, U.S. Committee on Fair Employment Practices (1941–1945), Reel 75FRA.

35. Letter from Grace C. Estelle to President Roosevelt dated 10 November 1942. *Records of the FEPC*, U.S. Committee on Fair Employment Practices (1941–1945), Reel 75FRA.

36. Anderson, p. 86. Another example occurred at the Advanced Aluminum Casting Corporation that was "unable to consider the employment of colored women because of the objections voiced by [their] white women employees, who steadfastly maintain that they will not share washroom facilities with the [black] help." Taken from a letter to Committee on Fair Employment from Advance Aluminum Corp., February 23, 1945. *Records of the FEPC*, Reel 74FRA. Also see George Lipitz, *Rainbow at Midnight.*

37. *Chicago Defender*, July 18, 1942, p. 9.

shaping wartime labor experience of African American women because they often used their work records as evidence to keep their jobs. Unlike white female workers, African Americans were sometimes fired, even if they were good workers, because this social distance had been violated.

Elizabeth Smith and Edna Toombs reported another such case to the FEPC.[38] Both women were at the Ahlberg Ball-Bearing Company, which had a government contract producing parts for the military. During a 15 minute break period in November 1943, Smith and Toombs entered one of the female break-rooms in order to sit and relax with other employees, all white. Following the break, the two women were called to the personnel department office and told that they received complaints from the white women because Smith and Toombs were "sitting on the bed" in the room. It would also appear from this case that the practice of segregation within Ahlberg was both unspoken and understood, but it became obvious that these practices would no longer be tolerated—at least by these two women. Smith and Toombs saw this idea of separate but equal accommodations as unacceptable and spoke out against it even if it meant losing their jobs. What this demonstrates is that these women were accosted and Smith lost her job not because of workplace ineptness, but because Smith and Toombs violated the white women's private space within the factory.

It was this protest over shared space by white women which prompted some employers to resist hiring African American women because of the possibility of losing white workers. The George A. Detterbeck Company was one example of this. When informed that refusing to hire African American women was a violation of an executive order, a company representative said that applications for African American women would be taken but the women would not be hired. Lester Detterbeck, vice-president of the company, commented that his company refused to hire any African American women because they "[did] not propose to risk losing a single one of his present employees," and that he was convinced that "the employment of Negro workers would entail that risk."[39] He continued to say that, "he [knew] beyond a shadow of a doubt that a number of women workers would leave rather than work with Negroes."[40] This is important because if Detterbeck felt that his workers would quit over the employment of black women this must have been a common occurrence during the time. As a result, the government moved to have the contract with the Detterbeck

38. *Records of the FEPC,* U.S. Committee on Fair Employment Practices (1941–1945), Reel 74FRA.

39. *Records of the FEPC,* U.S. Committee on Fair Employment Practices (1941–1945), Reel 76FR.

40. Ibid.

Company cancelled and it is unclear whether the Detterbeck Company ever complied with the Executive Order.

These obstacles made the work experiences of working-class African American women difficult. While, the examples highlight some of the difficulties black women experienced when they attempted to challenge the racial hierarchies that existed in wartime industries, other contributing factors made everyday life for these people a challenge.

Along with demanding equal employment, black Chicagoans sought equal access to wartime housing. By 1940, there were over 80,347 African Americans employed in Cook and DuPage counties in Illinois (which contain Chicago and surrounding areas)—this total made up less than 5% of the total number of people employed. By 1945, these numbers increased to more than 222,500 African Americans in Cook and DuPage counties; they now made up 10% of all those working.

Between 1940 and 1945, 70,000 to 100,000 black workers moved to Chicago from the South. As a result, the population in Bronzeville rose to 375,000; 85,000 more than could be housed comfortably.[41] As a result, the number of non-whites living in overcrowded conditions jumped from 19% in 1940 to 24% in 1950.[42] The employment opportunities that were created in the growth of wartime industries placed a tremendous strain on the already precarious housing availability.

During the war, the lack of housing in Chicago was an issue that faced African American women who remained on the home front during the war. Substandard living conditions that were often found in black neighborhoods posed an added problem for African American women and black families. Many African Americans lived in oneroom kitchenettes. According to a 1944 report by the Mayor's Commission on Race Relations, a total of 11,160 one-room apartments housed 2 to 6 people each.[43] These were cramped, cluttered and often three to five different families shared single family apartments that were divided into smaller units. Darlene Clark Hine describes how "black urbanites in Chicago, Cleveland, Philadelphia and New York . . . lived in overcrowded, poorly ventilated, vermin-infested housing."[44]

---

41. Christopher Robert Reed, *The Chicago NAACP and the Rise of Professional Leadership, 1910–1966* (Bloomington, Ind.: Indiana University Press, 1997), p. 120. Also see Chicago Branch, A Statement on Rising Prices, October 1947, p. 1 and p. 2, NAACP MSS., Branch Files.

42. Arnold R. Hirsch, *Making of the Second Ghetto: Race and Housing in Chicago, 1940–1960* (Cambridge: Cambridge University Press, 1983), p. 24.

43. Mayor's Commission on Race Relations, *Race Relations in Chicago,* 1945, p. 27.

44. Darlene Clark Hine, *Black Women in White: Racial Conflict and Cooperation in the Nursing Profession, 1890–1950* (Bloomington, Ind.: Indiana University Press, 1989), pg.8.

Continued neighborhood segregation and an increase in Southern black migrants to Bronzeville left many little alternatives but to occupy kitchenettes. In addition to being cramped, these units according to a report by the Metropolitan Housing and Planning Council in 1944, was "far below the minimum mandatory for healthful sanitation." Consequently, aside from the increased probability of the spread of disease, it was not at all uncommon to hear of rat attacks on sleeping black children that severely maimed and sometimes killed.[45] Novelist Richard Wright described these housing units in the following manner, "the kitchenette, with its filth and foul air, with its one toilet for thirty or more tenants, kills our black babies so fast that in many cities twice as many die as white babies."[46]

The overcrowded and squalid conditions of the kitchenette left lasting impressions in the minds of Black Chicagoans who resided there. Bronzeville resident Cecelia Donald remembers living in a two-room kitchenette with two other families as a teenager in 1941. She recalls sharing a kitchen and bathroom with other residents of the building and being forced to bathe in a tin washtub in her grandmother's kitchen because her grandmother did not want her bathing in the communal bathroom. For Donald the shared spaces were never sanitary enough and often posed health concerns and "even though we all took turns cleaning them;" the lack of carpeting also contributed to the "rotten living conditions" she had as a child. For the Donald family the war brought some hope of better times. Robert Lowery, Cecelia's uncle, was drafted into the Army. Although he was the chief supporter of the family and offered his family some sense of stability with his presence, Donald hoped that his participation in the military would bring a better life for her family in the future.[47] Donald also remembers that for her uncle his participation in the war did foster a new sense of opportunities and did allow him better chances to aid his family. After returning from the war, Lowery quickly found employment in the Post Office in Chicago and was able to better support his family financially.

Developments such as the Ida B. Wells homes, Altgeld Gardens and Wentworth Gardens on the South Side of Chicago as well as the Frances Cabrini and the Robert Brooks homes on the city's West side were some of the housing projects that were open to African American war workers. Although these projects were not exclusively built for African Americans, they quickly became major battlegrounds in the war for equality. Although it was the policy of the

---

45. Hirsch, p. 25.

46. Richard Wright, *12 Million Black Voices* (New York: Thunder's Mouth Press, 1941), p. 107.

47. Cecelia Donald. Interview by author. Chicago Illinois, 20 March, 1998.

Housing Authority not to discriminate based on race, debate and controversy surrounded the construction of these units. Unlike Detroit, which suffered race riots in 1943, these did not arise in Chicago until after the war ended. Nonetheless, the availability for improved housing made access into these facilities a heavily contested issue.

Wentworth Gardens, a housing development on the city's South side, serves as a vivid example of how housing and war work were closely related. Construction of this development was started in 1942 in order to provide adequate housing for black war workers, but what made this housing so valuable was its close proximity to the Wisconsin Steel Company, Carnegie-Illinois Steel Company, and the Aircraft Division of the Pullman Company.[48] African Americans constituted an important part of Chicago's war workers thus making housing for them essential.

Institutions such as the YWCA and African American churches served as mechanisms within the Black community through which this fight for wartime housing for those engaged in war work was waged. Black churches and the YWCA tried to alleviate some of the burden for black women who ventured to Chicago in search of both work and housing by supplying job training and providing rooms or access to room registries for women to find places to live. Until the 1960s the YWCA ran a separate branch for blacks called the Blue Triangle branch of the YWCA. Although this branch was segregated, many of the programs for the women were interracial except for the living quarters. Many of the other benefits of the organization were comparable for both blacks and whites.

Nationwide, the YWCA started room registries in order to provide single women housing options. As stated, this "offering of a home to a war worker was seen [as something more than] just a business proposition—it was a patriotic service."[49] Ella Moseberry, director of the South Parkway YWCA in Chicago, probably best summed up this linkage of democracy and housing. She saw these women as "soldiers of the homefront," and asked, "how can a girl keep up her morale if she isn't comfortably and safely housed?"[50] The initiatives put forth, for African Americans, by the YWCA supported the fight for civil rights by moving to ensure that African American women gained access to better living and working conditions. It was through this that black women could fully participate in the war effort on a par with white women. As one YWCA official put it, the programs offered at the YWCA gave black women ". . . the

48. *Chicago Defender,* October 24, 1942, p. 1.

49. *Chicago Bee,* February 7, 1943, p. 10.

50. Ibid.

privilege and responsibility of offering to these [African American] girls the same opportunities as those enjoyed by the white girls" and thus demanding equal treatment.[51]

When African Americans tried to find clean and safe housing outside of Bronzeville, they faced racial covenants that restricted the areas in which Blacks were allowed to live, even if they did manage to find housing. White Chicagoans were often very hostile to any effort to integrate white neighborhoods and as a result, many signed restrictive covenants—agreements by property owners in a neighborhood not to sell or rent to African Americans, and thus keep their neighborhood all white. In Chicago this practice was put into wide use. It was estimated that by 1945, nearly 80% of the city functioned under such agreements.[52]

In 1929, a NAACP investigator managed to attend a meeting of white Chicago residents as they discussed how to bar African Americans from moving into an all-white neighborhood. He stated that a group of white Chicagoans held a meeting with the intent to "extend a segregation program against colored people."[53] According to the report, a man claiming to be a representative of the Chicago Real Estate Board, who was identified in the report simply as Carroll, led the meeting. Using blatantly racist language, Carroll cited that the "Chicago Negro population" increased from 25,000 in 1912 to 200,000 in 1928 and had been responsible for property depreciation amounting to approximately 3 million dollars. The general attitude by many in this meeting was that "restricting was a job"[54] and African Americans who refused to comply "should die or sell."[55] The attendees believed this largely because they saw that "they [African Americans] had gotten possession of one of the finest thoroughfares in the world, Grand Boulevard, a street that now bears the name Martin Luther King, Jr. Drive.[56] They concluded the meeting by having members vote to bar African Americans between 63rd and 69th streets between Halsted and Racine avenues (an

51. Paper of the YWCA of Greater Des Moines. Box 20, Iowa's Woman's Archives. University of Iowa.

52. Gunnar Myrdal, *An American Dilemma* (New York: Harper & Brother Publishers, 1944), p. 624. The Bronzeville district here was nearly 100% African American during this era.

53. This and the following notes have been taken from a rough draft of a NAACP press release dated 18 January 1929. This document gives insight into these meetings which were often highly secretive and apparently supported by real estate agents. *Papers of the NAACP: Segregation and Discrimination, Complaints and Responses, 1940–1955*. Part 15, Series B, Reel 4.

54. Ibid.

55. Ibid.

56. Draft of a press release. *Papers of the NAACP: Segregation and Discrimination, Complaints and Responses, 1940–1955*. Part 15, Series B, Reel 4.

area of approximately 1 square mile) for the protection of the "great Christian democracy."[57]

However, instead of being mere victims of these racial covenants, African Americans exercised their rights as American citizens and looked to the courts for satisfaction. The NAACP's legal department was often called to help blacks combat these discriminatory practices. Dozens of housing discrimination cases were filed all across the United States. The most famous of these cases is *Hansberry v. Lee* (1940), by Earl B. Dickerson, FEPC committee-member and lawyer of the Chicago NAACP.[58] Following the case, Dickerson warned, the "Hansberry case assure[d them] only the right to live in Washington Park area . . . [and that they] must continue to fight to live anywhere [they pleased]."[59] The victory of *Hansberry* eventually set the stage for *Kraemer v. Shelley* (1948) which made discrimination in housing unenforceable under the Constitution by stating that such covenants violate the Fourteenth amendment. *Hansberry v. Lee* served as an important benchmark for African American women. As residential segregation was challenged in the courts, the ability to attain and maintain adequate living conditions was linked directly to the ability to form and maintain families—a task that fell largely on black women.

The fight for better living and working conditions by black women in Chicago challenges prevailing ideas about gender, race, war, and labor militancy during the Second World War. For individuals like Smith, Toombs, and Brown the federal Government's need to fully utilize the labor force, changes in federal policy, and growing labor militancy of the period afforded African American women the opportunity to challenge existing racial barriers. Additionally, by demanding equity in hiring practices during the war, black women helped shape the face of Chicago politics from "machine politics" to "politics of protest" through which established ideas of race relations are challenged. Lastly, the battle over homes and work during World War II sets the stage for a postwar Chicago in which work and housing become major political and social issues for black and white Chicagoans.

---

57. Ibid.

58. For more information on this case and the role that the NAACP played in Chicago see Christopher R. Reed's *The Chicago NAACP and the Rise of Black Professional Leadership, 1910–1960*.

59. "NAACP fights for Homes," *Chicago Defender*, November 30, 1940, p. 6.

11. From the Near West Side to 18th Street

Mexican Community Formation and Activism in Mid-Twentieth Century Chicago

LILIA FERNANDEZ

IN LATE 1971, A GROUP OF MEXICAN AMERICANS gathered in Chicago's Pilsen/18th Street neighborhood to discuss the naming of a new Mexican community center opening in the area's east end.[1] The center would occupy the building of an old Catholic grammar school and adjoining church and rectory, which lay vacant for several years. St. Joseph's, or St. Joe's as it was known in the neighborhood, had long served a Slovakian immigrant population, but those residents and their second and third generation descendants had abandoned the neighborhood and the parish years before. The growing Mexican community in the area had obtained permission from the Archdiocese of Chicago to lease the facilities and operate a community center to serve local youth and families.

At their meeting, community members and leaders interested in the establishment of the center expressed passionate opinions about what the site should be

---

LILIA FERNANDEZ received her Ph.D. in 2005 from the Ethnic Studies Department at the University of California, San Diego. Her dissertation, "Latina/o Migration and Community Formation in Postwar Chicago: Mexicans, Puerto Ricans, Gender, and Politics, 1945–1975," explores Mexican and Puerto Rican immigration and community activism in Chicago in the mid-twentieth century. During the 2005–2006 academic year Dr. Fernandez is a postdoctoral fellow in the Latina/Latino Studies Program at the University of Illinois, Urbana-Champaign; the following year she will join the History Department at Ohio State University as assistant professor.

1. I use the terms "Mexican" and "Mexican American" interchangeably (and sometimes jointly) throughout this essay to denote both immigrants and American-born or raised people of Mexican descent.

Journal of the Illinois State Historical Society Vol. 98, No. 3 (Autumn 2005): 162–183

named. Older professionals in the community, such as physician Dr. Jorge Prieto and Judge David Cerda, supported the name "Latin American Youth Center," a label that would clearly identify the community's purpose and ethnic identity. Younger, more militant participants who had embraced the nationalism of the Chicano Movement of the Southwest ardently called for a name in Spanish that would reflect the politics of a racialized national minority, not the traditional ethnic immigrant identity of the previous generation. According to one of the center's founders, Phil Ayala, "The more radical side [of the group] came up with [the name] El Centro de la Causa" (The Center for the Cause). Tense debates over the center's name consumed the lengthy meeting. Ultimately, the group reached a compromise that would seemingly satisfy all involved. Since state law at the time did not allow incorporation under a non-English name, the group decided to adopt both names—the Spanish one to appease the younger radicals and the English version to satisfy state incorporation laws and more moderate middle class sponsors.[2]

Regardless of the contrasting political views or generational differences, the establishment of the center marked an important moment for the Mexican people of Chicago's 18th Street neighborhood: they had laid claim to the community and began efforts to draw resources and establish services for the growing Mexican and Mexican American population. The creation of institutions such as El Centro de la Causa helped make 18th Street the quintessential Mexican *barrio* in Chicago and the largest in the Midwest for the past four decades.[3]

EARLY HISTORICAL DEVELOPMENT OF A COMMUNITY

The settlement of Mexican Americans in Chicago's Pilsen neighborhood did not occur by accident. Their presence there was embedded in a history of racially-based urban planning that had dislocated them from the neighboring Near West Side, known affectionately as "Taylor Street" (see map 1). Mexican immigrants had a decades-long history on the Near West Side, but by the 1960s the construction of federal expressways, urban renewal, and the construction of the new University of Illinois, Chicago Circle Campus, had displaced much

---

2. The debate over naming the center reflected the disagreements within the community over the utility and appropriateness of nationalist Chicano ideology and rhetoric. As in the Southwest, some older generation Mexicans/Mexican Americans took much more reformist, or moderate approaches to social change and community empowerment; Ayala interview, 25 March 2004. El Centro eventually became a Catholic Charities agency and remains so to this day.

3. This designation generally refers to the larger area that includes the contiguous neighborhood of Little Village.

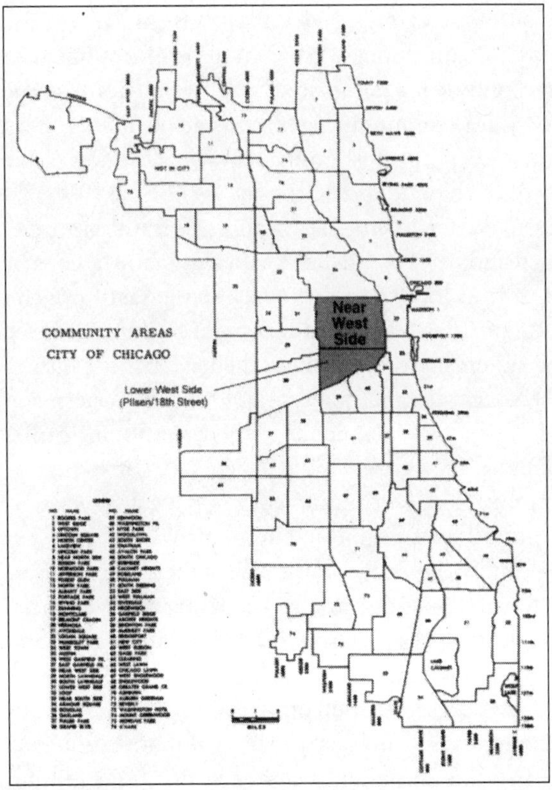

Map 1: Near West Side and Lower West Side (Pilsen/18th Street)

of the population. As a result, most families moved across the railroad tracks that divided the two areas and settled in the historically Eastern European Pilsen community (known officially by the Chicago Community Inventory as the Lower West Side). This essay traces the movement of the city's Mexican community from the Near West Side to 18th Street/Pilsen and the efforts at community formation and activism in both neighborhoods. I argue that the displacement of the thriving Mexican community on the Near West Side in many ways contributed to the emergence of community activism in the 18th Street neighborhood.[4]

The history of Mexican Americans in Chicago, and specifically the Near West Side neighborhood, dates back to World War I when Mexican workers came

4. Due to limited space, I do not provide an exhaustive treatment of these dynamics. For a more in-depth analysis, see Lilia Fernandez, "Latina/o Migration and Community Formation in Postwar Chicago: Mexicans, Puerto Ricans, Gender, and Politics, 1945–1975" (Ph.D. dissertation, University of California, San Diego, 2005), chapter two.

to labor on the city's railroads and steel mills. Mexicans settled in the area and established traditional ethnic organizations while making connections with local institutions. The Community Area designated by University of Chicago sociologists as the Near West Side (Community Area #28) had historically been a port of entry for immigrants to Chicago. Just south and west of the downtown business district, it was one of the oldest neighborhoods in the city.[5]

The area received Northern/Western European immigrants in the late nineteenth century. Impoverished and overcrowded, the area was made famous by social reformer Jane Addams, who chose it for her social settlement work and established Hull House in 1889. The dilapidated tenement buildings, which lacked plumbing or sewage systems, provided crude shelter for thousands of European immigrants. At the beginning of the twentieth century Eastern and Southern Europeans (mostly Greeks, Italians, and Jews) began replacing earlier German and Irish immigrants.[6]

When European immigration decreased dramatically in 1924, greater numbers of Mexicans and southern Blacks began making their way to the Near West Side. The aged and neglected neighborhood was one of the least expensive places to live and one of the few areas besides the Black Belt that accepted racial minorities.[7] The Near West Side housed a diverse working class immigrant and second generation population. Though the population was also racially diverse, this diversity belied the rigid physical segregation of African Americans. Blacks lived *within* Near West Side boundaries, but they generally did not live *among* Italians, Greeks, or other European immigrant neighbors. European ethnics often had slightly more tolerance for Mexicans than they did for Blacks. In general, Mexicans enjoyed a more ambiguous racial position, at times considered just another immigrant group, but at other times viewed as racially distinct.[8]

---

5. In their community studies, University of Chicago researchers divided up the city into seventy-five "community areas." Such designations, however, did not often match the names that community residents themselves gave to their neighborhoods. Moreover, these community areas often encapsulated multiple smaller neighborhoods, known to their inhabitants by street names, such as Halsted-Roosevelt, Taylor Street, Maxwell Street, or by other nicknames, such as "Black Bottom."

6. For a historical description of the Near West Side, see for example, Thomas L. Philpott, *The Slum and the Ghetto: Neighborhood Deterioration and Middle-Class Reform, Chicago 1880–1930* (New York: Oxford University Press, 1978).

7. Blacks formed an enclave within the Jewish section of the neighborhood. According to sociologist Louis Wirth, Jews on the Near West Side were less resistant to incoming Blacks than Whites in other areas; Carolyn Eastwood, *Near West Side Stories: Struggles for Community in Chicago's Maxwell Street Neighborhood* (Chicago: Lake Claremont Press, 2002), 204.

8. Thomas Philpott argues that Mexicans were considered an immigrant group similar to European immigrants. Yet researcher Paul Taylor noted as early as 1932 that Mexicans had a shifting racial position in the local social order, at times ranked above African Americans,

Throughout the first half of the twentieth century the neighborhood's large institutional presence brought stability to the area. Jane Addams's Hull House settlement figured among one of the largest social service agencies in the city. During the 1920s and 1930s Americanization programs at Hull House reached out to some Mexican families. The settlement incorporated Mexicans into their arts and crafts activities, for example, specifically their pottery making program.[9] The Institute for Juvenile Research, the Juvenile Justice Courts, and a sprawling medical complex consisting of Cook County Hospital, the University of Illinois Medical School and Center, Rush-Presbyterian Hospital, and St. Luke's Hospital occupied the western end of the region. The Institute for Juvenile Research began working with Mexicans in the 1940s to combat juvenile delinquency. Various Catholic and Protestant churches dotted the area as well. Finally, the eastern and northern boundaries of the Near West Side contained small factories, the railroads, and other industrial employers.

Mexicans and the small number of other Latin American immigrants in the area had opened their own businesses as early as the 1920s, including restaurants, boarding houses, small grocery stores, and other shops that catered to their cultural tastes and preferences. They also established mutual aid societies, athletic and fraternal clubs, and patriotic organizations. A handful of Spanish-language publications produced newspapers and periodicals in the neighborhood during the 1920s and 1930s, for varying lengths of time.[10]

In the 1930s, Chicago's Mexican population dropped to a third of its size as a result of the Great Depression and accompanying deportation and repatriation policies. The various social groups and service organizations that Mexicans managed to create on the Near West Side by the 1940s attest to the stable presence that Mexican immigrants and their children were able to maintain despite these challenges. Mexican and Mexican American area residents initiated

---

but at other times viewed as similar or even inferior to them. Gabriela Arredondo also argues that Mexicans experienced a great deal of racial discrimination from European immigrants and were racialized distinctly from them. See Philpott; Paul S. Taylor, *Mexican Labor in the United States,* Vol. II (New York: Arno Press, 1970, 1932); and Gabriela Arredondo, "Navigating Ethno-Racial Currents: Mexicans in Chicago, 1919–1939," *Journal of Urban History* 30 (2004).

9. Such Americanization programs focused largely on European immigrants such as Italians, Poles, Greeks, and Russian Jews. For an overview of Mexicans on the Near West Side in the 1920s and 1930s, and specifically their relationship to Hull House and St. Francis of Assisi parish, see David A. Badillo, "Incorporating Reform and Religion: Mexican Immigrants, Hull-House, and the Church," in Cheryl R. Ganz and Margaret Strobel, eds., *Pots of Promise: Mexicans and Pottery at Hull-House, 1920–40* (Urbana: University of Illinois Press, 2004).

10. For more on the Mexican community during the 1920s and thirties, see Louise Año Nuevo Kerr, "The Chicano Experience in Chicago: 1920–1970" (Ph.D. dissertation, University of Illinois, 1976) and Gabriela F. Arredondo, *Mexican Chicago: Race, Ethnicity and Nation: 1916–1939* (Urbana: University of Illinois Press, forthcoming).

various community organizations and groups designed to serve the largely immigrant, and largely impoverished ethnic Mexican community. St. Francis of Assisi parish, which held its first Spanish-language mass in 1926, continued to be an organizing institution in the community after the depression. Mexican men who attended St. Francis established a fraternal organization, the Wildcats, in 1938. Their newsletter, the *St. Francis Crier,* regularly reported news about neighborhood residents, especially returning young men who had served in the military during World War II. The church also sponsored youth clubs and offered recreational outings for second-generation teens. St. Francis's grammar school served many Mexican children as well.

Census data from 1940 provide a sketch of the existing Mexican population and the neighborhood more generally. Mexicans officially numbered over 2,700 persons on the Near West Side, making up 9.5 percent of the foreign-born population and two percent of the neighborhood's total population. While this may seem quite small, Mexican settlement, like that of most other immigrants, was concentrated in a specific set of blocks, thus making them highly visible as a distinct racial group.[11]

By the mid-1940s the city's Mexican population began increasing again, numbering over 20,000. This growth included both Mexican and Mexican American (im)migration, but increasingly a new group of Spanish-speaking migrants, Puerto Ricans, began arriving in the city and the Near West Side. The neighborhood continued to serve as a port of entry for many incoming Mexican immigrants, braceros, Mexican American migrants, and Puerto Rican labor migrants.[12]

Throughout the 1940s, Mexicans on the Near West Side developed various initiatives to address community needs and further plant roots in the neighborhood. In 1943, Mexican Americans formed the Mexican Civic Committee (MCC), under the sponsorship of the Chicago Area Project (CAP), a juvenile delinquency prevention initiative born out of the Institute for Juvenile Research. The Mexican Civic Committee drew some of the city's few Mexican professionals to its board. The chair, Frank Paz, a Mexican immigrant from Michoacan, Mexico, had an engineering degree from the University of Illinois at Urbana-Champaign and worked in the steel mills. University of Chicago instructor Luis Leal, who would later become a renowned Chicano literary scholar, served as

11. Louis Wirth and Eleanor H. Bernert, eds., *Local Community Fact Book of Chicago* (Chicago: University of Chicago Press, 1949). See also the following oral histories: Phil Ayala interview with the author, 4 December 2003, Chicago; Adrian Canales, Mikale Haepp, Josue Olivas, and Amanda Rojas, "Movement and Settlement: A Lower West Side Story," based on an oral history interview with Jovita Duran, in *Telling Historias: Oral Histories from Chicago Based on the Curiosity of Youth and the Memories of Elders* (Chicago: n.p., 2002–2003).

12. For a comparative analysis of Mexican and Puerto Rican labor migration to Chicago during the 1940s and 1950s, see Fernandez, chapter one.

an officer as well.[13] In its goal of preventing juvenile delinquency, the MCC sponsored summer camps, classes, and other recreational programs for children. Overall, the MCC promoted education as the key to Mexican American upward mobility. The organization adopted a self-help philosophy, espousing notions of civic responsibility, community problem-solving, and education as the means for social improvement.

RECOGNIZING AND STANDING UP TO DISCRIMINATION

In 1945 Mexican Americans called upon the citywide Council of Social Agencies to better serve Mexican social needs. The Council served as an umbrella organization for social service agencies throughout the metropolitan area and had a Committee on Minority Groups that addressed minority concerns in matters of education and recreation.[14]

That year at a welfare conference that the Council sponsored, Mexican American participants (including some from the Mexican Civic Committee) protested their status as a "forgotten minority," a group that had gone overlooked by the Committee on Minority Groups.[15] After much urging from Frank Paz and the MCC, the Committee on Minority Groups established a special Subcommittee on Mexican American Interests in February 1947. Paz, who served on the Committee on Minority Groups, became the subcommittee's first chair.[16]

The Subcommittee began planning and organizing for a city-wide conference for social service providers in the metropolitan area. On May 22, 1949, the Council of Social Agencies along with the Chicago Commission on Human

---

13. Nelson A. Rockefeller to Ernest Burgess, February 10, 1943, Box 89, Chicago Area Project Collection (hereafter CAP), Chicago Historical Society (hereafter CHS). "Report on the Conference on The Mexican Americans in Chicago," n.d., Box 147, Welfare Council of Metropolitan Chicago Records (hereafter WC), CHS; Jesse A. Jacobs, "Notes on conversation with Clifford Shaw re: Future of the Mexican Civic Committee," 17 February 1944, Box 373, WC, CHS. Clifford Shaw to Mexican Civic Committee, n.d., Box 89, CAP, CHS.

14. The Committee on Minority Groups operated with the Council's Division III (focused on education and recreation) and addressed issues affecting Chicago's Black population, as well as other "minority" issues such as Japanese American resettlement. Horace Cayton, one of the authors of the famous *Black Metropolis: A Study of Negro Life in a Northern City* (1945) chaired the committee. See Box 145, WC, CHS.

15. See "Minutes of the Meeting of the Committee on Minority Groups, Wednesday, October 23, 1946," Box 145; and "A Brief History of the Committee on Minority Group Relations, Division of Education and Recreation, Welfare Council of Metropolitan Chicago," October 1950, Box 145, WC, CHS.

16. "Minutes of the Meeting of the Committee on Minority Groups, Feb 26, 1947," Box 145; "Minutes of Meeting of the Executive Committee of Division on Education and Recreation, Feb 20, 1947," Box 147; "Minutes of the meeting on Mexican American interests," 7 May 1947, Box 147, WC, CHS.

Relations, social and welfare agencies, and leaders of the Mexican American community, held a conference entitled, "The Status of the Mexican American in Chicago." Frank Paz provided opening remarks and set the tone for the conference by examining the discrimination that Mexicans suffered in Chicago and how it had kept them at the bottom of the social ladder. With respect to housing, Paz remarked, "There is no neighborhood, that I know of, which has a publicly announced policy which says 'We do not rent to Mexicans,' yet it happens—could it be accidentally?—that we find ourselves congregated in particular districts."[17] Paz pointedly asked questions about employment discrimination as well. Why, he asked, were there no Mexican brakemen, conductors, firemen, or switchmen on the railroads? "There is nothing wrong with working as a railroad section hand but when a group of people are branded for employment only in one particular task there is something radically wrong," he contended. Paz cited similar employment patterns in the steel mills and packinghouses. Mexicans worked only in the dirtiest, most dangerous, low-paid, and unskilled jobs. These conditions had not improved for Mexicans despite more than three decades in Chicago.[18]

Finally, Paz made an incisive critique against Hull House, but without naming the institution explicitly. He cited the settlement house's failure to incorporate Mexican Americans into its leadership, though it had worked with Mexican Americans for more than a generation: "A settlement house on the West Side . . . has served the Mexican community for the last thirty years. During these thirty years there has *never* been a Mexican American on the settlement's Board of Directors. From time to time the settlement has had *one* Mexican on the staff (emphasis added)."[19] Paz's critical analysis of the condition of Mexicans in Chicago in the late 1940s represented one of the earliest attempts to address civil rights for Mexican Americans in the city.

Attendees at the 1949 "Status of the Mexican American" conference participated in workshops on employment, education, and health, welfare, and recreation and concluded by making several recommendations in these three areas.[20] In the end, they "proposed the formation of a city-wide, self-directed, non-profit organization for the purpose of serving as [the] representative voice for persons of Mexican American descent in Chicago." By the following June, the organization was incorporated as the Mexican American Council (MAC),

17. "Report on the Conference on the Mexican Americans in Chicago"; Frank Paz, "Status of the Mexican American in Chicago," speech given at conference, Box 147, WC, CHS.

18. Ibid., 8.

19. Ibid.

20. "Report on the Conference on the Mexican Americans in Chicago," n.d., Box 147, WC, CHS.

with Paz as the Council's first chair.[21] MAC noted, "The Mexican American is confronted with/ manifold inter-related social problems. As a recent immigrant his income is low, his employment security uncertain, and his 'acceptance' by other ethnic groups in doubt. He faces numerous problems occasioned by his differences from his neighbors in language, culture, and educational opportunity. Judged by even the minimum of American standards of health and decency, he is in general 'ill-housed, ill-clothed, and ill-fed.'" The Mexican American Council sought "the better integration of the Mexican American into the life of his community in metropolitan Chicago." Mexican Americans had lived in Chicago for more than a generation, as Paz had noted, and deserved their turn to reap the benefits of "the American dream."[22]

Mexican American leaders on the Near West Side addressed the plight of Mexican Americans in Chicago throughout the 1940s. Because deportation and repatriation had effectively diminished new immigration during the thirties, organizations like MAC served a largely settled immigrant and second generation population. By the 1950s, however, service organizations faced new challenges from increasing numbers of Mexican immigrants, Texas Mexicans, or *Tejanos,* and a new group, Puerto Ricans. In March of 1953, MAC estimated that over 28,000 Spanish-speaking people (including Puerto Ricans) lived in the area.[23]

New migrants brought with them all of the attendant problems of poor, recent arrivals, something that further compounded the already austere social conditions of Mexican American residents. Those who settled in the Near West Side area were drawn by the relatively low rents, proximity to jobs, and the presence of an already established Spanish-speaking community. As more Mexicans and Puerto Ricans arrived in the crowded, deteriorated community, they faced high unemployment rates, substandard housing, crowded schools, and high rates of poverty.[24] Many sought social services at Hull House, others turned to the Cordi-Marian sisters, a Mexican order of nuns who provided daycare and programs for school children.[25]

---

21. The Sub-Committee on Mexican American Interests had accomplished its goals and thus disbanded. See "A Brief History of the Committee on Minority Group Relations, Division of Education and Recreation, Welfare Council of Metropolitan Chicago," October 1950, Box 145, WC, CHS; Untitled document, Mexican American Council, April 1953, Box 88, CAP, CHS.

22. Untitled document, Mexican American Council, April 1953, Box 88, CAP, CHS.

23. Louise Hutchinson, "Quiet 'Revolt' Making City Happier Place for Mexicans," Chicago *Tribune* (March 29, 1953).

24. See for example, Tom Littlewood, "Mexicans Are Chicago's Least Understood Group," Chicago *Sun-Times* (October 19, 1953).

25. Phil Ayala, interview with the author, 4 December 2003; Jovita Duran oral history.

MAC's committees provided assistance and referrals for those in need as well. Their health committee helped translate information for the Spanish-speaking. The housing committee assisted those who needed emergency shelter. The labor committee met with union representatives. The educational committee awarded scholarships to Mexican American high school graduates. Finally, the youth committee addressed the issue of juvenile delinquency.[26]

THE NEAR WEST SIDE COMMUNITY DISRUPTED

The Mexican Civic Committee and the Mexican American Council represented two of the most visible initiatives of Mexican Americans on the Near West Side. The neighborhood also had an active interethnic community planning group, the Near West Side Planning Board (NWSPB), which in 1949 began plans for rehabilitating, improving, and conserving the neighborhood. The Near West Side Planning Board regularly held open forums for community residents to provide input to future plans for the area. A meeting in March of 1952 illustrates the level of sponsorship the NWSPB received: over eighty groups including neighborhood churches, public housing developments, schools, social service agencies, and civic groups sponsored the event. Mexican Americans participated in good numbers, represented by the Cordi-Marian Settlement, the Mexican American Council, the Mexican Civic Committee, the Mexican Methodist Church, the Manuel Perez American Legion Post #1017, and St. Francis of Assisi Church.[27]

The NWSPB succeeded in getting the area near Harrison and Halsted Streets, the heart of the Mexican neighborhood, designated by the federal government for "urban renewal," and proposed new affordable housing for the site.[28] The urban renewal designation, however, inadvertently led to the neighborhood's demise. Initially, City Hall supported the project, but soon it betrayed the community's plans for redevelopment.[29] In a typically unilateral decision in late 1960, Mayor Richard J. Daley offered the neighborhood's Harrison-Halsted site for the construction of a new University of Illinois campus in Chicago, without consulting the Near West Side Planning Board. NWSPB members and local residents learned of the decision in local newspapers. Although community women, some of them Mexican American, organized and challenged the city

26. See Hutchinson.

27. Near West Side Planning Board, flyer, March 1952, Box 88, CAP, CHS.

28. Near West Side Planning Board pamphlet, n.d.; James C. Downs to Clayton C. Meyers, 21 July 1955; "Proceedings of the Fifth Anniversary Meeting of the Near West Side Planning Board," 27 October 1953; all in Box 92, CAP, CHS.

29. See Near West Side Community Council, *Near West Side Chronicle* (October 1958): 7, in Near West Side Community Committee Records (NWSCC), Special Collections, University of Illinois at Chicago (UIC).

through pickets and federal courts, they lost their battle. The construction of the University of Illinois, Circle Campus went forward in 1963.[30]

Mexicans composed nearly forty-five percent of families and thirty-three percent of single residents displaced by the university. Between 1960 and 1970, the area lost 47,000 residents, 9,000 of whom were Mexican Americans.[31] The Mexican business district on Halsted Street, which provided Mexicans throughout the city, suburbs and even further away imported food products, *tortillerias, panaderias,* and other ethnic shops, had to relocate. Neighborhood institutions such as social agencies and ethnic organizations dispersed or folded all together as well. Hull House closed its doors and turned to city-wide, rather than neighborhood-specific social services.[32]

The displacement of Mexican Americans from the Taylor Street neighborhood has become part of a collective historical narrative for Mexican Americans throughout the Chicago area, but particularly for the Mexican community of Pilsen/18th Street. Countless families tell stories of growing up in the neighborhood and eventually being forced to move as buildings were torn down for university facilities, athletic fields, parking lots, or housing for university and medical students. Maria Ovalle, who grew up near Taylor Street, remembers as a child, coming home from the fourth grade every day to see which buildings had been marked for demolition on her block: "I have a very, very clear recollection of this. . . . You would come home and if your [apartment building] was ready [to be torn down] it would have a circle with a cross on it. . . . And so, it would be really, really sad! You'd come home and the kids would [say], 'Oh, our house is going next,' and you'd have to move."[33]

Families who had known each other for decades, or more recent arrivals who had just begun to establish roots in the neighborhood, were forced to find new housing elsewhere. As bulldozers razed area buildings, the majority of Taylor Street's Mexican families reluctantly packed up and moved just south and west to the neighboring Lower West Side, more popularly known as Pilsen or 18th Street.

---

30. For more details, see Eastwood; George Rosen, *Decision-Making Chicago-Style: The Genesis of a University of Illinois Campus* (Urbana: University of Illinois Press, 1980); and Fred W. Beuttle, Melvin G. Holli, and Robert V. Remini, *The University of Illinois at Chicago: A Pictorial History* (Charleston, S.C.: Arcadia Publishing, 2000).

31. Eastwood, 269; Evelyn Kitagawa, and Karl E. Taeuber, eds., *Local Community Fact Book: Chicago's Metropolitan Area, 1960* (Chicago: Chicago Community Inventory, University of Chicago, 1963), 71.

32. Unfortunately, a historic mural, the first ever painted by a Mexican in Chicago, Adrian Lozano, was torn down during the demolition of Hull House; see Badillo, 50–51.

33. Maria Ovalle, interview with the author, 6 June 2004, Chicago. The term "house" did not necessarily mean a single-family home, but rather a family residence. Most buildings in the area, in fact, were multi-family apartments.

MAKING COMMUNITY ANEW: FROM TAYLOR STREET TO 18TH STREET

The geographical movement of Mexicans from Taylor Street to 18th Street in the 1960s precipitated the emergence of social and political activism, particularly among second generation Mexican Americans. As families began establishing new social networks and community ties, many of the second generation more stridently began claiming 18th Street/Pilsen as a permanent Mexican community. Several factors and forces influenced this activism. During the sixties Chicago had vocal leftist and militant minority movements, such as Students for a Democratic Society, the Black Panther Party, and the Young Lords Organization. Nationally, the women's movement, anti-war protests, civil rights demonstrations, and the Chicano Movement of the Southwest also influenced Chicago's Mexican activists. But the experience of displacement from the Near West Side, and the new position in which Mexicans found themselves within the area's ethno-racial landscape played an important role as well.

Eighteenth Street resembled much of the rest of Chicago, layered with generations of immigrants, highly segregated, and characterized by residential succession.[34] The Pilsen neighborhood had historically been a port of entry for European immigrants. German and Irish immigrants settled the area first during the mid-1800s. By the late 1800s and early 1900s, Czechoslovakian, Bohemian, Slovenian, Lithuanian, and Polish workers and their families settled in the area as they searched for housing close to their industrial workplaces.[35] Pilsen lay in the center of an industrial corridor, fringed by railroad tracks on the north, factories and warehouses on the east and south, and the south branch of the Chicago River. To the west, Pilsen flanked the neighboring Little Village/South Lawndale community, which had a similar industrial and demographic composition. Pilsen was a decidedly working class community.

The neighborhood was impoverished and neglected. Housing stock was considerably older than other parts of the city: less than one percent of Pilsen's

34. For a discussion of race and housing (and specifically, the issue of public housing, which in Chicago has come to represent the confluence of race and housing), see chapter five of Gregory D. Squires, Larry Bennett, Kathleen McCourt, and Philip Nyden, *Chicago: Race, Class, and the Response to Urban Decline* (Philadelphia: Temple University Press, 1987). For the quintessential study of race, housing, and the creation of low-income African American public housing in Chicago, see Arnold R. Hirsch, *Making the Second Ghetto: Race and Housing in Chicago, 1940–1960* (Cambridge: Cambridge University Press, 1983).

35. In 1940 Pilsen was populated entirely by European immigrants and their descendants. Seventy-one percent of residents were "native white," and twenty-nine percent "foreign born white." This foreign born population consisted of Poles (31%), Czechs (23%), Yugoslavians (13%), Lithuanians (12%), Italians (8%), and other smaller ethnic groups; Wirth and Bernert.

housing had been constructed after 1940, while in some areas of Chicago as much as thirty percent of housing stock had been built since that year. Multi-family apartment buildings outnumbered single family homes.[36] Moreover, many property lots contained two buildings, one in the front and one in the rear, each of which was often divided into several small apartments to increase occupancy. Pilsen residents lived in very crowded conditions. For Mexicans and Puerto Ricans, relocation from Taylor Street to 18th Street did not signal much of an improvement.

This contrasted sharply with the experience of European Americans. By the early 1960s, many of Pilsen's second and third generation white ethnics had moved out to less crowded, better quality housing in neighborhoods south and west of Pilsen. Some of these families lived in neighboring Little Village (South Lawndale), with its slightly larger homes, while the better heeled moved further south and west to middle class suburbs like Cicero and Berwyn. The simultaneous process of white flight and Mexican in-migration changed 18th Street and eventually the contiguous Little Village area as well. The construction of the University of Illinois-Circle Campus had quickened the change in the racial composition of these neighborhoods.[37]

When Mexicans and Puerto Ricans began arriving to 18th Street and Little Village, they encountered an already deteriorated community with an aging immigrant population that often expressed racial resentment toward these recent arrivals, regardless of whether they were American-born urban renewal transplants or recent immigrants from Mexico.[38] Mexicans had historically held an ambiguous

36. By 1960, however, twenty-three percent of housing units were owner-occupied, a higher proportion than the Near West Side; Kitagawa and Taeuber, 76–77. See also Mary Bakszysz and Kay Guzder, "Description of the 18th and 26th Street Communities," n.d. (ca. 1970); "Pilsen," n.d., El Centro de la Causa private archives (hereafter ECC). Chicago Association of Commerce and Industry, *Community Area Data Book for the City of Chicago: 1975 Census Data by 75 Community Areas* (Chicago: Chicago Association of Commerce and Industry, ca. 1976), vi.

37. A white pastor at the Millard Congregational Church in Little Village, Pastor Anderson, explained to researchers in 1969 that he was leaving the neighborhood because the congregation could not support him anymore. There were only 130 members remaining in his church, and fifty percent of them had moved out of the area to Cicero or Berwyn but still came back to the neighborhood on Sundays for church. Bohemian families, Anderson claimed, moved out after their children graduated from 8th grade because they did not want to send their children to Farragut High School where they would mix with Black students. See Sister Marla del Rey and Mary Bakszysz, "Operation of the Millard Congregational Church," 9 September 1969, ECC.

38. Alicia Amador, interview with the author, 26 March 2004, Chicago; also, Mrs. and Mrs. Brevenick interview with Elisabeth Houston, 21 July 1969; Sister Marla Del Rey and Mary Bakszysz, "Operation of Millard Congregational Church," 9 September 1969; Cathy Alaniz, interview with Emile Schepers, 15 September 1970, all in ECC.

position within the city's racial order. Although they were immigrants, their cultural differences and the darker skin color of some marked them as racially distinct, especially in relation to European ethnics. Although many European immigrants and their descendants had deep-seated ethnic and national antagonisms toward each another (that is, Poles, Slavs, Czechs), they came together on the basis of their shared "whiteness" to battle the encroaching threat of darker people. By the 1970s, research conducted in Pilsen and Little Village revealed European immigrant anxieties about the changes in the community:

> [They] view the exodus of Mexicans, and to some extent the closeness of the blacks, as a threat to their very existence in every sense of the word. Informants often say that they do not object to Mexicans and blacks as such, but cannot hide a deep-seated anxiety concerning the changes they may bring in their own style of life and in the cultural and social atmosphere of the whole community.[39]

Researchers explained that in the face of incoming Mexicans and nearby Blacks, whose children attended their neighborhood public high school, "Czechs, Slovaks, Poles and Slovenians [were] sufficiently drawn together to overcome their historical pasts."[40]

Second generation Mexican Americans grew up with the experience of racial resentment from their neighbors. Alicia Amador, a Mexican American woman, remembered experiencing discrimination from Whites as a child in Little Village in the early 1960s when Mexicans had first begun breaking through neighborhood boundaries.

> Racism was awful over there. People can not believe what we went through. I remember walking into a store with my brother and we were waiting [to be attended] and people were walking ahead of us [in line]. Finally, I told the

---

39. Anonymous, "The Middle-European Community of South Lawndale," n.d. (ca. 1970), 6, ECC. See also Bakszysz and Guzder.

40. Anonymous, "The Middle European Community of South Lawndale," 7, ECC. Numerous scholars have documented this dynamic of "investing" in whiteness. See, for example, George Lipsitz, *The Possessive Investment in Whiteness: How White People Profit from Identity Politics* (Philadelphia: Temple University Press, 1998), David Roediger, *Wages of Whiteness: Race and the Making of the American Working Class* (New York: Verso, 1991), and Thomas J. Sugrue, *The Origins of the Urban Crisis: Race and Inequality in Postwar Detroit* (Princeton: Princeton University Press, 1996). Arnold Hirsch traces how European American "ethnics" became White through their opposition to blackness in *Making the Second Ghetto,* chapter six. Thomas Guglielmo notes that although Italians were always racialized as White, they consciously claimed their whiteness beginning in the 1940s to distinguish themselves from African Americans in Chicago; see his *White on Arrival: Italians, Race, Color, and Power in Chicago, 1890–1945* (Oxford: Oxford University Press, 2003).

proprietor, "We've been standing here. My brother wants to buy some candy." And he said, "We don't serve niggers here."[41]

On 18th Street, Mexicans and Mexican Americans had similar experiences. Carlos Valencia, who moved to Pilsen in 1958 when he was a teenager, remembered very tense relations in the predominantly Polish area. As one of the first Mexican families to cross the western racial boundary along Ashland Avenue (where Mexican families simply did not live in those years) the Valencias encountered prejudice from their Polish neighbors. Valencia noted, "We were always fighting with the Polish guys. There was lots of tension."[42] Resident Cathy Alaniz told researchers in 1970 about an elderly Polish neighbor, Mrs. Zapolsky: "Whenever the [Mexican children] go down the stairs and pass her on the way, they hear her muttering, 'Mexicans!'" Zapolsky also referred to Alaniz's dark-skinned niece as "that black Mexican."[43]

Despite these conflicts, by the late sixties signs of a new ethnic community began to emerge on 18th Street. The 1970 census officially counted a population of more than 24,000 Spanish-speaking people, composing fifty-five percent of the neighborhood's total population.[44] The community's poverty remained unchanged. Median family income measured less than $8,600, with sixteen percent of families in the neighborhood living below the poverty line. In contrast, median family income in Chicago's loop (downtown) district approximated $21,000, with only five percent of families living below poverty there. Forty-nine percent of those employed in Pilsen worked in manufacturing. The community had one of the city's lowest levels of school completion: the median for adults over twenty-five was only 8.5 years of schooling. Residents were very young, with thirty-nine percent under eighteen years of age.[45]

Such conditions prompted Mexican American women and men to begin organizing and working on social issues in their community. Some local activists worked in social service agencies, formed community-based organizations, and

41. Alicia Amador interview.

42. Carlos Valencia, personal communication with the author, 20 June 2004. Poles had a history of racial enmity towards Mexicans dating back to the 1920s. See, for example, Arredondo, *Mexican Chicago,* and Taylor.

43. Emile Schepers interview with Cathy Alaniz, 15 September 1970, ECC. Arredondo has documented the particular ethno-racial enmity that Poles had for Mexicans in *Mexican Chicago.*

44. Researchers and community leaders assumed a *significant* undercount, especially of the undocumented. The issue of an accurate census count of Latinas/os in the Chicago metro area would become a cause which some Latina/ o leaders in the city took up in the mid-seventies.

45. Chicago Fact Book Consortium, *Local Community Fact Book Chicago Metropolitan Area: Based on the 1970 and 1980 Censuses* (Chicago: Chicago Review Press, 1984), 364, 453.

began building coalitions with other groups across the city. Others had more strident critiques of American society and envisioned radical social changes that struck at the root of inequality. Those attracted by cultural nationalism gravitated to the burgeoning Chicano Movement of the southwestern United States. Like their counterparts in places like Los Angeles, those who identified as Chicanos in Chicago made demands for self-determination and community autonomy, protested against local power structures, and demanded greater social services. Unlike in the Southwest, however, this activism emerged in a context of traditional Chicago-style ethnic politics, racially shifting neighborhoods, and coalitions with other Latin American migrants, namely Puerto Ricans.[46] The particularities of Chicago's political history and ethno-racial landscape tempered some radical activism and promoted more moderate and "accommodationist" community politics among those who preferred to identify themselves as immigrants, akin to Europeans, rather than embrace a racial minority status.

The establishment of El Centro de la Causa, a community youth center, represented one effort at claiming space for Mexicans in Pilsen, challenging social inequalities, and bringing social services to the community. In 1970, Father John Harrington of the Providence of God parish in Pilsen's east end, informed two Mexican American workers at the Howell Settlement House, John Velasquez and Phil Ayala, about a vacant Catholic school and church building.[47] He suggested that they could possibly be re-opened and used by the neighborhood. The school facilities included classrooms and a large gym that could be put to use by local youth as a recreational center and meeting place. Velasquez and Ayala successfully negotiated with the Archdiocese to lease the buildings and secured two paid staff positions as well. In November of 1971, the building officially opened as El Centro de la Causa, the Latin American Youth Center, Inc.[48]

El Centro initially focused on recreational and athletic programs aimed at gang violence prevention. The director hired street workers to reach Mexican youth and draw them into the Center. Staff soon began applying for funding

---

46. By Chicago-style politics, I refer to the tradition of white ethnic political bosses who often controlled neighborhoods through patronage jobs, nepotism, and political machines. Such politics were also characterized by pork-barreling and other forms of corruption. From 1956 to 1976, Richard J. Daley reigned as city mayor, epitomizing such practices.

47. Mexican Americans also transformed Howell House into Casa Aztlán during this time.

48. Reverend John M. Harrington, "A Ministry of Social Justice: A Parochial Model in a Mexican American Community," Doctor of Ministry dissertation (St. Mary of the Lake Seminary, 1981), 10. See also, John Harrington, personal communication with the author, 10 December 2004 and Archdiocese of Chicago, *A History of the Institutions of the Archdiocese of Chicago,* Vol. II (Chicago: Archdiocese of Chicago, 1981), 857.

for other projects and quickly expanded their services to programs such as Servicios Sociales del Barrio, Project Quetzalcoatl, the Chicano Mental Health Training Program, BASTA (Brotherhood Against Slavery to Addiction), and Dar A Luz, a motherinfant health program. A fundraising press release from the early 1970s explained why El Centro had been formed: "Over the years this community [the Mexican community of 18th Street] has been ignored by federal, state, and city agencies that have been established to meet some of the needs of inner city residents. . . . There has been little interest on the part of city agencies to [expend] energy or monies to provide needed services for our community." The Center aimed "to provide an atmosphere which encourages adults to use their civil rights and responsibilities and which enables youth to realize their full potential."[49]

The Chicano Mental Health Training Program (CMHTP) symbolized one of the Center's most successful, though short-lived, initiatives. The program sought to train local community residents as "bilingual bicultural paraprofessionals in the ever broadening field of mental health."[50] CMHTP received funding from National Institutes of Mental Health in July of 1972. El Centro recruited Chicana/ o and Mexican American instructors from among local university researchers, graduate students, and social service professionals. They developed a Chicano-centric curriculum which included units on Child Psychology, Machismo, and Marriage, among other topics. CMHTP's director, Phil Ayala negotiated to have students receive college credit through Malcolm X Community College, a branch of the City Colleges of Chicago.[51] Over two dozen neighborhood residents enrolled in the courses. Classes were conducted at El Centro and students completed internships in local mental health or social service agencies. Within four years, the program had successfully trained forty-eight students, thirty-eight of whom received Associates Degrees, while fifteen continued on toward advanced degrees. The program placed a total of twenty students in mental health service positions, and fifteen in other human service jobs.[52]

---

49. "El Centro de la Causa/Latin American Youth Center, Inc," press release, n.d., ECC; Archdiocese of Chicago, 859.

50. Chicano Mental Health Training Program, funding application to the Department of Health, Education, and Welfare, 30 September 1972, ECC.

51. "Chicano Mental Health Training Program," n.d.; syllabi, Chicano Mental Health Training Program; "The Chicano Mental Health Training Program–Abstract," (August 1973), 1, ECC; Ayala interview, 25 March 2004.

52. Phil Ayala to Dr. Bertrand Brown, Director of Department of Health, Education, and Welfare, National Institutes of Mental Health, 12 May 1976, ECC; Ayala interview, 25 March 2004.

Two years after opening, El Centro received a $75,000 grant for a demonstration project they called Servicios Sociales del Barrio (Neighborhood Social Services). The program provided assistance to families and youth, largely in the form of casework, and included a research component that sought to identify needs and services that were not being met in the community.[53] A group of men in the neighborhood also obtained funding to initiate a drug rehabilitation program they called BASTA—Brotherhood Against Slavery to Addiction. They ran a methadone clinic in the basement of El Centro. Some nearby residents opposed having the clinic in the area, fearing that it would attract drug users. European American residents in particular opposed BASTA's presence in the neighborhood.[54]

El Centro established a community library as well. The neighborhood had long been without a public library, and while many had petitioned the city to open one in the area, El Centro's staff saw an opportunity to develop their own community-controlled space. Their community-focused, Chicano-centric philosophy was evident in the mission statement:

> Library service in America traditionally has been aimed at the white, middle-class majority, maintaining and reflecting their ideologies, at the expense and exclusion of minority communities. – Our primary goals are to supply the community with the information it needs to survive within a hostile environment, and to improve self-concepts by raising the level of consciousness about ourselves and our culture.[55]

El Centro's activities represented Mexican American activists' efforts to develop *community-controlled* projects that reflected the community's values, culture, and needs.

The militant nationalist posture of organizations like El Centro represented one among a broad range of political positions, strategies, and ideologies in Pilsen's Mexican community. El Centro took a reformist approach to social service provision, similar to many civil rights initiatives of the times. Radical, leftist groups made more direct critiques of social inequality and class relations. A coalition of Mexican and Puerto Rican workers, for example, began the group Asociación Pro Derechos Obreros/The Association for Workers' Rights (APO)

---

53. El Centro Board of Directors, "Meeting Minutes," 22 March 1973, ECC. See also *Servicios Sociales* case files, ECC.

54. Humberto Martinez, "BASTA: A Chicano Addict Rehabilitation Program," n.d., ECC. Documents reveal that Euro-Americans had more negative opinions overall towards El Centro. A survey done in September of 1973 within a two-block radius of the center revealed that some Euro-Americans had not heard of the center and many of those who had held very negative views of its activities, "Research Results of Community Survey," n.d., ECC.

55. "El Centro de la Causa Library," n.d., ECC.

in the late 1960s. APO staged bus boycotts and sit-ins to protest employment discrimination against Latinos by the Chicago Transit Authority. Leftist organizations such as Centro de Acción Social Autónomo-Hermandad General de Trabajadores (CASA-HGT) waged campaigns for immigrants' rights. Moderate and reformist activists led more traditional initiatives. In 1968 Mexican Americans successfully assumed leadership of the Pilsen Neighbors Community Council (PNCC), a Saul Alinsky-style Industrial Areas Foundation organization that focused on neighborhood beautification and operated a credit union and buying cooperative. A League of United Latin American Citizens (LULAC) chapter composed of attorneys, small businessmen, and skilled workers, operated in the slightly more middle class neighborhood of Little Village. LULAC provided scholarships for high school students and promoted greater educational attainment.

Education became a central organizing issue especially among women. In the early seventies, mothers and other residents fought for the construction of a high school in Pilsen. The protracted struggle, which included school boycotts and demonstrations, ended in victory for local Mexican residents who, until then, had to send their children a long distance to the only area high school. Residents named their new school Benito Juarez, after Mexico's first indigenous president. Still another group of activists established an alternative school for those labeled as "problem" students and those who dropped out or were "pushed out" of the school system. They called the institution Latino Youth Alternative High School.

These community organizations, campaigns, and struggles emerged within a span of only a few years, from 1968 to 1974. Such efforts symbolized an adamant claim on the community by Pilsen's Mexican and Mexican American residents. This activism was influenced to a great extent by civil rights and radical politics of the times. The war in Vietnam, student protests across the country, and colonial struggles for independence around the world certainly played a role in politicizing Mexican Americans on 18th Street and transforming some of them into militant Chicanas and Chicanos. But social, political, and economic dynamics at the local level provided more direct inspiration and motivation to act. The displacement of the Mexican community in the early 1960s from the Near West Side, their encounter with prejudice and discrimination, and their need to establish community roots in a new neighborhood influenced the response of Mexican Americans to the social conditions of the *barrio*. Working within their specific environment and sociopolitical context, Mexican Americans shaped their conditions and sought to improve their lives as best they could.

This article has briefly touched upon the broad contours of the social development of Mexicans and Mexican Americans as they were dislocated from their original settlement to a new community in Chicago. The conclusions about Pilsen's Mexican community do not necessarily apply to other Mexican populations in the city, such as South Chicago and Back of the Yards, where people experienced more residential stability and did not undergo the displacement of urban renewal initiatives. Indeed, Pilsen is a unique case.

Ironically, the university campus, which originally displaced Mexicans and Mexican Americans from Taylor Street and pressed them into Pilsen, now threatens to displace the community once more. As the university has expanded and central city neighborhoods have become fashionable for middle to upper-income residents across the nation, condominiums, townhouses, and lofts are replacing empty lots, dilapidated frame houses, and abandoned factories and warehouses around 18th Street. Students, professors, artists, and young professionals today encroach on the neighborhood where working class Mexican and Mexican American residents sought refuge four decades ago. This cycle of urban renewal, gentrification, and displacement, which is now repeating itself, should prompt us further to examine the past for clues about how such dynamics may unfold in the future. The history of the Near West Side and 18th Street might also inform contemporary activists' responses to this most recent threat to their community.

12. A Final Push for National Legislation

The Chicago Freedom Movement

RONALD E. SHAW

CHICAGO'S PREDOMINANTLY BLACK WEST SIDE erupted in violence on Tuesday, July 12, 1966, over a fire hydrant being turned off by police in ninety degree heat. Because of de facto segregation, black children had access to only one public swimming pool; therefore, they sought to cool themselves by using the city's fire hydrants. Turning on fire hydrants for cooling purposes probably started in Chicago when the city first introduced them. In any case, it had become a tradition established by countless generations prior to 1966. As soon as the police departed, residents again opened the hydrant. Apparently determined to show their authority, police returned and turned the illegally opened hydrant off again. Shortly thereafter, the neighborhood erupted into violence. By Friday of that week, two people had been killed, about eighty injured, two policeman shot, and over four hundred arrested, mostly young black teenagers. The damage to West Side businesses and property exceeded two and one half million dollars. Mayor Richard J. Daley requested mobilization of the National Guard from Governor Otto Kerner in order to quell the riot. The fact that such

---

RONALD E. SHAW is a Ph.D student in history at Northern Illinois University under the direction of Professors Sundiata Djata and Barbara Posadas. He is the recent recipient of an Illinois Consortium for Educational Opportunity (ICEOP) Fellowship and the Jeffrey T. Lunsford Fellowship. In preparation for his dissertation, he is currently researching civil rights in Chicago both before and after the Chicago Freedom Movement.

Note: Throughout footnotes, PMLK = The papers of Martin Luther King, Jr. and KLAA = King Library Archives, Atlanta

Journal of the Illinois State Historical Society Vol. 94, No. 3 (Autumn 2001): 304–332

a minor incident involving a fire hydrant sparked such violence revealed the existence of underlying problems in the city of Chicago.

Forty days later, two opposing groups of community leaders convened a meeting in the Monroe Room of the Palmer House, a famous downtown Chicago hotel. Two influential individuals led the separate groups; Dr. Martin L. King of the Chicago Freedom Movement (CFM) and Mayor Richard J. Daley of Chicago. Although they met with a mutually agreed upon agenda on paper, each group held different ideas on what should be accomplished. King and the black community wanted verification of the right of all African-Americans to purchase housing in any neighborhood of their choice, thus relieving pressure in the overcrowded black ghettos of Chicago. Daley and the affected white communities wanted a discontinuation of the month long nonviolent demonstrations conducted by King and the CFM throughout the Chicago area, and a verification that blacks would be kept in separate neighborhoods as in the past.

When Daley, the man who wanted peace restored to Chicago, and King, the man of peace and nonviolence, emerged from the ten hour meeting, both felt reasonably good about what had been accomplished. However, the resulting agreement, which contained no guarantees or schedules for compliance, drew criticism from both black and white segments of the Chicago community. Daley was unaccustomed to being criticized by anybody in the city of Chicago, which he ruled with an iron hand. Nonetheless, white citizens from the Northwest and Southwest sections of the city challenged his dictatorship and picketed the Mayor's office, claiming that Chicago had been sold out by Daley.[1] King supposedly held the upper hand upon entering the negotiations; therefore, Meyer Weinberg, a Chicago teacher and civil rights activist, felt that King had won nothing by signing the agreement.[2] Weinberg also assumed that King signed the agreement as an excuse to bail out of Chicago.[3] Chester Robinson, leader of the West Side Organization (WSO), a neighborhood activist group, grumbled that the black citizens of Chicago had been sold out by King.[4] Robert Lucas, chairman of Chicago's Congress of Racial Equality (CORE), who was not invited to participate in the summit meeting, thought the agreement represented nothing but promises on paper.[5] Albert Raby, chairman of the Coordinating Council

---

1. Roger Biles, *Richard J. Daley: Politics, Race, and the Governing of Chicago* (DeKalb, Ill.: Northern Illinois University Press, 1995), 134.

2. Stephen Oates, *Let the Trumpet Sound: The Life and Legacy of Martin Luther King* (New York: New American Library, 1982), 416.

3. Ibid.

4. Jacques Nevard, "Housing Pact Set, Dr. King Calls Off Chicago Marches," *New York Times*, 27 August 1966, 1.

5. Ronald G. Berquist, "King, Chicago Leaders Agree on Broad Open Housing Plan," *Los Angeles Times*, 27 August 1966, 5.

of Community Organizations (CCCO), an alliance of seventy-five Chicago neighborhood rights groups, King, and other civil rights activists who attended the summit meeting felt that the agreement represented the best they could get.[6] Considering the complaints received about previous agreements King had made in Birmingham and St. Augustine, the reproachful reaction of civil rights activists seemed normal. The possibility of a wider agenda or the further avoidance of violence by King never seemed to enter the minds of those who publicly stated their opinions.

This paper takes exception to the variety of public statements expressed by others concerning King's reasons for signing the agreement. The statements of Weinberg, Robinson and Lucas represent a narrow rather than a broad view of King's motivation. The paper will address King's determination to dramatize the lack of civil rights for the Black American by using nonviolent demonstrations as a tactic, and seeking federal intervention for assistance. It will analyze previously made agreements by King in Birmingham, Alabama, and St. Augustine, Florida, as well as Chicago, Illinois, and show an established pattern of King using local situations to emphasize the need for national legislation that would address these rights. The Birmingham campaign forced the Kennedy Administration to see the need for and to propose federal legislation; St. Augustine insured passage of that bill intact with no radical changes; and Chicago heightened the need for passage of the 1%[6] Civil Rights Bill on housing.

Very few scholars address the subject of King and SCLC's use of local situations to enhance national legislation. James R. Ralph in *Northern Protest: Martin Luther King, Jr., Chicago, and the Civil Rights Movement,* implies that the national debate on housing discrimination was awakened by the demonstrations in Chicago, but makes no comment about King's motivation for signing the agreement. Aldon Morris in *The Origins of the Civil Rights Movement: Black Communities Organizing for Change,* feels that in addition to getting Birmingham's white power structure to agree to five specific demands, King and SCLC's second objective was to use Birmingham as an example for other black communities and convince the federal government to act on racial domination. He indicates that more than local concerns were being sought by SCLC. Morris only applies this second objective to the Birmingham campaign since his book ends with that period of the Civil Rights Movement. Adam Fairclough, in *To Redeem the Soul of America: The Southern Christian Leadership Conference and Martin Luther King, Jr.,* mentions that SCLC had always used local situations to dramatize the need for national solutions, but like Ralph, fails to connect this statement with King and the Chicago agreement. David J. Garrow, in *Bearing the Cross: Martin Luther King, Jr., and the Southern Christian Leadership Conference,* provides

6. Oates, 415.

a legal activist's thoughts about SCLC's exploitation of local crisis situations for national objectives prior to Chicago, but no thoughts on the agreement are expressed. This paper will address King's larger motivation for signing the Chicago agreement. This information is important to show that those who criticized King for being naive in negotiating sessions held a narrow view and were wrong in their assessment of King's abilities.

Because King held the position of president in the Southern Christian Leadership Conference (SCLC), one of the most prominent civil rights organizations of the time, an examination of SCLC's purpose will be helpful in verifying the previously stated hypothesis. The Southern Christian Leadership Conference was a black civil rights organization founded in February 1957 by civil rights activists Bayard Rustin, Ella Baker, Stanley Levison, and Martin L. King, Jr. An early pamphlet distributed by SCLC indicates that, "SCLC is a service agency to facilitate coordinated action of local community groups within the frame of their indigenous organizations and natural leadership."[7] In practice, this statement translated into limited action on the part of SCLC field workers in any involvement undertaken in local campaigns. King, expressing his feelings to James Orange concerning SCLC field workers' close involvement in local communities, stated: "Our job was to get stuff started and then move on and get stuff started in other areas."[8] Field worker Dorothy Tillman explains further: "What we would do is hit cities, organize, mobilize, and move on."[9]

The tendency to remain in one place on a limited basis suggests that SCLC had a larger agenda. Fairclough confirms that "SCLC had always used local situations to dramatize the need for national solutions."[10] A disgruntled civil rights activist expands on this theory, commenting that "SCLC's exploitation of local crisis situations in the interest of its larger, national objectives has been a scandal for years."[11] While SCLC addressed local segregation problems in Birmingham, St. Augustine, and Chicago, it also maintained a determination to influence the introduction and passage of national legislation aimed at the civil rights of all Black Americans.

---

7. Board Meetings, September–October 1964, TD [photocopy], PMLK, 1954–1968, Box 29, Folder 4, KLAA.

8. James Orange, "With the People," *Southern Exposure* (Spring 1981): 110–16.

9. Dorothy Tillman, "Movement Activism from Martin Luther King to Harold Washington," in Terry N. Clark, ed., *Research in Urban Policy: Managing Cities* (Greenwich, Conn.: JAI Press Inc., 1986), Vol. 2, Part B, 155–61.

10. Adam Fairclough, *To Redeem the Soul of America: The Southern Christian Leadership Conference and Martin Luther King, Jr.* (Athens, Ga.: University of Georgia, 1987), 286.

11. David J. Garrow, *Bearing the Cross: Martin Luther King Jr. and the Southern Christian Leadership Conference* (New York: Vintage Books, 1986), 468–69.

This paper's first example, Birmingham, Alabama, provides a typical situation where this theory can be assessed. Birmingham, in 1963, carried the distinction of being the largest industrial city in the South, as well as the most racially segregated one. The Alabama Christian Movement for Human Rights (ACMHR), an affiliate of SCLC, and the National Association for the Advancement of Colored People (NAACP) comprised the main civil rights organizations operating in the city, although a 1956 injunction had outlawed the NAACP in Alabama. ACMHR's dynamic civil rights leader, the Reverend Fred Shuttlesworth, who had been fighting against Birmingham's immoral system of racism and white supremacy since 1956, invited King and SCLC to assist his organization in ending segregation in that city.

Consideration of a direct action campaign to end segregation in Birmingham took place as early as May of 1962 in an SCLC board meeting. As rumors spread about the impending demonstrations, store owners in the downtown area contacted Shuttlesworth and agreed to eliminate the Jim Crow signs and desegregate their stores' water fountains and toilet facilities. SCLC had previously planned to hold its annual convention in Birmingham during September 1962 and decided to postpone the protest campaign to give the store owners a chance to show their good faith. As soon as the convention ended, however, the merchants replaced their Jim Crow signs because of pressure brought to bear by Eugene 'Bull' Connor, the city's police commissioner.[12]

During a two-day retreat in Dorchester, Georgia, in January 1963, SCLC made a definite decision to move into Birmingham.[13] King voiced one of the conclusions reached: "While a campaign in Birmingham would surely be the toughest fight of our civil rights careers, it could, if successful, break the back of segregation all over the nation."[14] King and other SCLC members clearly had thoughts of success beyond the limits of Birmingham. Stanley Levison, a lawyer and close advisor of King, points out another major concern which arose. King said: "'I have to tell you that in my judgment, some of the people sitting here today will not come back alive from this campaign. And I want you to think about it.'"[15] The probable use of brutal methods to stop their demonstrations by police commissioner Connor weighed heavily on King's mind.

12. Glenn T. Eskew, "The Alabama Christian Movement for Human Rights and the Birmingham Struggle for Civil Rights, 1956–1963," in David J. Garrow, ed., *Birmingham, Alabama, 1956–1963: The Black Struggle for Civil Rights* (Brooklyn, N.Y.: Carlson Publishing Inc., 1989), 72.

13. Fairclough, 114.

14. Martin L. King Jr., *Why We Can't Wait* (New York: The New American Library, 1963), 54.

15. Garrow, ed., *Birmingham, Alabama, 1956–1963*, 75.

The Birmingham campaign began on April 3, 1963 with sit-ins and a boycott of downtown stores. The strategy centered around splitting the political community and economic community with the primary goal of black access to public facilities in downtown stores. A lack of support by the Black community caused the campaign to begin slowly, although Connor arrested small numbers of demonstrators almost every day. On April 7, Palm Sunday, Connor used police dogs for the first time. This resulting altercation involved the black citizens of Birmingham who were spectators, watching the demonstration from the sidelines. The participants in the march had already been taken to jail by the police. The confrontation lasted only briefly, but it provided an indication of the future violence that could be expected.

Since participation in the campaign by the blacks of Birmingham continued to be low, King and Ralph Abernathy, vice-president of SCLC, decided that they themselves would have to be arrested to drum up support. Connor accommodated them by obtaining a temporary restraining order which prohibited King, Shuttlesworth and various other leaders from demonstrating. King decided to break the injunction and go to jail, accompanied by Abernathy. While behind bars, King wrote his now famous "Letter From Birmingham Jail." In one section, King explained to the local clergy, which questioned his methods and timing, the reason for direct action: "In any nonviolent campaign there are four basic steps: collection of the facts to determine whether injustices exist; negotiation; self-purification; and direct action."[16] After explaining that the first three steps had already been taken in Birmingham, King made clear that, "We had no alternative except to prepare for direct action, whereby we would present our very bodies as a means of laying our case before the conscience of the local and the national community."[17] King's statement was undoubtedly intended to affect not only Birmingham, but a larger national audience.

Immediately after King and Abernathy broke the injunction, Wyatt Walker, executive director of SCLC, sought federal government intervention by sending telegrams to the White House and the Justice Department. One of the telegrams stated in part that "these two distinguished Americans are political prisoners, and not criminals. We ask that you use the influence of your high office in persuading the city officials of Birmingham to afford at least a modicum of humane treatment. Neither of these men have mattresses or bed linen."[18] Walker and other leaders feared for King and Abernathy's lives, since they remained in solitary confinement with no visitors or communication with the outside

16. King, 78.

17. Ibid.

18. Abernathy, Ralph D., *And the Walls Came Tumbling Down* (New York: Harper & Row Publishers, 1989), 256.

allowed. These telegrams brought a mild but effective response from the Kennedy Administration. President Kennedy and his brother Robert, Attorney General of the United States, arranged for King to place a telephone call to his wife, Coretta Scott King, from the Birmingham jail. President Kennedy provided no ready support since he had attempted to get King to delay the demonstrations. What other reasons caused President Kennedy to be so cautious in his support of King? In 1960, the Kennedy administration was voted into office by a slim margin, but blacks had voted overwhelmingly for Kennedy. Despite Democratic platform promises, the Kennedy Administration sought no civil rights laws in 1961. In 1962, Kennedy issued an Executive Order banning discrimination in federally financed housing as promised during the election campaign. But black leaders expected major civil rights legislation from the Kennedy Administration. President Kennedy remained concerned, however, with the future support of Southern Democrats both in getting future legislation passed and for support in future election campaigns. Levison believed "that if the civil rights movement could arouse the country and create the demand, this Administration would hear it and respond."[19] For the time being, however, the Kennedy Administration remained fairly cautious in its dealings with King and the civil rights movement. That mode of thinking would change rapidly because of events developing in Birmingham, and Levison's statement would eventually prove to be correct. After his release from jail in late April, King continued to urge the black community in Birmingham to support the demonstrations. The movement, however, began to run out of adult troops willing or able to demonstrate and face jail terms. James Bevel, a member of the recruiting committee, suggested the use of students, but King resisted this suggestion because of his concern for their safety. While King, Abernathy, Shuttlesworth and Walker attended an SCLC board meeting in Memphis, Bevel and the recruiting committee organized a children's march for May 2, 1963. When King and the SCLC leadership returned on May 1, the demonstration had already been planned, therefore King endorsed it. Since the student's parents faced loss of employment if they demonstrated, the children took over, thus breathing life into a faltering movement. Consequently, the next day, several thousand students left the Sixteenth Street Baptist Church in groups of fifty for city hall. Connor and his police arrested approximately six hundred students. The first day proved a great success, but Connor probably became the movement's best ally with actions taken on the following day.

On May 3, 1963, Connor authorized and directed the use of dogs and fire hoses on demonstrators. The dramatic images in the nation's newspapers and

---

19. George Plimpton, ed., *American Journey: The Times of Robert Kennedy* (New York: Harcourt Brace Jovanovich Inc., 1970), 114–15.

on television the next day probably did more for the Civil Rights Movement in the South than any other individual act. "Television coverage of the clubbings and hosings in Birmingham stirred indignation among Americans who had been complacent about racist mistreatment of Negroes."[20] Andrew Young, future SCLC executive director, explained: "The movement was really about getting publicity for injustice. The injustice was there under the surface and as long as it stayed below the surface, nobody was concerned about it. You had to bring it out in the open."[21] In commenting on the nonviolent determination and bravery of the demonstrators that day, King stated that "the moral conscience of the nation was deeply stirred and, all over the country, our fight became the fight of decent Americans of all races and creeds."[22] With his sites fixed on educating the nation as a whole, King and SCLC utilized this tactic in future encounters with segregated communities. The graphic television coverage not only raised the consciousness of the average citizen, but also opened some eyes in Washington.

After witnessing the brutality of Connor's forces the previous day, Robert Kennedy sent Burke Marshall, the administration's chief civil rights assistant, to Birmingham. King questioned Marshall's intentions initially, but grew to respect his ability to open lines of communication with the Senior Citizens Committee, a group of store owners in downtown Birmingham.[23] With Marshall's assistance, secret negotiations between the Senior Citizens Committee and SCLC's leadership went on for six days with a public agreement being announced on Friday, May 10, 1963. Black and white negotiators agreed to the following:

1. Within three days after the close of demonstrations, fitting rooms will be desegregated.
2. Within thirty days after the city government is established by court order, signs on wash rooms, rest rooms and drinking fountains will be removed.
3. Within sixty days after the city government is established by court order, a program of lunchroom counter desegregation will be commenced.
4. When the city government is established by court order, a program of upgrading Negro employment will be continued and there will be meetings with responsible local leadership to consider further steps.[24]

---

20. Robert Weisbrot, *Freedom Bound: A History of America's Civil Rights Movement* (New York: W.W. Norton & Co., 1990), 72.

21. Garrow, *Bearing the Cross*, 264.

22. Clayborne Carson, ed., *The Autobiography of Martin Luther King, Jr.* (New York: Warner Books, 1998), 209.

23. Ibid., 212.

24. Abernathy, 268–69.

King read a lengthy statement at the press conference afterwards beginning with: "I am very happy to be able to announce that we have come today to the climax of a long struggle for justice, freedom and human dignity in the City of Birmingham."[25] In keeping with his belief in the goodness of all men, he also praised "the white persons of the community who worked so diligently for just solutions to our mutual problems."[26] In explaining the accord's potential influence, King noted: "As a matter of fact, I believe sincerely that this victory cannot even be confined within the limits of this sprawling metropolis, for Birmingham now stands on the threshold of becoming a great, enlightened symbol, shedding the radiance of its example throughout this entire nation."[27] King's statement supported earlier comments concerning the national scope of SCLC's program.

Outside individuals proved instrumental in the success of the negotiations. In a telephone conversation taped by the Federal Bureau of Investigation (FBI), Levison tells an unidentified party concerning the agreement that "they are dealing with the business interests that control the city; who employ 80% of all the labor in the city. He says U.S. Steel and all the big people are involved so that he says the guarantees that they are giving on employment are not vague."[28] The fact that national companies with local concerns had an influence on the final agreement provides an idea of its scope.

The demonstrations and agreement produced numerous statements and some soul-searching from individuals on both sides of the segregation question. In commenting on the stores that agreed to desegregate, Connor declared: "The white people and other people of this city should not go in these stores. That's the best way I know to beat down integration in Birmingham."[29] *Time* reported that "under prodding from Justice Department lawyers in the city, a 77-man group called the Senior Citizens Committee had erected a fragile truce built on pallid promises to King's Negro negotiators."[30] Shuttlesworth spent the negotiating time in the hospital because of three broken ribs suffered at the hands of the Birmingham fire department and its water hoses; he stated that "he would not let King stop short of victory, as in Albany; he would sooner die in the streets than accept these terms."[31] Considering these previous two statements, why did King sign the agreement?

---

25. "Negro Leaders' Statements on Birmingham Accord," *New York Times,* 11 May 1963, 8.
26. Ibid.
27. Ibid.
28. David J. Garrow, ed., *The Martin Luther King Jr., FBI File, Part II: The King-Levison File* (Frederick, MD: University Publications of America, Inc., 1987), 10 May 1963, 100-111180-7-417a, 1.
29. "Bombs Touch Off Widespread Riot at Birmingham," *New York Times,* 12 May 1963, 53.
30. "Races: The Resounding Cry," *Time,* 24 May 1963, 22.
31. Fairclough, 128.

Historian Robert Cook in *Sweet Land of Liberty?* states that "on 7 May they [the Birmingham merchants] reached an agreement with SCLC leaders who were themselves concerned that mounting black frustrations might erupt in violence and thereby damage the spectacular public relations victory already won."[32] King also considered the attempts of die-hard segregationists who were "trying to sabotage any agreement by provoking a bloody clash between angry blacks and the bellicose state troopers who had been sent into Birmingham by Governor George Wallace."[33] Another problem became apparent after the signing of the agreement. The Ku Klux Klan held a rally outside Birmingham on Saturday, May 11, 1963. That same evening, the Gaston Motel, Birmingham's best black-owned motel, and the home of A. D. King, brother of Martin L. King, were bombed. These were major concerns for King, a man who advocated nonviolence.

Why did King sign an agreement which depended on the good graces of the Birmingham merchants, and nothing else? In summing up King's and SCLC's accomplishment in getting the businessmen to capitulate on a set of demands, historian Aldon D. Morris argues that "their second objective was to score a victory that would serve as a pivotal example to be used by other black communities and would force the federal government to take a firm stand against racial domination."[34] After the agreement became public knowledge, Burke Marshall, the Kennedy Administration's chief civil rights assistant, provided an enlightening reason for King's trust in the Birmingham merchants: "He [King] wanted recognition of what was right and what was unfair. And, once he got that in a way that was public, that was enough."[35] This line of reasoning would recur in future undertakings by King and SCLC, but what happened nationally?

Referring to Robert Kennedy, Fairclough argues, "Birmingham finally convinced him that crises would recur with such frequency and magnitude that the federal government, unless it adopted a more radical policy, would be overwhelmed."[36] The demonstrations also influenced the thinking of President Kennedy. Levison maintains that the Birmingham demonstrations encouraged Kennedy to consider civil rights legislation, something Kennedy earlier thought to be impossible.[37] President Kennedy finally acted by sending a civil rights bill

32. Robert Cook, *Sweet Land of Liberty?: The African-American Struggle for Civil Rights in the Twentieth Century* (New York: Addison Wesley Longman, 1998), 133.

33. Fairclough, 130.

34. Aldon D. Morris, *The Origins of the Civil Rights Movement: Black Communities Organizing for Change* (New York: The Free Press, 1984), 251.

35. Plimpton, 116.

36. Fairclough, 134.

37. Plimpton, 114.

to Congress on June 19, 1963. The Birmingham campaign had succeeded in both its local and national concerns.

Prior to the spring of 1964, four events provided the potential for accelerated action on the part of Congress concerning President Kennedy's legislation: civil rights advocates staged a March on Washington on August 28, 1963 to support the civil rights proposal presented to Congress by President Kennedy on June 19; an assassin killed Mississippi's NAACP leader Medgar Evers on June 12; four young Negro girls, attending Sunday school at the Birmingham Sixteenth Street Baptist Church, died in a bombing on September 15; and President John F. Kennedy was assassinated in Dallas on November 22, 1963. These events failed to inspire the House of Representatives; therefore, the Civil Rights Bill continued to languish in the Rules Committee. On January 8, 1964, Kennedy's successor, President Lyndon B. Johnson, called for passage of the civil rights bill in his State of the Union address. Finally, the House announced that debate would begin on Friday, January 31. During this same period, problems with desegregation continued to seethe in a small town in Florida.

St. Augustine has the distinction of being the oldest permanent settlement in the United States. In 1963 its primary income came from tourists' dollars; consequently, a visit from vice-president Lyndon B. Johnson that spring became extremely important in furthering support for the town's four hundredth birthday celebration scheduled for 1965. The town had sought almost $400,000 in federal funds for restoration and preservation projects primarily in the downtown area before the 1965 celebration. Dr. Robert B. Hayling, NAACP Youth Council advisor, and the local NAACP leaders contacted Johnson and advised him of the racial problems that existed. Hayling threatened mass demonstrations if Negroes remained outside the plans for Johnson's spring, 1963 visit and if public facilities remained segregated. As in Birmingham, desegregation lasted only until Johnson flew out of town; then the situation returned to what local officials considered normal.

Throughout the remainder of 1963, Hayling continued to contact the city commission about meaningful negotiations, with no positive results. He also picketed local businesses, mostly in the downtown area. Finally, on June 28, the commission met with Hayling and other black leaders and rejected all their demands, including the establishment of a bi-racial committee. During the months of July and August, Hayling conducted more pickets and several sit-ins at St. Augustine businesses. The police and sheriff's deputies used electric cattle prods and dogs from the very beginning on demonstrators who resisted. After failing in an appeal to vice-president Johnson, Hayling finally convinced the Florida Advisory Committee to the United States Commission on Civil Rights to hold hearings in August of 1963. The committee's conclusion warned that "St.

Augustine is a segregated superbomb aimed at the heart of Florida's economy and political integrity—the fuse is short."[38] Between the commission's report and March of 1964, a local Grand Jury ruled that the city's problems stemmed from extremists like Hayling. Roy Wilkins, national director of the NAACP, asked Hayling to resign and sought reconciliation with the city. Local white officials never acknowledged the NAACP's letter, again missing the opportunity for negotiations. In the meantime, Hayling attended an SCLC meeting in Orlando on March 6, 1964, and planned a desegregation campaign for St. Augustine during the Easter holiday with King and SCLC.

In a March 9, 1964 article published by *The Nation,* King commented on one of the future directions of the Civil Rights Movement, stating: "The new level of strength in the civil rights movement is expressed in plans it has already formulated to intervene in the Congressional deliberations at the critical and necessary points."[39] Author David R. Colburn in *Racial Change and Community Crisis: St. Augustine, Florida, 1877–1980,* observes that "the SCLC thus went into St. Augustine to prevent southern senators from tying the civil rights bill up in committee or successfully filibustering it on the floor of the Senate."[40] The St. Augustine campaign became the first application of this new direction.

The Easter campaign began in earnest on Saturday, March 28, with assistance from college students recruited from northern universities and individuals such as Mary Peabody, mother of the governor of Massachusetts. Their presence, along with King and the SCLC, gave the demonstrations immediate national press coverage. The city commission buried its head further into the sand and refused to negotiate or comment on the segregation situation in their city. This represented a leadership crisis, since the national media wanted to hear the local white leaders' assessment of the situation. Further, it opened up a perfect opportunity for individuals like Holstead "Hoss" Manucy and the Reverend Charles Conley (Connie) Lynch to fill the leadership vacuum, and provide the media with local comments. Manucy lived about five miles north of St. Augustine and supposedly commanded the allegiance of fifteen hundred whites known as "Manucy's Raiders." His colorful comments appeared almost daily in the press. Lynch grew up in Clarksville, Texas and helped to organize the Klan in St. Augustine during the fall of 1963. His fiery speeches at Klan meetings gained media attention, but made the situation worse.

---

38. David J. Garrow, *St. Augustine, Florida, 1963–1964: Mass Protest and Racial Violence* (Brooklyn, N.Y.: Carlson Publishing Inc., 1989), 26.

39. Martin L. King, "Hammer of Civil Rights," *The Nation,* 9 March 1964, 231.

40. David R. Colburn, *Racial Change and Community Crisis: St. Augustine, Florida, 1877–1980* (New York: Columbia University Press, 1985), 63.

Once the Easter demonstrations ended, the students returned to their studies, and Mrs. Peabody and her friends returned to Boston. Although St. Augustine commanded national attention, nothing changed in the way of eliminating the city's racial problems. SCLC field workers stayed behind to organize for the next stage of the campaign, scheduled for the summer, with the help of white college students and a small number of Negro residents. The combination of Manucy's Raiders and the Ku Klux Klan on one side and SCLC and its forces on the other meant that "the curtain was now ready to open on one of the longest and bloodiest civil rights campaigns of the early 1960s."[41]

On May 27, the first march of the second phase took place in St. Augustine around the symbolic "Old Slave Market" without incident or arrests. On the following night however, white onlookers, using tire irons and similar items, beat demonstrators. King immediately contacted President Johnson for federal protection with no positive result. The police banned demonstrations in downtown St. Augustine, but, to the joy of SCLC, federal judge Bryan Simpson rescinded this action. Simpson would be instrumental in aiding SCLC's efforts by reducing bonds, condemning county jail conditions, and generally adhering to the law.

The demonstrations resumed immediately. While the police stood by and watched, the white population became more brutal. King sent a telegram to the President, but Johnson took no action. As the nightly beatings continued, King decided to go public with his request for federal intervention. In a comment on the current conditions, he said: "For the last few days we have been in communication with state and federal officials concerning conditions in St. Augustine."[42] Colburn commented: "He [King] called St. Augustine the most lawless city SCLC had ever worked in, and asked the Justice Department to do something about the brutality and violence."[43] The Johnson Administration continued to ignore these requests for assistance.

Now that Johnson was President, what feelings did he express about the situation in St. Augustine, and why did he refuse government intervention for so long? Did the ongoing demonstrations affect the 1964 Civil Rights Bill, now on the Senate calendar since February 26, 1964? What factions kept the bill tied up in Senate committees? After voicing approval of the bill in his state of the union address, Johnson worked primarily behind the scenes for its passage. His concern with the upcoming 1964 presidential campaign in the fall, and his need

---

41. Garrow, *St. Augustine, Florida,* 39.

42. "Statement on Conditions in St. Augustine, Florida, 17 June 1964," 1, TD [photocopy], MLKP-Series III, Box 6, Folder 4, KLAA.

43. Colburn, 11.

for support from Southern Democrats, who kept the bill tied up in committee, dictated his approach. Knowing that the bill's passage depended on Republican support, which could be secured by Republican Senator Everett M. Dirksen of Illinois, Johnson offered Dirksen "favors which ranged from personal notes to federal projects, from photographs to judgeships."[44] He also queried civil rights leaders Roy Wilkins of the National Association for the Advancement of Colored People (NAACP), and Whitney Young, National Urban League, asking them: "When are you going to get down here and start civil-righting?"[45] On January 6, 1964, Johnson told Wilkins: "You're going to have to persuade Dirksen why this is in the interest of the Republican party. And let him know that you're going to go for the presidential candidate that offers you the best hope and the best chance of dignity and decency in this country."[46] In order to gain the necessary votes, Johnson felt passage of the bill needed assistance from outside sources, as well as executive pressure.

When it came to federal intervention in St. Augustine, Johnson remained behind the scenes for the same reason—Southern Democratic support in the upcoming Presidential election. On the day before the Senate passed the Civil Rights Bill of 1964, white citizens in St. Augustine kicked and beat demonstrators. On Friday, June 19, 1964, Johnson admitted to Wilkins: "I want to take some leadership. I'm just afraid of what's gonna happen this summer, like I saw yesterday at St Augustine."[47] Blacks in St. Augustine would, instead, retaliate by causing disturbances for the next two weeks. The need for Southern Democratic support continued to limit the actions taken by Johnson throughout the summer of 1964. Because of Johnson's silence, other approaches needed to be developed to gain federal intervention for protecting demonstrators, and convincing the white establishment to negotiate.

King and SCLC turned up the heat by staging "wade-ins" at public beaches, and private motel pools, and by calling for civil rights workers from out of town to join the demonstrations. King, Abernathy, and approximately fifteen others were arrested for trying to eat at the Monson Motor Lodge. All this activity, plus the nightly confrontations between demonstrators and Klan-backed whites, erupted on the night of June 25, 1964. Earlier that day, a white youth had been injured by state officers in an attempt to control a melee between whites and blacks. Klansmen took out their revenge on blacks that same night when

---

44. Doris Kearns, *Lyndon Johnson and the American Dream* (New York: Harper & Row, Publishers, 1976), 192.

45. Ibid.

46. Michael R. Beschloss, ed., *Taking Charge: The Johnson White House Tapes, 1963–1964* (New York: Simon & Schuster, 1997), 148.

47. Ibid., 420.

two hundred civil rights marchers were attacked by about five hundred whites. Between fifteen and twenty seriously wounded civil rights marchers ended up in the hospital.

Finally, "responding to the violence of June 25 and King's pleas, President Johnson asked Florida's U.S. Senator George Smathers if he could arrange a settlement."[48] On July 1, Governor Farris Bryant "named an emergency committee to 'restore communications' between whites and Negroes."[49] In response, King called off further demonstrations, pending results of negotiations with the committee. Perceiving this advancement as the beginning of a long journey, King stated: "But it is a creative and important first step, for it at least opens the channels of communication, something that St. Augustine has needed so long."[50] King also reflected: "In combination with the local defense fund, we began to pave the way for compliance with the civil rights bill and rush through its passage."[51] Pat Watters in *Down to Now: Reflections on the Southern Civil Rights Movement* speculates: "If there is the suggestion that SCLC exploited the local Birmingham situation, the suggestion was stronger in St. Augustine."[52] St. Augustine provided Americans with a better understanding of King's remarks in *The Nation* concerning intervention in Congressional deliberations at necessary points in time. Colburn summed up the St. Augustine campaign: "In retrospect, there seems to be little question that King and SCLC were primarily interested in St. Augustine as a way to facilitate passage of the civil rights bill and having accomplished this, sought to retire as soon as protection could be assured for local residents."[53] Current scholarship and this paper support his opinion.

President Johnson signed the Civil Rights Bill on July 2, 1964. From the bill's passage to the second half of 1965, the Civil Rights Movement continued to press American society for changes. The Student Nonviolent Coordinating Committee (SNCC) and The Congress of Racial Equality (CORE), with the assistance of northern college students, conducted voters' registration drives in Mississippi, which they called "Freedom Summer." The Mississippi Freedom Democratic Party (MFDP), challenged the seating of an all-white Mississippi delegation at the Democratic National Convention; and riots broke out in the northern cities of New York (Harlem), Brooklyn, and Rochester over the subject of civil

---

48. Colburn, 11.

49. Homer Bigart, "Peace Unit Named for St. Augustine," *New York Times*, 1 July 1964, 1.

50. "Statement on Conditions in St. Augustine, Florida, 17 June 1964," 2, TD [photocopy], King Papers-Series III, Box 6, Folder 4, The King Library Archives, Atlanta.

51. Carson, 241.

52. Pat Watters, *Down to Now: Reflections on the Southern Civil Rights Movement* (New York: Pantheon Books, 1971), 278.

53. Colburn, 112.

rights. Meanwhile, the SCLC convention endorsed President Johnson in the November Presidential election, and Johnson won a landslide victory over Barry Goldwater. SCLC and SNCC planned and conducted a voters' rights campaign in Selma, Alabama. President Johnson addressed Congress on March 15, 1965, and recommended voting rights legislation. On March 22–25 the organizations conducted a march from Selma to Montgomery to demonstrate the need for voters' rights legislation. On August 6, the Voting Rights Act became law. Two days later, riots broke out in the Watts section of Los Angeles, California. Despite the advancements in civil rights over the previous ten years, riots in the black sections of northern cities presented a dilemma for the average white American, some black Americans, and President Johnson.

Prior to the riot in Watts, the Civil Rights Movement had concentrated its campaigns in the Southern states because of the obvious unfairness of *de jure* segregation. In the north, however, *de facto* segregation existed which constituted a change of focus for SCLC from constitutional rights to social rights. King felt the need to address the social rights of northern black citizens after a visit to Watts. The local leaders in Watts expressed their desires to King: "They wished to bring an appeal to the attention of the federal government: the rampant unemployment due to the effects of automation, decaying housing; police brutality, and so forth."[54] However, King focused on the widespread violence, which disturbed him greatly. King understood the cause of the violence, "but violence as retribution was against his principles, and he felt that the riot in Watts was evidence of his failure to get his message of nonviolence across to all Black Americans."[55]

The problems that existed in Los Angeles could be found in numerous northern cities, and King had expressed this concern as early as March 25, 1965, months prior to the signing of the Voting Rights Act. At the end of the Selma to Montgomery march, King told supporters: "Let us march on segregated housing until every ghetto of social and economic depression dissolves and Negroes and whites live side by side in decent, safe and sanitary housing."[56] As early as April 1, 1965, the SCLC discussed moving its civil rights efforts north to the city of Chicago in a board meeting.[57] In response to suggestions about other campaigns, Bayard Rustin said at that meeting: "SCLC must seriously consider going to northern communities this summer—Philadelphia, Detroit, Chicago,

---

54. Andrew Young, *An Easy Burden: The Civil Rights Movement and the Transformation of America* (New York: HarperCollins Publishers, Inc., 1996), 378.

55 Ibid.

56. Carson, 285.

57. Minutes of Board Meetings, April 1–2, 1965, TD [photocopy], Southern Christian Leadership Conference, PMLK, 1954–1968, box 29, folder 5, KLAA, 1.

Cleveland."[58] After some discussion on the matter, Young concluded: "The new direction is going to take us very shortly into the North. There must be some kind of hope given to the millions of Negroes in the Ghettoes to relieve the condition of desperation and poverty."[59]

In making the decision to go North, Young felt that King gave considerable thought to a statement Robert Kennedy made that "the civil rights movement, in focusing on the South, had neglected the problems of the North and the cities."[60] In a public statement two days after the April 1–2 board meeting, Young stated that "Dr. King, with the support of his board, had agreed to help the Northern Negroes organize nonviolent street demonstrations for decent housing, better job opportunities and improved education and against *de facto* segregation."[61]

King scheduled a tour of northern cities including Chicago, Cleveland, Washington, and Philadelphia. In response to an earlier invitation from Albert Raby, chairman of the Coordinating Council of Community Organization (CCCO), an alliance of seventy-five neighborhood civil rights groups, SCLC chose Chicago as its first stop. King led fifteen thousand marchers through the downtown section of Chicago on July 26, 1965, in an attempt to bring attention to the city's segregated schools. In an executive staff meeting on August 26–28, King confirmed that Chicago would be the target.[62] James Bevel, a close associate of King, arrived on Chicago's West Side as an initial force to organize the community. He insisted: "We're going to organize a movement for adequate housing of the Negroes in Chicago. Not equal. We're not Communists. Just adequate distribution of the wealth of this country."[63] Author Stephen B. Oates in *Let the Trumpet Sound: The Life of Martin Luther King Jr.* believed that "it [Chicago] was the most 'ghettoized' city in America, the symbol and capital of segregation in the North. If he and SCLC could solve northern problems here, King felt, they could solve them anywhere."[64]

On January 7, 1966, the SCLC met with the CCCO in Chicago and formed the Chicago Freedom Movement (CFM). The national scope of the campaign became apparent from the very beginning. Raby admitted that "SCLC needs us to help set a pattern for the entire nation, and we need them for their experience

---

58. Ibid., 3.

59. Ibid., 1–2.

60. Young, 380.

61. "Dr. King To Assist Protest In North," *New York Times*, 4 April 1965, 56.

62. Minutes of Executive Staff Meeting, August 26–28, 1965, TD [photocopy], Southern Christian Leadership Conference, Records of the SCLC, box 46, folder 8, KLAA, 6.

63. Roslyn Rosen, "Jim Bevel—He Turns Fear Into An Asset," *Chicago Sun-Times*, 12 September 1965, 36.

64. Oates, 379.

and inspiration."[65] King declared that "our objectives in this movement are federal, state and local. On the federal level we would hope to get the kind of comprehensive legislation which would meet the problems of slum life across the nation."[66] This public statement by King showed that Chicago would be different from Birmingham and St. Augustine in that federal legislation, as a goal, was a primary consideration. In support of King's goal of federal legislation, Levison wrote King that "just as the victory in Birmingham resulted in national legislation and affected the entire south I believe we may force Federal action in Chicago as well as Municipal action."[67] King proceeded to move into a ghetto apartment in the Lawndale neighborhood, using it as his base of operation in Chicago.

Both blacks and whites opposed the presence of King and the SCLC. Six black aldermen who benefited from Mayor Daley's patronage system belonged to this opposition. Even before the CFM became a reality, these aldermen, four black judges, and various other blacks founded a "community action" program in direct opposition to the civil rights movement in Chicago.[68] *The New York Times* reported Chicago Alderman Ralph H. Metcalfe's view: "Dr. King's [proposed] campaign was unnecessary and had an 'ulterior motive.' He did not elaborate."[69] Equally unhappy with King's presence, Mayor Daley employed a different strategy. On February 9, without making reference to King, "Daley announced a new program to clean up the city's slums by the end of 1967."[70] The CFM not only had to overcome this type of opposition, but the question of a united focus within the CFM persisted. "John McDermott [of the Catholic Interracial Council] was concerned that there still was no 'action program to unite SCLC and CCCO'. He appreciated the SCLC leaders giving more time to Chicago, but around what [issues] are we going to do things'?"[71]

The CFM initially focused on poverty in Chicago's ghettos, but that program, called the "Union to End Slums," proved to be unsuccessful. An inside observer revealed: "By late spring it had become apparent that the Union to End Slums

---

65. Alan B. Anderson and George W. Pickering, *Confronting the Color Line: The Broken Promise of the Civil Rights Movement in Chicago* (Athens, Ga.: The University of Georgia Press, 1986), 182.

66. "Statement Announcing the Chicago Plan, 7 January 1966," TD [photocopy], PMLK-Series III, box 10, KLAA, 7.

67. "Letter from S.D. Levison to Martin Luther King, 1 February 1966," TD [photocopy], MLKP-Series III, box 10, KLAA.

68. Austin C. Wehrwein, "Chicago Negroes Criticize Dr. King," *New York Times,* 8 September 1965, 24.

69. Ibid.

70. Biles, 121.

71. Anderson, 186.

would not be able to provide a very large base for a summer direct action program. Some other form of involving the Negro community would be needed if an action program was to be carried out."[72] James R. Ralph in his book *Northern Protest: Martin Luther King, Jr., Chicago, and the Civil Rights Movement,* suggests that "while the Chicago Freedom Movement initially seemed destined to turn on economic issues, it settled on a more traditional civil rights focus: the dual housing market that favored whites over blacks."[73] The CFM labeled its new initiative the "openhousing campaign."

With a clear-cut issue agreed upon, SCLC's executive board delivered the following statement on April 13, 1966: "SCLC therefore calls upon the Congress of the United States to enact compulsive federal fair housing legislation, prohibiting discrimination and segregation in the sale and rental of all housing accommodations, public and private."[74] President Johnson had introduced the Civil Rights Bill of 1966 in his State of the Union Address on January 12. Because of its controversial Title IV, an open housing provision which barred racial discrimination in the sale and rental of all housing, opponents surfaced immediately. As with the Civil Rights Act of 1964, Dirksen voiced initial disapproval along with the objections of the usual Southern Democrats.

Even President Johnson had his reasons for not being as supportive of this civil rights legislation. Besides concerns for black civil rights, President Johnson faced a growing foreign policy problem that began in 1965. He had sent thirty-five hundred U.S. marines to South Vietnam on March 8, and committed fifty thousand more troops on July 28, bringing the total number to one hundred and twenty-five thousand. Being a man of peace, King considered this military build-up a threat to that end. King had raised the question of peace in Vietnam several times in speeches, but decided to use SCLC's annual convention to announce a formal peace initiative.

On August 12, with the backing of his SCLC advisors, King addressed the convention asking ". . . Johnson to make an 'unconditional and unambiguous statement' declaring his willingness to negotiate with the National Liberation Front, the political arm of the Vietcong."[75] The speech produced unexpected negative replies from delegates at the convention and the White House. While

72. Mary Lou Finley, "The Open Housing Marches: Chicago, Summer '66," in David J. Garrow, ed., *Chicago 1966: Open Housing Marches, Summit Negotiations, and Operation Breadbasket* (Brooklyn, N.Y.: Carlson Publishing Inc., 1989), 6.

73. James R. Ralph, Jr., *Northern Protest: Martin Luther King Jr., Chicago, and the Civil Rights Movement* (Cambridge, Mass.: Harvard University Press, 1993), 5.

74. Minutes of Board Meeting, April 13, 1966, TD [photocopy], Southern Christian Leadership Conference, PMLK, 1954–1968, box 29, folder 6, KLAA, 1.

75. Fairclough, 271.

backing the idea of peace in general, the Committee on Resolutions suggested in its report: "We must still, however, affirm that the primary function of our organization is to secure full citizenship rights for the Negro citizens of this country and that our major contribution to world peace and brotherhood is to create a truly democratic society here in America."[76] Johnson "was incensed by King's naive attempt at peacemaking," and used flattery, deceit, and pressure in an attempt to convince him to drop the initiative.[77] Johnson had become obsessed with Vietnam, and any opponents of his policy quickly became enemies. King and SCLC now fell into that category.[78]

Another reason for Johnson's cold shoulder to the Civil Rights Bill of 1966 involved the situation in Chicago. Johnson knew that "Daley's clout extended far beyond the borders of his home state and the confines of the U.S. Conference of Mayors, because he controlled the largest bloc of votes in Congress that would reliably move on one person's orders."[79] Consequently, the Democratic Party relied on the political power which Daley held in his hands. Because of Daley's power, Johnson blatantly chose not to support CFM's demand for housing integration. In speaking about the political drawbacks of creating jobs for the poor in 1965, Nicholas Lemann in *The Promised Land: The Great Black Migration and How it Changed America* confirms: "Actual racial integration was even more politically perilous. Every elected politician who represented cities knew how intense white opposition was to integrated schools and housing."[80] Although Johnson made speeches backing the bill, there seems to have been very little indication of the behind the scenes pushing by him that marked earlier civil rights legislation. Nevertheless, CFM continued to prepare for its summer direct action campaign.

In late May, the CFM set a date of June 26, 1966, for a rally at Soldier Field to kick off its summer campaign. On June 6, however, James Meredith, the first black to attend the University of Mississippi, became the target of an assassin's bullet on a march through that state. The assassin only wounded Meredith, but King and numerous other civil rights leaders vowed to continue Meredith's "march against fear," and the Chicago rally had to be postponed. CFM rescheduled the rally for July 10, 1966. Between thirty and sixty thousand people, both black and white, attended in one hundred degree heat. Afterwards,

---

76. Convention, Report of the Committee on Resolutions, August 11, 1965, TD [photocopy], Southern Christian Leadership Conference, PMLK, 1954–1968, box 31, folder 11, KLAA.

77. Fairclough, 273.

78. Ibid., 293.

79. Nicholas Lemann, *The Promised Land: The Great Black Migration and How It Changed America* (New York: Alfred A. Knopf, 1991), 166.

80. Ibid., 195.

approximately five thousand marchers paraded from Soldier Field to city hall where King taped the CFM demands on one of the doors. The extensive demands included requirements for the city, state, and federal governments. Under the "Demands For Open Housing" appeared: "From the Federal Government: Passage of the 1966 Civil Rights Act with the provision to make it illegal to discriminate in the sale or renting of property on the basis of race, color, creed or national origin."[81] Although Chicago contained numerous local civil rights problems for the CFM, this direct request for federal legislation in its demands highlighted King's pattern of using local concerns to achieve a national outcome.

On the next day, Monday, July 11, the CFM met with Mayor Daley to discuss the demands. The meeting lasted about two hours with Daley being noncommittal about any action during the entire time. At the news conference afterwards, Daley acknowledged that he had listened to the CFM's demands, but felt "they have no solutions."[82] King responded that Daley misunderstood the depth of injustice in Chicago and insisted that "the members of the CFM would be forced to 'escalate' their confrontation."[83] The CFM intended to do just that, but on Tuesday, the West Side of Chicago erupted in violence.

The temperature in Chicago had reached ninety degrees for nine of the twelve days in July. As tradition dictated, black children played in the cool water coming from the city's illegally opened fire hydrants since segregation in most public pools prevented their use. When several youths stole merchandise from a disabled ice cream truck, the police arrived, shut off the hydrant, and departed. The youths promptly turned the water back on. When the police returned, residents began throwing bricks and bottles at them, and soon the entire neighborhood exploded into chaos. Residents threw objects at passing cars and walked through the neighborhood breaking store windows. CFM members, including King, rushed to the area in an attempt to quell the mounting disturbance, but failed to accomplish their goal. The disturbances died overnight, and on the next day, CFM held meetings throughout the affected neighborhood in an attempt to prevent a recurrence of the day before.

The city's response came just as quickly. In their infinite wisdom, city officials instructed city workers to secure fire hydrants on the West Side with devices so residents could not open them. By Friday, the mayor asked Governor Otto Kerner for mobilization of the National Guard to end the rioting. The riot's effect carried beyond Chicago: "Concern in Washington was high enough that John

81. Chicago Freedom Movement Action Demands, July 10, 1966, TO [photocopy], Coordinating Council of Community Organizations, box 1, folder 16, KLAA, 2.

82. Austin C. Wehrwein, "Dr. King Declares Daley Balks Him," *New York Times*, 12 July 1966, 26.

83. Ralph, 109.

Doar and Roger Wilkins of the Justice Department were dispatched to Chicago on an Air Force plane."[84] Meanwhile, Daley blamed members of the CFM staff, charging that they had "been talking for the last year of violence, and showing pictures and instructing people in how to conduct violence."[85]

King and the CFM responded to Daley's comments by scheduling their first direct action campaign, marching into the all white Gage Park section of the city's Southwest Side. CFM workers had been testing real estate offices, to see if service would be provided, and visiting local white businesses since early July. On Thursday, July 14, nearly one hundred civil rights activists marched peacefully through Gage Park with no response from local residents. On Saturday and Sunday of that week, demonstrations continued with a picnic in a city park and a walk through the Gage Park community. Besides a few hecklers, the demonstrations remained peaceful. Andrew Young complained: "The trouble here is that there has been no confrontation."[86]

CFM leaders continued their demonstrations by holding an all-night vigil at a real estate office in Gage Park on Thursday, July 28. That Saturday, two hundred activists marched, and on Sunday, five hundred more participated with the hope of getting real estate brokers to serve blacks. The Sunday march produced a violent reaction on the part of local residents. They threw bottles and rocks at the demonstrators, and shouted insults. The police attempted to protect blacks, but this only made the white crowd angrier. By the end of the day, the white mob had wrecked approximately twenty-four cars, and the injured list stood at thirty.

King personally led a march on August 5, but as soon as the march began, a rock hit him in the head. After regaining his feet, he commented, "It hurt, but it's not an injury."[87] King finally faced the same situation that SCLC had created in its successful Southern campaigns in Birmingham and St. Augustine—"a dramatic confrontation between his nonviolent forces and brutal, hateful whites, over a single, morally clear-cut issue."[88] As in the Southern cities, the situation in Chicago reached beyond its borders. After King's injury on August 5, McPherson informed President Johnson that "the situation in Chicago is extremely bad."[89] Why did Johnson keep such a close eye on the situation in Chicago considering his less than enthusiastic support of the civil rights bill?

---

84. Lemann, 238.
85. "Daley Links Outsiders To Lawlessness," *Chicago Tribune*, 16 July 1966, sec. 1, 2.
86. Ralph, 119.
87. Fairclough, 297.
88. Lemann, 238.
89. Ibid.

In a third run for Mayor in 1963, after being booed off the stage at an NAACP convention, "Daley was canny enough to see that his support among blacks had begun to erode; on the other hand, his support among whites, many of whom perceived him as being too pro-black, had eroded much more severely and dangerously."[90] Daley seemed to be facing the same state of affairs in 1966 because of police protection of black demonstrators. Any erosion of Daley's power had a direct effect on Democratic politics in Congress, so Johnson remained concerned. Johnson also wanted to protect the reelection chances of Senator Paul H. Douglas of Illinois, a constant backer of his policies and a liberal when it came to civil rights. Douglas received letters from Southwest Side voters "accusing Congress of mistreatment and of subversion of the Constitution."[91] Because of the amount of hatred, ugliness, and racism exposed by the marches, the CFM began to get feelers from city hall and black aldermen. Daley promised money for urban renewal and more city jobs for blacks; the black aldermen complained about being excluded from the movement and wanted a meeting with the CFM leadership.[92] King realized that "the marches have not only aroused consciences, but are threatening existing political alliances. To protect his 'vested interest', Daley will eventually 'choose to negotiate civil rights issues rather than face a complete collapse of the alliance."[93] All of this attention, however, failed to meet the movement's goal of "open housing," or obtain a negotiating session with the Mayor. The August 5 march did awaken Chicago's average black citizens, and they began supporting the movement in larger numbers.

On August 8, Jesse Jackson, coordinator of CFM's Operation Breadbasket, announced a march into Cicero, a white suburb bordering Chicago on the west. This announcement horrified many of CFM's white members as well as city and county officials. Cicero remained one of the most racist towns in Illinois. Most Chicagoans remembered the killing of a black teenager by four whites only a few months earlier and the 1951 riot in Cicero when a black family tried to move into the community. Consequently, a march through the town raised the possibility of a bloodbath and loss of life among the demonstrators. The press and white supporters of CFM, including Archbishop John Cody, and Robert Johnson of the United Auto Workers, called for an end to the marches. The *Chicago Daily News* viewed the CFM's lack of warning to police about where their demonstrations would be held as an attempt to produce publicity. The

90. Ibid., 94.
91. Ralph, 127.
92. Fairclough, 297–98.
93. Kathleen Connolly, "The Chicago Open-Housing Conference," in Garrow, ed., *Chicago 1966*, 70.

paper suggested that "the most rational course would be to call off the marches entirely and turn to more constructive pursuits."[94]

After a Tuesday, August 9 meeting between Robert W. Johnson and Raby, "it was learned, the officials called UAW President Walter P. Reuther, in Detroit. Reuther, in turn, called Dr. King in Jackson. Then Dr. King got in touch with Raby . . . the result was that the demonstrations were called off."[95] The final decision to call off a previously planned demonstration in Bogan the next day was made by the CFM Action Committee early Wednesday morning. Since the CFM Action Committee held the final decision, King's request for stopping the demonstrations was temporary. The board substituted an August 10 march on the headquarters of the Chicago Real Estate Board located downtown. Bevel predicted that CFM would march into Bogan by the weekend.[96] That same day, Archbishop Cody joined the voices calling for restraint, stating: "The leaders of the CFM ad a 'serious moral obligation' to consider a halt to the marches."[97]

Meanwhile, UAW officials consulted with the Chicago Commission on Human Relations (CCRR), a group of Chicago religious and civic leaders loyal to Mayor Daley, and scheduled a Thursday, August 11 meeting with Daley and union officials. On Friday, August 12, CCRR's executive director Eugene Callahan, with the approval of Daley, announced a summit meeting for the middle of the next week. Once Daley agreed to meet with King and the CFM, "This was tantamount to admitting that Chicago's housing and slum policies did need serious improvement—something Daley had steadfastly denied—and King, Raby, and other movement leaders regarded it as a tremendous breakthrough."[98]

No specific date had been stated by Jackson for the Cicero march, so ignoring the feeling of its white supporters, the CFM continued demonstrating in Chicago's all white neighborhoods. Simultaneous marches took place on August 14 in three sections of Chicago: Bogan, Gage Park, and Jefferson Park. This action stretched the resources of the Chicago Police Department, and diminished its ability to protect the demonstrators from white attacks. Concern from Washington began to appear as early as August 10th. Representative Roman Pucinski, Democrat of Illinois, met with President Johnson, and asked him to meet with civil rights leaders in an attempt to stop the demonstrations. Pucinski recommended that Johnson tell the leaders "that unless the legislative process is given full opportunity to work its way toward removing inequities they are protesting

94. "The Point Is Made," *Chicago Daily News*, 10 August 1966, 12.

95. Basil Talbott Jr., "Demonstrate At Loop Real Estate Board," *Chicago Sun-Times*, 11 August 1966, 4.

96. Ibid, 4.

97. Fairclough, 299.

98. Oates, 414–15.

the civil rights bill of 1966 will not pass the Senate."[99] Pucinski evidently believed that the CFM's marches were directed, at least in part, towards passage of that bill, but feared that too many of them might cause its defeat.

The first "summit meeting" took place on Wednesday, August 17, 1966 at St. James's Episcopal Church. King, Raby, Young, Bevel, Jackson, and William C. Berry of the Chicago Urban League among others represented the CFM. The other group consisted of Daley, Alderman Thomas Keane, members of the CCRR, and delegates from the real estate board, businesses, industry, and the banks. Ben W. Heineman, president of the Chicago and Northwestern Transportation Company presided as chairman. Once the meeting began, it was immediately clear that "Daley would agree to virtually anything in order to secure a cancellation of the marches."[100] This presented the CFM with an advantage; however, the stance taken by the Chicago Real Estate Board (CREB) remained the critical question. CREB representative Ross Beatty claimed no responsibility on the part of realtors for segregation, claiming they had no power to change social attitudes or solve problems.[101]

By the end of the day, all CFM demands had promises of good faith from the other side, except the request that CREB instruct its members to treat blacks equally in the housing market. Since open housing was CFM's major goal, its members refused to call off the marches. Heineman suggested the formation of a subcommittee to work out a settlement, and proposed they meet again on August 26. The subcommittee held its first meeting on Friday, August 19, the same day that a circuit court judge granted Daley a limited injunction on marches in Chicago.

King immediately voiced disapproval of Daley's injunction, and "indicated that he might defy it."[102] However, in the end, King decided against defiance. Why did King choose to abide by the terms of the injunction? In reality, the CFM could not afford the money necessary to stage massive violations. Also, it would take tens of thousands of people to fill up Chicago's jails, another questionable venture.[103] Instead, CFM leaders responded to the Chicago injunction by staging marches in suburban Chicago Heights, Evergreen Park, and South Deering. *The Chicago Tribune* reported that King's nonviolent campaign had actually brought violence to the city, and called it a plot to "sabotage" Chicago.[104]

---

99. Talbott, 4.

100. Fairclough, 300.

101. Ibid.

102. Donald Janson, "Chicago Injunction Limits Rights Drive; Dr. King May Defy It," *New York Times*, 20 August 1966, 1.

103. Fairclough, 305.

104. "The Sabotage of Chicago," *Chicago Tribune*, 18 August 1966, 22.

The leadership also set a date of Sunday, August 28, for the march into Cicero, if the second summit meeting produced no meaningful progress.

Once the date for the march became known, Cicero town leaders contacted Governor Otto Kerner with a request for help from the National Guard. Since the town's small police force would be inadequate to maintain order, Kerner agreed and made plans for mobilization.

The Heineman subcommittee continued negotiations on Monday, Wednesday and Thursday of the next week. Finally, the participants compromised on an agreement to present at the second summit meeting on August 26, 1966. In good faith, CFM discontinued its marches for the time being, but remained firm on the August 28 Cicero march. Actually, King saw the Cicero march more as a threat to encourage future implementation of any agreement obtained form Daley rather than a reality.[105] He later called the march off, but only temporarily.

On Friday, August 26, 1966, Heineman convened the second summit meeting in the Walnut Room of the Palmer House Hotel. The agreement of the subcommittee became the first order of business. After its reading, Mayor Daley immediately asked for a vote, but the CFM members wanted to discuss the particulars, questioning the "personal commitment" of some members backing Daley to the goals of open housing.[106] The negotiations continued for most of the day, but when the participants emerged, an agreement had been signed. Daley commented: "This is a great, historical day in the life of the City of Chicago. Chicago, as usual, is leading the way for all other major cities."[107] King saw the agreement as the "most significant program ever conceived to make open housing a reality in a metropolitan area. And on this historic occasion, Chicago is well on its way to becoming the nation's leading city in dealing effectively with the critical problems of racial segregation in housing."[108] When asked specifically about opening up white neighborhoods for blacks, King answered that the agreement "is the first step in a 1,000-mile journey, but an important step."[109]

Some participants remained cautious in their reaction to the agreement. When asked if he were satisfied, Bevel replied "I don't know, I'll have to think about it."[110] Illinois' black State Representative William Robinson commented, "I'll have to wait and see whether the program becomes reality."[111] Others

105. Young, 416.

106. Ralph, 169.

107. Hugh Hough and James Campbell, "The Text of Daley's Statement on Accord," *Chicago Sun-Times,* 27 August 1966, 41.

108. Hugh Hough and James Campbell, "Dr. King's Statement on New Agreement," *Chicago Sun-Times,* 27 August 1966, 41.

109. "Cicero Rights March Called Off in Pact," *Chicago Daily News,* 26 August 1966, 4.

110. Ibid.

111. Ibid., 39

acknowledged: "This agreement was seen by some as the necessary price paid to stop three weeks of white violence, violence which was seriously threatening the eleven-year-old political administration."[112] In fact, the agreement contained no guarantees, only pledges by its participants, and no timetable for implementation. Oates argues that "if the agreement mentioned no specific timetable, it was still the most comprehensive of any of King's previous accords, including that in Birmingham."[113] When West Side Organization leader Chester Robinson announced that "we will march into Cicero come hell or high water," King's idea for using the march as a future threat vanished.[114]

This question remains, why did King sign another agreement which allowed the local power base to comply or not once the majority of SCLC workers departed? After the House of Representatives sent the Civil Rights Bill of 1966 to the Senate, without the open-housing provision, a number of earlier public statements should be considered as positive encouragement for King to sign. On Monday, August 8, Senator Everett Dirksen (Republican of Illinois) had predicted: "Congress will pass the administration's civil rights bill, altho it may not contain a controversial open-housing bill . . . we are going to have a bill."[115] Since the bill's passage represented one of the CFM's demands, the leaders probably welcomed this statement. Three days later, a positive response to the bill came from Bill D. Moyers, White House press secretary, who said, "the administration will work to have the Senate restore the open housing section to its original form."[116] Considering the reticent nature of the Johnson Administration in prior months, this most likely added to the CFM's optimism about the bill's passage.

These positive statements however, were accompanied by negative ones, which can also be seen as encouragement for King to sign. On August 12, Vice President Hubert H. Humphrey voiced these concerns. Humphrey agreed with Cody, stating that "there should be a temporary halt in civil rights marches in the Chicago area. Demonstrators have gone so far they have created a backlash of resentment among whites and 'the cause is suffering—the cause of social justice.'"[117] White supporters in Chicago had already given the CFM their views, and a statement of agreement with those supporters from the Vice President surely caught the attention of some CFM leaders. By August 22, Congress indicated that the bill might not be passed in 1966. Dirksen called "this proposal

---

112. Connolly, "Open-Housing Conference," in Garrow, ed., *Chicago 1966*, 51.

113. Oates, 415.

114. Jacques Nevard, "Housing Pact Set, Dr. King Calls Off Chicago Marches," *New York Times*, 27 August 1966, 1.

115. "Civil Rights Bill Will Pass: Dirksen," *Chicago Tribune*, 8 August 1966, sec. 1, 13.

116. Russell Freeburg, "LBJ Hits Open Housing Action," *Chicago Tribune*, 11 August 1966, 11.

117. "Humphrey Asks a Halt in Civil Rights Protests," *New York Times*, 13 August 1966, L7.

to ban racial discrimination in the sale and rental of housing unconstitutional and has said House action to exempt home and small apartment owners hasn't changed his stand."[118] *The Wall Street Journal* questioned the effectiveness of King's efforts in Chicago, stating that "it's an open question whether the drive will strengthen or weaken civil rights legislation in Congress this fall or succeed in opening many all-white areas to Negroes."[119] While these positive and negative public statements may have been a consideration when King signed the Chicago Summit Agreement, another question remains unanswered. Did King use local problems in Chicago, as well as in Birmingham, and St. Augustine to advance passage of national civil rights legislation?

Consider the following facts. The SCLC considered itself a national organization, and in each city mentioned above, local leaders requested their assistance. Those local leaders naturally concerned themselves with the particular forms of segregation they had been fighting long before the SCLC arrived. King and the SCLC agreed to assist in defeating local segregation in these cities, but their national scope remained the basis of their organization. SCLC's presence and assistance in numerous areas of the country throughout the Civil Rights Movement confirms its national outlook.

In Birmingham, just prior to the settlement, black demands contained four conditions: (1) desegregation of lunch counters, rest rooms, fitting rooms, and drinking fountains in department stores; (2) upgrading and hiring of blacks on a nondiscriminatory basis; (3) dropping of all charges against demonstrators; and (4) formation of a biracial committee. On May 10, 1963 when the settlement became public knowledge, the white negotiators had agreed to the essential demands of the black community. A timetable had been negotiated, but no means of insuring implementation was included. Beyond continued SCLC presence, and the threat of further demonstrations, implementation by the local leaders remained the only solution. However, the most important result of the Birmingham campaign affected segregation not only on a local scale, but on a national one as well. On June 11, 1963, President Kennedy announced the outline of a civil rights bill, and sent it to Congress on June 19, 1963.

In St. Augustine, the demands had been cut to only one; creation of a bi-racial committee. Although Governor Bryant announced the formation of a four man bi-racial committee, once SCLC departed, the committee never met. Again, no means of insuring compliance had been put into place. But the Civil Rights Act of 1964 became the law of the land on July 2, 1964, thus providing civil rights for

118. "Dirksen's Stand Could Shelve '66 Civil Rights Bill," *Chicago Sun-Times*, 22 August 1966, 4.

119. Peter H. Prugh, "Selma in Chicago?," *Wall Street Journal*, 24 August 1966, 10.

all Black Americans. Because of the sheer number of Black Americans residing in Chicago, and the multitude of neighborhoods involved, the Chicago demands covered over two pages. The CFM cut those down to one, which in most respects, influenced the others. One demand, open housing, became the primary goal in the negotiations, although secondary measures also concerned the CFM leaders. Once again, the signed agreement contained absolutely no means of enforcement. The Chicago movement remains different from Birmingham and St. Augustine in that the Civil Rights Act of 1966 died in the Senate on September 19, 1966; nevertheless, the campaign heightened awareness of the need for federal housing legislation.

King and the SCLC addressed local concerns in Birmingham, St. Augustine, and Chicago by raising the consciousness of the American public. Citizens were thus able to see the racism that existed and the lack of civil rights experienced by Black Americans. King and the SCLC also used these local situations to dramatize the need for national legislation. They succeeded in getting legislation introduced in the Birmingham campaign, and the St. Augustine campaign insured that that legislation was passed intact. The Chicago campaign created no legislation, but its intentions to do so were obvious. Those individuals who criticized King for being credulous or gullible for signing the Chicago agreement, with no means of enforcement, represent a narrow rather than broad view and are wrong in their assessment of King's abilities. King was not only thinking locally, but sought to advance the lives of all Black Americans by striving for national legislation.

The United States is a country of laws; therefore, laws represent one way of insuring socially acceptable behavior. For Black Americans, legislation has been the single most important means for insuring their civil rights. King and SCLC understood this fact far more than most white or black Americans. Therefore, they kept their sights on the passage of national legislation which would affect all blacks rather than a few.

13. From Gang-bangers to Urban Revolutionaries

The Young Lords of Chicago

JUDSON JEFFRIES

You can arrest us,
You can bum us,
You can kill us,
But you can't stop us
—Cha Cha Jimenez

THE YOUNG LORDS WAS A FLAMBOYANT revolutionary Chicago-based group that was comprised mainly of second generation Puerto Ricans. Although the organization had a flair for the dramatic, its impact was felt far and wide. Very little of a scholarly nature has been written about this important piece of Illinois history, however. Most of what has been written is in the form of popular magazine articles and memoirs that lack the objectivity and rigor expected of a scholarly study.[1] This essay helps to fill that void. It addresses the origins of the Young Lords, the aims, inner-workings and objectives of the group, the impact

JUDSON L. JEFFRIES is Associate Professor of Political Science and American Studies at Purdue University. He earned a Ph.D. at the University of Southern California in 1997. He has held fellowships and teaching posts at Harvard University, Indiana University, and Morehouse College. He has authored three books: *Virginia's Native Son: The Election of Governor L. Douglas Wilder* (2000); *Huey P. Newton, The Radical Theorist* (2002), and *Urban America and its Police* with Harlan Hahn (2003). He is also a volunteer at the Lafayette Adult Resource Academy where he helps young adults earn their high school diplomas and GEDs.

1. Pablo Guzman, "A Lord of the Barrio," *Village Voice*, 21 March 1995: 1–14; Frank Browning, "From Rumble to Revolution: The Young Lords," *Ramparts* 9 (1970–1971), 19–25.

Journal of the Illinois State Historical Society Vol. 96, No. 3 (Autumn 2003): 288–304

the organization had on the Latino community, and the factors that contributed to the Lords' demise?[2]

Puerto Rico became an United States territory in 1898, after the Spanish-American War. It was a colony from 1898 until 1952, when it became a commonwealth. Immediately following the American acquisition, Puerto Ricans were in a state of limbo; they were neither citizens of the United States nor citizens of an independent nation. To make matters worse, the presence of American corporations on the island weakened Puerto Rico's economy.[3] Consequently, many Puerto Ricans immigrated to the United States in search of better economic prospects. A number of Puerto Ricans ventured to Chicago. The first massive immigration of Puerto Ricans to the windy city occurred between 1950 and 1965.[4]

From the outset, most Puerto Ricans were forced to live in the most run-down sections of the city. Many of them settled in an area around Ohio to North Avenue with Clark Street as its nucleus. Among Puerto Ricans this barrio was known as "La Clark." Most of "La Clark" consisted of dilapidated hotels and mansions that were divided into kitchenette apartments and single rooms.[5] Gambling, drugs, and prostitution were prevalent.

By 1970 nearly 250,000 Latinos lived in Chicago. Some were able to find decent-paying jobs, but changes in the labor force reduced the number of jobs available to those with low levels of education and limited skills Those who were able to find work were often under paid.[6] Employers could pay Puerto Ricans less because they were aware that many of them lacked alternative employment prospects. Not only were these jobs low-paying, involving dirty and unsafe working conditions, but they were often temporary and had little advancement potential. According to the 1960 United States Census Report on the "Social and Economic Data for Persons of Puerto Rican Birth and Parentage," the majority were employed in the business sector as messengers and deliverymen or in stock rooms. Others found jobs as janitors and in restaurants as busboys and waiters.[7]

---

2. "Young Lords" and "Lords" are used interchangeably to avoid repetition.

3. Judson L. Jeffries, "The New York State Black and Puerto Rican Legislative Caucus, 1970–1988," *Afro-Americans in New York Life and History* 24 (January 2000), 7–40.

4. Felix Padilla, *Puerto Rican Chicago* (Notre Dame: University of Notre Dame Press, 1987), 21.

5. Felix Padilla, *Puerto Rican Chicago* (Notre Dame: University of Notre Dame Press, 1987).

6. Ibid.

7. U.S. Census, Economic Characteristics of Persons of Puerto Rican Birth and Parentage for Selected Standard Metropolitan Statistical Areas, Chicago, IL: 1960, Table 13, 100.

While Chicago in some ways offered opportunities to Puerto Ricans, discrimination thwarted their progress.[8] In fact, throughout most of the twentieth century, most people of Spanish descent were relegated to the lowest paying and most menial jobs. And because Puerto Ricans were relatively small in population and did not vote in large numbers, they were unable to elect representation that could help provide better housing, more educational opportunities, and better paying jobs. Unlike other major cities such as New York where Puerto Ricans were able to elect some of their own into office as early as the 1930s, Puerto Ricans in Chicago had no political representation.[9] Furthermore, with the exception of Los Caballeros de San Juan, there were no organizations that championed Puerto Rican causes.[10] And, since Puerto Ricans wielded little political influence, those in power often overlooked their interests.

By 1966 things began to change. That summer, a White police officer shot Arcelis Cruz, an unarmed twenty-year-old Puerto Rican man. Parts of the Puerto Rican community erupted. People looted and burned neighborhood businesses, particularly those that were White-owned. The disorder lasted three days. When it was over, sixteen persons were injured, forty-nine people were arrested, and over fifty buildings had been destroyed.[11] The events of 12, 13, and 14 June would serve as a turning point for many Puerto Ricans. The climate would set the stage for a more aggressive Puerto Rican Chicagoan, unafraid to confront the ruling elite and demand that the community's concerns be taken seriously. The Westtown community where the upheaval occurred would later be fertile recruiting ground for the Young Lords.

Orlando Davila and six others founded the Young Lords in Chicago in 1959.[12] Davila served as the Lords' chairman until the mid 1960s. For the first seven years they were just one of Chicago's many street gangs. They responded to White gang violence by forming a Puerto Rican gang for protection. Besides

8. Sam King, "Puerto Ricans are Eager to Work, Want No Handouts," *Chicago Daily News*, 11 August 1959, 6.

9. Judith Ann Stewart, *NYS Black and Puerto Rican Legislators: 1917–1977* (New York: New York State Legislative Library, 1977).

10. Los Caballeros de San Juan, the first major Puerto Rican community organization was chartered in 1954 in the state of Illinois as a fraternal and civic entity for Spanish-speaking men. The organization worked to "cleanse" the stigma of an oppressed minority status. Los Caballeros hoped to accomplish this by relying on the assimilationist approach, which in the long run, resulted in very little success and a great deal of frustration for the Puerto Rican masses. For more detail see Felix Padillo, *Puerto Rican Chicago* (Notre Dame: University of Notre Dame Press, 1987).

11. Felix Padilla, *Puerto Rican Chicago* (Notre Dame: University of Notre Dame Press, 1987), 146.

12. Hilda Vasquez Ignatin, "Young Lords Serve-and Protect," *The Movement*, May 1969, 4.

protecting Latinos from White bullies, the Lords fought for control of hangouts and turf.[13] At one of the sessions that led to the founding of the gang, Davila asked Cha Cha Jimenez and several other youth to attend a meeting. Jimenez seemed uninterested at first, but later joined the gang as a rank and file member. He developed a reputation not only for being tough, but also for being loyal. Whenever he was arrested, he refused to make any deals that involved incriminating other gang members. This won him respect within the gang community. By the time he was seventeen, he had risen to Chairman of the organization.[14]

Jimenez was born on 8 August 1948 in El Millon, a slum of Caguas, Puerto Rico.[15] His mother Eugenia had been raised in a convent because her father was blind and unable to care for her. At the age of sixteen, she left the convent to marry Jimenez's father, Antonio. During her pregnancy, she went to Caguas to be near a doctor. Antonio Jimenez had already left to find a job in the United States; he was in a migrant camp near Boston when Jimenez was born.[16] When Jimenez was two years old, his father earned enough money to send for him and his mother. They lived outside of Boston for a year, and then moved to Chicago. As a boy Jimenez was attracted to Chicago's mean streets. He was arrested numerous times. Although once an altar boy, his inability to stay out of trouble as he got older was the reason a judge ordered him deported to Puerto Rico for one year. When Jimenez returned to Chicago, he soon found himself in jail once again. This time, Jimenez spent time reading. He recalled, "I started reading in jail, and I guess it was Martin Luther King's books about changing things that started my political education."[17] Jimenez also read about Malcolm X, the Massacre of Ponce, and don Albizu Campos.[18]

His thirst for knowledge led him to reflect on the plight of Puerto Ricans in the United States. He was shocked at the disproportionate number of people of color, especially Latinos, in America's jails and prisons.[19] He began to understand

---

13. Eric Mink, "Young Lords & Their Reign," *Daily News*, 17 October 1996, 126.

14. Ibid.

15. "Que Viva El Pueblo": A Biographical History of Cha Cha Jimenez. (Unpublished Manuscript, 1973), 1.

16. Ibid.

17. Jules Archer, *Revolution in our Time* (New York: Julian Messner, 1971), 51.

18. The Ponce Massacre occurred in 1937, when nineteen Puerto Rican Nationalists were killed by police, and another two hundred were wounded during a peaceful demonstration. The demonstration had been organized on Palm Sunday to protest the U.S. government's imprisonment of Nationalist Party leader Albizu Campos on sedition charges.

19. Frank Browning, "From Rumble to Revolution: The Young Lords," *Ramparts* 9 (1970–1971), 19–25.

that the real enemy was not other gangs like the Paragons or the Black Eagles but Mayor Richard Daley's administration and the United States government (whose imperial colonization policy had so ravaged Puerto Rico that many Puerto Rican families were forced to leave in search of a better life). A Young Lords field marshall said, for example, "What we had to realize was that it wasn't no good fightin' each other, what we were doing as a gang had to be done against the capitalist institutions that are oppressing us."[20]

One institution that seemed to cause Latinos a great deal of anguish was the Chicago police department.[21] As in many other major American cities, police harassment of minorities was an ongoing problem. Many Puerto Rican residents complained that the Chicago police did not treat residents like human beings but like animals and that their presence in the community made residents uneasy.

After Jimenez was released from jail, he developed a close friendship with Chicago Black Panther leader Fred Hampton. Hampton's influence on Jimenez proved to be fundamental to the latter's political development.[22] Not surprisingly, Jimenez held the Black Panthers in high regard. On one occasion, when asked about the Lords' affiliation with the Black Panther Party, Jimenez said, "we see and recognize the Black Panther Party as a vanguard revolutionary party. And we feel that as revolutionaries we should follow the vanguard party."[23]

By 1967, Jimenez had changed the Lords' orientation from a street gang to an agent of social change. The conversion was a long arduous process. Although he was not able to get through to all of his fellow gang members, he did muster enough support to redirect its focus. In the process Jimenez changed the group's name from the Young Lords to the Young Lords Organization. The Lords' metamorphosis coincided with the mood of the late 1960s. The Black Power, Chicano, and Women's Liberation movements were in the early phases of their development and the anti-war movement was at its apex—all parts of the political context within which the Young Lords Organization emerged. The Lords' first order of business as a political organization was to negotiate a truce with some of Chicago's major gangs, convincing them to redirect their hostilities toward the agents of repression. Among the gangs that the Lords were able to influence was the Latin Kings, which was reputed to have a membership of three thousand, making it the city's largest gang.[24]

---

20. Ibid.

21. *Chicago Sun-Times,* "Fight Area Residents Tell of Police Puerto Rican Relations," 13 June 1966, 2.

22. Andres Torres and Jose E. Velazquez eds, *The Puerto Rican Movement: Voices from the Diaspora* (Philadelphia: Temple University Press, 1998), 212.

23. "Interview with Cha Cha Jimenez Chairman—Young Lords Organization," *The Black Panther,* 7 June 1969, 17.

24. Hilda Vasquez Ignatin, "Young Lords Serve-and-Protect," *The Movement,* May 1969, 4.

The evolution of the Young Lords caught the attention of Latinos throughout the country. Jose Martinez, a member of Students for a Democratic Society (SDS), was intrigued by the Lords' transformation. At SDS's May 1969 convention in Chicago, Martinez met Jimenez and inquired about starting a chapter in New York.[25] With Jimenez's approval, Martinez returned to the Empire State and opened a branch of the Young Lords in East Harlem. In subsequent years other chapters sprouted in Boston, Bridgeport, New Haven, Philadelphia, Newark, New Jersey, and Puerto Rico. Like many radical organizations of color during the period, the Young Lords did not allow Whites to join. In the words of Young Lord Rafael Viera, "we refuse white people admittance into the YLO for the purpose that we are out there to serve the community, the Puerto Rican community. If white people want to serve their community then there is the Young Patriots in Yorkville or other respective white organizations."[26]

Although Whites were prohibited from joining the organization, the Young Lords were not racists. In fact, their hope was that one day White revolutionaries would join them and Blacks in a collective struggle to liberate all oppressed people. One member explained, "what we are trying to destroy is not white people, but a system created by white people."[27] While the organization was overwhelmingly Puerto Rican, African Americans and other Latinos were welcomed.[28] That Blacks would be permitted to join is not surprising. Both Blacks and Puerto Ricans share a common African historical background and both suffered from the American-American legacy of segregation and discrimination. Said one Young Lord, "before they called me spic they called me nigger."[29]

At its peak the organization claimed to have one thousand members.[30] They ranged in age from children of twelve years to men and women in their early thirties. Men held nearly all of the leadership positions. However, women played an integral role in the organization's success. The Lords considered themselves full-time revolutionaries. Some decided against holding jobs in order to devote all of their time to organizing and serving the people. Individuals who made such sacrifices were given a per diem for meals and other essentials.[31] The Young Lords Organization did not publicly reveal the size of its membership. To those

---

25. Pablo Guzman, "A Lord of the Barrio," *Village Voice*, 21 March 1995, 1–14.
26. Roland Young, "The Young Lords Organization on the Move: Interview with Rafel Viera," *Community News Reporter*, 8 February 1970, no page number.
27. Pablo Guzman, "A Lord of the Barrio," *Village Voice*, 21 March 1995, 1–14.
28. African Americans were more likely to be members of the Young Lords chapter in New York than in Chicago.
29. Pablo Guzman, "The Party," from *Palante! Young Lords Party*, in Robert Santiago ed., *Boricuas* (New York: Ballentine Books, 1995), 54.
30. Pablo Guzman, "A Lord of the Barrio," *Village Voice*, 21 March 1995b, 1–14.
31. Jose Yglesias, "Right on With the Young Lords," *New York Times*, 28 June 1970, 57.

who inquired, the Lords' standard reply was, "those who tell don't know and those who know don't tell."[32]

The organization helped to support itself by selling the *YLO*, a monthly newspaper. The *YLO*, published in both Spanish and English, printed articles on local, national and international affairs. The Lords envisioned the newspaper as a tool that would help heighten the level of political consciousness within the Latino community. Since the paper was published only once a month, it could not sustain the organization financially. Hence, the Lords also sold posters and buttons and secured donations from philanthropists and local businesses.

The organizational hierarchy and structure of the Young Lords Organization in many ways paralleled those of the Black Panther Party. Members would report in and get their daily assignments from the Officer of the Day. The organization's governing body was called the Central Committee, a term traditionally associated with the communist movement. The committee was organized into ministerial divisions, with specific lines of authority and levels of responsibility. The positions included Chairman, Minister of Information, Minister of Education, Minister of Finance, Minister of Defense, Minister of Health, Chief of Staff, Minister of Economic Development, and Communications Deputy. From the outset, Jimenez delegated much of the leadership responsibility to his ministers to counteract the government's proclivity for targeting an organization's leader as a way of undermining its effectiveness. Jimenez surmised that, in the event of his arrest, the organization would be strong enough to function without him.

The Young Lords saw themselves as revolutionary nationalists even though many of their ideological mentors espoused an internationalist world view. Political education classes were held where members discussed the works of Frantz Fanon, Malcolm X, Che Guevara, Karl Marx, and others. The purpose of these classes was to learn to apply theory to real world situations. In addition to setting up study groups, the Lords established classes in marital arts.

Although the organization did not have an official uniform, like the Black Panther Party or Us, the Young Lords wore a purple beret.[33] They devised a twelve-point program that appeared to be modeled after the Panthers and the Nation of Islam. It called for self-determination for all oppressed people, an

32. Michael T. Kaufman, "Black Panthers Join Coalition With Puerto Rican and Appalachian Groups," *New York Times*, 9 November 1969, 1.

33. The Black Panther Party was a revolutionary Black internationalist group that wore black leather jackets, black berets, and powder blue shirts as their uniforms. Us was a Black cultural nationalist group founded by Maulana Karenga in Los Angeles in 1965. Us means us against them. The group was known for wearing dashikis. Jose Yglesias, "Right on With the Young Lords," *New York Times*, 28 June 1970.

education that reflected the Latino experience and, an end to capitalism.[34] The Lords called for the liberation of Puerto Ricans in America as well as in Puerto Rico. From their standpoint, Puerto Ricans on the island lived in an oppressive colony of the United States, while Puerto Ricans in America lived under conditions of internal colonialism. The Lords believed that armed struggle would probably and eventually be the only way to achieve liberation. Yet unlike the Panthers, guns were not a part of the Lords' program.[35] Said Jimenez, "we have to educate the people before we think about guns."[36] Unlike some earlier groups, the Lords did not believe in plebiscites, such as the one held in 1967 in Puerto Rico, in which only one percent of the voters expressed a desire for national independence over statehood or commonwealth status.[37] The Lords were in accord with nationalist groups in Puerto Rico that called for a boycott of the referendum. They argued that a combined program of education and direct struggle by Puerto Ricans could only gain national independence, and that the political aims must be accompanied by economic ones that would break American domination of the island.

It would take two years after its conversion before many Chicago residents would learn of the Young Lords. In April 1969, just as a national conclave of Presbyterian ministers convened in Texas, the Lords along with the Panthers, the Young Patriots, and the SDS moved to take over Presbyterian McCormick Theological Seminary in Chicago.[38] They entered the premises, barricaded the doors, and set up security with walkie-talkies. During the occupation the Young Lords publicized the city's attempts to displace Puerto Ricans from the Lincoln Park community and charged that the seminary was complicit in this displacement. The seminary's president, Arthur McKay, threatened that he was going to call the police to remove the Lords. Jimenez remembers, "we made it clear that no warrant to leave, no piece of paper was going to evict us."[39] Classes at the seminary were suspended for four days as the Young Lords' occupation of the campus lasted almost a week. The Young Lords demanded that the seminary provide funds for low-income housing in the community, a children's center, a cultural center for Latin Americans, and legal assistance."[40]

34. See January issue of *YLO* for a detailed look at the twelve-point program.

35. Whether the Lords carried guns or not is debatable. What is true is that members did not openly carry firearms.

36. Jules Archer, *Revolution in our Time* (New York: Julian Messner, 1971), 51.

37. Jose Yglesias, "Right on With the Young Lords," *New York Times*, 28 June 1970, 57.

38. The Young Patriots was an organization comprised of poor White radicals from the Chicago area.

39. Frank Browning, "From Rumble to Revolution: The Young Lords," *Ramparts* 9 (1970–1971), 20.

40. "3 Protest Groups Occupy Seminary," *Chicago Sun-Times*, 16 May 1969: 46.

When the media learned of the occupation, reporters rushed to the scene. Jimenez recalls,

> McKay talked to the Board and dropped the charge, and we got a call from Texas saying we had got $600,000 for low-income housing in Lincoln Park. The Board agreed to meet our demands for housing, that their financial records be open, that McCormick join to help community groups, that it publicly oppose the racist policies of Urban Renewal, and that it open its facilities to the use of the community. We were in the building for five days before we got that decision.[41]

The action was taken by the Lords primarily to dramatize the situation of the poor in Lincoln Park and to demand that McCormick Theological Seminary and other institutions get involved. The media exposure garnered inadvertently helped the Young Lords with recruitment. The incident appealed to some younger Puerto Ricans, as many of them had never witnessed such a bold political act. Shortly thereafter, the Young Lords Organization experienced a rise in membership.

The Young Lords Organization implemented a number of substantive community service projects aimed at meeting the needs of the people in Chicago's barrios and ghettoes. They established a free breakfast program for children where the Puerto Rican national anthem was played each morning so that the children would stay connected to their culture. The Young Lords also set up a daycare center, much to the chagrin of some White residents and city officials. Leaders asked officials at the Armitage Avenue Methodist Church for permission to establish a daycare center, and although the minister of the church was receptive to the idea, the congregation was not.[42] Unwilling to take no for an answer, the Lords occupied the church. The take-over had been preceded by a sit-in, which began 11 June 1969 and ended four days later with the occupation of the church. Many White residents of Lincoln Park opposed the idea of a daycare center and asked city inspectors to conduct an investigation of the site to determine if it would be in compliance with state regulations. Residents were hopeful that the inspectors' findings would cause the Lords to drop the idea. Indeed, inspectors found eleven violations. The total cost for correcting the violations was estimated at ten thousand dollars.[43] Undeterred, the Young Lords raised the money and opened the daycare center two months later.

One of the organization's most laudable efforts involved a plan to establish a "poor people's" housing project on the west side of Lincoln Park near Larrabe

---

41. Frank Browning, "From Rumble to Revolution: The Young Lords," *Ramparts* 9 (1970–1971), 20.

42. Felix Padilla, *Puerto Rican Chicago* (Notre Dame: University of Notre Dame Press, 1987).

43. Ibid.

and Eugene streets.[44] Knowing that the Department of Urban Renewal (OUR) had approved the construction of a housing plan there, the Young Lords proposed that forty percent of the units be reserved for low-income families. The organization also demanded that the rent be subsidized by the United States Department of Housing and Urban Development under Section 8.[45]

The Lincoln Park Conservation Community Council (LPCCC), a group of community residents named by Mayor Daley to oversee and approve government urban renewal in the community, countered the Lords' proposal with one of their own. The LPCCC'S plan, aimed primarily at middle-income families, called for setting aside only the Federal Housing Authority minimum of fifteen percent for low-income family units. After the announcement of this plan, the Lords vowed to disrupt any open meeting held by this group to seek support of its plan. In July 1969, several meetings were disrupted when boisterous Young Lords stormed the stage and refused to allow the agenda to be implemented.[46]

On 11 February 1970 the Department of Urban Renewal rejected the poor people's plan. In an open meeting in the council chambers in city hall, the board turned down the bid to build a housing project for low- and moderate-income families. The OUR voted to award construction of a seventy unit project, which provided fifteen percent of the housing for poor people. Pandemonium nearly broke out in the council chambers following the OUR's decision. The *Chicago Tribune* reported that policemen subdued one person after he leaped over a spectator's partition to reach the area where the board members were sitting.[47] Although the Young Lords' demands were not met, their confrontation with the Lincoln Park Conservation Community Council signaled a new response among Puerto Ricans to their housing situation.

Determined not to become disillusioned, the Young Lords immediately began work to secure a clinic for the community. The free Health Clinic, which opened in late February 1970, was staffed with doctors, nursing students, and other healthcare professionals. A third year medical student at Northwestern University supervised the clinic. The clinic served nearly fifty people every Saturday, with services from prenatal care to eye examinations.[48] At first some residents were reluctant to visit the clinic. They were still leery of the Lords' old gang image and were frightened by what they read in the newspapers. Recognizing their

44. *Chicago Sun-Times,* "Federal Program Approved for Lincoln Park Area," 23 June 1969, 28.

45. Ibid.

46. "Council Chairman Calls Housing Biggest Need," *Chicago Tribune,* 14 December 1969, 8.

47. *Chicago Tribune,* "Assail Lincoln Park Decision," 12 February 1970: 1.

48. Frank Browning, "From Rumble to Revolution: The Young Lords," *Ramparts* 9 (1970–1971), 22.

credibility problem, the Young Lords started canvassing door-to-door, asking residents if anyone needed medical care and making arrangements for them to go to the clinic. If the people failed to appear, they were sent a follow-up letter inviting them to visit the clinic. Some of the time, members of the Health Ministry and doctors would make house calls, especially for those whose mobility was restricted.

Initially Grant Hospital (an area hospital) agreed to provide free follow-up examinations upon referral by the clinic's doctors. But the hospital soon began billing the clinic patients and initiating collection procedures. Consequently, the Lords severed its relationship with the hospital. By that time, however, the Lords had earned the trust of the people and were able to increase the level of its services in order to meet the community's growing needs. Through the Health Clinic the Lords were able to strengthen their bond with the community and to expose the inadequacies of the established social service institutions. The Health Clinic proved to be the most successful organizing tool for the Lords. Other community service activities included neighborhood clean-ups and free clothing drives. The Lords also pushed for bilingual education in public schools.

In addition to the tangible benefits that the Young Lords Organization provided, the Lords also played an important symbolic role for Puerto Ricans in Chicago. According to one member of the organization, before the Young Lords Organization was founded, Puerto Ricans used to walk with their heads down. Puerto Ricans had been socialized into being docile and submissive. Said another Young Lord, "from day one Puerto Ricans were told that Puerto Rico was small and the United States was big; Puerto Rico was poor and the United States was rich. Puerto Rico was weak and the United States was strong."[49] It is no wonder that, when many Puerto Ricans migrated to the states, they arrived with something of an inferiority complex.[50]

In striving for Puerto Rican equality, the Lords helped to instill in Puerto Ricans a sense of self-worth and pride in their heritage and culture. Marina Roseman said, "the Young Lords provided a rite of passage for a generation of politically conscious young people."[51] Full equality for the Lords was not simply about acquiring material benefits; it was also about dignity, integrity and self-respect for a people that had historically been consigned to an inferior place by many Whites. The Lords filled a leadership vacuum that seemingly could not be filled by any other organization. They risked their lives in the struggle for

49. Ibid.

50. Jennifer Lee, "The Young Lords: A New Generation of Puerto Ricans. An Oral History," *Culturefront*, Fall (1994): 1.

51. Marina Roseman, "The New Rican Village: Taking Control of the Image-making Machinery," *New York Folklore* 6 (1980): 45–54.

Puerto Rican self-determination and, in the process, they became folk heroes to some of the city's Latino residents.[52]

The Young Lords were in the process of setting up a free day care center and a substance abuse program when they were met with systematic repression by Mayor Daley's administration.[53] Although the Young Lords were able to put the daycare facility in place, the drug program never materialized. Daley apparently believed that the Young Lords stood in the way of his plans for urban renewal. In part, because he was receiving funds from the federal government, Daley could not allow representatives from the Department of Housing and Urban Development (HUD) to be intimidated by menacing-looking Young Lords who opposed his scheme for urban renewal. Hence, when the Young Lords began holding rallies and demonstrations in protest of Daley's plans, he called a press conference and announced a "War on Gangs." Daley proposed to put one thousand more police officers on the streets by the following year.[54] As part of this initiative the Gang Intelligence Unit (GIU) increased its number of officers from thirty-seven to two hundred.

Jimenez appeared to be the focus of Daley's GIU. On one occasion, in January 1969, Jimenez was standing on a street comer explaining urban renewal to a crowd of people when two policemen from the GIU drove up and ordered him to get into the car. "Am I under arrest?" Jimenez asked. "No, we just want to talk with you," replied an officer.[55] At the police station, the officers kept Jimenez for two hours while they perused their files for warrants. The officers reminded Jimenez of his record and advised him to stop his political activities. Jimenez replied that he did not see anything illegal about his activism. He had been put in jail before for stealing from his people. If he had to go to jail now for helping his people, then he would do so. The police used two warrants from 1967 to arrest Jimenez. He was released on bond a week later, but the harassment continued.

Shortly thereafter Jimenez was arrested again, along with twelve others, at a welfare demonstration and charged with "mob action." Of the thirteen arrested, Jimenez was the only one indicted. The arrests and indictments continued

52. U.S. Commission on Civil Rights, *Puerto Ricans in the Continental United States: An Uncertain Future* (Washington, DC: Government Printing Office, 1976), 5.

53. In *Political Repression in Modern America: 1870 to the Present,* Robert J. Goldstein defines political repression as government action that grossly discriminates against persons or organizations viewed as presenting a fundamental challenge to existing power relationships or key government policies, because of their perceived political beliefs. Robert J. Goldstein, *Political Repression in Modern America: 1870 to the Present* (New York: Schenkman, 1978), XIV.

54. "Gang Busters," *The Movement,* August 1969, 15.

55. "Que Viva El Pueblo": A Biographical History of Cha Cha Jimenez (Unpublished Manuscript, 1973), 19.

through 1969 and 1970. By mid 1970 Jimenez had been arrested eighteen times.[56] Because he had numerous cases against him, he not only had to appear in court three to four times a week, but he had to appear in different courts simultaneously. Jimenez's attorneys informed the court that he would be appearing late, the judge issueed a warrant for his arrest. While it appears that Jimenez was unfairly singled out by law enforcement, there were at least two occasions where he was found to be in possession of marijuana. And on another occasion Jimenez was arrested for stealing lumber from a construction site.[57] Initially, he claimed that he did not steal the lumber. However, his actions belied those of an innocent man when he jumped bail and disappeared for over a year. Jimenez eventually turned himself in during an emotional ceremony at the nineteenth precinct. He was sentenced to nine months in jail for theft. While it does appear that Jimenez was subjected to police harassment, some of his troubles were clearly self-initiated.

At any rate, Jimenez was not the only one subjected to Daley's repressive tactics. Several members of the Central Committee received four to five indictments for various offenses. Some of the Young Lords supporters, especially those who protested Daley's urban renewal, were also harassed. Members of the "Red Squad" photographed people from their squad cars and later visited them at their homes.[58] Police stopped and questioned people who wore buttons distributed by the Young Lords, such as one that read "Tengo Puerto Rico en mi Corazon" ("I have Puerto Rico in my heart.") Intelligence files were kept on some barrio residents. Oftentimes, anybody from the community who went to a meeting was labeled as an activist by the police.[59]

Perhaps the most crushing blow dealt the Young Lords occurred in May 1969. On the night of the 4 May the Lords were hosting a party as part of their fundraising activities when a White plain-clothes off-duty police officer entered the premises, ostensibly because of the loud music. What transpired next is murky. The Lords claimed that officer Robert Lamb shot and killed Manuel Ramos in cold blood and wounded another Lord.[60] Ramos had been one of the most dedicated members of the organization. The Lords claimed that the shooting was unprovoked. When uniformed officers arrived on the scene, Lamb

---

56. Ibid., 21.

57. Ibid., 21.

58. The Red Squad was an undercover police unit within the Chicago Police Department. The CPD used Red Squad officers to infiltrate groups, spy on their activities and at times provoke the group's members into foolish actions.

59. Felix M. Padilla, *Puerto Rican Chicago* (Notre Dame, IN: University of Notre Dame Press, 1987), 172.

60. Janet Jones, "You Can't Stop Us," *The Movement* (June 1969): 4.

pointed out four of the Lords who were then arrested. Lamb claimed that Ramos reached for his gun, causing him to fire in self-defense. The Lords claimed that Ramos was peacefully trying to break up a heated argument between Lamb and another person. What actually happened is still a matter for debate. What is clear is that government repression took its toll on the Young Lords Organization. Some argue that the Young Lords were targeted because they were associated with Puerto Rico's independence movement. In their book, *The Cointelpro Papers: Documents from the FBI's Secret Wars Against Dissent in the United States,* Ward Churchill and Jim Vander Wall show that the independence movement for Puerto Rico was under surveillance by the Federal Bureau of Investigation (FBI).[61] Former Young Lord Iris Morales recounts how police and federal agents would come to their homes at odd hours and question them about their views on Puerto Rican independence.[62]

As far as the city and the federal governments were concerned, the Lords were subversive and criminal. Consequently, the police and the FBI infiltrated the organization with the intention of destroying it from within. In addition, group leaders were harassed, beaten, and jailed, disrupting the organization's day-to-day operations. The main tactic used against the Lords was to arrest its members so that the organization would have to expend its resources on legal assistance and bail. Anthony Oberschall underscores this point when he writes "the government's strategy appeared to be to tie down movement leaders in costly and time consuming legal battles that would impede their activities and put a tremendous drain on financial resources regardless of whether the government would be successful in court."[63] The systematic arresting of Young Lords also served to discourage potential recruits.

Another way in which the government sought to neutralize the Lords was to intentionally misrepresent the ideology and intentions of the group. Local politicians such as Daley, Alderman George McCutcheon, State Attorney Edward Hanrahan, as well as certain segments of the news media, tried to portray the Lords as a group of rabble-rousing vandals. They attempted to manipulate Chicago's residents so that they would ignore the message that the Lords were trying to get out, and distrust and refuse to be moved by their rhetoric. Some argue that if the government could convince the public that left-wing ideologies were destructive and un-American, then dissident groups such as the Young Lords

---

61. Ward Churchill and Jim Vanderwall, *The Cointelpro Papers: Documents from the FBI's Secret Wars Against Dissent in the United States* (Boston: South End Press, 1990).

62. David Gonzalez, "Young Lords: Vital in 60's, A Model Now," *New York Times,* 16 October 1996, Section B: 1.

63. Anthony Oberschall, "The Decline of the 1960 Social Movements." In Louis Kriesberg ed., *Social Movements,Conflicts and Change* (Greenwich, CT: Jai Press, 1978), 277–88.

would gain fewer adherents and eventually fizzle out. The idea that a form of repression could be ideological has its major expositor in the Italian Marxist Antonio Gramsci. Gramsci who maintained that remain in power not only do so by force, but also by developing a certain set of ideas that become part of the culture, thereby making their rule seem just and normal.[64]

In the Young Lords' case, police were known to spread erroneous information about the group as a way of driving away sympathizers. In *The Police and the Ghetto,* J. C. Cooper notes that "undercover police officers were responsible for feeding the news media discoloring information about radical groups; with the result that to this day, most Americans do not know the message that some of these groups were trying to deliver."[65] In the beginning, law enforcement tried to paint the Lords as Communists and unpatriotic, which were considered serious offenses at that time. Later, FBI Director J. Edgar Hoover would try to convince many that the Lords were the Latino version of the Weather Underground, a White terrorist group known for its use of explosives.

Discouraging employers from hiring members of the Young Lords was another way that law enforcement tried to derail the Young Lords Organization.[66] Again, this tactic scared away potential recruits. Moreover, it proved a major hindrance to Lord members with families to support. Given the Young Lords long-time reputation as a street gang one can understand why the government may have felt compelled to investigate them. However, the "do whatever it takes to get them" attitude taken by various government agencies resulted in a violation of basic civil liberties.

By 1971 the organization's demise was in full swing. Aside from government repression, youthful inexperience led to errors in judgment. The Lords lacked discipline. One Young Lord complained that some members would consistently show up late for meetings, spend too much time hanging out on the street instead of organizing, and allow old programs to fall by the wayside when a new one caught their interest.[67]

Moreover, the organization developed an infatuation with ideological refinement. Originally built upon the concept of direct community action, the Lords

---

64. Giuseppe Fiori, *Antonio Gramsci: Life of a Revolutionary* (London: New Left Books, 1970) and John M. Cammet, *Antonio Gramsci and the Origins of Italian Communism* (Stanford: Stanford University Press, 1967), 28, 36.

65. J.C. Cooper, *The Police and the Ghetto* (Port Washington, NY: National University Publications, 1980), 72.

66. Pablo Guzman, "The Party: From Palante! Young Lords Party," in Roberto Santiago ed., *Boricuas* (New York: Ballantine Books, 1995a), 59–70.

67. Frank Browning, "From Rumble to Revolution: The Young Lords," *Ramparts* vol. 9 (1970–1971): 21.

became preoccupied with theory at the expense of their community service projects. This point is made abundantly clear in a 1969 interview of Jimenez who mentioned on several occasions, "The Young Lords are going to try to get a little more ideology. We have to do this to educate the Latin community, not just Puerto Ricans, but also Chicanos, Cubans, South Americans, the whole Latin scene."[68] Elaborate socialist ideas meant very little to the people whose immediate concerns were food, shelter, and clothing.

For the poor and disenfranchised, goals of social justice needed to be straightforward and immediately achievable. The Lords made the critical mistake of straying from immediate and foreseeable goals for the sake of theoretical development.[69] In the midst of the Black Power Movement, the Vietnam War, and liberation movements in Africa, Asia and Latin America, the Young Lords Organization was born. Within two years, the Lords had become one of the most widely-known radical groups in America, let alone Chicago. The organization consisted of young people who, through direct action, made an impact on the conditions and, more importantly, the consciousness of the Latino community.

To achieve what the Lords did in such a short time (1967–1972) required an unwavering desire and steadfast commitment. The leading activities undertaken by the Young Lords were designed to thwart Mayor Daley's plans to displace segments of the Puerto Rican community under the guise of urban renewal. The Lords' approach was based on the premise that the most powerful resource that they possessed was their ability to cause trouble—to disrupt institutions of the established system and produce political reverberations in order to heighten awareness and bring attention to the issues, thus forcing the authorities to respond. For the poor who attempt to initiate change, disruption is often their only recourse.[70]

The Lords instilled a sense of pride in many Puerto Ricans. And although the Young Lords Organization was relatively small in membership, the impact made by the group was in some ways immeasurable. They demonstrated that an organization does not have to be large in size in order to make a big and far reaching impact. Unfortunately, in the end the Young Lords Organization fell victim to many of the same problems that afflicted other left wing groups. The irony is that one of the Lords' mantras was to avoid repeating the mistakes that other groups had made. Yet, one of the Lords' most costly mistakes was to lose touch with the community. Perhaps the Lord's failed to realize that the success of

---

68. "We're Fighting Freedom Together . . . There is no other way," *The Movement* (1969), 13.

69. Frances Fox Piven and Richard Cloward, *Poor People's Movements* (New York: Pantheon, 1977), 101–2.

70. Ibid.

an organization is largely predicated on the support of the people that it claims to represent.

Despite the Young Lords' failures one could argue that the organization laid the groundwork for a new kind of Puerto Rican—a less passive generation willing to bring about faster and more substantive change. As a result, Young Lord chapters were formed in various parts of the country. These chapters became a vehicle for the political maturation of a sector of second and third generation Puerto Ricans. The impact of the Young Lords is also evident in the area of electoral politics and contemporary grassroots activism. For example, until the 1970s Latinos had been effectively kept out of Chicago politics. By 1975 three Latinos had been elected to public office. Since that time Latinos have been elected to a variety of local offices throughout the city. Organizations such as the Puerto Rican Cultural Center and the Centro Cultural Segundo Ruiz Belvis, the Westtown Concerned Citizens Coalition and the creation of Puerto Rican Students Unions are just a few examples of groups that drew inspiration from the dissident politics of the Young Lords. These endeavors serve to remind us of the continuing legacy of the Young Lords Organization. Surely, the voice of the Young Lords was not the first time that the clamor of Puerto Rican protest had been heard, but it was certainly the first time it reached a national audience.

14. The Decline of Decatur

ROGER BILES

DEINDUSTRIALIZATION EXACTED A SEVERE TOLL on Chicago, the economic bellwether of the midwestern Rustbelt, but much smaller cities scattered throughout Illinois also suffered considerably due to the loss of manufacturing jobs and population in the last decades of the twentieth century. These cities enjoyed less economic diversification than the Windy City and frequently relied on a few key employers for their continued prosperity. As a result, communities outside the sprawling metropolitan region abutting Lake Michigan felt the sting of economic contraction just as keenly if not more so than Chicago and its suburbs. The population of East St. Louis at the end of the Second World War plummeted by roughly two-thirds during the next sixty years (from 82,366 in 1950 to 27,006 in 2010) along with the demise of the city's meatpacking, steel, aluminum, and asphalt industries. Rockford's population declined by nearly 6 percent between 1980 and 2000 as much of its furniture and metal works industries relocated elsewhere. Galesburg lost 1,600 jobs when Maytag left town in 2004—the company had employed as many as 8,000 workers there in its heyday—and the closing of the General Motors foundry in 1996 cost Danville more than 1,000 jobs. When other firms such as General Electric, Bohn Aluminum, and Anchor Hocking Glassware departed, Danville saw its population fall 8.4 percent in the 1980s and 13.2 percent in the 1990s. After the disappearance

---

ROGER BILES is Professor Emeritus of History at Illinois State University. A specialist in urban history, he is the author of *The Fate of Cities: Urban America and the Federal Government, 1945–2000* (2011), among many other works.

Journal of the Illinois State Historical Society Vol. 110, No. 2 (Summer 2017): 183–210

of Peoria's distilleries and breweries in mid-century, the fortunes of the local economy overwhelmingly rose and fell with manufacturing giant Caterpillar. Population loss in the 1980s (2.2 percent) and 1990s (8.6 percent) reflected the tractor company's frequent decisions to impose massive layoffs. In all, however, no medium-sized Illinois community came to embody the travails of deindustrialization as vividly in the national consciousness as Decatur.[1]

Boastfully calling itself "the pride of the prairie," Decatur flourished as a bustling middle-sized city where blue collar workers readily found manufacturing jobs and lived comfortably during the golden age of American prosperity immediately after World War II. Beginning in the 1980s, however, the city suffered a dramatic decline caused by deindustrialization, rising unemployment, and severe population loss. Factories closed or operated at reduced capacity, department stores and small retail shops fled the central business district, much of the housing stock deteriorated as cash-strapped home owners failed to make needed repairs, and statistics measuring increases in crime, drug usage, and violent gang activity threatened the community's long-standing reputation as a peaceful, family-centered community. By the closing decades of the twentieth century, Decatur's plight mirrored the fate of countless other industrial cities in the midwestern Rustbelt laid low by sweeping changes in the nation's economy. The wholesale abdication of manufacturing for service employment nationally left cities such as Youngstown, Ohio, Gary, Indiana, Flint, Michigan, and many other gritty industrial centers with little hope of regaining the prosperity they had enjoyed in earlier times. Technology replaced people in the work place, and a new fluidity of capital allowed multinational corporations to open and close factories with dispatch. Organized labor's inability to save jobs, sustain high wages, and preserve humane working conditions hastened management's triumph over workers, a development highlighted in Decatur when unions went toe-to-toe with three corporate leviathans simultaneously in the 1990s—and lost. By the turn of the twenty-first century, Decatur had become a forlorn national symbol of neoliberalism's triumph in the American heartland.[2]

---

1. *Chicago Tribune*, February 2, 1994, September 14, 2004, September 8, 2013; Robert Loerzel, "Impoverished in Illinois," *Illinois Issues* (January 2014), http://illinoisissues.uis.edu/archives/2014/01/poverty1.html, accessed May 3, 2016; Roger Biles, *Illinois: A History of the Land and Its People* (DeKalb: Northern Illinois University Press, 2005), Chapter Fifteen. On deindustrialization in Chicago, see Dominic A. Pacyga, *Chicago, A Biography* (Chicago: University of Chicago Press, 2009); Joel Rast, *Remaking Chicago: The Political Origins of Urban Industrial Change* (DeKalb: Northern Illinois University Press, 1999); and Larry Bennett, *The Third City: Chicago and American Urbanism* (Chicago: University of Chicago Press, 2010).

2. Kevin McDermott, "Decatur, Down and Out," *Illinois Issues* 27 (November 2001), http://illinoisissues-archive.uis.edu/features/2001nov/decatur.html, accessed February 29, 2016;

Platted at a bend in the Sangamon River in the early 1820s approximately 180 miles southwest of Chicago and 120 miles northeast of St. Louis, Decatur grew slowly as an isolated outpost in the sparsely populated rural interior of Illinois. In its infancy, the city developed as a processor for agricultural products and a distribution center of retail goods to the surrounding hinterland. The coming of the first locomotive in 1854 and the statewide expansion of a railroad network in subsequent decades led to commercial expansion and population growth in the 1880s and 1890s. Early industries included the maintenance shops of the Wabash Railroad, farm implement factories, a rolling mill that produced rails for the railways, and several metal shops that supplied parts for railroad engines as well as plumbing equipment for homes located in the region. (In the twentieth century, local machinists converted from the manufacture of railroad components to automobile motors). Despite its failure to realize the hopes of local boosters that the community would become one of the Midwest's leading iron and steel producers, Decatur grew steadily and its population reached 20,000 by the end of the nineteenth century.[3]

Between 1900 and 1930, Decatur's population nearly tripled as it became a national leader in the processing of certain crops for consumption worldwide. In the years between the world wars, as the market for wheat and other cereal grains diminished, soybeans emerged as the second leading crop in the state (behind corn). Agronomists at the state's agricultural experiment stations created new

---

Kevin Clarke, "Dispatches from Decatur," *U.S. Catholic* 73 (June 2008), http://www.uscatholic.org/print/270, accessed April 18, 2016. On deindustrialization, see Barry Bluestone and Bennett Harrison, *The Deindustrialization of America: Plant Closings, Community Abandonment, and the Dismantling of Basic Industry* (New York: Basic Books, 1982); and Jefferson Cowie, *Capital Moves: RCA's 70-Year Quest for Cheap Labor* (Ithaca: Cornell University Press, 1999). For specific cities, see Sean Safford, *Why the Garden Club Couldn't Save Youngstown: The Transformation of the Rust Belt* (Cambridge, Mass.: Harvard University Press, 2009); S. Paul O'Hara, *Gary, the Most American of All Cities* (Bloomington, Ind.: Indiana University Press, 2010); Andrew R. Highsmith, *Demolition Means Progress: Flint, Michigan, and the Fate of the American Metropolis* (Chicago: University of Chicago Press, 2015); Allen Dietrich-Ward, *Beyond Rust: Metropolitan Pittsburgh and the Fate of Industrial America* (Philadelphia: University of Pennsylvania Press, 2016); and Tracy Neumann, *Remaking the Rustbelt: The Postindustrial Transformation of North America* (Philadelphia: University of Pennsylvania Press, 2016). On neoliberalism, see David Harvey, *A Brief History of Neoliberalism* (New York: Oxford University Press, 2005).

3. Maren Allan Stein, "The Agricommercial Tradition on the Metropolitan Frontier: Decatur," in *Cities of the Prairie Revisited: The Closing of the Metropolitan Frontier*, ed. Daniel J. Elazar (Lincoln, Neb.: University of Nebraska Press, 1986), 221–22; *History of Macon County*, ed. O. T. Branton (Decatur, Ill.: Macon County Historical Society, 1976), 120–22, 220; Biles, *Illinois*, 225–26. On Decatur's early years, see John W. Smith, *History of Macon County, Illinois: From its Organization to 1876* (La Crosse, Wisc.: Brookhaven Press, 2001).

strains of soybeans that thrived in the soil and climate of central Illinois, and University of Illinois chemists developed a host of new food products and industrial uses for the commodity. In 1922 the A. E. Staley Company, a manufacturer of starch and glucose, relocated to Decatur from Baltimore, Maryland, and opened the nation's first soybean-processing plant. Later that year, needing more water for its production, Staley pressured the city to construct Lake Decatur; to accommodate rising production, the municipality expanded the lake from 2,800 acres to 3,300 acres in 1953. Having increased its production of corn-based sweeteners, Staley's became the world's leading manufacturer of high fructose corn syrup (a substitute for sugar in most major soft drinks and beer) in the 1970s.[4]

In 1939 the Archer Daniels Midland (ADM) Company moved its mammoth soybean milling operations to Decatur from Minneapolis, Minnesota. ADM developed edible soy protein and discovered a process for extracting lecithin, an important compound for use in food additives, dietary supplements, and medical treatments, from soy oil. The company also pioneered in the manufacture of ethanol and high fructose corn sweeteners. When the Second World War disrupted the importation of vegetable oils from Asian nations, Illinois farmers planted even more acres of soybeans. After the war, ADM became the nation's leading soybean processor, its agricultural plant complex the largest globally. In 1969 the firm moved its corporate headquarters to Decatur, which became known as the soybean capital of the world. Supplying additives to an expanding list of food items, including grains, meats, salad oils, yogurt, and chocolate, the agribusiness titan began calling itself the "supermarket to the world."[5]

Already fully established as a leading agribusiness hub, Decatur parlayed its importance as an armaments and munitions manufacturer during World War II into a home for a variety of heavy industries in later decades. Caterpillar Tractor Company, headquartered in nearby Peoria, operated the Victory Military Engine plant in Decatur during the war and then returned in 1954 to open a factory on a 340-acre tract of land on the city's northeast side. Four subsequent expansions increased the Caterpillar production space to four million square feet and, with more than 5,000 workers, the company became the city's largest employer by 1975. The U.S. army converted the Victory Military Engine plant after the war into a warehouse for military communication equipment and continued using the structure for that purpose until its closing in 1962. The following year, the

---

4. Dan J. Forrestal, *The Kernel and the Bean: The 75-Year Story of the Staley Company* (New York: Simon and Schuster, 1982), 25, 60–61, 78–79, 91, 205.

5. James B. Lieber, *Rats in the Grain: The Dirty Tricks and Trials of Archer Daniels Midland* (New York: Four Walls Eight Windows, 2000), 72–79; Biles, *Illinois*, 226.

Firestone Tire and Rubber Company (later, Bridgestone/Firestone) acquired the factory and immediately commenced production of automobile tires there. By the mid-1970s, the Decatur plant's production of tires ranked fourth among all Firestone facilities. Honeycombed with factories and warehouses owned by large corporations and smaller businesses, the community assumed the persona of a "soy-smelly . . . roughneck town." The Economic Development Corporation of Decatur happily reported in 1993 that 30 percent of the Decatur workforce, more than twice the national average, toiled in manufacturing occupations (Figure 1). And earned a good living. Steady blue collar jobs allowed workers to live in a comfortable ranch house, drive a late-model car, and enjoy an annual vacation. The city nestled among the corn and soybean fields, observed a local businessman, had morphed into a "miniature Chicago."[6]

The glossy picture of Decatur as a thriving industrial community faded in the 1980s, however, as substantial numbers of people and jobs left for greener pastures elsewhere. The 1980 population of 94,081 fell sharply to 83,885 in 1990, an 11 percent decrease. A severe recession that crippled the nation in 1981–82 drove Decatur's unemployment rate upward to 19.9 percent, the highest figure in Illinois (at a time when the overall rate for the state stood at 11.4 percent) and one of the highest in the country. The Good Samaritan Inn, a soup kitchen operated downtown by the Salvation Army, reported an increase in customers fed per day from fewer than fifteen in April 1982 to approximately 125 in September. Large local industries such as Borg-Warner (motor vehicle parts), the Mueller Corporation (plumbing components and fire hydrants), and Mississippi Valley Structural Steel also imposed substantial layoffs in 1982. When Caterpillar announced the release of 957 workers, Decatur Mayor Elmer Walton called the local situation "quite bleak." The largest private employer in Illinois, Caterpillar laid off an additional 8,000 workers later that year; the total manpower reductions in 1982 by the Peoria-based company brought its number of idled workers to 17,500 statewide, more than one-third of the company's hourly workers. In October the United Auto Workers (UAW) led Caterpillar workers out on strike and began picketing at plants in six states after the company sought reductions in wages and benefits when the existing bargaining agreement expired. UAW Local 751 followed suit in Decatur. The acrimonious work stoppage, covered exhaustively by the national media, concluded 205 days later. Many employees failed to reclaim their jobs for several years, and relations between Caterpillar

---

6. Banton, *History of Macon County*, 232–33; Becky Bradway, *Pink Houses and Family Taverns* (Bloomington, Ind.: Indiana University Press, 2002), 8; Steven K. Ashby and C. J. Hawking, *Staley: The Fight for a New American Labor Movement* (Urbana, Ill.: University of Illinois Press, 2009), 15.

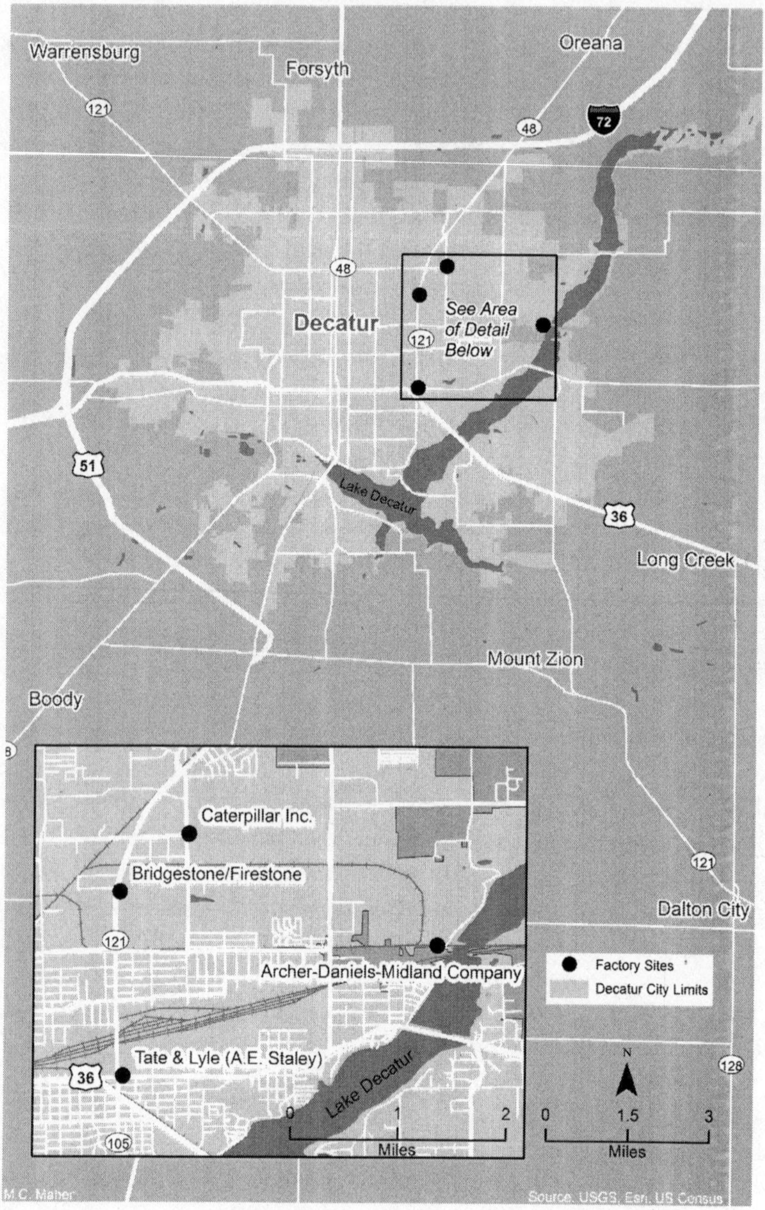

Figure 1. Location of Decatur factories involved in labor confrontations. Courtesy Illinois State University, Institute for Geopolitical Analysis and Mapping.

and union members soured further as the company relegated strikers to a new hiring pool. Needy job applicants in Decatur, who had scraped by precariously for nearly seven months during the strike, then exhausted their remaining savings waiting for the summons to rejoin the Caterpillar work force and belatedly did so at sharply reduced wage levels.[7]

Several years of uneasy labor peace ensued. Deeply disheartened by the outcome of the 205-day struggle, the UAW avoided another rift and reluctantly ratified disappointing contracts in 1986 and 1988. Having weathered the 1982–83 strike but lost an estimated $500 million in the process, Caterpillar pledged to improve relations with the union for the mutual benefit of both parties. But the joint desire for reconciliation evaporated with the elevation of Don Fites to the Caterpillar chairmanship in 1990. As he had ascended the Caterpillar corporate ladder during the previous thirty-four years, Fites had become convinced that the company desperately needed a complete overhaul to improve efficiency—most importantly including the imposition of a new approach to labor-management relations. Believing that the unions had become too powerful and that the company needed to reassert its unimpeded "right to manage," he argued that higher returns for company shareholders overwhelmingly depended upon cutting production expenses. The indiscriminate paring of labor costs meant rolling back safety measures, a reckless decision that produced tragic consequences when an inexperienced mechanic in the Caterpillar's Decatur plant lost his life in 1990 due to inadequate training and supervision. After investigating the casualty, the Occupational Safety and Health Administration (OSHA) fined Staley $1.6 million for 298 health and safety violations.[8]

In November 1991, Fites initiated new contract talks with the UAW brandishing a list of aggressive demands that stunned union officials. He sought additional layoffs, the conversion from eight-hour to twelve-hour shifts, wage cuts, the replacement of annual raises with productivity bonuses, less rigorous grievance procedures, relaxed safety rules, and reduced wage levels for starting

---

7. U.S. Department of Commerce, Bureau of the Census, *General Social and Economic Characteristics of the Population: 1980*, Volume I, Part I, Section 2 (Washington, D.C.: General Printing Office, 1983), 15–13; U.S. Department of Commerce, Bureau of the Census, *Census of Population, 1990: Social and Economic Characteristics*, Section I (Washington, D.C.: General Printing Office, 1993), 3; *Chicago Tribune*, May 14, 1982, October 2, 3, 1982; *New York Times*, April 25, 1983; Stephen Franklin, *Three Strikes: Labor's Heartland Losses and What They Mean for Working Americans* (New York: Guilford Press, 2001), 73.

8. Kevin Kelly, "Caterpillar's Don Fites: Why He Didn't Blink," *Business Week* 3278 (August 1992), 56; Tom Frank and Dave Mulcahey, "This is War," *Chicago Reader* 24 (January 1995), http://www.chicagoreader.com/chicago/this-is-war/Content?oid=886520, accessed March 28, 2016.

workers. In December, after several weeks of spirited negotiations, the membership of UAW Local 751 in Decatur joined another national strike against Caterpillar (Figure 2).[9]

As in 1982–83, print and electronic media gave considerable attention to the dramatic events in central Illinois as the rancorous strike dragged on for months in the bitterly cold winter of 1991–92. An estimated 2,000 striking workers and sympathizers lined the long road to the Decatur plant every morning as a show of unity. Daily telecasts showed irate strikers shouting epithets at company security officers at factory gates, violence often resulting when strike breakers ("scabs") attempted to force their way through picket lines. Decatur, Macon County, and Illinois State police escorted scabs into the factory when UAW members partially blocked the entrance with their automobiles. The prolonged battle to fend off financial calamity left strikers and their families increasingly restive, and the number of union members crossing picket lines began to increase as winter turned to spring. In April, after a five-and-a-half-month standoff, Fites brought the union to heel with a threat to supplant personnel at all Caterpillar facilities with permanent replacement workers. The UAW abdicated totally, accepting all of the conditions Fites had proffered in his original contract proposal. Caterpillar allowed most of the strikers to return to work, but commented ominously about 15 to 20 percent work reductions in coming months. "The UAW was forced into a major strategic retreat," concluded the *Decatur Herald and Review*, "in agreeing to end its strike and return to work under a Caterpillar-imposed contract that the UAW had vowed it would never accept."[10]

Keenly aware of the hardships suffered by UAW members in their disastrous confrontation with Caterpillar, workers at A.E. Staley warily considered the prospects of conducting a strike throughout the spring and summer of 1992. They believed that the situation in the Decatur plant had deteriorated substantially after Tate & Lyle, a British multinational agribusiness conglomerate, had acquired Staley in a hostile 1988 takeover. In particular, workers inveighed against the unsafe working conditions that had become commonplace since the change of ownership. The company promptly hired a law firm and management team known for union-busting. In October Tate & Lyle offered a retrograde contract, which the company deemed its "best and final offer," to the union representing Staley workers, Local 837 of the Allied Industrial Workers

9. Franklin, *Three Strikes*, 41–42; Kelly, "Caterpillar's Don Fites," 56.

10. *New York Times*, April 16, 1992; *Chicago Tribune*, April 17, 1992; Kelly, "Caterpillar's Don Fites," 56–57; Franklin, *Three Strikes*, 102–6; *Decatur Herald and Review*, April 17, 1992.

Figure 2. Striking workers picket Caterpillar plant in 1991. Photo Courtesy of Jim West.

(AIW). The contract called for twelve-hour rotating shifts, reduced seniority, and emasculated safety and grievance procedures. The rank-and-file rejected the contract but also eschewed a strike, which they feared would end with Staley following Caterpillar's lead and hiring permanent replacements. Instead, the workers commenced an "in-plant" strategy whereby they remained on the job and utilized a number of subtle strategies to slacken pace and reduce productivity. Workers followed instructions for each task in their operating manuals to the letter but applied no initiative and ignored the experience that had allowed them to maximize output in the past; as a result, production fell between a third and a half in the ensuing months. At 3:00 A.M. on June 27, 1993, calling the in-plant strategy "sabotage," management implemented a plant shutdown. Shop foremen assembled AIW members working the overnight shift and summoned the other workers from home to be given an ultimatum: sign the contract offer or vacate the plant indefinitely. All 762 Staley workers left. Some supervisors allowed workers to retrieve belongings from their lockers, while others ushered the employees out immediately; still others subjected exiting workers to humiliating strip searches on their way out of the building.[11]

Determined to capitalize on the bold initiative, Staley kept the pressure on its labor adversaries in subsequent months. The company painted yellow stripes on the pavement at each plant entrance and announced that any AIW 837 member crossing the line would be arrested for trespassing. Tate & Lyle discontinued its payments to health care insurance for union members. A phalanx of security guards fanned out opposite picket lines at the gates and ushered replacement workers into the plant. Company executives mailed several hundred letters to Decatur merchants that presented a detailed justification for the lockout. The letter charged union members with destructive behavior, labeling their in-plant strategy a form of guerilla warfare. Management invited newspaper and television reporters into the plant to view examples of the "sabotage" purportedly effected by workers. Staley ran a full-page advertisement in the *Decatur Herald and Review*, headlined "Why a Lock-out?" that defended its unprecedented move. Because of the union's provocative actions in the plant, the missive argued, the company had "no other choice" but to "take a defensive action" to "save our Decatur business."[12]

AIW 837 leaders lamented that the company's efforts to stitch together a corporate alliance against the Staley work force were succeeding. The *Decatur Herald and Review*, a time-honored apologist for the city's corporate interests, eagerly endorsed management's argument that cuts in labor costs had become unavoidable for Staley to remain profitable. Accordingly, the newspaper's editorial supported twelve-hour shifts and higher worker contributions for health insurance as necessary changes to safeguard the company's financial bottom line. Staley also benefited from the aid offered by ADM, ostensibly its agribusiness competitor. Owning 8 percent of Tate & Lyle stock, ADM had every reason to see the union squelched and helped fill orders at Staley during the lockout via a recently completed pipeline linking the two corn-processing plants. Impressionistic readings of local public opinion indicated mixed feelings about the lockout, with the citizenry split about evenly between supporters of labor and management. But Staley's backing within the Decatur business community, especially

---

11. Rita Koselka, "'Back to What We Do Best,'" *Forbes* 147 (June 1991), 48; Frank and Mulcahey, "This Is War;" Eric Jarosinski, "Labor War Zone in Illinois," *Progressive* 58 (February 1994), http://web.a.ebscohost.com/ehost/detail/detail?vid=2&sid=fd386ad3-8879-4280-a277-4db, accessed March 27, 2016; *New York Times*, June 29, 1993; Ashby and Hawking, *Staley*, 74–76; Thomas Frank, *Listen, Liberal: Or, What Ever Happened to the Party of the People?* (New York: Henry Holt and Company, 2016), 74.

12. *New York Times*, June 29, 1993; Ashby and Hawking, *Staley*, 79–83; *Decatur Herald and Review*, June 28, 1993.

the direct intervention by ADM, a local economic powerhouse, augured well for its ability to win a battle of attrition against the vulnerable workers.[13]

Convinced that succumbing to the lockout would result in a decisive loss of influence in the industry, AIW marshaled all of its resources for a prolonged struggle. The locked-out workers argued that if they surrendered, all other unionized shops in Decatur would suffer as well. "It's our solidarity versus theirs," Local 837 defiantly proclaimed. The union objected most strenuously to the imposition of rotating twelve-hour shifts, a portentous change that threatened to impair the lives of workers, undermine family life, and disrupt community cohesiveness. Confined to the workplace for so many hours, blue collar employees would forfeit time for recreation, church attendance, and political activities, among other leisure pastimes. Rotating schedules exacerbated the problem, insuring that parents and children would see each other irregularly if at all. "If you want to see the destruction of the American family," argued a professor of labor studies at Indiana University, "there is no better way than to put the head of the household on a rotating shift."[14]

Fighting back, Local 837 filed a grievance with the National Labor Relations Board (NLRB), calling the lockout illegal under existing law. Other union members in Decatur rallied around their Staley counterparts. UAW Local 751 at Caterpillar, United Rubber Workers (URW) Local 713 at Bridgestone/Firestone, and two unions at ADM raised tens of thousands of dollars for the AIW strike fund and made regular food donations to aid the Staley workers. More than four thousand union members staged a boisterous demonstration in downtown Decatur on Labor Day, September 1, 1993, to underscore the special significance of the holiday that year. Staley workers distributed to local politicians, clergy, and media outlets a copy of a new documentary film, "Deadly Corn," which chronicled unsafe working conditions at the plant. The union also organized boycotts of Domino and GW sugar, the best-selling Tate & Lyle products in the United States, and the State Farm Insurance Company, the largest holder of ADM stocks and bonds. Local 837 demonstrated at State Farm headquarters in neighboring Bloomington and at branch offices in Champaign, Peoria, and other central Illinois communities. Moreover, AIW mailed sixty thousand brochures to union supporters throughout the country urging them to cancel their insurance policies unless State Farm persuaded Staley to end the lockout. The union also targeted the Miller Brewing Company, whose purchase of high fructose corn syrup accounted for 11 percent of Staley's income, and won a

---

13. *Decatur Herald and Review*, August 2, 1993; Lieber, *Rats in the Grain*, 94; Jarosinski, "Labor War Zone."

14. Jarosinski, "Labor War Zone;" Frank and Mulcahey, "This is War."

notable victory when the beer manufacturer announced that it would cut ties with its Decatur supplier when the existing contract expired on January 1, 1995.[15]

Meanwhile, management and labor at Staley remained deadlocked. The small number of picketers stationed at the plant's entrances proved inadequate to stop the steady stream of scabs from entering the workplace and maintaining production levels, and the standoff continued through the winter months. Officials at the United Paperworkers International Union (UPIU) Local 7837, which had subsumed the AIW in September 1993 and become the official bargaining agent of the Staley work force, launched a new program of mass protest in the spring to attract wider public attention to the situation. The union conducted nonviolent civil disobedience training sessions in April–May 1994 before initiating activities at the Staley plant on June 4. On that day, five hundred workers, spouses, and supporters crossed the yellow property line at the plant's west gate and sat down. Police arrested fifty sit-down protesters, who immediately became known as the "Decatur Fifty," and disbursed the remaining participants without incident. In addition to the *Decatur Herald and Review*, Chicago newspapers, several Illinois television stations, the Associated Press, and National Public Radio sent journalists to cover the story. Buoyed by the favorable reporting afforded its venture by the media, Local 7837 eagerly announced another sit-down for June 25.[16]

Unlike the earlier event, in which disciplined law enforcement authorities calmly took sedate protesters into custody, June 25 took a very different turn. A crowd of several hundred demonstrators waving placards and American flags at a city park included autoworkers from Flint, Michigan, Pittsburgh steelworkers, and Caterpillar employees from Peoria, as well as local union members. The peaceful assemblage listened to a series of speeches extolling union solidarity and then followed rows of Harley-Davidson motorcycles to the Staley plant a mile away. As they had done on June 4, the sit-downers took up position on company property inside the west gate. This time, however, Decatur police acted without the restraint and professionalism for which they had been praised the previous three weeks. Without warning, a police commander and several other officers wearing gas masks and gloves turned pepper spray on the unsuspecting protesters who sat arm-in-arm facing the opposite direction (Figure 3). With cold calculation, many of the policemen repositioned themselves to aim the gas canisters directly into the eyes of their cringing targets. Several bystanders and young children fell victim to the attack as well. In keeping with the decision

15. Jarosinski, "Labor War Zone;" Ashby and Hawking, *Staley*, 83–85, 112–23.

16. Frank and Mulcahey, "This Is War;" Ashby and Hawking, *Staley*, 169–93; *Decatur Herald and Review*, June 5, 1994.

Figure 3. Decatur police unleash pepper spray on unsuspecting strikers at Staley's west gate. Photo courtesy of Jim West.

made earlier by the Decatur city manager, Macon County state's attorney, and Decatur Police Department to use pepper spray rather than detain the protesters, the authorities only made one arrest. Surprised and fearing further violence, union officials hurriedly terminated the sit-in and sent the crowd away. The police department's official statement explained that the order to use pepper spray came only after demonstrators had charged the officers' ranks, a claim later disproved by a videotape taken at the scene by a local television station.[17]

The violent attack on peaceful protesters at the Staley plant underscored the heightened climate of labor strife in Decatur by 1994, which had become known nationally in labor circles as the "War Zone." Just three days before the pepper spray incident, UAW Local 751 went out on strike again against Caterpillar. Having worked for more than two years without a contract, the union charged the company with having adopted unfair labor practices on the shop floor (especially the summary firing of union activists) since the last work stoppage. Management

17. *Decatur Herald and Review*, June 26, 1994; Ashby and Hawking, *Staley*, 188–92.

at first kept the factory thrumming by transferring white collar employees from their desks to the assembly lines and then by importing unemployed migrants from southern states, farmers seeking additional income, and renegade union members who had deserted the UAW picket lines as replacement workers. Another protracted standoff developed at Caterpillar.[18]

On July 12, 1994, the URW called a strike against Bridgestone/Firestone, a multinational corporation headquartered in Japan that operated eighty-five plants in nineteen countries. The previous contract had expired four months earlier, and the company was insisting that a new agreement include significant alterations. Among other notable changes, management demanded adoption of twelve-hour shifts and seven-day weeks without overtime rates, relinquishment of seniority rights, a two-tier wage system, elimination of cost-of-living increases, reductions in health care coverage, fewer vacation weeks, and mandatory holiday work. (Workers at the Decatur plant had not received a general wage increase since 1985.) Having provoked the union with a series of audacious demands in the contract negotiations, Local 713 officers suspected, management was surreptitiously preparing for a work stoppage. In the months prior to the walkout, accelerated production at the Decatur plant had resulted in the accumulation of huge inventory surpluses that would presumably allow the company to continue filling orders in the early stages of the strike. Referring to the corporation's foreign ownership, striking workers unfurled a large banner outside the factory gate that read: "1941, Japan Attacks Pearl Harbor. July 12, 1994, Bridgestone/Firestone Attacks American Workers." At the time and for years afterward, angry workers referred to the company's treatment of its American labor force as a "second Pearl Harbor."[19]

The walkout of 1,270 employees at the Bridgestone/Firestone plant, in addition to the number of striking and locked-out laborers at Caterpillar and Staley respectively, brought the number of idled workers in Decatur to approximately 3,800. Thus, in the summer of 1994, virtually one-third of the workers in the city were taking their turns on picket lines. The idea of widespread labor discord dominating the daily rhythms of an entire community, an image promulgated by the national media, left Decatur with the dramatic appellation, "Striketown, U.S.A." Embattled Mayor Erik Brechnitz, whose son had been spotted crossing a picket line to work at Staley, told a National Public Radio reporter: "It's a very tough situation, and the atmosphere is becoming more and more electric." A Republican financial analyst who made no effort to conceal his pro-business bias, the wealthy Brechnitz quickly earned the enmity of the city's blue collar populace. He soon received a number of threatening telephone calls at home. At

---

18. Franklin, *Three Strikes*, 226–31; Frank and Mulcahey, "This War."

19. *Decatur Herald and Review*, July 13, 1994; Ashby and Hawking, *Staley*, 196.

Decatur's Celebration Days, an annual downtown celebration commemorating the community's founding, a union sympathizer dumped a beer on the mayor's head. Unmoved by the anger and destructiveness all around him, Brechnitz refused to meet with strikers and continued to motor around the city flamboyantly in his red Jaguar convertible. Several city council members, former executives at Staley, ADM, Caterpillar, and Bridgestone/Firestone, likewise openly sided against the unions.[20]

The bitter clash in Decatur proved emblematic of the labor-management battles being fought nationwide, the fundamental issues at play in the central Illinois community a microcosm of the challenges facing the U.S. economy in the last decades of the twentieth century. J. Patrick Mohan, an executive vice-president and principal spokesman for corporate interests at Staley, matter-of-factly explained from management's point of view the underlying cause of the mid-1990s turmoil: the unions' unwillingness to accommodate to the new realities of global competition. Lower employment rates and reduced wages could not be avoided if modern corporations hoped to remain competitive in international markets, he said. Modernization inevitably precluded the retention of the skilled workers who had once formed the backbone of mass production. "We rely more now on brain than on brawn," Mohan explained. Workers could no longer expect the kind of job security that had allowed generations of high school graduates an entry into the middle class.[21] Mohan articulated the rationalization for the decisive steps taken by Staley and replicated by Caterpillar and Bridgestone/Firestone:

> Our responsibility is to make sure the corporation continues to survive and prosper. We have to look to the good of the corporation as a whole and the good of all the other workers, not just for a small pocket of workers. We want the jobs that do exist to be viable and sustainable. Is it morally responsible for a corporation to operate in a fashion that forces it to go out of business and close factories?[22]

On the other hand, workers and union leaders in Decatur echoed the sentiments expressed elsewhere in disputing the neoliberal view espoused in corporate boardrooms. Father Martin Mangan of the St. James Roman Catholic Church, located in a tired Decatur neighborhood southeast of downtown, sided early on with the unions, went to jail with sit-downers, and emerged as a leading

---

20. *Decatur Herald and Review*, July 14, 1994; McDermott, "Decatur, Down and Out;" Franklin, *Three Strikes*, 191; Ashby and Hawking, *Staley*, 203–4.

21. *Christian Science Monitor*, November 29, 1995, http://www.lexisnexis.com/1nacui2api/frame.do?tokenKey=rsh-20.659456.964784161&tar, accessed March 30, 2016; Clarke, "Dispatches from Decatur."

22. Clarke, "Dispatches from Decatur."

advocate for the strikers. Father Mangan invoked social gospel ministers of industrialism's early days in arguing for society's need to treat the working classes and the downtrodden humanely. His sermons and public addresses eloquently defended worker activism as vital to economic equity and democracy, noting that corporate rapacity was nullifying the sense of community in Decatur. The introduction of twelve-hour shifts, the erosion of safety standards, and the wholesale withdrawal of benefits rescinded hard-earned improvements that workers had achieved only after decades of undaunted union effort. Such surrenders to management demands also threatened to impose undue hardships on working class families. "It's like going back to the company town," he said. "It's an insidious form of control over people's lives."[23]

While picketing continued at the three factories, the cooperating unions launched other initiatives to publicize their cause to a number of different audiences nationally as well as locally. Thousands of strikers and their supporters stood arm-in-arm fashioning a human chain that spanned the two miles along 22nd Street between the Caterpillar and Staley facilities; for thirty consecutive days, workers chained themselves to a metal fence outside the Staley factory for twelve hours at a time, symbolically lodging their protest against twelve-hour workdays. "Road warriors" fanned out across the Midwest speaking to union locals, church congregations, and civic organizations about the issues behind the labor confrontation in Decatur and seeking financial contributions to the respective strike funds. UPIU Local 7837 member Dan Lane began a hunger strike at St. James Church that he pledged to continue until the soft drink giant PepsiCo and its subsidiaries, Kentucky Fried Chicken, Pizza Hut, and Taco Bell, stopped buying corn sweetener from Staley. Still fasting after fifty-four days, Lane addressed the American Federation of Labor-Congress of Industrial Organizations (AFL-CIO) annual convention in New York City on October 26, 1995, and urged a national boycott of all Pepsi Cola products. Lane ended his hunger strike after sixty-four days only after he received assurances from John Sweeney, the newly-elected AFL-CIO president, that the labor federation had decided to make Local 7837's crusade against Staley its top priority for the coming months.[24]

---

23. Marc Cooper, "Harley-Riding, Picket-Walking Socialism Haunts Decatur," *The Nation* 262 (April 1996), 24–25; Mark Singer, "Town on a String," *The New Yorker* 76 (October 2000), 60–61; Ashby and Hawking, *Staley*, 202. Also see Robert Sampson, "A Priest on the Front Lines: Father Martin B. Mangan in the Decatur 'War Zone,'" *Journal of the Illinois State Historical Society* 106 (Summer 2013), 243–80.

24. Thomas Frank and David Mulcahey, "Hunger Striking in the Corn Belt," *The Nation* 261 (November 1995), 540–42; Franklin, *Three Strikes*, 215–20; *Decatur Herald and Review*, November 5, 1995.

Their perseverance and creative tactics notwithstanding, each of the three unions eventually lost its face-off against corporate antagonists. The pervasiveness of labor-management confrontation, which made Decatur famous as "Strike City, U.S.A.," began to dissipate in 1995. Last to enter the fray, the workers at Bridgestone/Firestone became the first to desert the field. In May 1995, just less than a year after walking out, Local 713 ended its strike and signed a new contract. Company officials at the Decatur tire plant announced that the strikebreakers employed during the preceding ten months were providing adequate manpower and that the strikers would be brought back only as necessary. Bridgestone/Firestone rehired just 376 of the 1,250 union workers in the ensuing six months.[25]

Workers at Caterpillar capitulated later in 1995. UAW Local 751 rejected the company's latest contract offer in early December of that year, but shortly thereafter the international union decided to end the strike in all locations. Workers in Decatur terminated the protracted seventeen-month walkout and returned to the plant later that month without a binding agreement, and the company unilaterally imposed the contractual terms the local had recently spurned. The specifics of the unofficial contract included workdays in excess of eight hours with no overtime pay, a two-tier wage structure, and a new code of conduct that included restrictions on freedom of speech in the workplace. The company began suspending and firing workers for speech infractions such as affixing union stickers on lunch pails and pejoratively uttering the word "scab" on the shop floor. Replacement workers enjoyed preferential treatment, receiving better job assignments with more responsibility and higher pay, while shop foremen assigned union members to "work pools" that directed them to perform less desirable tasks that yielded smaller remuneration. Management insisted that former-strikers wear their safety goggles and ear plugs at lunch, an encumbrance that plant officials and strikebreakers were not forced to endure.[26]

The lockout at Staley ended after three and a half years when UPIU Local 7837 members voted on December 21–22, 1995 to accept the company's latest contract offer. Despite AFL-CIO President John Sweeney's avid pledge of support to Dan Lane less than two months earlier, the federation hierarchy had grown weary of depleting its national strike fund when the chances of success seemed not to be improving; the international union informed Local 7837 that support would

---

25. Frank and Mulcahey, "Hunger Striking in the Corn Belt," 541; Franklin, *Three Strikes*, 232–34.

26. *Decatur Herald and Review*, December 7, 1995; "Labor Takes Its Lumps," *Progressive* 60 (March 1996), http://web.b.ebscohost.com/ehost/detail/detail?vid=2&sid=3cdffob9-2ad9-4918-ba03-b313, accessed March 23, 2016.

evaporate if the Decatur membership failed to approve the contract. After 908 days of exile, 56 percent of the workers approved an agreement that differed little from the versions they had soundly rejected in October 1992 and July 1995. The union agreed to withdraw all charges filed against the company with the NLRB. The twelve-hour shifts remained in force with employees actually obligated to work sixteen-hour days (including four hours of mandatory overtime). The contract also weakened arbitration and grievance procedures. Management agreed to welcome back into the plant just 350 of the 762 workers locked out in 1993; 146 of the demoralized employees decided to return. More than 600 union members retired immediately, accepted a severance package, or sought employment elsewhere rather than tolerate the onerous working environment. The company estimated that the number of personnel in the Decatur factory would be pared to 220 within the next two years. The downcast president of Local 7837 grimly admitted, "We lost this war."[27]

Indeed, Decatur workers lost the war on all fronts in the mid-1990s. The three defeats for the unions coming in quick succession engendered a sense of fatalism, a resignation to the transcendence of the employer and to the undisputable loss of influence by the employee. The fact that international conglomerates headquartered in distant nations owned two of the three companies that prevailed in the contest with labor—and a corporation exercising control from another U.S. city owned the other—left local residents feeling powerless against impersonal outside market forces. For a manufacturing town such as Decatur, no longer able to rely on a robust trade union movement to guard against the recurring fluctuations of the capitalist economy, the onset of deindustrialization proved especially debilitating.

An already fraught economic situation in the community worsened soon after the conclusion of the strikes. In 1998 a State Farm Insurance researcher informed the National Highway Traffic Safety Administration (NHTSA) that he had found an inordinate number of flawed Bridgestone/Firestone tires in use on U.S. roadways. The federal agency took no action at the time, but two years later a Houston, Texas, television station reported having identified a number of fatal crashes involving sport-utility vehicles (mostly Ford Explorers) equipped with the company's tires. As an NHTSA investigation proceeded, Bridgestone/Firestone and Ford jointly announced the recall of 14.4 million tires. The Japanese company at first defended its product but later admitted that the tire treads peeled apart at high speeds, resulting in a spate of lethal automobile accidents. In the fall of 2000, the U.S. government agency linked the defective tires to 119 fatalities and more than 500 injuries. Legislators in Washington, D.C., opened

27. *Decatur Herald and Review*, December 23, 1995; Cooper, "Harley-Riding," 21–22; Ashby and Hawkins, *Staley*, 272.

congressional hearings, and aggrieved family members of the deceased brought lawsuits against Bridgestone/Firestone seeking hundreds of millions of dollars in damages. Negative publicity led to steeply falling sales. The embattled company announced that it was closing three of its twelve U.S. factories, including the antiquated thirty-eight-year-old Decatur edifice, for unspecified amounts of time while assessing the situation. Stopping short of blaming the Decatur plant exclusively, corporate executives in Japan nonetheless indicated that the Central Illinois site seemed to be the principal source of the problem.[28]

Union officials and members of the rank-and-file, who saw themselves as scapegoats, adamantly refused to accept responsibility for the accidents. "Tires do fail," observed the president of Local 713 in blaming Ford. "But when tires fail, vehicles shouldn't turn over and kill somebody." The union also pointed to substandard quality control practices on the shop floor, most notably inadequate training and supervision, as the most likely causes of the problem. Veteran workers at the Decatur plant charged that the blame rested overwhelmingly with poorly trained replacement laborers whom the company had rushed onto the assembly line to maintain high production levels. "I knew there'd be some kind of problem with the tires," commented a shaken worker. "I just didn't know it would be this serious."[29]

On June 27, 2001, Bridgestone/Firestone announced that it would begin laying off the Decatur plant's remaining 1,380 workers in the coming months and close the facility altogether by the end of the year. A company vice-president explained that the decision to terminate production at the factory should be seen strictly as a business matter and not as an indictment of the local workforce. The firm was seeking to streamline its operations abroad and the Decatur plant, both the oldest of Bridgestone/Firestone's holdings in the U.S. and the one with the smallest annual output, became a logical target for elimination. Whether the result of a cold-blooded business calculation, the reaction to a public relations disaster, or a combination of both, the determination to close the factory produced devastating consequences for a community so dependent upon manufacturing jobs. Local officials predicted that the shuttering of the plant would severely harm Decatur's economy, the lost payroll alone totaling approximately $100 million annually. In addition to throwing 3 percent of the city's work force out of a job, economists noted, a ripple effect would course through the city. Bridgestone/Firestone, one of Macon County's largest sources of revenue, would no longer be paying $250,000 in property taxes per annum. The loss of purchasing power would also curtail retail sales, resulting in reduced

28. *Chicago Tribune*, August 20, 2000; *Wall Street Journal*, September 13, 2000; Franklin, *Three Strikes*, 268–72.

29. *New York Times*, December 14, 2001; Singer, "Town on a String," 60.

profits for merchants in Decatur's already contracting downtown, shopping centers scattered throughout the city, and stores in neighboring towns.[30]

Decatur's municipal government estimated that approximately 600 workers, less than half of the number released by the company, lived within city limits. For the most part, the remainder resided in a number of small, incorporated places in Macon, Christian, Moultrie, DeWitt, and Shelby counties. For nearly four decades, occupants of Mt. Zion, Forsyth, Maroa, Pana, Taylorville, Sullivan, Shelbyville, Cerro Gordo, Clinton, and a few other nearby communities had found in Decatur the relatively high paying, low-skill manufacturing jobs unavailable at home. From the many small towns dotting the Central Illinois landscape, workers traveled by automobile (usually less than an hour's drive) to Bridgestone/Firestone, Caterpillar, Staley, ADM, and other purveyors of employment in Macon County's metropolis. Many of those workers found the size of Decatur uninviting and preferred to commute from one of the small towns in its orbit. Indeed, crossroads communities that had originated in the nineteenth century as marketing centers for agricultural products were serving by the mid-twentieth century as bedroom communities for people who worked in Decatur but preferred to live elsewhere.[31]

Many inhabitants of the bedroom communities moved there from Decatur, fueling a striking increase in the size of the small towns and a corresponding decrease in the central city's population during the last decades of the twentieth century. Contiguous to the central city, Forsyth to the north and Mt. Zion to the south led the way in attracting newcomers during the 1980s and 1990s. Residents of Macon County traced Forsyth's remarkable population growth and economic development to the opening of Hickory Point Mall in 1978. The Decatur City Council voted in 1974 not to allow the construction of the massive shopping emporium within city limits, ostensibly in deference to downtown merchants seeking to oppose decentralization, so the region's only mall opened instead in the inviting suburban location. The heavy traffic stream of shoppers north from Decatur created a sales tax bonanza and fueled a twenty-four-fold increase in Forsyth's annual budget, enabling the village to provide improved services that included new schools, parks, and a public library. Ruefully recalling the city council vote in 1974, Decatur Mayor Paul Osborne called it "the worst decision ever made."[32]

Population decentralization occurred for a number of reasons, including high taxes, the rising fear of crime, the deterioration of public education, inadequate housing stock, and an aversion to dense urban living, but many observers

30. *Decatur Herald and Review*, June 28, December 15, 2001; *New York Times*, December 14, 2001; McDermott, "Decatur, Down and Out."

31. *Decatur Herald and Review*, June 28, 29, 2001.

32. Ibid., January 13, 2000, November 30, 2003.

explained the demographic change principally in terms of the steadily rising African American population in Decatur and the concomitant white flight. (The percentage of blacks in the city rose from 11.0 in 1970, to 15.3 in 1980, and to 17.4 in 1990.) Contemporary observers ascribed the rapid growth of places such as Mt. Zion and Forsyth, whose populations were 97.8 percent white and 96.5 percent white in 2000 respectively, to the desire of middle-class Decaturites to escape an increasingly diverse city; many of these migrants expressed a desire to reside in all-white neighborhoods and to avoid the racial desegregation of public schools by relocating to suburban school districts. Blacks accounted for almost 45 percent of Decatur's public school enrollment, approximately three times their numbers in the city. A Commission on Community Integration drafted a school desegregation plan based upon busing that met fierce opposition from an ad hoc organization, United School Action, composed of white professional and blue collar groups. Referendum campaigns for public education improvements in 1998 and 1999 fell short of passage as white voters, speaking in coded idioms, objected to spending more money when schools were allocating more resources for discipline than education. As superannuated school buildings in the central city decayed year after year, blacks gazed longingly at gleaming new academies and athletic venues at suburban sites. Feeling themselves the overriding cause of white flight, African American residents of Decatur characterized race relations in the region as volatile.[33]

Simmering racial disquietude boiled over in 1999, the result of an incident that thrust Decatur into the national news once more. A fight at a high school football game, captured on videotape and shown repeatedly on national television broadcasts, singled out the Illinois city as an example of the kind of racial tension plaguing heterogeneous blue collar communities in the midwestern Rustbelt. The fracas began as a dispute among African American adolescents and escalated as a group of combatants pursued a single male through the crowded bleachers. Hundreds of spectators scattered as the altercation halted the game for ten minutes. Police made several arrests but reported taking no participants or bystanders to the hospital for treatment. What the chief of police termed a relatively minor tussle, blown out of proportion because of the sensational film footage, became a national *cause célèbre* when the Board of Education meted out draconian punishment to the seven black students apprehended

---

33. U.S. Department of Commerce, Bureau of the Census, *Characteristics of the Population: 1970*, Volume 1, Section 1 (Washington, D.C.: Government Printing Office, 1973), 15–104; U.S. Department of Commerce, Bureau of the Census, *General Social and Economic Characteristics of the Population: 1980*, 15–32; U.S. Department of Commerce, Bureau of the Census, *Census of the Population, 1990: Social and Economic Characteristics*, Section 1, 44; Stein, "The Agricommercial Tradition," 229; Singer, "Town on a String," 62; *Decatur Herald and Review*, January 13, 2000.

during the melee. The school board expelled the students through September 2001—in other words, for the remainder of the 1999–2000 school year as well as the 2000–2001 school year. School officials justified imposing the maximum punishment allowed by state law as consistent with its "zero tolerance policy." Arguing that the punishment far exceeded the seriousness of the crime, the incident having been more a fistfight than a brawl, dissenters attributed a racial element to the Board of Education's stringent actions. Without allowing for some form of alternative schooling, protesters complained, the sanctions consigned the seven black students to "educational death sentences."[34]

Frustrated by the ruling, a member of Decatur's Rainbow/PUSH coalition chapter sought help from the group's national headquarters in Chicago. The Reverend Jesse Jackson, founder and president of the organization, sent an emissary to confer with school officials. After a meeting between the education director for Rainbow/PUSH and school board members ended in a stalemate, Jackson became directly involved himself. His stature as one of the nation's foremost civil rights activists and a two-time presidential candidate kept the matter squarely on the front pages of the nation's newspapers. At the same time, his staunch defense of the seven students rankled many Decatur residents, who resented the meddling of an outsider with no ties to the community. A local social worker observed that Jackson's suddenly ubiquitous presence "rocked the very foundations of the white community."[35] He continued:

> Traditionally, white people enjoy the positions of power and authority. And here comes a man who has international power and authority, and all of a sudden everybody closed ranks to make sure they had all their ducks in a row to fight this international figure.[36]

Intransigent school board members affirmed their decision and defiantly rejected the idea that Jackson's intervention would yield any positive results. "There is nothing Reverend Jackson can say or do," declared School Board president Jacqueline Goetter, "that would make me change my mind."[37]

The impasse persisted for several weeks until Illinois Governor George Ryan interceded to broker a compromise. On November 9, after a tendentious day of negotiations supervised by the governor, the school board reduced the expulsions to one year and agreed that the seven students could continue their educations elsewhere until the beginning of the next academic year; Ryan agreed to make the arrangements for the students to be taught in alternative venues.

---

34. *Decatur Herald and Review*, September 18, 19, October 8, 1999; Singer, "Town on a String," 61.

35. *Decatur Herald and Review*, October 8, 1999; Singer, "Town on a String," 61.

36. Singer, "Town on a String," 61.

37. *Decatur Herald and Review*, October 8, 1999; Singer, "Town on a String," 61.

Even after the announcement of the compromise, however, tensions remained elevated in the city. Dissatisfied that the settlement had not allowed the students to return to their high schools in January 2000, Rainbow/PUSH filed a law suit in U.S. District Court challenging the Board of Education's authority to impose such sanctions. On November 14 a Ku Klux Klan expedition from Butler, Indiana, conducted a rally in a Decatur park to register their support for the school board's original disciplinary measures. Two days later, Decatur police arrested Jackson when he, parents of the expelled students, and other demonstrators crossed a barrier onto the grounds of Eisenhower High School as an act of nonviolent civil disobedience. Only after a federal judge affirmed the legitimacy of the school board's actions in a January 13, 2000 decision did the expulsion story begin to recede from the local headlines.[38]

Still, the controversy continued. Invoking his success as a peacemaker in Decatur, Jackson fashioned a national Rainbow/PUSH campaign to publicize the much higher expulsion rate for black high school students than for white students throughout the country. At a summit meeting held at the Prairie Capital Convention Center in Springfield, Illinois, on January 25, 2000, he further posited that expelled black students rarely graduated, enjoyed less success finding jobs without high school diplomas, and eventually ended up being incarcerated in the many prisons being operated and built across the nation, thus creating more jobs for white prison guards. Explicating his conspiracy theory throughout the country, Jackson pointed to the recent events in Central Illinois as a textbook example of how the nefarious process worked. Elected officials, influential community leaders, and the local media vigorously objected when he gave this phenomenon a name: the "Decatur syndrome."[39]

Decaturites blanched at the unflattering image of their hometown that formed in the last decades of the twentieth century. A sequence of calamities sketched a sorrowful picture of decline in which a thriving industrial center found itself reeling from one financial reversal after another. More than anything else, strikes, lockouts, and other work stoppages tied to setbacks for unions tarnished Decatur's image as an energetic community with abundant economic opportunity for men and women willing to work hard. Toxic relations between management and workers culminated in the clashes of the mid-1990s when thousands of residents walked picket lines and the city became known as the "War Zone" and "Striketown, USA." As a consequence of the metropolitan region's economic stagnation, the commercial airlines linking Decatur with Chicago canceled passenger service. Job losses and plant closures occurred with

---

38. *New York Times*, November 17, 1999; *Decatur Herald and Review*, November 9, 15, 17, 1999, January 14, 2000; Singer, "Town on a String," 61.

39. *Decatur Herald and Review*, January 26, 2000; Singer, "Town on a String," 62.

unsettling frequency, as one observer glumly noted, because "working-class Americans were in the crosshairs of a merciless new economic order."[40]

While struggling against a prolonged economic torpor, Decatur suffered from other maladies as well. Population loss continued unabated, as overall the number of residents fell 19 percent from 1980 to 2010. Latent racial unease, fed by white flight and public school desegregation, surfaced with the suspension dispute of 1999 and the attendant confrontation between the school board and the Reverend Jesse Jackson. An international price-fixing scandal at ADM in 1995, which led to a $100 million fine and sent three of the firm's top executives to prison for high-tech corporate espionage and embezzlement, brought additional opprobrium. The concatenation of unfortunate developments left many residents muttering about a rumored "Decatur curse."[41]

Economic revitalization stalled in twenty-first century Decatur. In its quest to retain manufacturing enterprises and attract new industrial employers, the city constructed a new water tower, replaced sewer lines, and completed a new freight-rail terminal. Federal dollars made possible a face-lift for portions of downtown. Yet Decatur's vital signs remained worrisome. After the shuttering of Bridgestone/Firestone in 2001, Zexel Valeo (automobile components) closed in 2002 followed by the Intermet Corporation (metal castings) three years later. In 2015 the *Wall Street Journal* found the recent reports of modest improvement in the community's employment situation misleading. The financial newspaper deduced that the purported decline in the number of jobless workers owed to the fact that, as when evaluating conditions in other midwestern industrial cities, U.S. Department of Commerce statisticians were removing from the unemployment rolls the names of people who had not rejoined the labor force. In fact, many Decatur residents no longer classified as unemployed had moved away, retired, or, most importantly, stopped trying to find jobs. The hyperbolic accounts of urban renaissance notwithstanding, the newspaper noted, the city was still saddled with the highest jobless rate in Illinois. As well, Decatur's population loss accelerated in the twenty-first century. The number of people the city lost in the 1990s nearly doubled during the next decade, and the U.S. Census Bureau termed the 1.0 percent population decline suffered in 2013–2014 the steepest among all of the nation's metropolitan areas. The future prospects for a city of factories and foundries that flourished during the earlier manufacturing age remained worrisome in the post-industrial world, its uncertain fate a microcosm of the story being repeated in countless blue collar communities throughout the region.[42]

---

40. Frank, *Listen, Liberal*, 75.

41. McDermott, "Decatur, Down and Out." The best account of the ADM scandal is Lieber, *Rats in the Grain*.

42. *Wall Street Journal*, May 10, 2015; *Decatur Herald and Review*, February 16, 2011; Frank, *Listen, Liberal*, 251.

The University of Illinois Press
is a founding member of the
Association of American University Presses.

Composed in 10.5/13 Minion Pro
by Kirsten Dennison
at the University of Illinois Press

University of Illinois Press
1325 South Oak Street
Champaign, IL 61820-6903
www.press.uillinois.edu